HTML:
A Beginner's Guide

Wendy Willard

Osborne/**McGraw-Hill**

New York   Chicago   San Francisco
Lisbon   London   Madrid   Mexico City   Milan
New Delhi   San Juan   Seoul   Singapore   Sydney   Toronto

Osborne/**McGraw-Hill**
2600 Tenth Street
Berkeley, California 94710
U.S.A.

For information on translations or book distributors outside the U.S.A., or to arrange bulk purchase discounts for sales promotions, premiums, or fund-raisers, please contact Osborne/**McGraw-Hill** at the above address.

HTML: A Beginner's Guide

34567890 DOC DOC 0198765432

ISBN 0-07-213026-1

Publisher   Brandon A. Nordin
Vice President & Associate Publisher   Scott Rogers
Acquisitions Editor   Jim Schachterle
Project Editor   Monika Faltiss
Acquisitions Coordinator   Timothy Madrid
Technical Editor   Matt Brown
Copy Editor   Marcia Baker
Proofreader   John Gildersleeve
Indexer   Claire Splan
Computer Designers   Tara Davis & Gary Corrigan
Illustrator   Michael Mueller
Series Design   Gary Corrigan
Cover Design   Pattie Lee

This book was composed with Corel VENTURA™ Publisher.

To Corinna—

*That you might remember your mom
once knew some "cool stuff",
even when HTML becomes for you
what 8-track tapes are to me.*

*"Therefore do not worry about tomorrow,
for tomorrow will worry about itself.
Each day has enough trouble of its own."*

Matthew 6:34

About the Author

Wendy Willard is founder and owner of WILLARDESIGNS, a firm specializing in cutting edge Web-based design and development for businesses of all sizes and varieties, and in education and consulting about web-related concepts. She holds a degree in Illustration from Art Center College of Design in Pasadena, California. Wendy teaches and lectures on Web design and development throughout the U.S. and Europe.

Wendy's passions include all aspects of digital design, drawing, painting, photographing Maine, and anything related to the Web. She lives and works in Dresden, Maine with her husband, Wyeth, and young daughter, Corinna.

Contents

PART 2

Beyond HTML

Acknowledgments

Thanks to Rachel, my *non-technical* editor, for spending hours reading this material with a critical eye, pointing out things she didn't understand in the text and points I needed to clarify. I wouldn't turn a chapter in without you reading it first!

Thanks to Wendy, Jim, Tim, Monika, Marcia and Matt, for believing in me, and turning my random thoughts into a cohesive book, and to Molly and David for setting this whole thing in motion.

A special thanks to the Woolwich Historical Society, for providing the real-world project in the book.

And finally, thanks to my family and friends for putting up with my "addiction" for three months. Without your love and support I never would have met all my deadlines or been able to accomplish much of anything at all. Mom and Dad—you're owed half the credit. Wyeth and Corinna—you are my inspiration and my reward.

Introduction

When I was first approached about writing this book, I must admit that my thought was, "Another HTML book—how many do we need?" I learned HTML by experience when there was only one version of Netscape, and it had been a long time since I'd even looked at an HTML book. But after I researched the other HTML books on the market, I felt compelled to write a book that gives readers a realistic, easy-to-understand approach to learning HTML, while at the same time offering real-world practice activities and advice on related issues.

HTML: A Beginner's Guide is that book, offering you practical tools and knowledge that can easily be applied to a variety of development situations, without the boring rhetoric or lengthy technical fluff. This book tells you what you need to know, when you need to know it.

Who Should Read This Book

Since this book is geared toward anyone with little or no prior HTML knowledge, it's perfect for anyone wishing to learn HTML. If you are a stay-at-home mom wanting to create a Web site for your family, you've come to the right place. If you are a business professional seeking to acquire Web development skills, this is the book for you. If you are interested in learning HTML, this book is for you.

You don't need to know anything about computer programming or Web development in order to learn HTML, and you certainly don't need to know either of those things to get a lot from this book.

What This Book Covers

The book is separated into three distinct parts—HTML Basics, Beyond HTML, and Resources.

Part 1, "HTML Basics" covers all you need to know in order to start coding effective and efficient Web pages with HTML. Part I consists of eleven modules, where information is broken up into manageable chunks. Each module contains one or more step-by-step, real-world projects to give you practice performing the concepts taught.

Module 1, "Getting Started" helps you understand the Web by answering common questions such as "Who created HTML?" and "Who maintains HTML?" and tackling the anatomy of a Web site, Web browsers, and XHTML. Issues surrounding how to plan your Web site, using HTML editors, and learning from the pros are also discussed.

Module 2, "Basic Page Structure" explains beginning terminology such as tags, attributes, and nesting while also describing naming conventions and proper page structure.

Module 3, "Color" gives you details on how to work with and reference color in your Web pages. Hexadecimal color and the Web-safe color palette are also discussed.

Module 4, "Working with Text" teaches you how to use HTML to format text within your Web pages, whether that means changing the font style or color, or adding line breaks and emphasis.

Module 5, "Working with Links" discusses the core of HTML: hypertext links. This module gives details on how to add and customize links in your Web pages, whether you're linking to another Web page, a section of a Web page, or an email address.

Module 6, "Working with Images" helps you use images in your Web pages by describing different image types, how to add them to a page, and how to link to and from them. Additional tips on using images in Web pages are also provided.

Module 7, "Working with Multimedia" explains different types of multimedia you can add to your pages, and tells how to do so in ways that work in multiple browsers.

Module 8, "Creating Lists" teaches you how to create and format the three different types of lists available in HTML.

Module 9, "Using Tables" tackles the somewhat difficult but very useful topic of HTML tables. In a step-by-step fashion, this module takes you through creating a very basic table structure all the way to formatting nested and seamless tables for the purposes of page layout.

Module 10, "Developing Frames" offers you ways to break your Web pages up into separate window frames, each with different pieces of content. Both standard and inline frames are discussed, as well as how to format each.

Module 11, "Employing Forms" discusses a key ingredient for most Web sites—forms providing communication methods for customers. Various types of input controls are taught, including textfields, check boxes, file uploads, select menus, and buttons, as well as information about processing forms with scripts and additional formatting techniques.

Part 2, "Beyond HTML" gives you an introduction into several additional areas related to building Web pages with HTML. If you're only interested in learning HTML, you might be able to skip these sections, but if you're wondering what comes next after you learn HTML, I recommend checking out the modules in Part II. All of the modules in Part 2 also include sections called "Learning More", which provide additional resources for those interested in pursuing the topic.

Module 12, "Creating Your Own Web Graphics" contains a review of popular Web graphics software, as well as guidelines you can use when creating images for the Web. This module also discusses issues that impact design decisions and Web graphics file formats. Even if you don't have a graphics editor, the module lists several places where you can download demos for free to practice the concepts taught.

Module 13, "Web Content" discusses ways to ensure the on-screen readability of your Web pages, how to create effective links and printer-friendly pages. In addition, this module provides essential dos and don'ts for working with Web content.

Module 14, "JavaScript" offers you an introduction into JavaScript, a technology used to add dynamic aspects to otherwise static HTML pages. Sample scripts allow you to add the current date and time to a Web page, make form fields required, and change page elements when users point to them.

Module 15, "Cascading Style Sheets" gives an introduction into using Cascading Style Sheets to control page layout and formatting. Essential terminology is discussed, and detailed tables are included to identify the various properties used.

Module 16, "Making Pages Available to Others" teaches you to prepare your pages for online distribution before guiding you to making important decisions such as, where to host your site, what domain name to use, and how to upload it. Testing, submission to search engines and directories, and general marketing tips are also discussed.

Part 3, "Resources" provides additional information in quick-reference formats, and puts commonly used details at the fingertips of both beginning and advanced HTML coders.

Resource A, "HTML 4 Reference Table" outlines all of the HTML tags taught in the book in an easy to read and reference format.

Resource B, "Special Characters" lists the character entities used to embed special characters (such as the copyright symbol and an ampersand) into a Web page.

Resource C, "Troubleshooting (FAQ)" provides answers to commonly asked questions from beginning and advanced HTML coders.

Resource D, "Locating Images, Clip Art, Multimedia, Software, etc." contains links to additional resources that can be used within your Web pages.

Resource E, "File Types" includes a list of the file types you are most likely to encounter while creating Web pages, as well as a brief description and MIME type for each.

Resource F, "Mastery Checks Answers" gives the answers to the questions asked at the end of each module.

How to Read This Book

The content is structured such that you can read a single module as needed, or the entire book from cover to cover. Although beginners should most likely read through the book, module by module, in order to efficiently grasp the concepts taught, intermediate and advanced users can use certain modules as reference materials.

The projects at the end of each module build upon each other, but you could certainly adapt a specific module to your own needs if you read them out of order. If you're using this book within a classroom setting, be sure to visit **www.willardesigns.com/htmlbook** for instructor tips and additional notes.

Since this book is part of the iGeneration Professional Certification Program, you are already on your way toward receiving certification as an Internet professional. Visit iGeneration's Web site (**www.igeneration.com**) to learn more or to register for the companion exam.

Special Features

Each module includes *Hints*, *Tips,* and *Notes* to provide additional reference information wherever needed. Detailed *code listings* are included in gray boxes, many times with certain tags or features highlighted with further explanation.

Many modules contain *Ask the Expert* question-and-answer sections to address potentially confusing issues. Each module contains step-by-step *Projects* to give you a chance to practice the concepts taught thus far. These Projects are based on a real-world Web development project I worked on for the Woolwich Historical Society in Woolwich, Maine.

Mastery Checks are included at the end of each module to give you another chance to review the concepts taught in the module. The answers to the Mastery Checks are in Resource F.

You can download the content for the Woolwich Historical Society projects from Osborne's Web site (**www.osborne.com**) or the companion site to this book (**www.willardesigns.com/htmlbook**). Updated copies of Resource D, as well as additional troubleshooting tips and bulletin boards are also available on the companion book site.

Throughout the development of this book, our objective has always been to provide you with a cohesive, easy-to-understand guide for coding HTML to help you get up and running in no time. As you'll hear me say countless times, HTML is not that difficult and is definitely within your reach. I applaud your decision to learn HTML and encourage you to use the Internet to its fullest potential both during the learning process and in your ensuing Web development aspirations. As Module 1 discusses, visit the Web sites you love and love-to-hate to determine how they accomplished various features. Follow the links identified in the book for additional information, and don't forget to perform your own Web searches for related content. Have fun and good luck!

Part 1

HTML Basics

Module 1

Getting Started

Goals

- Understand the Internet as a medium for disseminating information
- Plan for the audience, goals, structure, content, and navigation of your site
- Identify the basic differences between the different types of HTML editors
- Learn from the pros using the VIEW SOURCE command of popular Web browsers

For as long as I have been involved in making Web pages, people have asked me to teach them the process. In the beginning, many people are intimidated at the thought of learning HTML. Fear not. One of the reasons I decided to go to art school was to avoid all math and science classes. So, as I tell my students . . . if I could learn HTML, so can you.

HTML is not rocket science. Quite simply, HTML is a means of telling a Web browser how to display a page. That's why it's called *HTML,* which is the acronym for *Hypertext Markup Language.* Like any new skill, HTML takes practice to comprehend what you are doing.

Before we dive into the actual creation of the Web pages, you need to understand a few things about the Internet. I could probably fill an entire book with the material in this first chapter, but the following should provide you with a firm foundation.

Understanding the Medium

When you are asked to write a term paper in school, you don't just sit down and start writing. First, you have to do research and learn how to format the paper. When you decide to write and design a Web page, the process is similar.

The Anatomy of a Web Site

Undoubtedly, you have seen a few Web sites by now. Perhaps, you know someone who is a Web geek, and you have watched him navigate through a Web site by chopping off pieces of the Web address. Do you ever wonder what he is doing? He knows a little bit about the anatomy of a Web site and how the underlying structure is laid out.

?—Ask the Expert

Question: I've heard the phrase "The World Wide Web" used so many times, but I'm a little confused about what it actually means and how it relates to the Internet.

Answer: The *World Wide Web* (*WWW* or the *Web*) is often confused with the Internet. While the Internet was originally created during the Cold War as a way to link sections of the country together during an emergency, the Web didn't really exist until the late 1980s. At that time, Tim Berners-Lee created a set of technologies that allowed information on the Internet to be linked together through the use of links, or connections, in documents. The language component of these technologies is HTML.

The Web was mostly text based until Marc Andreessen created the first Web browser in 1992, called Mosaic. This paved the way for video, sound, and photos on the Web.

As a large group of interconnected computers all over the world, the Internet comprises not only the Web, but also things like *newsgroups* (online bulletin boards) and e-mail. Many people think of the Web as the graphical or illustrated part of the Internet.

URLs

The fancy word for "Web address" is *uniform resource locator*, also referenced by its acronym *URL* (pronounced either by the letters U-R-L or as a single word, "url," which rhymes with "girl"). If you haven't heard a Web address referred to as a URL, you have probably seen one—URLs start with http://, and they usually end with .com, .org, .edu, or .net. Every Web site has a URL. An example is http://www.yahoo.com.

The following illustration shows another example of a URL, as it appears in a Netscape browser.

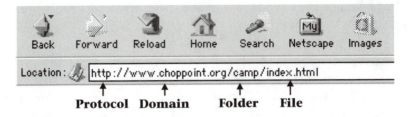

One part of a URL is the *domain name*, which helps identify and locate computers on the Internet. To avoid confusion, each domain name is unique. You can think of the domain name as a label or a shortcut. Behind that shortcut is a series of numbers, called an *IP Address*, which gives the specific address of where the site you are looking for is located on the Internet. To draw an analogy, if the domain name is the word "Emergency" written next to the first aid symbol on your speed dial, the IP Address is 9-1-1.

Note

Although many URLs begin with "www," this is not a necessity. Originally used to denote "*World Wide Web*" in the URL, using *www* has caught on as common practice. The characters before the first period in the URL are not part of the registered domain, and can be almost anything. In fact, many businesses use this part of the URL to differentiate between various departments within the company. For example, the GO Network includes ABC, ESPN, and Disney, to name a few. Each of these are departments of go.com: abc.go.com, espn.go.com, and disney.go.com.

Businesses typically register domain names ending in a .com (which signifies a commercial venture) that are similar to their business or product name. Domain registration is like renting office space on the Internet. Once you register a domain name, you have the right to publish a Web site under that name on the Internet for as long as you pay the rental fees.

Hint

Wondering whether *yourname.com* is already being used? You can check to see which domain names are still available for registration by visiting **www.networksolutions.com/**

Web Servers

Every Web site and Web page also needs a Web server. Quite simply, a *Web server* is a computer, running special software, which is always connected to the Internet.

When you type a URL into your Web browser or click a link in a Web page, you send a request to the server that houses that information. It's similar to the process that occurs when you dial a phone number with your telephone.

Your request "calls" the computer that contains all the files necessary to show you the Web page you requested. The computer then "serves" and displays all the pages to you, usually in your Web browser.

Module 16 discusses locating a Web server and publishing your Web page.

Sites

A URL is commonly associated with a Web site. You have seen plenty of examples on billboards and in television advertising. www.yahoo.com is the URL for Yahoo!'s Web site; www.cbs.com is the URL for CBS's Web site.

Most commonly, these sites are located in directories or folders on the server, just as you might have your C: drive on your personal computer. Then, within this main site, there may be several folders, which house other sections of the Web site.

For example, Chop Point is a summer camp and K-12 school in Maine. It has several main sections of its Web site, but the most notable are "camp" and "school." If you look at the URL for Chop Point's camp section, you can see the name of the folder after the site name:

www.choppoint.org/camp

If you were to look at the main page for the school, the URL changes to:

www.choppoint.org/school

Pages

When you visit a Web site, you look at pages on the site that contain all the text, graphics, sound, and video content. Even though a Web page is not the same size or format as a printed page, the word "page" is used to help us differentiate between pages, folders, and sites. Just as many pages and chapters can be within a single book, many pages and folders (or sections) can also be within a Web site.

Most Web servers are set up to look automatically for a page called "index" as the main page in any folder. So, if you were to type in the URL used in the previous example, the server would look for the index page in the "camp" folder.

www.choppoint.org/camp/index.html

If you want to look for a different page in the camp folder, you could type the name of that page after the site and folder names, keeping in mind that HTML pages usually end with `.html` or `.htm`

www.choppoint.org/camp/dayactivities.html

Web Browsers

A *Web browser* is a piece of software that runs on your personal computer and enables you to view Web pages. Web browsers, often simply called "browsers," interpret the HTML code and provide a visual layout displayed on the screen. Many browsers can also be used to check e-mail and access newsgroups.

The most popular browsers are Netscape Navigator and Microsoft Internet Explorer. These browsers can be downloaded from the respective company's Web site. Each company updates its browser regularly, changing to address new aspects of HTML or emerging technologies. Many people continue to use older versions of their browsers, however. This means, at any given time, there may be three or four active versions of one browser, and several different versions of other browsers being used by the general public.

What if there were several versions of televisions, which all displayed TV programs differently? Then, imagine your favorite television show looked different every time you watched it on anyone else's television. This would not only be frustrating to you as a viewer, it would also be frustrating for the show's creator.

Web developers must deal with this frustration every day. Because of the differences among various browsers and the large number of computer types, the look and feel of a Web page can vary greatly. This means Web developers must keep up-to-date on the latest features of the new browsers, but we must also know how to create Web pages that are backwards-compatible for the older browsers many people may still be using.

> ## Hint
> To help keep current on statistics about browser use, try visiting **www. browserwatch.com/**, a site that offers up-to-the-minute research and information about browsers, plug-ins, and Active-X controls.

Internet Service Providers

You use an *Internet service provider* (*ISP*) to gain access to the Internet. Usually, you can also obtain a free Web browser from your ISP. This connection can be made through your phone line with a company like MCI, RCN, or Earthlink, or you can connect through a cable line with a company like Comcast or Time Warner.

Many companies offer you a choice of browsers; however, some companies may support only one browser, such as *America Online* (*AOL*). To locate an ISP with local service in your area, visit **boardwatch.internet.com/isp/ac/index.html**, and click your phone number's area code.

What about AOL?

AOL runs what you might think of as a mini "Web-within-the-Web" because it maintains content on its own systems that non-AOL users cannot view. Whereas most ISPs don't maintain proprietary content for their users, AOL is both an ISP and a content provider. Its software provides you with access to the entire Web, in addition to AOL user-restricted content. Many people think of AOL as "the Internet with training wheels"—it walks beginning users through the experience of surfing the Web.

Hint

Most browsers can be easily customized, meaning you can change the text sizes, styles, and colors, as well as the first page that appears when you start your browser. This is usually called your "home" page or your "start" page, and it's the page displayed when you click the "home" button in your browser. For easier access, many people change their home page to a search engine or a news site customized according to their needs. These personalized sites are often called *portals* and also offer free e-mail to users. A few examples are: Yahoo!, Excite, Netscape, and Snap.

Looking to the Future

Over the past few years, HTML has been through many iterations and, in many instances, this has led to a lack of standardization across the Internet. Currently, we are using HTML 4.01, a set of standards for Web development drafted by the *World Wide Web Consortium* (W3C—**www.w3.org**).

To help standardize everything without making our lives more difficult, the W3C has rewritten HTML 4.01 using the *Extensible Markup Language (XML)*. The resulting set of standards is called *Extensible Hypertext Markup Language (XHTML)*, and it even provides a way for HTML to handle alternative devices, such as cell phones and hand-held computers.

XHTML offers many new features to Web developers that will make life much easier in the long run but, at press time, no browser supports all these features. Because XHTML is here to stay, Web developers would be wise to learn the basics and begin to use them now. In fact, every new version of HTML will be built on the foundation of XHTML 1.0. How you can help prepare your documents for XHTML is discussed in upcoming modules. You can learn much more about XHTML from several online resources, including the following:

- "Squeaky Clean Markup," by Molly E. Holzschlag; *Web Techniques.* (**www.webtechniques.com/archives/2000/05/desi/**)

- "Molly Holzschlag: Everything You Never Need to Know About HTML 4.0," by David Sims; *webreview.com*(**www.webreview.com/wr/pub/1999/06/25/ feature/holzschlag_html4.html**)

- W3C's recommendation on XHTML 1.0: *The Extensible Hypertext Markup Language* (**www.w3.org/TR/xhtml1/**)

- whatis.com's definition of XHTML (**www.whatis.com/xhtml.htm**)

- Web Developer's Virtual Library discussion on XHTML (**www.wdvl.com/Authoring/Languages/XML/XHTML/**)

1-Minute Drill

- **What is a Web browser?**
- **List some parts of a URL.**

Planning

In addition to learning about the medium, you also need to do the following:

- Identify your target audience

- Set goals for your site

- Create your Web site's structure

- Organize your Web site's content

- Develop your Web site's navigation

- **A Web browser is a piece of software that runs on your computer and enables you to view Web pages**
- **domain name, folder, file**

Identifying the Target Audience

If you are creating a Web site for a business, a group, or an organization, you are most likely targeting people who might buy or use the company's products or services. Even if your site is purely for the purpose of disseminating information, you must be targeting a certain audience. Consider whether you have any existing research regarding your client or user base. This might include demographics, statistics, or other marketing information, such as age, gender, and Web experience.

Hint

If your site represents a new company or one that doesn't already have information about its clients' demographics, you might check out the competition. Chances are good that if your competition has a successful Web site, you can learn from them about your target audience.

Knowing who your target audience is can greatly affect how you design and develop your Web site. For example, if you are developing a site for beginners to learn about the Internet, you want to create a site that is extremely easy to use and does not stray from standard computer conventions.

Once you identify your target audience, you need to think about what functions each part of that audience can perform at your site. You might use a table like Table 1-1 to help you make your plans. The following example could be used for a bank, but you could use it as a starting place for any site you are creating.

You can use this information to determine the appropriate direction for the site. I like to break down the audience into two major sectors: the "accidental tourists" and the "navy seals." Most sites have a little of both. Have you ever been surfing a certain site, and then wondered how you got there from here? This is the "accidental tourist," a.k.a. the serendipitous visitor. At the other end of the spectrum is the student on a

Hint

Does your site target mostly "navy seals" visitors? These individuals prefer search engines, especially when trying to locate information quickly. Providing a good search engine on your site can greatly increase your repeat visitors.

User Group	Functions Performed	Ages	Gender	Web Experience
Current customers	bank online contact customer service research additional services/products	16+	male/female	varies
Potential customers	research services/products contact sales	16+	male/female	varies
Potential employees	search job openings research company contact HR	18-60	male/female	varies
Financial consultants	research services/products view company financials contact sales	30-60	male/female 60/40	savvy

Table 1-1   Functions Performed by a Target Audience

mission—looking for a specific piece of information for a homework assignment. I call these the "navy seals."

Setting goals

Since the Web's inception, millions of new Web sites have been created. To compete in such a large market, you need to set clear goals for the site. A few examples might be

● sell products/services

● recruit potential employees

● entertain

● educate

● communicate with customers

Always remember the goals when developing the site to avoid unnecessary content. If a page on your site doesn't meet one of the goals, it may confuse and/or turn away visitors.

Creating the Structure

Once you align your site's goals with the functions performed by the target audience, you can begin to see a structure appearing. Consider a site whose primary goal is to sell office supplies to businesses and whose secondary goal is to recruit potential employees. This site would most likely contain two main topic areas: shop for office supplies and browse available jobs.

Many people use tree diagrams, such as the one shown in Figure 1-1, to help define the structure of the site. Others use flow charts or simple outlines.

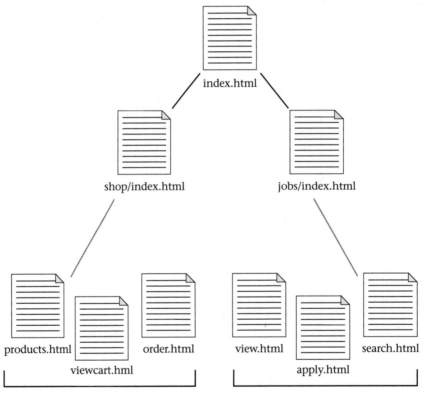

These pages are all stored in the "shop" folder. These pages are all stored in the "jobs" folder.

Figure 1-1 This example tree diagram shows how a portion of the structure for this sample office-supplies site might look

1

Organizing Content

All the content for the site should then fit under each of the topic areas in the site structure. You might have several subcategories in each topic area. So, the "shop for office supplies" section from the previous example might be broken down into several subcategories, according to the different types of products available. Table 1-2 shows how the category names might relate to the folder names.

Developing Navigation

After the site structure has been defined and the content has been placed into the structure accordingly, you will want to plan out how a visitor to this site navigates between each of the pages and sections. Good practice is to include a standard navigation bar on all pages for consistency and ease of use. This navigation bar probably should include links to your home page and any major topic areas. It should probably also contain the name of your business or a logo so a simple visual clue lets the user know she has not passed from your site by accident.

Highlighting the current section on the navigation bar is important, so visitors can more easily distinguish where they are in your site's structure. This means if your site has two sections — jobs and resumes — the jobs button would look different when you were inside that section and, in some way, should identify it as the current section.

Category Name	Folder Name
Paper	shop/paper/
Pens	shop/pens/
Software	shop/software/
Furniture	shop/furniture/
Furniture, Desks	shop/furniture/desks/
Furniture, Chairs	shop/furniture/chairs/
Furniture, Bookcases	shop/furniture/bookcases/

Table 1-2   Content Organization

In addition, consider giving your visitors as many visual clues as possible to aid in the navigation of your site (see Figure 1-2). This might be accomplished by repeating the page name in

- the page's title (the text that appears in the top of the browser window, as well as in search engines)

- the page's filename

- a headline

- buttons and links to the page (highlighted if you are viewing that page)

Using HTML Editors

At some point, you may wonder: "Why go to the trouble of learning HTML if I can use a program that does it for me?" With so many new software packages available to help you develop HTML, that's a valid question. The bulk of the software packages can be broken up into two main categories: text-based HTML editors and *What You See Is What You Get (WYSIWYG),* pronounced *wuzzywig* or *wizzywig* editors.

Text-based HTML Editors

Text-based editors require you to know some HTML to use them. They can be customized to help speed your coding process, and often have sophisticated checks and balances in place to check for errors in coding. The most popular text-based HTML editors are:

- **Allaire HomeSite**
  (**www.allaire.com/products/homesite/index.cfm**) ranked #1 in a 1999 InternetWorld Survey(**www.internetworldnews.com/ article_bot.asp?inc=110199/WDS/11.01WDS1&issue=11.01**). It offers features like automatic tag completion, tag recommendation, and customizable shortcuts.
  This product is only available for the PC.

This tab is a different color to show the visitor which section this page is located

The page title lists the name of the site as well as the page and section names

The URL clues the visitor to the name and location of the page being viewed

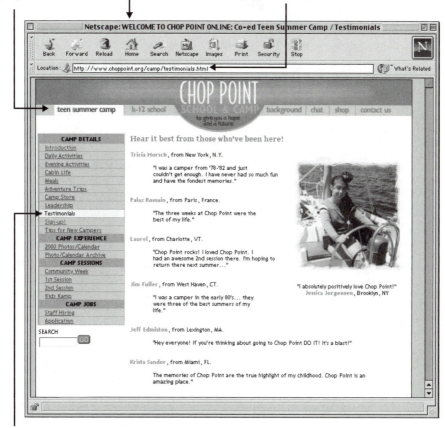

This link is highlighted to remind the visitor which page he/she is viewing

Figure 1-2   This example shows how the page name is repeated several times

● **Bare Bone BBEdit (www.barebones.com)** ranked #2 in the same survey and is only available for the Macintosh. Its features include an HTML checker, customizable shortcuts, and an HTML-aware spelling checker.

WYSIWYG HTML Editors

WYSIWYG editors don't require HTML knowledge. Instead of looking at the HTML of your pages, you are shown a "preview" of how the page will look in a browser. You can simply drag-and-drop pieces of your layout as you see fit. These types of programs can have many drawbacks, but they can also be quite useful for the purposes of learning different aspects of HTML or for quickly publishing a basic Web page. The most popular WYSIWYG editors are

● **Macromedia Dreamweaver (www.macromedia.com/software/ dreamweaver/)** is available for both the Macintosh and the PC. It offers benefits such as customizable features and automated production and is integrated with graphics tools such as Macromedia Fireworks.

● **Microsoft FrontPage (www.microsoft.com/frontpage/)** is also available for both the Macintosh and the PC (although in different versions). It boasts integrated support for other products in the Microsoft Office suite and advanced features, such as sample forms and site management tools.

Which Is Best?

Many Web developers prefer to use the text-based HTML editors, rather than have a WYSIWYG editor do it for them, for the following reasons:

● **Better control** WYSIWYG editors may write HTML in a variety of ways—although not all of them will have the same outcome. For example, Microsoft Front Page sometimes uses proprietary code that is not understood by Netscape's browsers. This means your pages can look different in each browser. Unfortunately, this has caused many of these programs to be labeled "WYSINWYG" or What-You-See-Is-NOT-What-You-Get.

- **Faster pages**   WYSIWYG editors often overcompensate for the amount of code needed to render a page properly, and they end up repeating code many more times than necessary. This leads to large file sizes and longer downloads.

- **Speedier editing**   The large-scale WYSIWYG editors often take a lot of memory and system resources, slowing both the computer and the development process.

- **More flexibility**   Many WYSIWYG editors are programmed to "fix" code they thinks is faulty. This may make you unable to insert code or edit the existing code as you want.

That said, the newest WYSIWYG editors have come a long way in terms of control and flexibility. They even offer Web developers advanced features such as the capability to code DHTML and JavaScript.
Note that:

- *Dynamic HTML* (or *DHTML*) is a newer version of HTML, in which page content is easily changed and customized on the fly, without having to send and receive additional information from the server. Style sheets, used especially in DHTML, are discussed in Module 15.

- *JavaScript* is a scripting language designed to give Web pages more interactivity than can be achieved through HTML. Even though the name might make you think otherwise, JavaScript is different from Java, which is a full programming language. You read more about JavaScript in Module 14.

So, both text-based HTML editors and WYSIWYG editors have their benefits. My recommendation is to download free trials of the various programs and decide for yourself which one works best for your needs.

For the purposes of this book, you are free to use any editor or software package you like, although to begin, I recommend you use the basic text editor that came with your computer system, such as SimpleText (Macintosh) or Notepad (PC). Once you have the basics of HTML down, you can move on and experiment with other available programs.

Learning from the Pros

One of the best ways to learn HTML is to surf the Web and look at the HTML for sites you like (as well as those you don't like). Most Web browsers enable you to view the HTML source code of Web pages, using the following commands:

- In Netscape, choose VIEW | PAGE SOURCE

- In Internet Explorer, choose VIEW | SOURCE

Hint

A few browsers don't let you VIEW SOURCE. If you find you cannot view the HTML source of a Web page, try saving the page to your local hard drive, and then opening it in a text editor instead.

You can even print or save these pages to review at a later time or to keep in a reference library. Because the Web is *open source*, meaning your code is free for anyone to see, copying other developers' code is tempting. But, remember, you should give credit where credit is due (you learn more about commenting HTML pages in Module 2) and never copy anything protected by a copyright, such as graphics and text content.

Project 1-1: Develop a Web Site

1

The best way to practice HTML is to develop Web sites. While developing a personal site might be fun, I think you can sometimes learn more about the whole development process by working on a site for a business or organization. In fact, volunteering your time to develop a Web site for a nonprofit organization is a wonderful way to start.

Throughout the course of this book, I give you projects that relate to the development of such an organization's Web site. If you already have an organization in mind for which you want to develop a site, then use that one. If not, you can use the organization I used while creating examples for this book—the Woolwich Historical Society, located in Woolwich, Maine.

All the files needed to complete the projects in this book for the Woolwich Historical Society can be downloaded from **www.osborne.com** or **www.willardesigns.com/htmlbook**. In addition, you can view my version of the Web site anytime by visiting **www.woolwichhistory.org**.

This specific project takes you through the planning phase of the Web development project. Goals for this project include

- Identify your target audience.

- Set goals for your site.

- Create your Web site's structure.

- Organize your Web site's content.

- Develop your Web site's navigation.

Step-by-Step

1. Spend some time researching your organization. Try to learn as much about its business as possible. If you know people within the organization, do some interviews to help you identify your target audience, as well as the site goals. If you can't speak with members of the organization, visit other similar sites to determine what type of people the competition is targeting. Some questions to ask and things to consider:

● What business problem(s) will the Web site address? What do you want to accomplish? What are your goals for the Web site?

● Who are the targeted users/visitors of the site? Do you have any existing research regarding your client or user base, such as demographics, statistics, or other marketing information?

● To determine the appropriate direction for the site, you must match the targeted users and the functions they will perform when visiting the site. For example, will the targeted users be "accidental tourists" directed to the site by an advertisement or potential investors looking for the financials? How do the audience demographics affect this? (You can use a table like the following one to help you plan the targeted users and the functions they might perform at the site. An example is shown for the Woolwich Historical Society.)

USER GROUP	Functions Performed at Site	Ages	Web Experience
1. students	research for school projects	6-18	moderate - high
2.			
3.			

2. After you decide on the target audience and goals for the site, it's time to evaluate your content. This is best accomplished through conversations with the people for whom you're developing the site. If this isn't possible, be creative and come up with a list of content you think could be appropriate.

Hint

For help with planning the Woolwich Historical Society's project, visit Osborne's Web site (**www.osborne.com**) to download the book's .zip file. Module 1's folder contains notes from my discussions with members of the Historical Society.

3. Use the answers to the following questions as a springboard for building the structure of your site. Then develop a tree diagram, similar to the one shown in Figure 1-1, to identify all the pieces of your site and where they fit within the overall structure.

- Does an official logo have to be used on the Web site?
- Is all the content written and available in digital format?
- What are the main sections of the site? Does all the content fit within those sections?
- List all the content for the site. Assign each piece of content to a section (as necessary) and define filenames.

Hint

If you're using the Woolwich Historical Society as your organization, you can find a sample tree diagram and a list of all the content for the site in the Module 1 folder of the book's .zip file (download it from **www.osborne.com**).

Project Summary

Before you begin writing the actual HTML for your Web pages, you need to know something about the site you are creating. The questions asked in this project should get you off to a good start and help you build a solid foundation for your Web site. In the next module, you continue working with this site, as you write the code for one of the pages.

☑ Mastery Check

1. What does HTML stand for?

   _____

   _____

2. What does the word "camp" in the following URL signify?

   http://www.choppoint.org/camp/index.html

   A. file name

   B. page name

   C. folder name

   D. domain name

3. Why is it important to know who your target audience is before developing your Web site?

   _____

   _____

4. What does WYSIWYG mean?

   _____

   _____

5. What is the easiest way to learn HTML from your favorite Web sites?

   _____

   _____

   _____

Module 2

Basic Page Structure

Goals

- Open, edit, and save a Web page
- Preview a Web page in a browser
- Recognize tags and attributes
- Understand and apply the basic HTML document format
- Add comments to your Web page

Now that you know a little about the Web and what to think about before creating a Web page, let's talk about the basic structure of an HTML page.

At their very core, HTML files are simply text files with two additional features.

1. **HTML files have an .html or .htm file extension.** A *file extension* is an abbreviation that associates the file with the appropriate program or tool needed to access it. In most cases, this abbreviation follows a period, and is three or four letters long. In the following example, notice that Yahoo!'s home page ends in an .html file extension.

2. **HTML files have *tags*,** which are commands or code used to tell the computer how to display the page content. After choosing **VIEW | SOURCE**, you can see some of the HTML tags in Yahoo!'s home page.

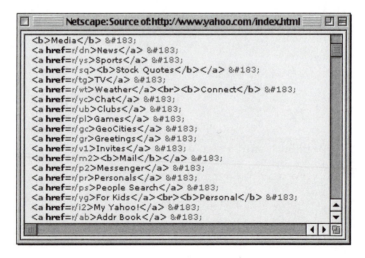

┼**Note**

You might also see more advanced types of pages on the Internet, such as Microsoft's Active Server Pages (.asp) or those written in the Extensible Markup Language (.xml). These are beyond the scope of the traditional HTML page and follow different standards.

Naming Conventions

Remember these few things when naming your HTML files.

1. Although in most cases it doesn't matter whether you use `.html` or `.htm`, you should always be consistent to avoid confusing yourself, the browser, and your users.

┼**Note**

Windows 3.1 and DOS systems cannot understand four-letter file extensions. Because the first three letters of `.html` and `.htm` are the same, those systems simply ignore the "l" and recognize the file type without any problems.

2. Some Web servers are case-sensitive, so remember this when naming and referencing filenames and try to be consistent. If you name your file `MyPage.html`, and then reference it later using `mypage.html`, you may end up with a broken link. One good technique is to use only uppercase or lowercase to name your files. This way, if you see a file with a letter in it that doesn't match, you know instantly that file is probably the problem. Even the pros run into case sensitivity problems on an almost daily basis.

3. Use simple filenames with only letters and numbers. Don't use spaces, punctuation, or special characters. [Dashes (-) and underscores (_) are allowed.] Good examples might be `home.html`, `my-story.html`, and `contact_me.html`.

Hint

If you decide to use Microsoft Word or WordPad to type your HTML, you need to choose the file type "Text Document" or "Text Only" and to give the file an `.html` extension the first time you save your file. This is because both of those programs default to saving "Word for Windows" or "Microsoft Word" documents with a .doc extension.

These same recommendations hold true for any folder names you use. If you were creating a Web site that had your favorite links, family photos, and résumé, you might find it useful to put each of those things in a separate folder.

Viewing in a Browser

You can view HTML files located on your personal computer within your own Web browser. It isn't necessary for your files to be stored on a Web server until you are ready to make them visible on the Internet.

When you want to preview a page, open your Web browser and choose FILE | OPEN PAGE (Netscape) or FILE | OPEN (Internet Explorer), and then browse your hard drive until you locate the HTML file you want to open.

If you are going to make frequent changes to the HTML file in a text editor, and then switch back to a Web browser to preview the page, keeping both programs (a text editor and a Web browser) open at the same time makes sense. The steps to edit and preview HTML files are

1. Open/return to your HTML file in a text editor.

2. Edit your HTML file in a text editor.

3. Save your HTML file in a text editor.

4. Open/return to your HTML file in a Web browser.

5. Click the REFRESH button in Internet Explorer or RELOAD button in Netscape in your Web browser to update the HTML page according to any changes you just made to it.

By keeping your HTML file open in both a text editor and a browser, you can easily make and preview changes.

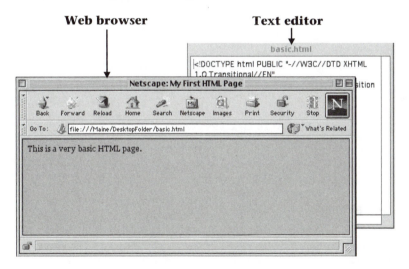

Understanding Tags

An *HTML entity* or *tag* is a command used to tell the computer how to display content on a page. This command is similar to what happens behind the scenes when you highlight some text in a word processor and click the BOLD button to make the text boldface.

Ask the Expert

Question: Are you sure I don't need to buy a special program to write and preview HTML files on my home computer?

Answer: No. If you have a basic text editor (which nearly every new computer comes with) and a Web browser, you have everything you need! As I mentioned in Module 1, you could certainly purchase some programs that would help you write and preview HTML, but they aren't necessary at this point. While you are learning, it's best to use a basic text editor, such as SimpleText (Mac) or NotePad (PC), and then preview your pages in whichever Web browser you normally use to access the Internet.

With HTML, instead of clicking a button to make text bold, you type a tag before and after the text you want to make bold.

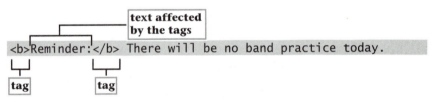

You can easily recognize tags because they are placed within *brackets* (< >), or less-than and greater-than symbols.

Did you notice the tag for bold is b? Given that piece of information, can you guess the tags to make text italic or underlined?

Desired Effect	Tag
Bold text	<b>
Italicized text	<i>
Underlined text	<u>

Now do you believe me when I say HTML is not rocket science? Don't worry—most of the tags are pretty intuitive and easy to remember.

Types of Tags

In HTML, there are usually both *opening* and *closing* tags. For example, if you use <b> as an opening tag to signify where to start making text bold, you have to use a closing tag to signify where to stop making text bold (unless you want your entire page to be boldface). To do so, you use the same tag with a forward slash placed before it: </b>. Table 2-1 shows a list of basic HTML page tags.

Hint

Even though HTML doesn't require every tag to be closed, XHTML does require it. Because all future versions of HTML are based on XHTML, you might as well get used to closing all your tags now. Throughout the rest of this book, I will add notes whenever we come across a tag that HTML doesn't require closing.

Attributes

Many tags have additional aspects that you can customize. These options are called *attributes* and are placed after the tag, but before the final bracket. You might think of attributes as ice cream flavors and toppings. After you choose what type of ice cream dessert you are going to have (cone, banana split, sundae), you get to choose what flavor you want (vanilla, chocolate, strawberry), as well as any additional toppings (sprinkles, hot fudge). The same is true for tags, in that after you select which tag you want to use, you often have a variety of optional attributes from which to choose.

Specific attributes for each tag are discussed as we move through the book. But to give you an idea of how specific attributes work, let's look at an example using the font tag.

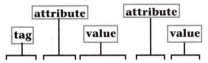

```
<font face="arial" size="+1">This text is in the Arial font
face, one size larger than</font> this text, which is not
in Arial.
```

In this example, the base tag is font, and the attributes are face and size. Each attribute has a *value*, which comes after an equals sign (=) and is placed within quotation marks.

There's no need to repeat the font tag because multiple attributes can be included in a single tag. Note, even though two attributes are listed in the opening tag, you only need to close the tag (not the attributes).

Required Tags

All HTML pages need to have the html, head, and body tags. In addition, XHTML also requires the DOCTYPE identifier. This means, at the very least, your pages should include the following:

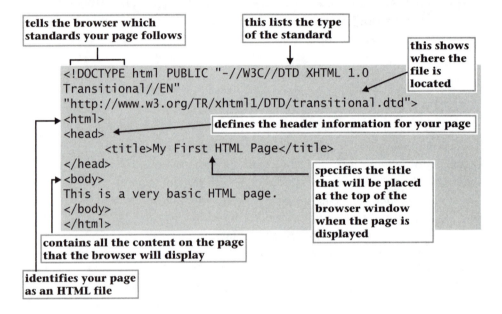

tells the browser which standards your page follows

this lists the type of the standard

this shows where the file is located

```
<!DOCTYPE html PUBLIC "-//W3C//DTD XHTML 1.0
Transitional//EN"
"http://www.w3.org/TR/xhtml1/DTD/transitional.dtd">
<html>
<head>
        <title>My First HTML Page</title>
</head>
<body>
This is a very basic HTML page.
</body>
</html>
```

defines the header information for your page

specifies the title that will be placed at the top of the browser window when the page is displayed

contains all the content on the page that the browser will display

identifies your page as an HTML file

Here is the result of this page when displayed in a browser.

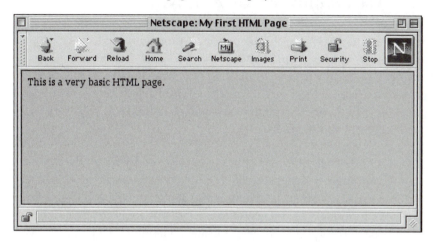

To test this basic HTML page for yourself, try the following:

1. Open SimpleText (Mac) or Notepad (PC).

2. Copy the previous code into a new text document.

3. Save it as a text-only file (ASCII text) and name it test.html.

4. Launch your browser and choose FILE | OPEN PAGE (Netscape) or FILE | OPEN (Internet Explorer).

5. Browse your hard drive to locate the test.html file, and you are off and running!

The Three Flavors of XHTML

The W3C has specified that XHTML 1.0 be available in three flavors, or versions, to accommodate the transition time during which developers and browsers migrate from HTML 4.0 to XHTML 1.0. You need to identify your page with one of these three flavors to help the browser validate it. Because most of your pages will probably fall into one of the three categories, you can simply copy-and-paste the DOCTYPE from one page on to all the others.

1. XHTML Transitional—This is the category under which the majority of your pages will probably fall. It enables you to use those HTML 4.0 tags that are deprecated, as long as you also follow the XHTML rules, such as closing all tags (even ones like br, that aren't required to be closed in regular HTML). Pages that are transitional are prepared for XHTML, but are also compatible with older browsers that don't understand XHTML. To validate your pages against this flavor of XHTML, use

```
<!DOCTYPE html PUBLIC "-//W3C//DTD XHTML 1.0 Transitional//EN"
"DTD/xhtml1-transitional.dtd">.
```

2. XHTML Strict—Pages that fall into this category don't contain any deprecated tags. These pages may not be compatible with older browsers. To validate your pages against this flavor of XHTML, use

```
<!DOCTYPE html PUBLIC "-//W3C//DTD XHTML 1.0 Strict//EN"
"DTD/xhtml1-strict.dtd">.
```

3. XHTML Frameset—Sites using HTML frames to divide the pages must identify with the frameset flavor of XHTML. To validate your pages against this flavor of XHTML, use

```
<!DOCTYPE html PUBLIC "-//W3C//DTD XHTML 1.0 Frameset//EN"
"DTD/xhtml1-frameset.dtd">.
```

2

Opening Tag	Closing Tag	Description
!DOCTYPE	n/a	tells the browser which set of standards your page adheres to —lists the standard (see more about XHTML later in this module) —identifies the location of the standard by linking to the URL
\<html\>	\</html\>	frames the entire HTML page
\<head\>	\</head\>	frames the identification information for the page, such as the title, that is transferred to the browser and search engines
\<body\>	\</body\>	frames the content of the page to be displayed in the browser window
\<title\>	\</title\>	gives the name of the page that will appear at the top of the browser window and be listed in search engines —is contained within \<head\> and \</head\>

Table 2-1   Basic HTML Page Tags

1-Minute Drill

● **What is an attribute?**

● **How can you preview your Web page in a browser?**

● An attribute is an optional feature of a tag that can be customized.
● Choose FILE I OPEN page (Netscape) or FILE I OPEN (Internet Explorer) and browse your hard drive until you locate the file you want to preview.

Ask the Expert

Question: I typed the previous HTML into a text file, but when I tried to preview the page in my browser, nothing happened. Why?

Answer: There are several possible reasons why your page would appear blank. First, review the code in the previous example and compare it line by line with the code you typed. Forgetting a closing tag or maybe just a forward slash (/) is easy. Sometimes it's helpful to take a quick break before returning to scrutinize your page. If you do make a change, be sure to save the file in your text editor, before clicking REFRESH or RELOAD in your Web browser.

If you are certain the code in your page matches the example, try resaving your file under a new name. Close your browser. Relaunch your Web browser and open the page in the browser again.

Additional troubleshooting techniques are located in Resource C.

Capitalization

HTML is case-insensitive and, in fact, very forgiving. This means all of the following three examples would be considered the same by the browser:

1. `<html>`

2. `<HTML>`

3. `<HTml>`

That said, I should point out that XHTML is case-sensitive and requires all tags to be lowercase. Of the three previous examples, the browser would properly interpret only the first. I recommend getting into the habit of using all lowercase tags.

Quotations

HTML doesn't require quotation marks unless the value of an attribute contains a hash mark or a space, as in the following case:

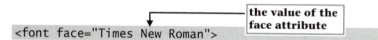

the value of the
face attribute

`<font face="Times New Roman">`

XHTML does require all attribute values to be placed within straight quotation marks, however, so a good idea is to begin doing this now.

Hint

Most word processors can output two different types of quotation marks: straight " " and curly " ". Whenever you use quotation marks in HTML documents, be sure to only use straight quotation marks. The curly quotes are sometimes misinterpreted by the browser and may produce random characters such as ? or Ö. In Microsoft Word, for example, the quotation marks default to the curly type. However, you can use choose INSERT | SYMBOL to add straight quotes instead.

Nesting

The term *nesting* appears many times throughout the course of this book, and it refers to the process of containing one HTML tag inside another.

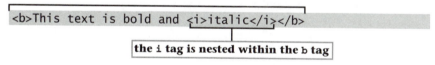

`<b>This text is bold and <i>italic</i></b>`

the i tag is nested within the b tag

There is a proper and improper way to nest tags. All tags should begin and end starting in the middle and moving out. Another way of thinking about it involves the "circle rule." You should always be able to draw semicircles that connect the opening and closing versions of each tag. If any of your semicircles intersect, your tags are not nested properly.

Using the following example, the first one is proper because the b tags are both on the outside and the i tags are both on the inside.

```
<b><i>These tags are nested properly.</i></b>
<b><i>These tags are not nested properly.</b></i>
```

Even though both may work in some browsers, you need to nest tags the proper way to ensure that your pages display the same across multiple browsers.

Spacing and Breaks

Let's look more closely at some example HTML to identify where proper spacing should occur.

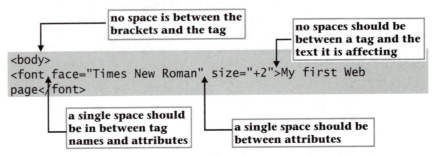

There are two places within an HTML file where you might like to add breaks:

- In between tags, to help you differentiate between sections of the page

- In between lines of text within the body of the page

Spacing and Breaks Between Tags

The first place you might like to add breaks is in between tags, as in the following example.

```
<html>                    the head tag is on a line
<head>                    below the html tag
    <title>My First web Page</title>
</head>
                              the title tag is indented to
                              show it is nested in the head tag
```

Although this is not required, most people use the ENTER or RETURN key to separate tags with line breaks. Others also indent tags that are contained within another tag, as in the previous example, the `title` tag is indented, to show it is contained or nested within the head tag. This may help you to identify the tags when viewing the page in a text editor more quickly.

Spacing Between Lines of Text

The second place you add breaks is between the lines of text in the body of the page. If you use the RETURN or ENTER key on your keyboard to add a line break in between two lines of text on your page, that line break will not appear when the browser displays the page.

```
<!DOCTYPE html PUBLIC "-//W3C//DTD XHTML 1.0
Transitional//EN"
"http://www.w3.org/TR/xhtml1/DTD/transitional.dtd">
<html>
<head>
    <title>My first web page</title>
</head>
<body>
Welcome.
                          here the RETURN was pressed twice after "welcome"
Thank you for visiting my first web page. I have several
other pages that you might be interested in.
</body>
</html>
```

In the previous code, I typed the RETURN key twice after the word "Welcome." In this example, you can see the browser ignored my returns and ran both lines of text together.

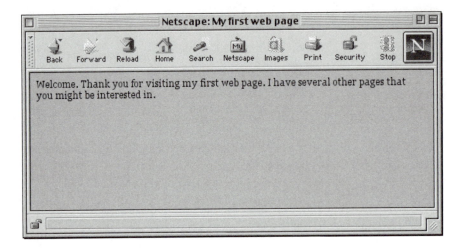

To make those line breaks appear, I'd have to use a tag to tell the browser to insert a line break. Two tags are used for breaks in content.

- `<br>`

- `<p>`

The `br` tag inserts a simple line break. It tells the browser to drop down to the next line before continuing. If you insert multiple `br` tags, the browser will drop down several lines before continuing.

The `p` tag signifies a paragraph break. The difference between the two is that paragraph breaks cause the browser to skip a line, while line breaks do not. Also, the `p` tag is considered a *container* tag because its opening and closing tags should be used to contain paragraphs of content. The `<br>` and `<p>` tags are discussed in more detail in Module 4.

If I enclose each of these paragraphs in `p tags`,

```
<p>Welcome.</p>
<p>Thank you for visiting my first web page. I have several
other pages that you might be interested in.</p>
```

the browser will know to separate them with a blank line. The following screen shows how the browser displays the text now that I have contained each of the paragraphs in `p` tags.

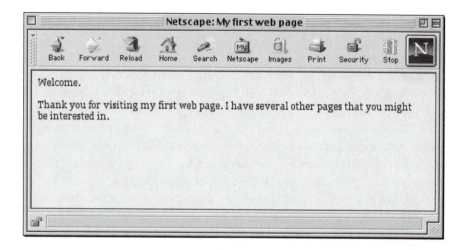

In addition, HTML neither recognizes more than a single space at a time nor does it interpret a TAB as a way to indent. This means to indent a paragraph or to leave more than one space between words, you must use style sheets (see Module 15) or special characters.

1-Minute Drill

What's wrong with these tags?

- `<b><i>This text is bold and italic.</b></i>`
- `< b >This text is bold.< / b >`

Using Special Characters

As crazy as this sounds, you shouldn't include any characters in your HTML files that you can't type with only one finger. This means, if you have to hold down the SHIFT key to type an exclamation mark or a dollar

---

- **These tags aren't nested properly. The correct order would be:**
  `<b><i>This text is bold and italic.</i></b>`
- **No spaces should appear within the tags**

sign, you will need to use a *character entity* to include that special character in your HTML file.

Even though you might be able to type a certain character on your computer system without any problems, some characters may not translate properly when visitors to your Web site view your page. So, I recommend you use character entities to maintain consistency across computer systems.

Character entities can be typed either as a numbered entity or a named entity. All character entities begin with an ampersand (&) and end with a semicolon (;). Although every character entity has a numbered version, not every one has a named version. While a full list of special characters is included in Resource *B*, a few are listed here to give you an idea of what they look like.

Hint

A few characters are reserved and given special meaning in HTML. For example, the brackets (< and >) are used to signify HTML tags, and the ampersand (&) is used to begin these entities. If you need to use a bracket within the content of your HTML page, such as when a greater-than symbol is needed, in the case of 3 > 2, you will use the character entity (>) to do so.

Character	Numbered Entity	Named Entity
"	&#34;	&quot;
&	&#38;	&amp;
(nonbreaking space)		
©	&#169;	&copy;
®	&#174;	&reg;
é	&#233;	&eacute;
<	&#60;	&lt;
>	&#62;	&gt;

> ## Hint
>
> Having made the case for using character entities, it's been my experience that certain characters *can* be used in a Web page without causing any problems. These include straight—not curly—quotation marks ("), exclamation marks (!), question marks (?), colons (:), and parentheses ( ). While I haven't noticed any of these to cause problems in the majority of browsers, you should still test your pages thoroughly when using any special characters.

Adding Comments

Sometimes, you might not want visitors to your Web site to see comments or notes you need to add to your Web pages. These notes might be directions to another person or reminders to yourself.

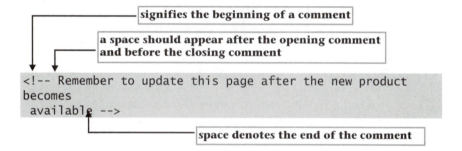

signifies the beginning of a comment

a space should appear after the opening comment and before the closing comment

```
<!-- Remember to update this page after the new product
becomes
 available -->
```

space denotes the end of the comment

Comments are not restricted in size and can cover many lines at a time. The end comment code (-->) doesn't need to be on the same line as the beginning comment code. If you forget to close your comment tag, the rest of the page will not appear in your browser. If this happens, don't be alarmed. Simply go back to the code and close that comment. The rest of the page will become visible when you save the file and reload it in the browser.

Project 2-1: Create the First Page of Your Site

To continue with the site you began planning for in the first module, we now begin the first page in your site. Goals for this project include

- Use all the necessary tags to create a basic Web page.
- Use a character entity to add a copyright symbol to the page.
- Save the page as an HTML file that can be read by a Web browser.
- Preview the page in a Web browser.

Note

All the files needed to complete the projects in this book for the Woolwich Historical Society can be downloaded from **www.osborne.com** or **www.willardesigns.com/htmlbook**. In addition, you can view my version of the Web site anytime by visiting **www.woolwichhistory.org**.

Step-by-Step

1. Open a text editor on your computer (such as SimpleText on the Mac or Notepad on the PC). Copy the following code to begin your Web page. Feel free to make edits wherever necessary to personalize your site for your organization.

```
<!DOCTYPE html PUBLIC "-//W3C//DTD XHTML 1.0 Transitional//EN"
"http://www.w3.org/TR/xhtml1/DTD/transitional.dtd">
<html>
<head>
    <title>Welcome to the Woolwich Historical Society, located in Woolwich,
Maine</title>
</head>
<body>
<p>Woolwich Historical Society, Woolwich, Maine</p>
<p>The Woolwich Historical Society's 19th Century Rural Life Museum is
located at the corner of Route 1 and Nequasset Road in Woolwich, Maine.</p>
</body>
</html>
```

2. After the end of the second paragraph, add two breaks and a copyright symbol (©), followed by the year and the name of the organization. (Example: © 2000 Woolwich Historical Society.)

3. Create a new folder on your hard drive, called `woolwichhistory` (or the name of your organization or Web site). Save this file as `index.html` in the folder you just created.

4. Open your Web browser and choose FILE I OPEN PAGE (or OPEN FILE or OPEN, depending on the browser you are using). Locate the file `index.html` you just saved.

5. Preview the page and compare it to Figure 2-1. If you need to make changes, return to your text editor (SimpleText or NotePad) to do so. Once you have made those changes, save the file and switch back to your Web browser. Click the RELOAD or REFRESH button in your browser to update your page according to the changes you just made. The complete code for your page might look like this:

```
<!DOCTYPE html PUBLIC "-//W3C//DTD XHTML 1.0 Transitional//EN"
"http://www.w3.org/TR/xhtml1/DTD/transitional.dtd">
<html>
<head>
    <title>Welcome to the Woolwich Historical Society, located in Woolwich,
Maine</title>
</head>
<body>
<p>Woolwich Historical Society, Woolwich, Maine</p>
<p>The Woolwich Historical Society's 19th Century Rural Life Museum is
located at the corner of Route 1 and Nequasset Road in Woolwich, Maine.</p>
<br />
<br />
&copy; 2000 Woolwich Historical Society
</body>
</html>
```

Hint

Does your browser window appear blank when you try to preview your page? If so, return to your text editor and make sure you have included all the necessary closing tags (such as </body> and </html>). In addition, if you are using any editor other than SimpleText or NotePad, don't forget to save the file as "text only" with an .html file extension. For more tips, see Resource C: Troubleshooting.

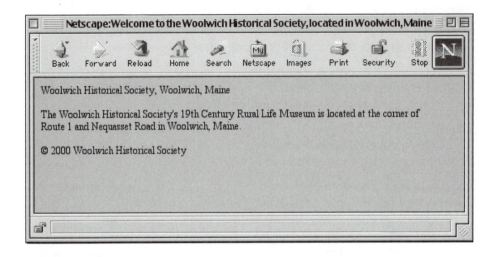

Figure 2-1   Your page should look similar to this one when displayed in a browser, depending on the organization and content you are using

Project Summary

Every Web page needs a few tags to display properly in the browser. This project helps you practice typing those tags and placing them in the correct order on the page.

Getting used to the process of editing, saving, and previewing pages is good because this is used throughout the rest of this book and during the course of your continued Web development.

✓ *Mastery Check*

1. What file extension should HTML files have?

_____

_____

2. What is this tag missing?

`<b`

3. At the very least, which tags should be included in a basic HTML page?

_____

_____

4. Which word in this tag is the attribute? What is the value of that attribute?

`<font size="+1">`

5. What might cause a random character, such as ? or Ö, to appear by mistake in a Web page?

_____

_____

6. How can you make line breaks appear within the content of a Web page?

_____

_____

Module 3

Color

Goals

- Understand the use of hexadecimal color
- Recognize Web-safe colors by their hexadecimal values

Each browser has a set of standard colors for Web pages that can be customized by the user (see Figure 3-1). If you don't specify otherwise, your pages will display according to the browser's settings.

To change colors on your Web page, you need to know the color to which you want to change it, as well as the corresponding hexadecimal color value.

Understanding Hexadecimal Color

The "normal" number system in the U.S. is *decimal*, or based on the number 10. This means we have 10 units (0-9) to use before we have to repeat a unit (as with the number 10, which uses the 0 and 1).

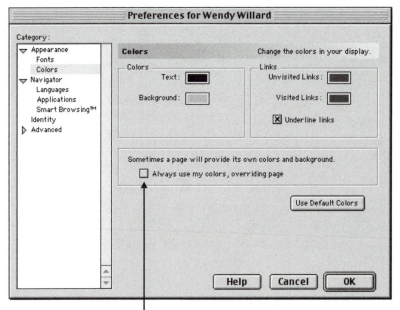

With most versions of Netscape, users have the ultimate control over how the colors on a page display

Figure 3-1   This screen shot shows how the user can customize Netscape color settings

3

The *hexadecimal* system (hex) uses the same concepts as the decimal system, except it's based on 16 units (see Table 3-1). Because HTML cannot handle decimal color values, the hexadecimal system is used to specify color values on Web pages. Instead of making up new characters to represent the remaining units after 9, the hexadecimal system uses the first six letters of the English alphabet (*A-F*).

Computer monitors display color in *RGB* mode, where R = Red, G = Green, B = Blue. Each letter (R, G, & B) is represented by a value between 0 and 255, with 0 being the darkest and 255 is the lightest in the spectrum. In RGB, the white and black have the following values:

	Red Value	**Green Value**	**Blue Value**
White	255	255	255
Black	0	0	0

This is how one graphics program—Adobe Photoshop—displays the RGB values for blue (R:00 G:00 B:255). Most other graphics programs have similar ways of helping you determine the RGB values of your colors.

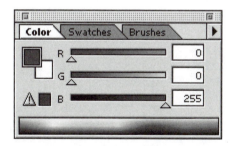

Decimal	0	1	2	3	4	5	6	7	8	9	10	11	12	13	14	15
Hex	0	1	2	3	4	5	6	7	8	9	A	B	C	D	E	F

Table 3-1   Decimal and Hexadecimal Units

In Photoshop, one way to find out what the hexadecimal values are for that shade of blue is to click the triangle in the upper-right corner of that color window and choose **WEB COLOR SLIDERS** from the menu.

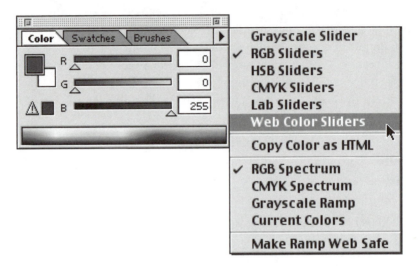

The resulting window shows the corresponding hex values for that same blue are R:00 G:00 B:FF. To reference this color in your Web page, you would use #0000FF.

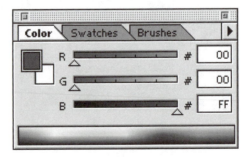

Whenever you want to use a color in an HTML page, you need to translate that color from decimal (RGB) to hex. Each red, green, or blue value translates into a two-digit hex value. You then combine all three of those two-digit hex values into a single string, preceded by a hash mark.

Here's an example where a hexadecimal color is used to change the text to blue.

```
<font color="#0000FF">
```

While you previously needed a scientific calculator to convert between decimal and hexadecimal values, many charts, software programs, converters, and even Web pages are now available to do this for you. Links and additional resources can be found in Resource *D*.

Using Color Names

HTML 3.2 and 4.0 have defined a standard set of 16 colors, which can be referenced by names in addition to hex values. See table 3-2.

Netscape and Internet Explorer also enable you to specify additional colors according to their own list of names. However, I caution against the use of these nonstandard color names—even though they are easier to remember—because most other browsers don't support them.

Color Name	Hex Value
black	"#000000"
white	"#FFFFFF"
silver	"#C0C0C0"
gray	"#808080"
lime	"#00FF00"
olive	"#808000"
green	"#008000"
yellow	"#FFFF00"
maroon	"#800000"
navy	"#000080"
red	"#FF0000"
blue	"#0000FF"
purple	"#800080"
teal	"#008080"
fuchsia	"#FF00FF"
aqua	"#00FFFF"

Table 3-2   **Standard Colors**

Note

Although HTML requires you to specify colors with hexadecimal values or names, the use of styles (discussed in Module 15) also enables you to specify colors using the decimal (RGB) values.

Using Web-safe Colors

Have you ever looked at your favorite Web site on someone else's monitor and noticed the colors seemed a bit different? This may have been because of different monitor settings. For example, most newer computer systems and monitors are capable of displaying millions of colors. But that wasn't the case only a few years ago, when most DOS-based PCs were set up to display 256 colors or fewer. This reduced color palette means you can't always be assured the color you choose for your Web page will be available on the viewer's system.

To compound the problem, Macintosh systems display a different set of 256 colors than their DOS-based PC counterparts. Only 216 colors between the two computer systems (Mac and PC) are the same! Those 216 colors have come to be known as the *Web-safe color palette* (see inside panel of front cover for a full-color reproduction of the Web-safe palette). You can feel safe that if you use a color from this palette, the majority of your viewers will see approximately the same color you selected.

You can easily recognize Web-safe colors by their hexadecimal values. Each of the Web-safe colors has RGB values that are multiples of 51. So, every color in the 216-color Web-safe palette has a hex value made up of the values shown here. This makes it easy to recognize if a color you're using is Web-safe.

RGB	Hex
0	00
51	33
102	66
153	99
204	CC
255	FF

The color selected in this illustration is not Web-safe. This is evident because the green value is #55, which is not a Web-safe hex value. To make this color Web-safe, you would have to change the green value to #66.

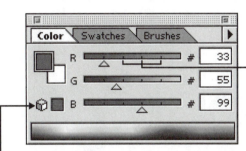

Photoshop's color window has little black lines along each of the three color bars (red, green, and blue) to show where the Web-safe values are

This symbol warns that the color currently selected is not Web-safe. Clicking the square box next to the cube causes Photoshop to change the color to the closest Web-safe color

Ask the Expert

Question: What happens if I don't use a Web-safe color?

Answer: The answer depends on what your viewer's color settings are. If the viewer's system is set up to view 256 colors or fewer, then the browser may use dithering to try to approximate the color.

Dithering causes colors to have a somewhat "dotty" or "speckled" appearance (as shown in Illustration 5) because it often requires two or more similar colors placed next to each other in a checkerboard-style pattern to approximate a color not within the 256-color palette. However, if you use a non–Web-safe color and the viewer's system can handle more than 256 colors, then you most likely won't have any problems.

For example, the color used to create this image was not Web-safe. Because it was viewed on a system capable of displaying 256 colors or fewer, the browser dithered the colors that weren't within its standard color palette. (A portion of the image is magnified 2*x*.)

Question: I used Web-safe colors on my Web site, but they still look different on some other machines. Why?

Answer: A variety of other reasons exist why colors may appear differently, but the most common reason has to do with gamma. Loosely defined, *gamma* refers to the relationship between your monitor's power supply and its light intensity. Most monitors have a gamma setting of 2.5 but, left unchecked, they can produce irregular results. To fix any irregularities, software makers have developed gamma correction tools. Macintosh systems have built-in *gamma correction tools* that set the gamma to 1.8, while DOS-based PCs are typically set to 2.5. This can cause images to appear lighter on a Mac and darker on a PC.

Another possible reason for color differences could be the ambient light in the room containing the monitor, as well as the brightness and contrast settings on a monitor.

Specifying Document Colors

Document colors, such as the background and the text, can be changed using attributes within the body tag. The default colors vary according to the browser, and they can also be customized by the user, as shown at the beginning of the module in Figure 3-1.

Attribute	Values	Description
bgcolor	"#rrggbb" (hexadecimal value) or "color name"	changes the background color of the page
text	"#rrggbb" (hexadecimal value) or "color name"	changes the default font color of the page

These attributes can be separated by spaces and added to the body tag, as the following shows. The order in which you specify colors (of the background, text, and so forth) doesn't matter.

```
<!DOCTYPE html PUBLIC "-//W3C//DTD XHTML 1.0 Transitional//EN"
"http://www.w3.org/TR/xhtml1/DTD/transitional.dtd">
<html>
<head>
<title>My First HTML Page - with new document colors</title>
</head>
<body bgcolor="#000000" text="#ffffff">
This is a very basic HTML page.
</body>
</html>
```

You can see how the previous code would change the look of the Web page, by viewing Figure 3-2

Given how different colors can appear on various computer systems, picking text colors that are in contrast to your background colors is a good

Figure 3-2 This screen shows how the browser displays the page after I changed the background color to black (#000000) and the text color to white (#ffffff)

idea. For example, dark blue text on a dark purple background may not be easily distinguished by all viewers.

In addition, remember, the majority of people who are color-blind cannot differentiate between red and green.

Project 3-1: Change the Colors of Your Page

Let's take the `index.html` page from the previous module, and change the background and text colors of that page. Goals for this project include

- Choose colors from the Web-safe palette.

- Add the `bgcolor` and `text` attributes to the `body` tag.

- Reference the colors with the appropriate hexadecimal color codes.

   Note that: All the files needed to complete the projects in this book for the Woolwich Historical Society can be downloaded from **www.osborne.com** or **www.willardesigns.com/htmlbook**. In addition, you can view my version of the Web site anytime by visiting **www.woolwichhistory.org**.

Step-by-Step

1. Open your text editor (SimpleText on the Mac or Notepad on the PC) and load the `index.html` page saved from Module 2.

2. Add the bgcolor and text attributes to the `body` tag on your page as the following shows, where *n* is equal to a number in the hexadecimal color code, and save the file. You can find a color in several different ways:

```
<body bgcolor="#nnnnnn" text="#nnnnnn">
```

- Pick one from the Web-safe color palette on the inside front cover of this book.

- Choose one from the color-picker in your favorite graphics program (such as Adobe Photoshop).

- View an online Web-safe color palette by visiting **www.lynda.com/hexh.html.**

- Download the HTML Beginner's Guide .zip file, which has your very own Web-safe color palette in the Module 3 folder.

3. Open your Web browser and choose FILE I OPEN PAGE (or OPEN FILE or OPEN, depending on the browser you're using). Locate the file `index.html` you just saved.

4. Preview the page to determine if you approve of your color choices. If you don't, return to your text editor to make changes. After making any changes, save the file and switch back to the browser. Choose REFRESH or RELOAD to preview the changes you just made.

Project Summary

Using attributes to change the colors of your Web page is not difficult, but it does require some planning to find a set of colors that works well together. Viewing your pages on several different computer systems can help ensure they all appear as you would like.

Hint

Do any of your colors look drastically different than you imagined they would? Make sure you surrounded your color value with straight quotes (such as "#003366"). If you are missing either the beginning or ending set of quotes, the browser may interpret your color as a different one than you intended. For more tips, see Resource C: Troubleshooting.

☑ Mastery Check

1. What is the difference between decimals and hexadecimals?

2. The first two numbers in a six-digit hexadecimal code refer to which color?

3. How many colors are in the Web-safe palette?

4. Which color is not Web-safe?

    A. #FFCC33

    B. #FFCCFF

    C. #FFCC44

    D. #FFCC66

5. How do you change the background color of a Web page?

Module 4

Working with Text

Goals

- Format and align paragraphs of text
- Use logical and physical style tags to format text
- Use the font tag to alter the face, color, and size of text

61

Now that you've learned the basics of planning for, opening, editing, and saving a Web page, you can learn about editing the content. HTML allows for many ways to format text on a Web page. However, some of these ways were *deprecated* by the W3C when they set up the XHTML standards. This means the W3C discourages the use of these tags, in favor of style sheets (discussed in Module 15).

If you wonder why you should spend time learning something that is deprecated, don't worry—browsers are expected to continue supporting these deprecated tags for some time. These tags are simple to learn and easier to use than their style sheet counterparts, particularly because browser support for style sheets is, at this point, a bit variable.

Formatting Paragraphs

As discussed briefly in Module 2, HTML is different from traditional word processors because you cannot simply click the RETURN or ENTER key to end a paragraph, and then the TAB key to indent a new one. Instead, you have to use tags to tell the browser where to start and end paragraphs, as well as any other types of breaks.

Paragraph Breaks

In the earlier versions of HTML, the p tag was used as a one-sided tag (with no closing tag) to signify the end of a paragraph. When the browser saw the <p> in the page, it knew to stop where it was, skip a line, and begin again on a new line to differentiate between paragraphs. Here's an example of how the p tag might have been used originally.

```
Jack and Jill went up a hill<p>
To fetch a pail of water<p>
Jack fell down and broke his crown<p>
And Jill came tumbling after<p>
```

While it is still perfectly legitimate to use the p tag without a closing tag, as previously shown, the W3C changed the specifications in the recent versions and is recommending otherwise. The p tag now functions specifically as a container for paragraphs. This means you need to use an

opening p tag at the beginning of your paragraph and a closing p tag at
the end. If each line in this nursery rhyme were a paragraph, it might look
like this:

Note

Additional reasons to use both the opening and closing versions of the
p tag are it's required in XHTML and is especially important when using
style sheets.

4

```
<p>Jack and Jill went up a hill</p>
<p>To fetch a pail of water</p>
<p>Jack fell down and broke his crown</p>
<p>And Jill came tumbling after</p>
```

Figure 4-1 shows how the browser would render this code. Notice how
the p tag forces a blank line in between each of the paragraphs or sections.

Even though the p tag is most often used to contain paragraphs of text,
it doesn't automatically indent them. There's no regular HTML tag to
indent and, as discussed in Module 2, the browser ignores any tabs and
multiple spaces you enter using the keyboard.

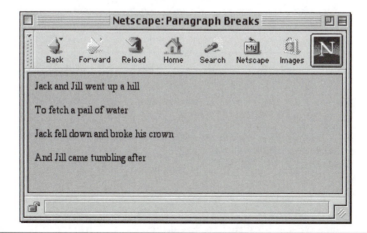

Figure 4-1 Notice the **p** tag forces a blank line in between paragraphs

Hint

Don't worry—using both the opening and closing p tags won't cause the browser to render more than one blank line in between each section or paragraph. In fact, most browsers ignore multiple p tags placed one after the other. This means <p><p><p><p> will produce the same single paragraph break as <p>.

Instead, you can use the nonbreaking space character entity ( ) several times to indent your paragraphs. In the following example, I used   four times at the beginning of each paragraph to achieve a short indent.

This is the named character entity for nonbreaking space; you have to use this special character to force spaces

```
<p>    Jack and Jill went up a hill to fetch a pail of
water. Jack fell down and broke his crown and Jill came tumbling after.</p>
<p>    Mary had a little lamb, its fleece was white as
snow. Everywhere that Mary went, the lamb was sure to go.</p>
<p>    Twinkle, twinkle, little star, how I wonder what
you are. Up above the world so high, like a diamond in the sky... Twinkle,
twinkle, little star, how I wonder what you are.</p>
```

Figure 4-2 shows how the nonbreaking space character entity can help you achieve indented paragraphs.

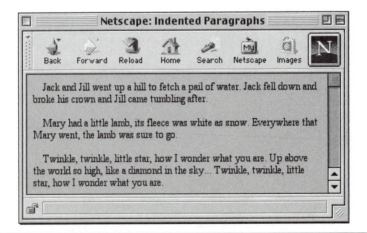

Figure 4-2   Here we see how the nonbreaking space character entity can help you achieve indented paragraphs

Line Breaks

You can also use the `br` tag to add a line break in your HTML page. Typing the `br` tag in HTML is the same as clicking the RETURN or ENTER key on your keyboard in a word processor. It causes the browser to stop printing text on that line and drop down to the next line on the page. The following code uses the same nursery rhyme with line breaks instead of paragraph breaks in between each line. Figure 4-3 shows how the browser would display this code.

Note

Earlier, I mentioned some HTML tags aren't required to be closed. The tag used to add line breaks, `<br>`, is one such tag. To make the `br` tag XHTML-compliant, however, you can add a space and a forward slash before the final bracket. Although this won't alter the page display in the browser, it may cause problems for some WYSIWYG HTML editors who don't understand XHTML. As long as you are using a simple text editor for the examples in this book, you won't have any problems.

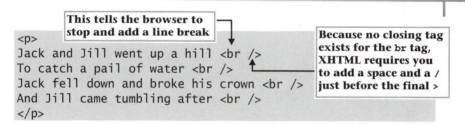

```
<p>
Jack and Jill went up a hill <br />
To catch a pail of water <br />
Jack fell down and broke his crown <br />
And Jill came tumbling after <br />
</p>
```

This tells the browser to stop and add a line break

Because no closing tag exists for the `br` tag, XHTML requires you to add a space and a / just before the final >

In most cases, it doesn't matter if you click the RETURN or ENTER key after typing `<br  />` to begin again on the next line (as shown in the previous code). In fact, that code would have the same output if you let all the text run together as in the following example:

```
<p>
Jack and Jill went up a hill<br />To catch a pail of
water<br />Jack fell down and broke his crown<br />And Jill
came tumbling after<br />
</p>
```

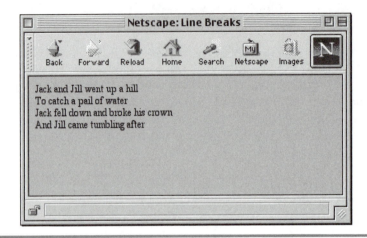

Figure 4-3 The browser understands the **br** tag as a signal to stop and begin again on the next line

Unlike the p tag, which cannot be repeated to add multiple paragraph breaks in a row, you can use the br tag to add several line breaks. To do so, simply repeat the tag in your HTML file. Figure 4-4 shows how the browser renders this code.

```
<p>
Jack and Jill went up a hill <br /><br /><br /><br />
To fetch a pail of water
</p>
```

Preformat

The only time pressing the RETURN or ENTER key in your page creates line breaks in the browser view is when the pre tag is used. Short for *preformat*, the pre tag renders text in the browser exactly as you type it. Why, then, wouldn't I just use the pre tag for everything because it sounds so much easier? Two reasons:

1. The pre tag usually displays text in a monospaced font, such as Courier, that looks similar to what a typewriter prints. While this may be appropriate for examples of programming code, it probably isn't the look you want for your entire Web site.

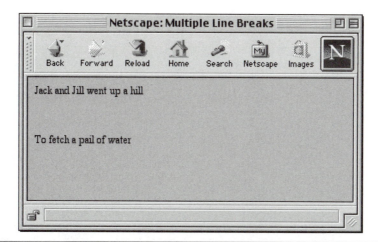

Jack and Jill went up a hill

To fetch a pail of water

4

Figure 4-4 You can use multiple **br** tags to add as many breaks as you want to your page

2. The output isn't guaranteed to remain as you envisioned it. Even though you are able to use the tab key to format text in the pre tag, browsers may interpret a tab as a greater or lesser number of spaces than your text editor did. This could cause any tables you lay out to render incorrectly.

With that said, the pre tag is quite useful for displaying code examples or even creative illustrations.

```
<pre>
This text will display exactly as I type it. Watch this:
     x  |  o  |  o
     ---------------
     x  |  x  |
     ---------------
     o  |     |  x
</pre>
```

Here's how Netscape displays the previous code:

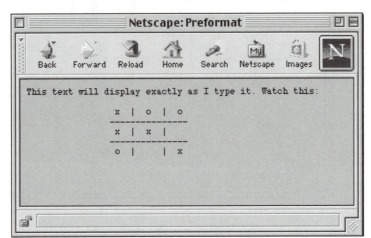

Quotation Blocks

The `blockquote` tag gives you the option of setting off a long quotation or note that might otherwise get lost within a paragraph of text. This tag indents the entire selection on both the right and the left, and also adds a blank line above and below. The browser determines the exact amount of the indentation, and it may vary from browser to browser. The result of the following code is shown in Figure 4-5.

```
<p>Campers sleep in cabins that hold 10-12 people,
including 2 college-age counselors. The girls' cabins all
have showers and toilets, whereas the boys share a
latrine.</p>
```

This tells the browser to begin indenting this section of text

```
<blockquote>Would you like to see a video clip of a cabin?
The cabin shown is called "Manana" and usually houses the
oldest girls.</blockquote>
```

The browser continues to indent the text until it sees the closing `blockquote` tag

```
<p>Each summer campers, ages 12-18, come from all over the
world to spend 3 or 6 weeks at Chop Point. In recent years,
we have had campers from foreign countries such as Italy,
Switzerland, France, Canada, Mexico, Puerto Rico, Japan,
Germany, Ireland and Brazil (just to name a few).</p>
```

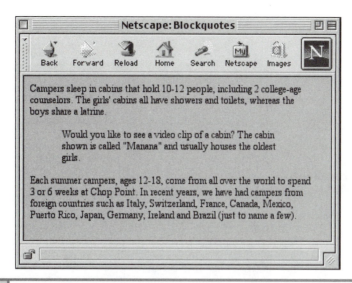

Figure 4-5 Notice how the `blockquote` tag causes the text to be indented on both sides

You can include `br` tags within the content of your blockquote, to create a group of text lines that are all indented. In addition, you can nest `blockquote` tags to indent text further.

Horizontal Rules

One way you can separate sections of your Web page is to use the `hr` tag. By default, this tag produces a thin, gray horizontal line called a *horizontal rule*.

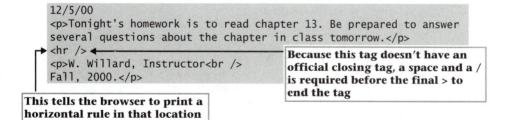

```
12/5/00
<p>Tonight's homework is to read chapter 13. Be prepared to answer
several questions about the chapter in class tomorrow.</p>
<hr />
<p>W. Willard, Instructor<br />
Fall, 2000.</p>
```

Because this tag doesn't have an official closing tag, a space and a / is required before the final > to end the tag

This tells the browser to print a horizontal rule in that location

Although many browsers display horizontal rules a bit differently, a basic one usually looks like the one shown here.

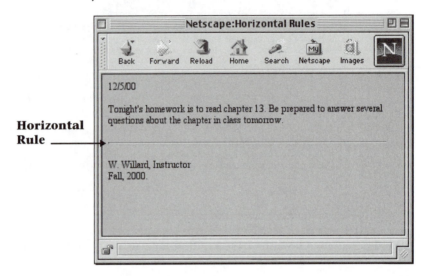

Horizontal Rule

Several attributes can change the appearance of the horizontal rules you use on your pages (see table 4-1). The use of these attributes is deprecated in favor of style sheets, but they are still supported in HTML 4.0.

Attribute	Possible Values	Description
align	left, center, right, justify (the default is "center")	aligns the rule within the browser window
noshade	noshade *Although no required value exists for this attribute, XHTML requires all attributes to have a value. To comply, simply repeat the attribute name as the value	changes the look of the rule from 3-D to flat
size	# of pixels (the default—also the smallest—is 2)	changes the thickness or height of the rule
width	# of pixels or % of screen (the default is "100 %")	changes the horizontal length of the rule as it appears across the screen

Table 4-1   **Attributes for Horizontal Rules**

The following example uses each one of these attributes to give you an idea of how they appear in the browser.

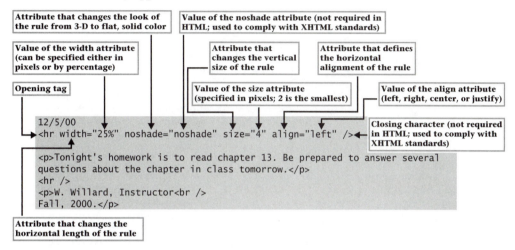

| Attribute that changes the look of the rule from 3-D to flat, solid color | Value of the noshade attribute (not required in HTML; used to comply with XHTML standards) |

| Value of the width attribute (can be specified either in pixels or by percentage) | Attribute that changes the vertical size of the rule | Attribute that defines the horizontal alignment of the rule |

| Opening tag | Value of the size attribute (specified in pixels; 2 is the smallest) | Value of the align attribute (left, right, center, or justify) |

```
12/5/00
<hr width="25%" noshade="noshade" size="4" align="left" />
<p>Tonight's homework is to read chapter 13. Be prepared to answer several
questions about the chapter in class tomorrow.</p>
<hr />
<p>W. Willard, Instructor<br />
Fall, 2000.</p>
```

| Closing character (not required in HTML; used to comply with XHTML standards) |

| Attribute that changes the horizontal length of the rule |

This illustration shows how the previous code might appear in the browser. The top horizontal rule that is just below the date has a width of "25 %," a size of "4", is aligned left, and contains "noshade."

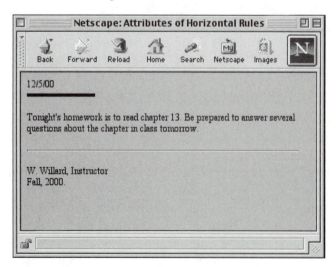

Alignment

When you want to align whole sections of text, you use the same attribute you just learned in the section on horizontal rules: `align`. In this case, add the `align` attribute to the `p` tag, as in the following example (see Figure 4-6 for a visual representation):

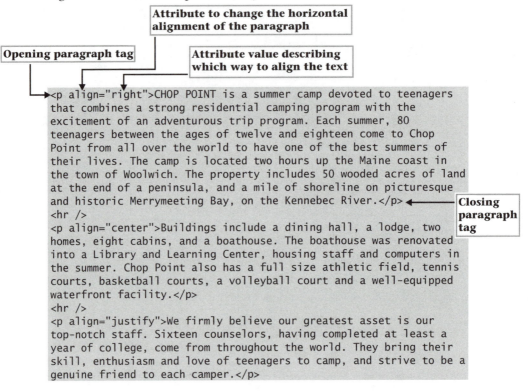

Attribute to change the horizontal alignment of the paragraph

Opening paragraph tag

Attribute value describing which way to align the text

```
<p align="right">CHOP POINT is a summer camp devoted to teenagers
that combines a strong residential camping program with the
excitement of an adventurous trip program. Each summer, 80
teenagers between the ages of twelve and eighteen come to Chop
Point from all over the world to have one of the best summers of
their lives. The camp is located two hours up the Maine coast in
the town of Woolwich. The property includes 50 wooded acres of land
at the end of a peninsula, and a mile of shoreline on picturesque
and historic Merrymeeting Bay, on the Kennebec River.</p>
<hr />
<p align="center">Buildings include a dining hall, a lodge, two
homes, eight cabins, and a boathouse. The boathouse was renovated
into a Library and Learning Center, housing staff and computers in
the summer. Chop Point also has a full size athletic field, tennis
courts, basketball courts, a volleyball court and a well-equipped
waterfront facility.</p>
<hr />
<p align="justify">We firmly believe our greatest asset is our
top-notch staff. Sixteen counselors, having completed at least a
year of college, come from throughout the world. They bring their
skill, enthusiasm and love of teenagers to camp, and strive to be a
genuine friend to each camper.</p>
```

Closing paragraph tag

The normal text alignment depends how text is read across the page in the browser's default language. If text is read from left to right, the normal alignment is left. If text is read from right to left, however, the normal alignment is right.

In either case, when text is aligned to one side or the other, the opposite side is *ragged*, in that it doesn't continue all the way to the margin. When text does continue to both margins, it is called *justified*.

Another way to align sections of text involves the `div` tag. This tag doesn't have any formatting properties of its own but, instead, carries the properties of whichever attribute is used with it. This means placing a `<div>` in your page won't affect the look of it in the browser. But, placing `<div align="right">` aligns the elements after that tag to the right margin.

**This paragraph is aligned
to the right margin**

This paragraph is centered

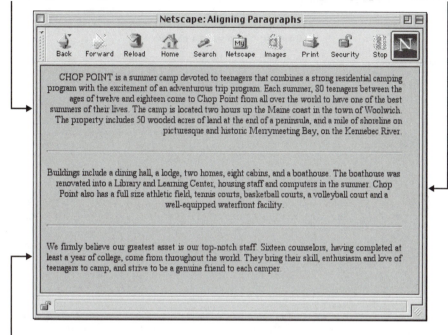

This paragraph is justified

4

Figure 4-6   The previous example code is illustrated here, showing different alignment possibilities using the **p** tag and the **align** attribute

---

Hint

Although using `<center>` as a shortened version of `<div align="center">` is acceptable, it isn't recommended by the W3C. They prefer you use the `div` tag for consistency.

One significant benefit of the `div` tag, as compared to using the `align` attribute with the p or hr tag, is it can be used to align many different types of elements on your page. In fact, with a single `div` tag, you can align paragraphs, horizontal rules, and many other page elements.

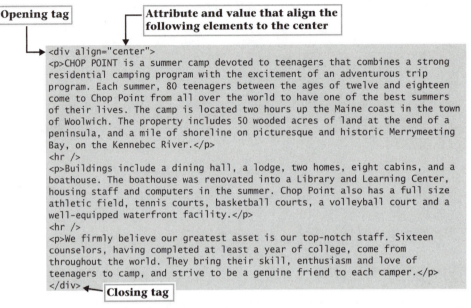

Opening tag

Attribute and value that align the following elements to the center

```
<div align="center">
<p>CHOP POINT is a summer camp devoted to teenagers that combines a strong
residential camping program with the excitement of an adventurous trip
program. Each summer, 80 teenagers between the ages of twelve and eighteen
come to Chop Point from all over the world to have one of the best summers
of their lives. The camp is located two hours up the Maine coast in the town
of Woolwich. The property includes 50 wooded acres of land at the end of a
peninsula, and a mile of shoreline on picturesque and historic Merrymeeting
Bay, on the Kennebec River.</p>
<hr />
<p>Buildings include a dining hall, a lodge, two homes, eight cabins, and a
boathouse. The boathouse was renovated into a Library and Learning Center,
housing staff and computers in the summer. Chop Point also has a full size
athletic field, tennis courts, basketball courts, a volleyball court and a
well-equipped waterfront facility.</p>
<hr />
<p>We firmly believe our greatest asset is our top-notch staff. Sixteen
counselors, having completed at least a year of college, come from
throughout the world. They bring their skill, enthusiasm and love of
teenagers to camp, and strive to be a genuine friend to each camper.</p>
</div>
```

Closing tag

Here is how the previous code is displayed in the browser. Notice how all of the page elements contained within the `div` tags take on the characteristics of that `div` tag. In this case, this means all of that content is centered.

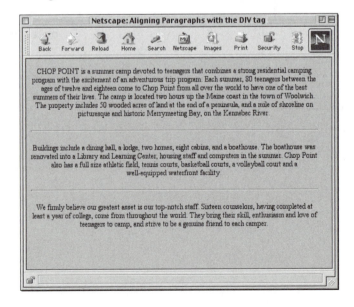

⊣ *Note* ────────────────

The `align` attribute is deprecated, in favor of style sheets, but is still valid in HTML 4.0.

Project 4-1: Format Paragraphs and Page Elements

This initial project in Module 4 gives you practice formatting paragraphs and other page elements using the `p`, `blockquote`, and `div` tags. Goals for this project include

● Add `p` tags to format the paragraphs

● Use the `div` tag to format a section of the page

● Use the `blockquote` tag to format a long quotation

● Add a horizontal rule to separate sections

Note that: All the files needed to complete the projects in this book for the Woolwich Historical Society can be downloaded from **www.osborne.com** or **www.willardesigns.com/htmlbook/**. In addition, you can view my version of the Web site anytime by visiting **www.woolwichhistory.org**.

Step-by-Step

1. Open your text editor (SimpleText on the Mac or Notepad on the PC) and load the `index.html` page saved from Project 3.1. Make the following changes and save the file.

2. Add two to four more paragraphs of text in between the existing paragraphs and the copyright information. (Those using the Woolwich Historical Society can use the text included in the .zip file available from the Osborne Web site, also shown after this numbered list.)

3. Add `p` tags around each of the paragraphs on the page.

4. Add a quotation (also shown after this numbered list) in between two of the paragraphs. Format it using the `blockquote` tag. Italicize any part of the quotation contained within quotation marks.

5. Add a horizontal rule in between the last paragraph and the copyright information.

4

6. Use the `div` tag to align both the horizontal rule and the copyright information to the right margin.

7. Open your Web browser and choose FILE | OPEN PAGE (or OPEN FILE or OPEN, depending on the browser you are using). Locate the file `index.html` you just saved.

8. Preview the page to check your work. If you need to make changes, return to your text editor to make changes. After making any changes, save the file and switch back to the browser. Choose REFRESH or RELOAD to preview the changes you just made.

Added Paragraphs

The following paragraphs are the added text (mentioned previously in step two) and can be added to your Web page. The text is also included in the .zip file available from the Osborne Web site.

Woolwich is a rural community on the east shore of the Kennebec River, opposite the historic city of Bath and approximately 12 miles from the Atlantic Ocean. It is bordered by waterways: the Sasanoa, the Sheepscot and Merry Meeting Bay, which is the confluence of five rivers. First settled in 1600's and incorporated in 1759, the town is named for Woolwich, England, which in like manner is situated on a large, navigable river.

The Kennebec brought to the territory explorers, settlers, traders and fishermen. Indians from the hinterland used this route for summer visits to the coast, and harried early settlers with attacks. The first settlement was abandoned in 1600. Subsequently, the area was resettled by inhabitants whose courage, perseverance, strength and ingenuity enabled the survival of their town.

The Woolwich Historical Society's 19th Century Rural Life Museum affords the visitor an opportunity to step back in time and experience life as it was for earlier generations, while touring an eight room authentic country farmhouse, shed and barn. On display are home furnishings, quilts, garments, household implements and the tools and equipment of local employment: farming, blacksmithing, dairying, brick and pottery making and seafaring.

History and genealogy researchers visiting the museum will be directed to a substantial collection of resources, among them *The History of Woolwich, Maine: A Town Remembered,* which may be purchased in soft cover. Other items for sale include a beautiful watercolor print by Betsy Bisson, historical maps, note cards, recipe booklet, and postcards. All items require an additional shipping and handling fee. Contact us for more information.

Quotation

The following quote is the added text (as mentioned previously in step four) and can be added to your Web page. It is also included in the .zip file available from the Osborne Web site.

"They lived between the dark forest and the Kennebec River that empties into the lonely Atlantic. They did for themselves. They had to. They left after them lilac bushes, stone walls, deeply dug wells, tall elms now dying, old cellar holes, old things in old houses, and the Next Generation." From Carlton Day Reed Sr's Proceedings (Taken from 1760-1800 town records.)

Check Your Work   If you are using the Woolwich Historical Society, you can compare your files to the following code and Figure 4–7.

```
<!DOCTYPE html PUBLIC "-//W3C//DTD XHTML 1.0 Transitional//EN"
"http://www.w3.org/TR/xhtml1/DTD/transitional.dtd">
<html>
<head>
    <title>Welcome to the Woolwich Historical Society, located in
Woolwich, Maine</title>
</head>
<body bgcolor="#ffffff" text="#000000">
<p>Woolwich Historical Society, Woolwich, Maine</p>
<p>The Woolwich Historical Society's 19th Century Rural Life Museum
is located at the corner of Route 1 and Nequasset Road in Woolwich,
Maine.</p>
<p>Woolwich is a rural community on the east shore of the Kennebec
River, opposite the historic city of Bath and approximately 12
miles from the Atlantic Ocean. It is bordered by waterways: the
Sasanoa, the Sheepscot and Merry Meeting Bay, which is the
confluence of five rivers. First settled in 1600's and incorporated
in 1759, the town is named for Woolwich, England, which in like
manner is situated on a large, navigable river.</p>
<p>The Kennebec brought to the territory explorers, settlers,
traders and fishermen. Indians from the hinterland used this route
for summer visits to the coast, and harried early settlers with
```

```
attacks. The first settlement was abandoned in 1600. Subsequently,
the area was resettled by inhabitants whose courage, perseverance,
strength and ingenuity enabled the survival of their town.</p>
<blockquote>"They lived between the dark forest and the Kennebec
River that empties into the lonely Atlantic. They did for
themselves. They had to. They left after them lilac bushes, stone
walls, deeply dug wells, tall elms now dying, old cellar holes, old
things in old houses, and the Next Generation." From Carlton Day
Reed Sr's Proceedings (Taken from 1760-1800 town
records.)</blockquote>
<p>The Woolwich Historical Society's 19th Century Rural Life Museum
affords the visitor an opportunity to step back in time and
experience life as it was for earlier generations, while touring an
eight room authentic country farmhouse, shed and barn. On display
are home furnishings, quilts, garments, household implements and
the tools and equipment of local employment: farming,
blacksmithing, dairying, brick and pottery making and
seafaring.</p>
<p>History and genealogy researchers visiting the museum will be
directed to a substantial collection of resources, among them The
History of Woolwich, Maine: a Town Remembered, which may be
purchased in soft cover. Other items for sale include a beautiful
watercolor print by Betsy Bisson (shown below), historical maps,
note cards, recipe booklet, and postcards. All items require an
additional shipping and handling fee. Contact us for more
information.</p>
<div align="right">
<hr />
<br />
<br />
&copy; 2000 Woolwich Historical Society
</div>
</body>
</html>
```

Project Summary

Page elements can be aligned and formatted using the p tag or the div tag. Because text and element formatting are used on almost every Web page, practicing and understanding the capabilities for doing so within HTML is important.

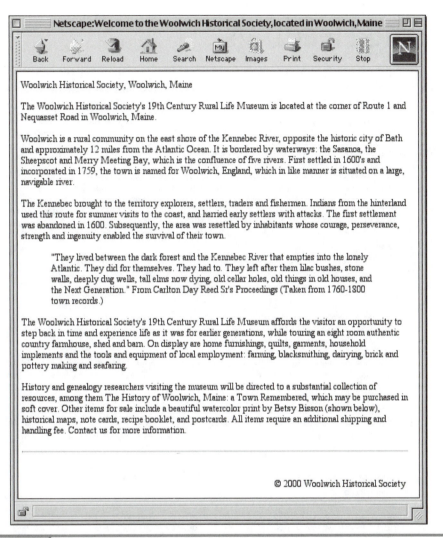

Woolwich Historical Society, Woolwich, Maine

The Woolwich Historical Society's 19th Century Rural Life Museum is located at the corner of Route 1 and Nequasset Road in Woolwich, Maine.

Woolwich is a rural community on the east shore of the Kennebec River, opposite the historic city of Bath and approximately 12 miles from the Atlantic Ocean. It is bordered by waterways: the Sasanoa, the Sheepscot and Merry Meeting Bay, which is the confluence of five rivers. First settled in 1600's and incorporated in 1759, the town is named for Woolwich, England, which in like manner is situated on a large, navigable river.

The Kennebec brought to the territory explorers, settlers, traders and fishermen. Indians from the hinterland used this route for summer visits to the coast, and harried early settlers with attacks. The first settlement was abandoned in 1600. Subsequently, the area was resettled by inhabitants whose courage, perseverance, strength and ingenuity enabled the survival of their town.

> "They lived between the dark forest and the Kennebec River that empties into the lonely Atlantic. They did for themselves. They had to. They left after them lilac bushes, stone walls, deeply dug wells, tall elms now dying, old cellar holes, old things in old houses, and the Next Generation." From Carlton Day Reed Sr's Proceedings (Taken from 1760-1800 town records.)

The Woolwich Historical Society's 19th Century Rural Life Museum affords the visitor an opportunity to step back in time and experience life as it was for earlier generations, while touring an eight room authentic country farmhouse, shed and barn. On display are home furnishings, quilts, garments, household implements and the tools and equipment of local employment: farming, blacksmithing, dairying, brick and pottery making and seafaring.

History and genealogy researchers visiting the museum will be directed to a substantial collection of resources, among them The History of Woolwich, Maine: a Town Remembered, which may be purchased in soft cover. Other items for sale include a beautiful watercolor print by Betsy Bisson (shown below), historical maps, note cards, recipe booklet, and postcards. All items require an additional shipping and handling fee. Contact us for more information.

© 2000 Woolwich Historical Society

Figure 4-7   If you are using the Woolwich Historical Society, your page might look similar to this one

Using Headings

One of the earliest means of formatting text was the heading tag. It is available in six levels of importance from <h1> down to <h6>, as shown in the following code and Figure 4-8. You might think of these headers as headlines for chunks of text.

This is the opening tag that tells the browser to begin treating this text as a level 1 header

This closing tag tells the browser to stop treating the text as a level 1 header and to return to the default text formatting

```
<!DOCTYPE html PUBLIC "-//W3C//DTD XHTML 1.0 Transitional//EN"
"http://www.w3.org/TR/xhtml1/DTD/transitional.dtd">
<html>
<head>
      <title>Header Example</title>
</head>
<body>
<h1>This is an example of a level 1 header.</h1>
<p>This is the text that follows the level 1 header. This is the text that
follows the level 1 header. This is the text that follows the level 1
header.</p>
<h2>This is an example of a level 2 header.</h2>
<p>This is the text that follows the level 2 header. This is the text that
follows the level 2 header. This is the text that follows the level 2
header.</p>
<h3>This is an example of a level 3 header.</h3>
<p>This is the text that follows the level 3 header. This is the text that
follows the level 3 header. This is the text that follows the level 3
header.</p>
<h4>This is an example of a level 4 header.</h4>
<p>This is the text that follows the level 4 header. This is the text that
follows the level 4 header. This is the text that follows the level 4
header.</p>
<h5>This is an example of a level 5 header.</h5>
<p>This is the text that follows the level 5 header. This is the text that
follows the level 5 header. This is the text that follows the level 5
header.</p>
<h6>This is an example of a level 6 header.</h6>
<p>This is the text that follows the level 6 header. This is the text that
follows the level 6 header. This is the text that follows the level 6
header.</p>
</body>
</html>
```

Heading tags are similar to the headings you might use in a word processor like Microsoft Word. They are also like headings in outlines because they should only be used in the proper order, from h1 down to h6.

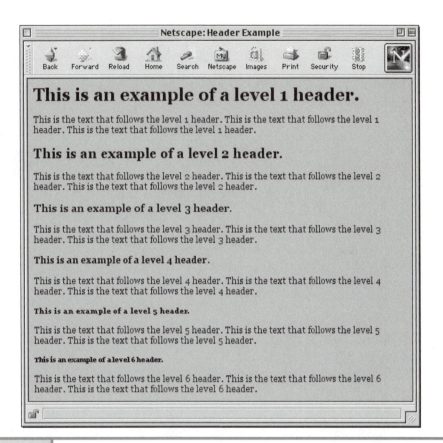

Figure 4-8 Six levels of header tags exist, with **h1** producing large text that is approximately 24 points in size, and level 6 creating small text sized at 8 or 9 points

For example, you wouldn't create an outline that began with a small letter *a* and was followed by the Roman numeral *I*. Instead, you would begin with the Roman numeral *I*, follow that with a capital *A*, and, most likely, follow with a number 1. In like manner, an <h1> should be followed by an <h2>, as opposed to an <h3>.

Note

Using a header tag automatically adds breaks before and after the headline.

You can add an attribute to each header to change the alignment of the text to which it applies. For example, if you add `align="right"` to the h3 tag from Figure 4-8, the entire phrase contained within the h3 tags would be aligned to the right of the browser window, as shown in the following.

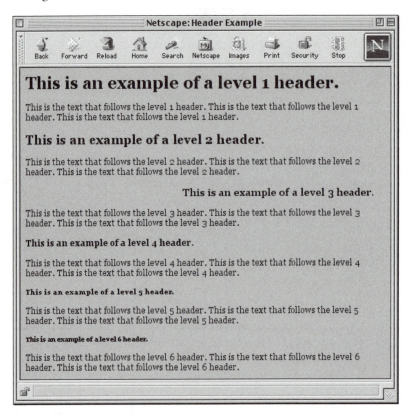

align is an attribute of this tag

right is one possible value for the align attribute. Others are left, center, and justify

```
<h3 align="right">This is an example of a level 3 header.</h3>
<p>This is the text that follows the level 3 header. This is the
text that follows the level 3 header. This is the text that follows
the level 3 header.</p>
```

1-Minute Drill

● **Which h tag creates the largest and most important headline?**
● **How can you center a headline in the page?**

Adding Emphasis

HTML allows for different types of formatting tags to add emphasis. Most of the tags available can be classified under one of two styles:

● logical

● physical

You might consider logical styles to be similar to a person's personality traits, whereas physical styles more closely resemble a person's physical appearance.

Logical Styles

Logical styles define how the affected text is to be used on the page, but not how it will be displayed. This means the browser ultimately decides how to display the text (see table 4–2). For example, if you were writing the HTML for the first sentence in this paragraph, you could use the dfn tag to tell the browser the phrase "logical styles" should be highlighted as a defined term.

```
<dfn>Logical styles</dfn> define how the affected text will
be used on the page.
```

Note

The h tag is also a type of logical style.

● **<h1>**
● **Use the align="center" attribute in your h tag or add a dir tag and align attribute around the headline.**

In the previous expample, the `dfn` tag would tell the browser to differentiate between the phrase "logical styles" and the rest of the sentence. Exactly how it does so depends on the different browsers. Netscape ignores the `dfn` tag, but Internet Explorer displays it as italicized text.

All logical styles must be opened and closed when they are used in an HTML document. Figures 4–9 and 4–10 show how these tags are displayed in Netscape 4 and IE 5.

Physical Styles

Contrary to logical styles, *physical* styles define how to display the affected text. For the most part, these styles display the same, regardless of the browser type. Because they are more reliable with regard to browser display, physical styles are more frequently used than logical styles.

Tag	Description	Typical Graphical Browser Display
`<abbr>`	indicates an abbreviation	not displayed in graphical browsers (each letter is spoken in audio browsers)
`<acronym>`	indicates an acronym	not displayed in graphical browsers (each letter is spoken in audio browsers)
`<cite>`	marks a reference to another source or a short quotation	italic
`<code>`	displays a code example	monospace font (such as Courier)
`<dfn>`	highlights a definition or defined term	italic * not supported by Netscape
`<em>`	provides general emphasis	italic
`<kbd>`	identifies text a user will enter (*kbd* is short for *keyboard*)	monospace font (such as Courier)
`<samp>`	describes sample text or code, typically output from a program	monospace font (such as Courier)
`<strong>`	provides a stronger general emphasis than with `<em>`	bold
`<var>`	suggests a word or phrase that is variable and should be replaced with a specific value	italic

Table 4-2 Logical Styles

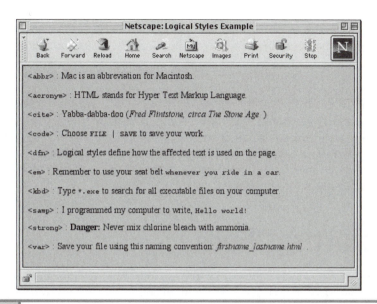

Figure 4-9 Netscape 4 supports all these logical styles except for **dfn**, **abbr**, and **acronym**

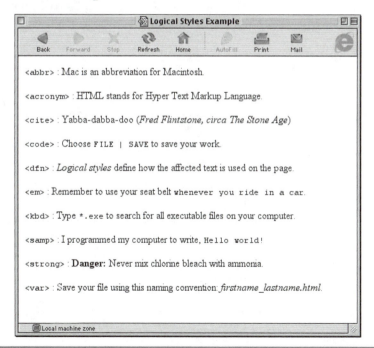

Figure 4-10 The only two logical styles tags Internet Explorer 5 doesn't support are **abbr** and **acronym**

As shown in Table 4-3, all physical styles need to be opened and closed when used in HTML documents. A visual representation of these styles is available in Figure 4–11.

Note

The <strike> and <u> tags have been deprecated. The W3C recommends using style sheets instead of these tags. Because more browsers currently support these tags than style sheets, however, many people use a combination of both style sheets and these tags to ensure their pages display the same across a wide variety of browsers.

Formatting Fonts

Before you begin changing the font characteristics of a Web page, note that visitors to your Web site have the ultimate control over these font characteristics is important. The following screen shows how the user can customize Netscape. Users can even choose to use their fonts, overriding page-specified fonts, so you should consider these tags as recommendations for the browser, but never rely on them for your page display.

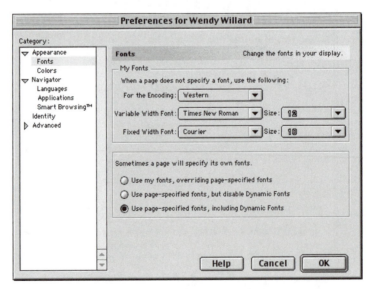

Tag	Description
`<b>`	**bold**
`<big>`	increases the font size by 1 each time it is used (maximum size is 7, default size is 3)
`<i>`	*italic*
`<tt>`	`typewriter font`
`<small>`	decreases the font size by 1 each time it is used (minimum size is 1, default size is 3)
`<strike>`	Strikethrough
`<sub>`	subscript
`<sup>`	superscript
`<u>`	underline

Table 4-3 | Physical Styles

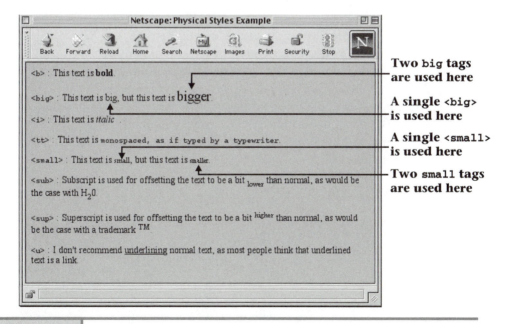

Figure 4-11 | This screen shows how the physical styles are typically rendered (in this case, in Netscape on the Mac)

With that said, the font tag enables you to customize various aspects of the text on your pages, specifically the font face, size, and color. No need exists to repeat font tags; you can define the face, size, and color of text all within a single font tag.

Hint

The W3C recommends using style sheets instead of the font tag to format text. However, given that more browsers currently support the font tag than do style sheets, many people use a combination of both style sheets and the font tag to ensure that their pages display the same across a wide variety of browsers.

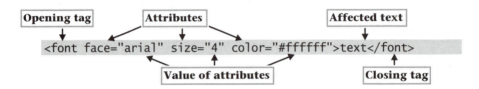

If you want to change the default font face or size for a Web page, you can use the basefont tag. Unfortunately, the basefont tag doesn't always affect text inside a table (described in Module 9) and headings. (For example, Netscape doesn't use basefont specifications inside a table, but IE does.) In addition, the basefont tag is deprecated in favor of style sheets. Because it doesn't have a closing tag, you should include a space and a forward slash (/) before the final bracket to prepare for XHTML compatibility.

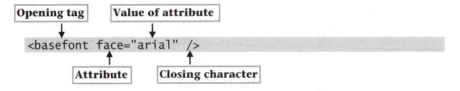

Faces

When used in conjunction with the term *font*, the term *face* refers to the name of the font you'd like to use on your page. You can use the face attribute to specify virtually any font name you can think of, but the person viewing your Web page will be unable to see your page in that font face unless he already has it loaded on his computer. So, if you specify your page be displayed in Gill Sans font, but the person viewing your page doesn't have Gill Sans, he will see your page in the browser's default font face (usually Times New Roman).

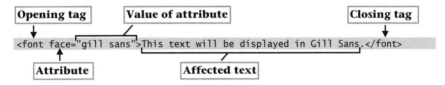

To compensate for the possibility that not all visitors will have the font face you specify, you can specify backup fonts in the value of the `face` attribute. If the browser cannot find the first font face listed on the viewer's computer, it then looks for the second font face, and the third, and so forth until it comes up with a match. Once again, if the browser doesn't find a font face listed in your HTML file that is actually installed on the viewer's system, it displays the page in the default font (usually Times New Roman).

Hint

This process of providing a backup font name in the face attribute is also referred to as *cascading*.

In this example, the browser would first look for Gill Sans

```
<font face="gill sans,verdana,arial,helvetica">Here I have
given the browser 4 choices, in hopes that it will find one
of them on the viewer's system.</font>
```

In the previous code, the browser first looks for Gill Sans. If it doesn't find that font face, it looks for Verdana, followed by Arial and Helvetica. If none of those font faces are available, it would display the text in the browser's default font.

Several font faces have become quite popular on the Web. This is because these faces offer the best chance of being installed on a majority of viewers' systems. Table 4–4 shows many of these to help you when you choose font faces for your pages.

Hint

Remember, font names may be a bit different across computer systems. Therefore, I recommend using lowercase names and sometimes even including two possible names for the same font. For example, the font Comic Sans can sometimes be installed as Comic Sans or Comic Sans MS. You can code your page to allow for both instances by using:
`<font face="comic sans,comic sans ms">`.

Font Name	Example Text	Availability
Arial	abcdefg 1234567890 !?@	comes with Microsoft Office, IE 3-4, Windows 3.1, 95, and NT also available in Microsoft's Web fonts (**www.microsoft.com/typography/fontpack/default.htm**)
Courier New	abcdefg 1234567890 !?@	comes with Microsoft Office, most versions of IE, Windows 3.1, 95, and NT also available in Microsoft's Web fonts (**www.microsoft.com/typography/fontpack/default.htm**) * Courier is a common font supplied by Xfree on UNIX ** Courier comes with Macintosh System 7+ and Adobe Type Manager (versions 3.8, 3.9)
Comic Sans	abcdefg 1234567890 !?@	comes with Microsoft Plus! for Windows 95 and most versions of IE
Georgia	abcdefg 1234567890 !?@	comes with the supplemental pack of add-ons for IE 4 also available in Microsoft's Web fonts (**www.microsoft.com/typography/fontpack/default.htm**)
Helvetica	abcdefg 1234567890 !?@	a common font supplied by Xfree on UNIX comes with Adobe Type Manager (versions 3.8, 3.9) comes with Macintosh System 7+
Impact	abcdefg 1234567890 !?@	comes with Microsoft Office, IE 3-4, Windows 3.1, 95, and NT also available in Microsoft's Web fonts (**www.microsoft.com/typography/fontpack/default.htm**)

Table 4-4   Popular Web Fonts

Font Name	Example Text	Availability
Times New Roman	abcdefg 1234567890 !?@	comes with Windows 3.1, 95, and NT * Times is a common font supplied by Xfree on UNIX ** Times comes with Macintosh System 7+ and Adobe Type Manager (versions 3.8, 3.9)
Trebuchet	abcdefg 1234567890 !?@	comes with the supplemental pack of add-ons for IE 4 also available in Microsoft's Web fonts (**www.microsoft.com/typography/ fontpack/default.htm**)
Verdana	abcdefg 1234567890 !?@	comes with most versions of IE also available in Microsoft's Web fonts (**www.microsoft.com/typography/ fontpack/default.htm**)
Webdings	✔ ✿☐♥🏠🚗🏢■ ☐🗗◀ ▶ ▲ ▼ ◀◀ ▶▶ ◀◀ _ ✳🐾✗	comes with IE 4.0 also available in Microsoft's Web fonts (**www.microsoft.com/typography/ fontpack/default.htm**)

Table 4-4 Popular Web Fonts *(continued)*

The more products a font ships with, the more likely it is that viewers of your Web site will have the font installed. The information on the availability of fonts was drawn from Microsoft's discussion on Web Typography. To learn more, visit **www.microsoft.com/typography/web/**.

1-Minute Drill

● **Which tag could you use to change the default font information for a page?**

● **What is the benefit of listing more than one font name in the `face` attribute of the `font` tag?**

● `<basefont>`
● If a visitor to your site doesn't have the first font listed in the `face` attribute, the browser then looks for the next font name. Using more than one font name increases the chances that one of the fonts is installed on the visitor's computer system.

Sizes

You can also use the font tag to change the size of text. This is accomplished with the size attribute and either an absolute or a relative value.

An *absolute* font size uses a single digit between 1 and 7, as in `<font size="4">`.

A *relative* font size uses a value relative to the default font size of the page. For example, a value of "+2" would be rendered as two sizes larger than the default font size of the page, which would usually display as 5 because the default font size for the majority of browsers is 3.

Although these sizes loosely correspond to the point sizes you use in a word processor, most text in a Web page looks a bit smaller on a Mac than it does on a PC (because the two systems render type differently). Figures 4–12 and 4–13 show how the same code might appear differently on a Mac and a PC.

```
<p><font size="1">This text is size 1.</font></p>
<p><font size="2">This text is size 2.</font></p>
<p><font size="3">This text is size 3.</font></p>
<p><font size="4">This text is size 4.</font></p>
<p><font size="5">This text is size 5.</font></p>
<p><font size="6">This text is size 6.</font></p>
<p><font size="7">This text is size 7.</font></p>
```

These are the tags used in Figures 4–12 and 4–13

Absolute Size	Approximate Point Size
1	8-9
2	10
3 (default)	12
4	14
5	16
6	18
7	24

Table 4-5   Font Size

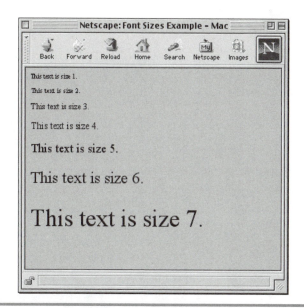

Figure 4-12   This screen shows how the HTML font sizes are typically rendered on the Mac.

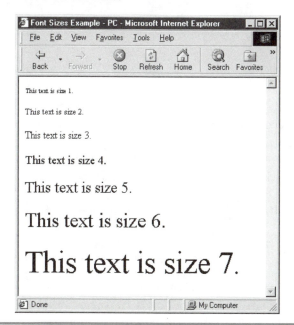

Figure 4-13   This screen shows how the HTML font sizes are typically rendered on the PC.

Ask the Expert

Question: **I'm not sure I understand the difference between relative and absolute font sizing. What reasons would I use one instead of the other?**

Answer: Every browser is set up with a default font size. Typically, this is size 3 but, because it can be customized by the user, the default font size could conceivably be any size between 1 and 7. When you use absolute font sizes, in effect, you override any browser settings in favor of the size you specify (again, a value between 1 and 7, with 7 being the largest). The benefit of absolute sizing is you are assured your text will appear about the same size on most browsers.

By contrast, relative font sizes work *with* any browser settings instead of overriding them. This is a drawback because you cannot guarantee your font sizes will remain the same from browser to browser. A benefit of relative sizing, however, is users can more easily control the look of text in their browsers. If a person prefers to view all Web sites in a larger font size, such as 18 pt, the use of relative font sizing on a Web site won't interfere with that, whereas absolute font sizing will interfere.

Colors

Whereas the `text` attribute of the `body` tag (see Module 3) enables you to specify text colors for an entire document, the `font` tag and `color` attribute enable you to specify text colors for particular sections of text on a Web page.

As discussed in Module 3, you reference the color by either a hexadecimal value or a predefined color name, as in the following examples:

This shows how you reference a hexadecimal color
↓
```
<font color="#333333">This text is dark gray.</font>
<font color="black">This text is black.</font>
```
↑
This shows how you reference a predefined color name

Always remember to include both sets of quotation marks around your hexadecimal values. If you forget one set, you may end up seeing a completely new color in place of the one you thought you would get.

Hint
Check the inside cover for a chart of Web-safe colors, complete with hexadecimal color values.

1-Minute Drill

- **The b tag is classified as which type of style?**
- **Which attributes are available for the font tag?**

4

Project 4-2: Add Styles to Your Web Page

Returning to the `index.html` page, let's vary the font characteristics of the text on that page, and add some physical and logical styles. Goals for this project include

- Add emphasis to the page with physical and logical styles

- Use the `font` tag to change the face, size, and color of the text on a page

Note that: All the files needed to complete the projects in this book for the Woolwich Historical Society can be downloaded from **www.osborne.com** or **www.willardesigns.com/htmlbook/**. In addition, you can view my version of the Web site anytime by visiting **www.woolwichhistory.org**.

Step-by-Step

1. Open your text editor (SimpleText on the Mac or Notepad on the PC) and load the index.html page saved from Project 4-1.

2. Make "The Woolwich Historical Society, Woolwich, Maine" a Level 1 headline.

3. Add "Historical Riverfront Community" as a Level 2 headline in between the first and second paragraphs. Align this headline to the center of the page.

- physical
- face, size, and color

4. Use a logical style to emphasize the phrase "The Woolwich Historical Society's" in the first paragraph.

5. Change the font face of the first paragraph to one listed in Table 3.

6. Change the size of the first paragraph to +1.

7. Use a physical style to emphasize the three waterways that border Woolwich (the Sasanoa, the Sheepscot, and Merry Meeting Bay).

8. Change the color of the copyright symbol and the text that follows it to a lighter color than the rest of the text on the page.

9. Open your Web browser and choose FILE | OPEN PAGE (or OPEN FILE or OPEN, depending on the browser you are using). Locate the file `index.html` you just saved.

10. Preview the page to check your work. If you need to make changes, return to your text editor to make changes. After making any changes, save the file and switch back to the browser. Choose REFRESH or RELOAD to preview the changes you just made. If you are using the Woolwich Historical Society, you can compare your files to the following code and figure.

```
<!DOCTYPE html PUBLIC "-//W3C//DTD XHTML 1.0 Transitional//EN"
"http://www.w3.org/TR/xhtml1/DTD/transitional.dtd">
<html>
<head>
    <title>Welcome to the Woolwich Historical Society, located in Woolwich,
Maine</title>
</head>
<body bgcolor="#ffffff" text="#000000">
<h1>Woolwich Historical Society, Woolwich, Maine</h1>
<p><font face="verdana" size="+1"><em>The Woolwich Historical Society's</em>
19th Century Rural Life Museum is located at the corner of Route 1 and
Nequasset Road in Woolwich, Maine.</font></p>
<h2 align="center">Historic river-front community</h2>
<p>Woolwich is a rural community on the east shore of the Kennebec River,
opposite the historic city of Bath and approximately 12 miles from the
Atlantic Ocean. It is bordered by waterways: <i>the Sasanoa, the Sheepscot
and Merry Meeting Bay,</i> which is the confluence of five rivers. First
settled in 1600's and incorporated in 1759, the town is named for Woolwich,
England, which in like manner is situated on a large, navigable river.</p>
<p>The Kennebec brought to the territory explorers, settlers, traders and
fishermen. Indians from the hinterland used this route for summer visits to
the coast, and harried early settlers with attacks. The first settlement was
abandoned in 1600. Subsequently, the area was resettled by inhabitants whose
courage, perseverance, strength and ingenuity enabled the survival of their
town.</p>
```

```
<blockquote><i>"They lived between the dark forest and the Kennebec River
that empties into the lonely Atlantic. They did for themselves. The had to.
They left after them lilac bushes, stone walls, deeply dug wells, tall elms
now dying, old cellar holes, old things in old houses, and the Next
Generation."</i> From Carlton Day Reed Sr's Proceedings (Taken from
1760-1800 town records.)</blockquote>
<p>The Woolwich Historical Society's 19th Century Rural Life Museum affords
the visitor an opportunity to step back in time and experience life as it
was for earlier generations, while touring an eight room authentic country
farmhouse, shed and barn. On display are home furnishings, quilts, garments,
household implements and the tools and equipment of local employment:
farming, blacksmithing, dairying, brick and pottery making and
seafaring.</p>
<p>History and genealogy researchers visiting the museum will be directed to
a substantial collection of resources, among them The History of Woolwich,
Maine: a Town Remembered, which may be purchased in soft cover. Other items
for sale include a beautiful watercolor print by Betsy Bisson (shown below),
historical maps, note cards, recipe booklet, and postcards. All items
require an additional shipping and handling fee. Contact us for more
information.</p>
<div align="right">
<hr />
<br />
<br />
<font color="#999999">&copy; 2000 Woolwich Historical Society</font>
</div>
</body>
</html>
```

4

Project Summary

Physical and logical styles enable you to add emphasis to your pages. The
font tag offers you the capability to customize the look of your page by
changing the font face, size, and color. All these things can help make
your pages more readable onscreen.

Hint

Do any of your changes continue past where you want them to stop?
Make sure to use the appropriate closing tag to tell the browser
where to stop. For more tips, see Resource C: Troubleshooting.

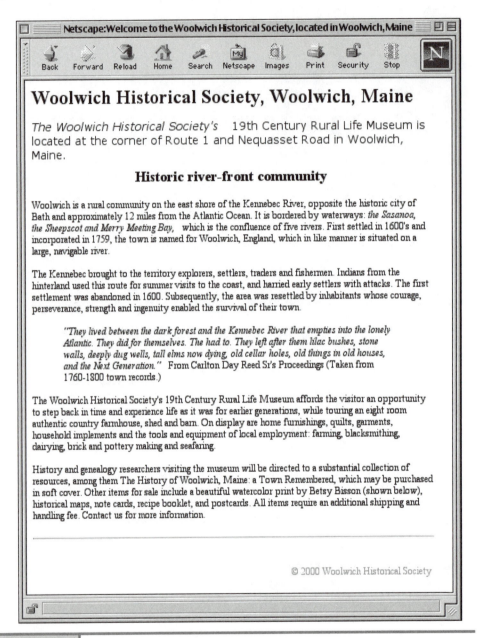

Mastery Check

1. List two characteristics of the h tag.

2. What is the difference between physical and logical styles in HTML?

3. How can you change the font in which the text on a Web page is rendered?

4. How do you close the br tag?

5. List two characteristics of the blockquote tag.

6. List two ways to align text.

4

Module 5

Working with Links

Goals

- Add links to other Web pages
- Add links to sections within the same Web page
- Add links to e-mail addresses, newsgroups, and downloadable files
- Use an attribute of the body tag to change the link colors on a Web page
- Customize links by setting the tab order, keyboard shortcut, and target window

The crux of HTML is its capability to reference countless other pieces of information easily on the Internet. This is evident because the first two letters in the acronym HTML stand for Hypertext, or text that is linked to other information.

HTML enables us to link to other Web pages, as well as graphics, multimedia, e-mail addresses, newsgroups, and downloadable files. Anything you can access through your browser can be linked to from within an HTML document. In fact, one of the easiest ways to identify the URL of a page you want to link to is to copy it from the location (Netscape) or address (Internet Explorer) toolbar in your Web browser. You can then paste it directly into your HTML file.

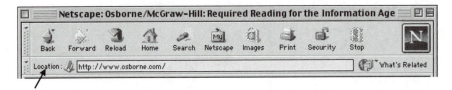

Adding Links to Other Web Pages

You can add links to other Web pages, whether they are part of your Web site or someone else's. To do so requires using the a tag:

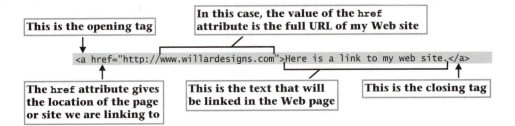

Hint

While adding a link to your favorite Web site on your page is usually considered acceptable, it is never acceptable to copy someone else's content without their permission. If you have any doubts, check with the site's Webmaster whenever you are linking to a site that isn't your own.

The a tag itself doesn't serve much purpose without its attributes. The most common attribute is href, which is short for *hypertext reference:* it tells the browser where to find the information to which you are linking. Other attributes are name, title, accesskey, tabindex, and target, all of which are discussed in this module.

The text included in between the opening and closing a tag is what the person viewing your Web page can click. In most cases, this text is highlighted as a different color from the surrounding text and is underlined, as shown in Figure 5–1.

This is the text in between the opening and closing a tag in the example code

When a visitor to your Web site moves the mouse over a link, it usually changes to a hand to show the text can be clicked

The location of the link is usually printed in the bottom part of the browser window, which is also called the *status bar*

| **Figure 5-1** | This screen shows the browser view of the previous example code |

Hint

When you are creating links, carefully consider the wording you want to use to highlight your links. I discourage you from using the phrase "Click here" as your link because it doesn't tell visitors what they will find when they "click here." Most people scan Web pages and look for links of interest. If all the links on your pages say "click here," visitors will be forced to read the content in detail to determine where to click. Unfortunately, given the short amount of time most people spend on the typical Web site, you probably will lose more visitors than you will gain with this practice. Compare the Figures 5–2 and 5–3 to see how more descriptive links are easier to use.

In deciding what to use as the value of your `href` attribute, consider what type of link you want to use. Two basic types of links exist:

- absolute

- relative

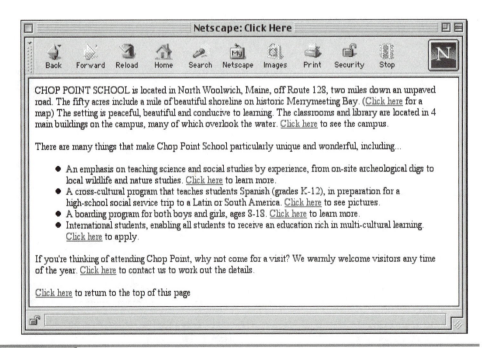

Figure 5-2 This screen shows a page with "Click here" used for each link

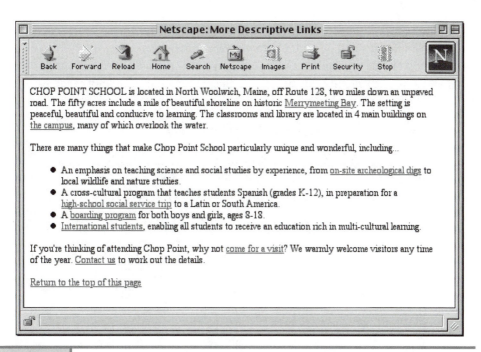

Figure 5-3   This screen shows the same page with much more descriptive link names, which make it easier to scan the content of the page

Absolute Links

Absolute links are those that include the entire pathname. In most cases, you use absolute links when linking to pages or sites that are not part of your own Web site. For example, if you are linking from your Web site to Yahoo!, you type "http://www.yahoo.com" as your link.

```
<a href="http://www.yahoo.com">Visit Yahoo!</a>
```

This absolute link includes the entire pathname—everything the browser needs to locate the site in question

Relative Links

Relative links are called so because you don't include the entire pathname of the page to which you are linking. Instead, the pathname you use is relative to the current page. This is similar to saying, "I live in Summershade Court, about three miles from here," which is relative to wherever "here" is. A more *absolute* way to say this might be "I live at 410 Summershade Court in Anytown, USA 55104."

These types of links are most commonly used when you want to link from one page in your site to another. Here's an example of what a relative link might look like:

```
<a href="contactme.html">Contact Me</a>
```

This link looks for the contactme.html file in the same folder that contains this page. If you were linking to a file in another folder below the current one, the value of your `href` might look like this:

```
<a href="wendy/contactme.html">Contact Me</a>
```

If you need to link to a file in a folder above the folder your page is in, you can add "../" for each directory up the tree. So, if the file you are linking to is two folders higher than the one you are in, you might use

```
<a href="../../contactme.html">Contact Me</a>
```

Suppose you were building a Web site for yourself and your family, using the following directory structure. You might remember something similar from Module 1, where we talked about file naming and the anatomy of a URL. Folders and files are indented to indicate that they are located on a different level.

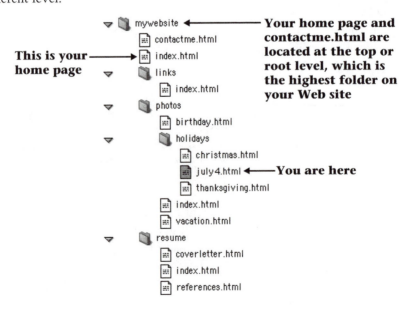

You are working on the highlighted file: july4.html. This file is located two folders down from the home page (index.html) in a folder called *holidays*. If you want to link back to that home page from the july4.html page, you would include a relative link similar to this one:

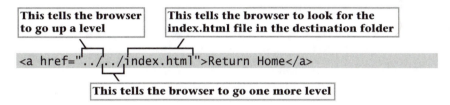

Now, suppose you are working on the birthday.html file and you want to link to the july4.html page. Can you imagine how you would do that?

To link from birthday.html to july4.html, use the following code:

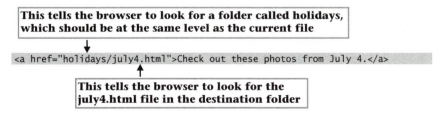

Because the july4.html file is one folder below the birthday.html file you are currently working on, you simply list the folder name followed by a forward slash and the filename (as shown in the preceding example).

1-Minute Drill

● **Using Illustration 4 as a guide, identify the pathname you would use to link from references.html to contactme.html.**

● **Identify the pathname you would use to link back from contactme.html to references.html.**

Ask the Expert

Question: How do I know when to use relative or absolute pathnames?

Answer: Whenever you are linking to a page *that is not contained within your Web site,* you will probably want to use an absolute pathname. For example, if you are working on the Woolwich Historical Society's Web site and you want to link to a historical society for another town, you need to use the full (absolute) pathname to do so.

However, if you are linking to *a page on your own Web site* that contains information about that other historical society, then you could use a relative pathname.

Remember, if you do decide to use absolute pathnames to link to a page located in the same folder on your Web site, this may cause problems for maintenance in the long run. If, at a later date, you decide to change the name of the folder these files are located in, you need to go back and change all the absolute links. If you used a relative link, though, you wouldn't have to change anything.

● **../contactme.html**
● **resume/references.html**

Adding Links to Sections Within the Same Page

When you link to a page, the browser knows what to look for because each page has a name. But sometimes you may want to link to a section of text *within* a page on your Web site (see Figure 5–4 for an example). To link to a section of a Web page, you must first give that section a name.

Figure 5-4   When you have multiple sections on a single page that you want to link to, you can use an anchor to name them

Creating an Anchor

An *anchor* is a place within a page that is given a special name, enabling you to link to it later. Without first naming a section, you cannot link to it. Here is an example of an anchor:

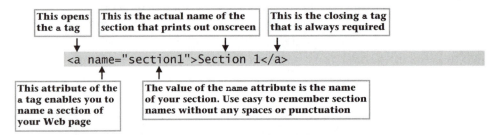

In this example, the phrase in between the opening and closing a tag is displayed in the Web page and labels the anchor as "Section 1".

If you prefer not to include a label for your anchor, you can leave that space blank, as in the following example:

```
<a name="top"></a>
```

Here, you could use this invisible anchor at the top of your page, and then link to it from the bottom of your page. This would enable visitors to return to the top of a long page easily, with only one click and no scrolling (see Figure 5–5 for an example).

Linking to an Anchor

To create the link to an anchor, you also use the a tag and the href attribute, as you would when creating any other type of link. To finish the link, you need to include a hash symbol (#) and the anchor name as the value of the href attribute.

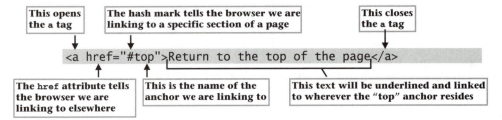

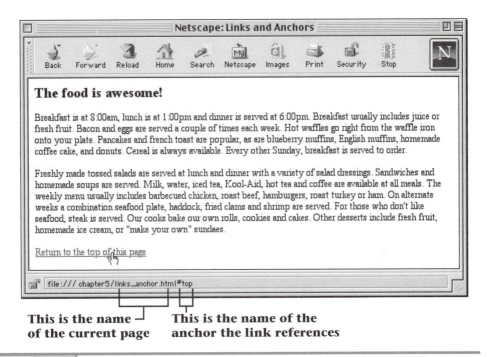

This is the name ⌐ **This is the name of the**
of the current page **anchor the link references**

Figure 5-5   This browser view (of links_anchor.html) shows how an invisible
anchor can be used to give visitors an easy link back to the top
of the page

Here's how it all might look when you code it in an HTML document:

```
<!DOCTYPE html PUBLIC "-//W3C//DTD XHTML 1.0 Transitional//EN"
"http://www.w3.org/TR/xhtml1/DTD/transitional.dtd">
<html>
<head>
     <title>Links and Anchors</title>
</head>
<body bgcolor="#ffffff" text="#000000">
<a name="top"></a>
```
> This anchors tells the
> browser where the "top"
> of the page is located

```
<a name="food"><h2>The food is awesome!</h2></a>
<p>Breakfast is at 8:00am, lunch is at 1:00pm and dinner is served
at 6:00pm. Breakfast usually includes juice or fresh fruit. Bacon
and eggs are served a couple of times each week. Hot waffles go
right from the waffle iron onto your plate. Pancakes and french
toast are popular, as are blueberry muffins, English muffins,
homemade coffee cake, and donuts. Cereal is always available. Every
```

```
other Sunday, breakfast is served to order.</p>
<p>Freshly made tossed salads are served at lunch and dinner with a
variety of salad dressings. Sandwiches and homemade soups are
served. Milk, water, iced tea, Kool-Aid, hot tea and coffee are
available at all meals. The weekly menu usually includes barbecued
chicken, roast beef, hamburgers, roast turkey or ham. On alternate
weeks a combination seafood plate, haddock, fried clams and shrimp
are served. For those who don't like seafood, steak is served. Our
cooks bake our own rolls, cookies and cakes. Other desserts include
fresh fruit, homemade ice cream, or "make your own" sundaes.</p>
<a href="#top">Return to the top of this page</a>
</body>
</html>
```

This tag links to the predefined anchor "top"

Another good case for using anchors involves a long page with many small sections, such as the example shown in Figure 5–4. Whenever you do have long pages with several sections, it's nice to offer your visitors a "Back to Top" link to bring them back to the index easily. The following shows the HTML code used to create this page.

```
<!DOCTYPE html PUBLIC "-//W3C//DTD XHTML 1.0 Transitional//EN"
"http://www.w3.org/TR/xhtml1/DTD/transitional.dtd">
<html>
<head>
    <title>Using Anchors on Long Pages</title>
</head>
<body bgcolor="#ffffff" text="#000000">
<a name="top"></a>
<a href="#section1">Jump to Section 1</a><br />
<a href="#section2">Jump to Section 2</a><br />
<a href="#section3">Jump to Section 3</a><br />

<hr />
<a name="section1"><b>Section 1</b></a>
<p>Text for section 1 goes here.</p>
<p><a href="#top">Back to top</a></p>
<hr />
<a name="section2"><b>Section 2</b></a>
<p>Text for section 2 goes here.</p>
<p><a href="#top">Back to top</a></p>
<hr />
<a name="section3"><b>Section 3</b></a>
<p>Text for section 3 goes here.</p>
<p><a href="#top">Back to top</a></p>
</body>
</html>
```

This links to the anchor lower on the page named "section1"

This links to the anchor lower on the page named "section2"

This links to the anchor lower on the page named "section3"

The anchor names this "section1"

The anchor names this "section2"

The anchor names this "section3"

Hint

If the anchor you are linking to is already visible on the screen (such as how the *A* section is already visible in Figure 5–4), then the browser may not jump to that anchor. Similarly, if the anchor being linked to is at the very bottom of the screen (such as the *C* section is in Figure 5–4), then the browser also may not jump to that anchor, according to your screen size. The reason for this is, if the browser is already to the bottom of the page, it cannot go any further and, therefore, can only try to get as close to the anchor as possible.

If you need to create a link to a specific section with another page (not the one you are currently working on), then you use that page's filename and the anchor name separated by a hash mark (#), as in the following example.

```
<a href="genealogy.html#intro">View names beginning with an
"A" on our genealogy page.</a>
```

In this case, the browser will first look for genealogy.html, and then locate an anchor named "intro" on that page.

Adding Other Types of Links

Although linking to and within Web pages are the most common types of links you create, you can also link to other types of content on the Internet.

E-mail Addresses

When you want to give someone easy access to your e-mail address, you can include it on your page as a *mailto* link. This means instead of using `http://` in front of your links, you use `mailto:` to preface your e-mail addresses.

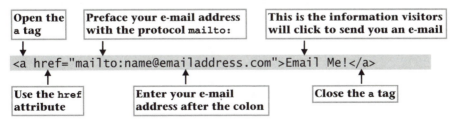

Clicking this link in a browser causes the visitor's e-mail program to launch. Then it opens a new e-mail message and places your e-mail address in the TO: box of that message.

Hint

For this to work, visitors to your Web site must have an e-mail program set up on their computers.

Customizing the E-mail Message

Some browsers will even let you add content to the subject and cc fields in the email, by entering additional text into the `href` value. To do so, you add a question mark after the end of your email address, and type the word "Subject" followed by an equals sign (=) and the word or phrase you'd like to use as your subject. This can be particularly useful in helping you distinguish mail sent through your Web site from your other email.

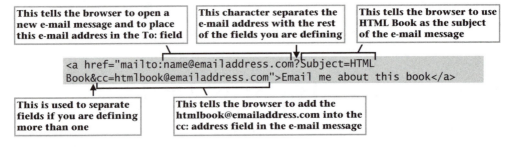

Remember, no spaces should be in the value of the `href` attribute, unless they are part of the subject line.

Newsgroups

Similarly, you can link to newsgroups by using `news:` instead of `http://` in the value of the `href` attribute. After `news:` you enter either the *name of the newsgroup* or *the identification number of the news article* you're linking to.

```
<a href="news:alt.html">Visit an HTML newsgroup</a>

<a href="news:123456.78910@netscape.com">Read this news article on Netscape</a>
```

When a visitor clicks one of these links, the browser should attempt to load the newsgroup or news article in the browser or in a newsreader.

Hint

Some browsers don't support this feature, while others aren't configured to use it. Remember this and consider offering alternative sources of information for visitors unable to use newsgroups. News articles eventually expire, sometimes as often as six days after they are posted. For this reason, linking to a specific article is discouraged, in favor of linking to the newsgroup sponsoring it.

Newsgroups defined

A *newsgroup* is an Internet discussion forum where people talk about a specific topic or series of topics. Literally thousands of newsgroups exist on almost every topic imaginable.

People post *articles* on these newsgroups (sometimes referred to as *electronic bulletin boards*) and when another person responds to an article, a *thread* is started. Other people can then add more articles to a thread, making it a sort of mini discussion about a topic.

You use a *newsreader* to access newsgroups. Newsreaders can be part of a browser package or stand-alone applications.

The full name of newsgroups is *Usenet Newsgroups*. You may hear it called *Usenet*.

FTP & Downloadable Files

The Internet provides many companies with an easy way to transmit files to customers. For example, suppose you purchased a piece of software to protect your computer against viruses. Eventually, your software must be updated, so it can recognize new viruses. The quickest and easiest way to obtain such an update is to download it from the company's Web site.

When you download files from the Internet that cannot be displayed in your Web browser (such as software applications and add-ons), you usually do so by accessing the company's FTP site.

FTP, which stands for *file transfer protocol*, is a way in which you send and receive files over the Internet. Many companies have both HTTP servers, which house their Web site, and FTP servers, which house their downloadable files.

To reference a file on an FTP site, you use the a tag and the `href` attribute, as in the following example:

```
<a href="ftp://sunsite.unc.edu/pub/">Visit the SunSite FTP</a>
```

Although many FTP files are anonymous and don't require a password for access, some are private. You won't be able to access a private FTP site without a qualified username and password. If you are linking to a private FTP site, you should also consider providing a way for visitors to register or sign up to receive a username and password.

Of course, in some cases, you could have downloadable files located right on your Web server with your Web page. These might be movies, sounds, programs, or other documents you want to make available to your visitors. You can link to these just as you would any other Web page, keeping the proper file extension in mind.

```
<a href="http://www.willardesigns.com/baby.mov">View the baby movie!</a>
```

Project 5–1: Add Links

Returning to the index.html page, let's vary the font characteristics of the text on this page and add links to the Web site. A reminder, all the files needed to complete the projects in this book for the Woolwich Historical Society can be downloaded from **www.osborne.com** or **www.willardesigns.com/htmlbook/**. In addition, you can view my version of the Web site anytime by visiting **www.woolwichhistory.org**.

Those of you who aren't using the Woolwich Historical Society can tailor the project to your particular needs. Goals for this project include

● Add links to Web pages

● Add links to sections within a Web page

● Add links to e-mail addresses

Step-by-Step

1. Open your text editor (SimpleText on the Mac, or Notepad on the PC) and load the `index.html` page saved from Module 4.

2. Add a link to `genealogy.html` that says, "View our online genealogy resources for Woolwich, Maine."

3. Save the file.

4. Create a new file named `genealogy.html`. Include the text included in `genealogy.txt` in the HTML Beginner's Guide .zip file. (For your convenience, a portion of that page is printed following these steps.)

5. Format the first sentence as a level 2 headline.

6. Format each paragraph with the `p` tag.

7. Format the word "emailed" at the end of the first paragraph as an e-mail link. Mail should be sent to "info@woolwichhistory.com." The subject should be "Genealogy."

8. Emphasize the *Note.

9. Format the sentence that starts with "To begin,..." as bold.

10. Add a horizontal rule in between the alphabetical listing and the sections below.

11. Format each section heading (such as *A, B, C,* and so forth) as a level 3 headline.

12. Save this file.

13. Open your Web browser and choose FILE I OPEN PAGE (or OPEN FILE or OPEN, depending on the browser you are using). Locate the file `index.html` you just saved.

14. Click the link you added to ensure it works. The link should bring up the genealogy.html page.

15. If you need to make changes, return to your text editor to make changes. After making any changes, save the file and switch back to the browser. Choose REFRESH or RELOAD to preview the changes you just made.

Hint

Does your link work? If not, make sure the pathname is correct. Both the index.html and genealogy.html pages should be located in the same folder. If they aren't, you need to change the pathname to reflect the proper folder name. In addition, be sure to check your capitalization (or lack thereof). Remember, links like this are case-sensitive, so if you named a section "Intro" with a capital *I*, but linked to "intro" with a lowercase *i*, then your link won't work. For more tips, see Resource C: Troubleshooting.

5

16. Return to the `genealogy.html` file in your text editor.

17. Add anchors to each of the section headings, using the section name (*A, B, C,* and so forth) as the anchor name.

18. Add links to each of the letters in the alphabetical listing at the top of the page to the corresponding section name.

19. Add an anchor to the top of the page named "top."

20. Add "Back to Top" links at the end of each section to enable a visitor to have easy access back to the alphabetical listing at the top of the page.

21. Save the file.

22. Return to your Web browser and choose REFRESH or RELOAD to confirm your changes. If you are using the Woolwich Historical Society, you can compare your files to the following code and Figure 5–6.

```
<!DOCTYPE html PUBLIC "-//W3C//DTD XHTML 1.0 Transitional//EN"
"http://www.w3.org/TR/xhtml1/DTD/transitional.dtd">
<html>
<head>
        <title>Online Genealogy Resources for Woolwich, Maine</title>
</head>
<body bgcolor="#ffffff" text="#000000">
<a name="top"></a>
<h2>Online Genealogy Resources for Woolwich, Maine</h2>
<p>We have some information about early Woolwich families and would be glad
to help you with basic searches. However, in depth searches do need to be
done in person, due to lack of sufficient volunteer time.  Thanks for
understanding! If you have additional information to share, we would very
much appreciate receiving a copy of it - <a
href="mailto:info@woolwichhistory.org?Subject=Genealogy">emailed</a> or via
USPS.</p>
<p>*Note: <em>original information and comments are the work of founding
society member Roland S Bailey.</em></p>
<p><b>To begin, please choose the letter of the alphabet that the family's
last name begins with.</b></p>
<p><a href="#a">A</a>  <a href="#b">B</a>  <a href="#c">C</a> D  E  F  G  H  I  J  K
L  M  N  O  P  Q  R  S  T  U  V  W  X  Y  Z</p>
<hr />
<h3><a name="a">A</a></h3>
<p>AMES, JACOB E          b. abt 1756  d. March 12, 1839</p>
<p><a href="#top">Back to Top</a></p>
<h3><a name="b">B</a></h3>
<p>BAILEY, JOSHUA SR      b. Nov 24, 1726      d. May 23, 1816 Woolwich<br />
BAILEY, JOHN (CAPT.)     b. Feb 2, 1737       d. July 29, 1813 Woolwich<br />
BLANCHARD, SAMUEL SR b. Sept 19, 1697      d. Feb 23, 1783 Woolwich<br />
BLINN, JAMES    b. abt 1725       d. Nov 13, 1813<br />
BROOKINGS, HENRY b. Mar 19, 1689 York ME      d. June 1748 killed by
Indians<br />
```

```
BUCK, EPHRIAM 5th     b. Mar 6, 1761      d. Mar 13, 1821</p>
<p><a href="#top">Back to Top</a></p>

<h3><a name="c">C</a></h3>
<p>CARD, WINCHESTER b. July 7, 1710        d. May 17, 1784<br />
CARLTON, JOHN SR b. July 1, 1740     d. Sept    1782</p>
<p><a href="#top">Back to Top</a></p>

</body>
</html>
```

5

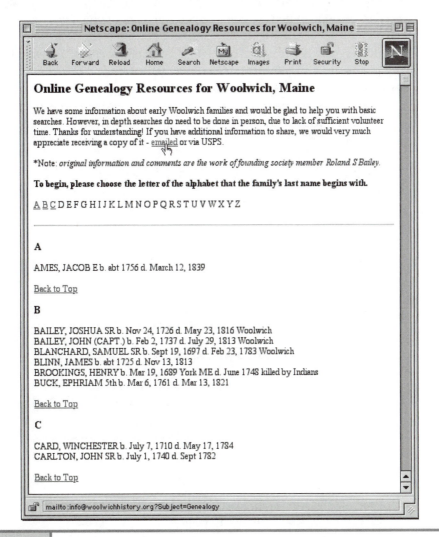

Figure 5-6 Our Online Genealogy Resources page for the Woolwich Historical Society

Paragraphs for genealogy.html

This is the text included in genealogy.txt in the HTML Beginner's Guide .zip file (as mentioned earlier in step 4):

Woolwich, Maine Genealogy Information
We have some information about early Woolwich families and would be glad to help you with basic searches. However, in depth searches do need to be done in person, due to lack of sufficient volunteer time. Thanks for understanding! If you have additional information to share, we would very much appreciate receiving a copy of it - emailed or via USPS
★Note: original information and comments are the work of founding society member Roland S Bailey.

To begin, please choose the letter of the alphabet that the family's last name begins with.

A B C D E F G H I J K L M N O P Q R S T U V W X Y Z

A

AMES, JACOB E   b. abt 1756 d. March 12, 1839

B

BAILEY, JOSHUA SR   b. Nov 24, 1726   d. May 23, 1816 Woolwich
BAILEY, JOHN (CAPT.)   b. Feb 2, 1737   d. July 29, 1813 Woolwich
BLANCHARD, SAMUEL SR b. Sept 19, 1697   d. Feb 23, 1783 Woolwich
BLINN, JAMES   b. abt 1725   d. Nov 13, 181
BROOKINGS, HENRY b. Mar 19, 1689 York ME   d. June 1748 killed by Indians
BUCK, EPHRIAM 5th b. Mar 6, 1761   d. Mar 13, 1821

C

CARD, WINCHESTER b. July 7, 1710   d. May 17, 1784
CARLTON, JOHN SR b. July 1, 1740   d. Sept   1782

Project Summary

The a tag enables you to add links to many types of information on the Internet. This project gives you practice using that tag to link to another Web page, an e-mail address, and sections within the same Web page.

> ### Hint
> Do each of your target links work? If not, make sure the anchor name is correct. Remember, links are case-sensitive, so if you capitalized the anchor name, you need to capitalize it again when you link to it. In addition, check to see you have included a hash mark (#) before each anchor name when you link to them (that is, href="#a") For more tips, see Resource C: Troubleshooting.

5

1-Minute Drill

- **Can you fix the following tag?**
  ```
  < ahref="http://www.yahoo.com" >
  ```

- **Can you fix the following tag?**
  ```
  <a name="top>
  ```

- **Can you fix the following tag?**
  ```
  <mailto:wendy@willardesigns.com>
  ```

Changing Link Colors

In Module 3, we discussed changing the text and background colors for pages, using attributes of the body tag. You can use three more attributes of the body tag to customize the three link colors of a Web page: normal *link* colors (link), *visited link* colors (vlink) and *active link* colors (alink). Table 5-1 lists attributes of the body tag.

```
<body bgcolor="#ffffff" text="#000000" link="#003366"
vlink="#999999" alink="#ff33cc">
```

- `<a href="http://www.yahoo.com">` **(the spacing was incorrect)**
- `<a name="top">` **(the final quotation mark was missing)**
- `<a href="mailto:name@company.com">` **(the a tag and href attribute were missing)**

Attribute	Value	Description
link		changes the color of the links on the page that haven't yet been visited
vlink		changes the color of the links on the page the viewer has already visited
alink	"#rrggbb" code (hexadecimal color code) or "name" code (predefined color name)*	changes the color displayed when a viewer presses the mouse button while it is placed over a link
bgcolor		(from Module 3) changes the background color
text		(from Module 3) changes the text color

* The value is the same for the five attrributes

Table 5-1   Attributes of the **body** Tag

Note

These attributes are deprecated in favor of style sheets. However, they are still valid in HTML documents.

As with other attributes that change color in HTML pages, you need to specify the color either by hexadecimal code or a predefined color name. A chart of Web-safe colors is on the inside of the front cover and a list of predefined color names is in Module 3.

In most cases, the default link color for browsers is blue. The default visited link color is purple, and the active link color is red. Remember, as with many other features of Web browsers, the user ultimately controls these default colors.

I recommend using the same link colors on all the pages in your Web site to give a consistent look and feel across the pages. In addition, it's wise

Hint

Although not required and certainly not always possible, staying within a blue/purple/red color scheme for your link/visited link/active link colors is nice. Visitors to your site may adjust to the navigation more quickly if the color scheme is similar to that of other Web sites.

to pick visited link colors that don't stand out as much as your unvisited links. Both of these recommendations enable visitors to scan your page easily and identify which pages they have been to and which they haven't visited.

Last, remember to test your colors on a number of different computer systems to ensure they appear as you intend.

Hint

Change your monitor settings to black and white for a minute, just to make sure your links are visible in a grayscale setting.

5

Customizing Links

You can further customize the links on your page by setting the tab order, keyboard shortcuts, and target windows. The first two of these features are new to HTML 4.0 and, therefore, are only supported by newer browsers. These are included in the hope they soon will be more widely supported, and then you can use them to benefit your users.

Tab Order

Frequent users of screen-based forms understand that pressing the TAB key advances your mouse pointer to the next available form field. Usually, the tab order of those fields is specified by the programmer who created the form.

In like manner, you can customize the tab order of links and form field elements on your Web page through the use of the `tabindex` attribute. Unfortunately, at press time, this attribute is only supported by versions 4 and higher of Internet Explorer and is not supported at all by Netscape.

Note

Although Netscape doesn't support this tag yet, the browser simply ignores it. This tag won't cause problems if you decide to use it.

> **This attribute defines the tab order**

```
<a href="page1.html" tabindex="1">Page 1</a><br />
<a href="page2.html" tabindex="2">Page 2</a><br />
```

> **The value of the `tabindex` attribute defines which link is to be highlighted first, and second, and so forth when a visitor uses the TAB key to navigate the Web page**

When a visitor uses the TAB key to navigate your Web page, each link or clickable element on the page is, in turn, highlighted. If no order has been specified by the `taborder` attribute (or if the browser doesn't recognize the `taborder` attribute), the browser will make its best effort to use a reasonable tab order, usually from top to bottom on the page.

After successfully using the TAB key to highlight the link the person wants to visit, he or she can press the RETURN or ENTER key to visit that link.

Hint

You can use any number between 0 and 32,767 for the value of the `tabindex` attribute or use a negative number to exclude an element entirely from the tab order.

Keyboard Shortcuts

Many computer users are familiar with some common keyboard shortcuts, such as copy (CTRL-C /WINDOWS or COMMAND-C /MAC) and paste (CTRL-V / WINDOWS or COMMAND-V /MAC). Similarly, you can assign keyboard shortcuts to links in your Web page. To do so requires adding the `accesskey` attribute to the a tag.

> **This attribute defines the keyboard shortcut**

```
Click the link or type the appropriate keyboard shortcut and press RETURN to
visit the page of your choice:
<a href="page1.html" tabindex="1" accesskey="1">Page 1</a> (Alt-1)<br />
<a href="page2.html" tabindex="2" accesskey="2">Page 2</a> (Alt-2)<br />
```

> **The value of the `accesskey` attribute specifies which key the user must enter**

A good idea is to include the keyboard shortcut next to your link; otherwise, visitors to your Web page wouldn't know it exists. Table 5–2 shows how browser support for the `accesskey` attribute varies.

Tip

Try to remember any universal keyboard shortcuts when you come up with your own. You wouldn't want to disable someone's ability to print, for example, in favor of a link in your Web page.

Target Windows

Have you ever visited a Web site and noticed a second instance of the Web browser opened when you clicked a link? This happens when Web developers use the `target` attribute to load links in a browser window other than the one you are currently using.

For example, you might want to offer visitors to your site a link to search Yahoo!, but you don't want to encourage them to leave your site. If you use "_blank" as the value of the target attribute in your link to Yahoo!, the browser will launch a new browser window to load http://www.yahoo.com.

> **This attribute is most commonly used to target browser windows other than the one you are currently using**

```
<a href="http://www.yahoo.com" target="_blank">Search Yahoo!</a>
```

> **This is one possible value for the `target` attribute**

Operating System	System Key Required to Use HTML Keyboard Shortcuts	Notes
Windows	ALT	supported by IE version 5+ not supported by Netscape* *As of press time
Macintosh	COMMAND or OPTION	not supported by either IE or Netscape* *As of press time

Table 5-2   Browser Support for the `accesskey` Attribute

Value of Target Attribute	Description
_blank	opens the link in a new unnamed browser window
_self	opens the link in the same window currently being used
name (where *name* is any name you have given to a window)	opens the link in the window of that name (if no window is currently open by that name, the browser launches a new window and gives it that name)

Table 5-3   **Target** Attribute Values

Aside from targeting new windows, you can also target specific windows you have named. For instance, instead of using "_blank" to launch a new window, you might use "cars" to launch a window that is named "cars." Then, any time you have a link related to cars, you can add `target="cars"` to your link and all those links will load into the "cars" window. Table 5–3 lists three of the possible options for the target attribute. Additional options are discussed in Module 10.

Project 5–2: Customize Links

This final project in Module 5 gives you practice customizing links by changing the default colors, tab order, keyboard shortcuts, and target windows. Goals for this project include:

● Change the link colors for a page using attributes of the `body` tag

● Target a link to open in a new browser window

   Note that: All the files needed to complete the projects in this book for the Woolwich Historical Society can be downloaded from **www.osborne.com** or **www.willardesigns.com/htmlbook/**. In addition, you can view my version of the Web site anytime by visiting **www.woolwichhistory.org**.

Step-by-Step

1. Open your text editor (SimpleText on the Mac, or Notepad on the PC) and open both the index.html page and genealogy.html page saved from Project 5–1.

2. Change the link colors on both pages to the color scheme of your choice. Save both files.

3. Close index.html.

4. Switch to genealogy.html and add a link to http://dir.yahoo.com/ Arts/Humanities/History/Genealogy/ somewhere on the page. Target a new browser window with this link.

5. Save the file.

6. Open your Web browser and choose FILE I OPEN PAGE (or OPEN RILE or OPEN, depending on the browser you are using). Locate the file `genealogy.html` you just saved.

7. Preview the page to check your work. If you need to make changes, return to your text editor to make changes. After making any changes, save the file and switch back to the browser. Choose REFRESH or RELOAD to preview the changes you just made. If you are using the Woolwich Historical Society, you can compare your files to the following code and Figure 5–7.

5

```
<!DOCTYPE html PUBLIC "-//W3C//DTD XHTML 1.0 Transitional//EN"
"http://www.w3.org/TR/xhtml1/DTD/transitional.dtd">
<html>
<head>
    <title>Online Genealogy Resources for Woolwich, Maine</title>
</head>
<body bgcolor="#ffffff" text="#000000" link="#333366" alink="#ff6633"
vlink="#663399">
```
Code that was added during this project
```
<a name="top"></a>
<h2>Online Genealogy Resources for Woolwich, Maine</h2>
<p>We have some information about early Woolwich families and would be glad
to help you with basic searches. However, in depth searches do need to be
done in person, due to lack of sufficient volunteer time.  Thanks for
understanding! If you have additional information to share, we would very
much appreciate receiving a copy of it - <a
href="mailto:info@woolwichhistory.org?Subject=Genealogy">emailed</a> or via
USPS. If you can't find what you are looking for here, you might try <a
href="http://dir.yahoo.com/Arts/Humanities/History/Genealogy/"
target="_blank">Yahoo's genealogy site</a>.
```
Code that was added during this project
```
<p>*Note: <em>original information and comments are the work of founding
society member Roland S Bailey.</em></p>
<p><b>To begin, please choose the letter of the alphabet that the family's
last name begins with.</b></p>
<p><a href="#a">A</a> <a href="#b">B</a> <a href="#c">C</a> D E F G H I J K
L M N O P Q R S T U V W X Y Z</p>
<hr />
<a name="a"><h3>A</h3></a>
<p>AMES, JACOB E         b. abt 1756  d. March 12, 1839</p>
<p><a href="#top">Back to Top</a></p>
<a name="b"><h3>B</h3></a>
<p>BAILEY, JOSHUA SR      b. Nov 24, 1726      d. May 23, 1816 Woolwich<br />
BAILEY, JOHN (CAPT.)     b. Feb 2, 1737      d. July 29, 1813 Woolwich<br />
BLANCHARD, SAMUEL SR b. Sept 19, 1697      d. Feb 23, 1783 Woolwich<br />
BLINN, JAMES      b. abt 1725      d. Nov 13, 1813<br />
```

```
BROOKINGS, HENRY b. Mar 19, 1689 York ME      d. June 1748 killed by
Indians<br />
BUCK, EPHRIAM 5th      b. Mar 6, 1761     d. Mar 13, 1821</p>
<p><a href="#top">Back to Top</a></p>
<a name="c"><h3>C</h3></a>
<p>CARD, WINCHESTER b. July 7, 1710      d. May 17, 1784<br />
CARLTON, JOHN SR b. July 1, 1740     d. Sept   1782</p>
<p><a href="#top">Back to Top</a></p>
</body>
</html>
```

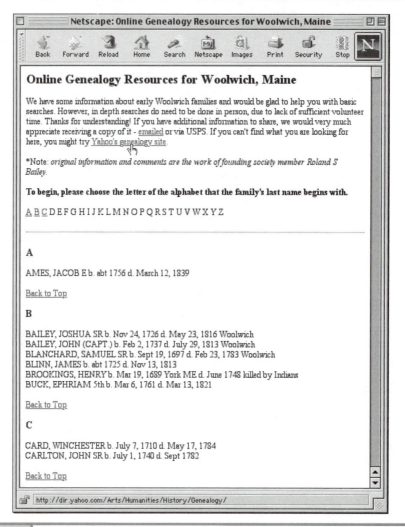

Figure 5-7 When you move the mouse over the link you added, you can see the location of the link in the status bar at the bottom of the screen

Project Summary

Although users and browsers ultimately control the link colors on your pages, you can make recommendations by using link, vlink, and alink attributes of the body tag. This project gives you practice changing those colors, as well as customizing the target windows for your links.

☑ *Mastery Check*

1. Which tag and attribute are used to give a name to a section of text on a Web page to which you want to link?

2. Which of the following would be classified as an absolute link?

   ● <a href="http://www.choppoint.org/camp/store.html">

   ● <a href="../camp/store.html">

3. How do you link to a newsgroup?

4. Which attribute enables you to change the color of the links on your page after someone has clicked them?

5. How can you tell the browser to launch a link in a new window?

Module 6

Working with Images

Goals

- Add images as elements in the foreground of a Web page
- Format images by specifying the height and width, and by sizing the borders and surrounding space
- Provide alternative text for images
- Link images to other content on a Web site
- Align images with other elements on the page
- Use images as elements in the background of a Web page

The first pages of information on the Internet were text only and didn't contain any images. We've come a long way from that, and many Web sites are comprised of only images. While, in most cases, I wouldn't advocate using only images, I do advocate using images to spice up your Web pages wherever they make sense. The saying "a picture is worth a thousand words" definitely holds true on the Internet.

Using Images in the Foreground

You can easily add images anywhere in your Web page by using the img tag, where img is short for *image*. Add the src attribute (short for *source*), the appropriate value, and you are off and running.

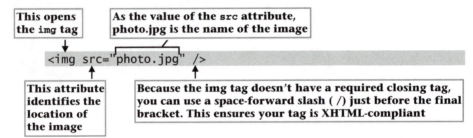

When you use the img tag, you are telling the browser to display the image right within the Web page, as shown in Figure 6-1. In doing so, remember these few things:

- Your image should be in a Web-friendly file format, such as GIF or JPEG. (See the next section on Image File Types).

- The value of your src attribute should include the correct path name and location of your file. So, if the image you want to use is not located in the same folder as the HTML page you are working on, you need to tell the browser in which folder that image is located. For example, if you want to include an image located one directory higher than the current directory, you would use src="../photo.jpg" where the ../ tells the browser to go up one directory before looking for the image file. If you want to reference an image from another Web site, you could use src="http://www.websitename.com/images/photo.jpg" where the URL is the full name of the image location on the other site.

- In general, each image should serve a unique purpose and add something to your Web page. Because visitors have to wait while images download to their computers, it's wise not to bog down your page with gratuitous graphics that serve little or no purpose.

Image File Types

The most common and most widely supported image file types are:

- GIF (usually pronounced with a soft *g*, just like the peanut butter—think "choosy designers choose GIF" to help you remember—but many people do pronounce it with a hard *g*)— is the acronym for *graphic interchange format*

- JPEG (pronounced *jay-peg*)—is the acronym for *joint photographers expert group*

6

Figure 6-1	The browser displays the image within the Web page wherever you typed the **img** tag. In this case, the image was the only content on the page, so it was placed at the top of the page

Because of its compression format, the GIF file type is best suited for flat-color graphics such as comics, illustrations, typography, and line art. In contrast, JPEG was created specifically for photographic imagery and shouldn't be used for flat-color graphics.

A third file type, PNG, is gaining popularity. *PNG,* which stands for *portable network graphic,* has many of the best characteristics from both JPEG and GIF. However, only the newest browsers currently support it. This causes PNG to be unusable for developers who want to create sites for the widest possible audience. As more people upgrade to newer browsers, this will change.

For more information on Web image file types, see Module 12.

Using Existing Graphics

Whenever your create a Web site, you will undoubtedly want to include some images. It isn't always necessary to create you own images. In fact, thousands of stock images are available either in computer stores or on the Internet. Some require minimal fees and others are free. Let's run through a few different types to help you decide.

Stock Photography

The use of photography can often add a sense of professionalism to a business Web site, but many businesses don't have the budget to hire photographers to do private photo shoots for them. If you are in this predicament, have no fear. Plenty of stock photography houses offer royalty-free photography to be used for almost any purpose, except for resale.

You can purchase entire CDs of photographs with a particular theme at your local computer or office supply store. These CDs range in cost from $40 to $500, depending on the quality of the work and the type of license you are given.

You can also search online and purchase the right to use an individual photograph. The costs vary according to how you plan to use the photograph. For example, if you want to purchase the right to use a photograph only on your Web site, you can expect to pay a minimal fee of $25–$50. If you want to use the same image in all your printed publications, as well as in any digital presentations, however, the fees typically start around $100 and go up from there.

You might also check the software licenses that came with your favorite graphics or presentation program. For instance, registered owners of Microsoft Office have access to Microsoft's free image gallery: **cgl.microsoft.com/clipgallerylive/**

When using any stock photography, be sure to read the terms of use and license carefully. While you may find free stock photography, it's often restricted only to noncommercial use. For more links, see Resource *D*.

Clip Art

Whenever you need a stock button, cartoon, line drawing, illustration, or other graphic, you might try searching through some clip-art libraries. You can find CDs filled with various types of clip art at your local computer or office supply store for $10–$150. (The cost typically depends on the quantity of graphics you receive.)

Probably thousands of online clip art galleries exist where you can search for the type of graphic you want. Many artists publish their clip art on the Internet and offer it free for personal use. License fees for commercial use of this clip art are usually affordable, and vary greatly according to the artist.

As with stock photography, you may receive some clip art free with the purchase of another software program. For instance, registered owners of Microsoft Office have access to Microsoft's free image gallery: **cgl.microsoft.com/clipgallerylive/**

For lists of online sources for stock photography and clip art, see Resource *D* in the back of this book.

Creating Your Own Graphics

If you do not use existing graphics on your pages, you may need to create some of your own or hire a Web designer to do so. The best Web designers typically have a background in graphic design and know how to make fast-downloading, good-looking graphics for the Web. You can locate Web designers either by word-of-mouth or by searching an online directory such as Design Shops: **www.designshops.com**

For more information about creating your own graphics, see Module 12.

Project 6–1: Add an Image to Your Web Page

Returning to the `index.html` page for the Woolwich Historical Society (or your own organization), let's add an image to the bottom of the page. Open your text editor (SimpleText on the Mac or Notepad on the PC) and load the `index.html` page saved from Module 5.

Note that: All the files needed to complete the projects in this book for the Woolwich Historical Society can be downloaded from **www.osborne.com** or **www.willardesigns.com/htmlbook/**. In addition, you can view my version of the Web site anytime by visiting **www.woolwichhistory.org.** Those of you who aren't using the Woolwich Historical Society can tailor your project to your particular needs.

Step-by-Step

1. At the bottom of the page, just above the horizontal rule, add the `painting.jpg` image located in your Module 6 folder of the .zip archive.

2. Save the file.

3. Open your Web browser and choose FILE I OPEN PAGE (or OPEN FILE or OPEN, depending on the browser you are using). Locate the file `index.html` you just saved.

4. View the page to ensure the image appears on the page. If you need to make changes, return to your text editor to make the changes. After making any changes, save the file and switch back to the browser. Choose REFRESH or RELOAD to preview the changes you just made. If you are using the Woolwich Historical Society, you can compare your files to the following code and Figure 6-2.

```
<!DOCTYPE html PUBLIC "-//W3C//DTD XHTML 1.0 Transitional//EN"
"http://www.w3.org/TR/xhtml1/DTD/transitional.dtd">
<html>
<head>
        <title>Welcome to the Woolwich Historical Society, located in Woolwich,
Maine</title>
</head>
<body bgcolor="#ffffff" text="#000000">
<h1>Woolwich Historical Society, Woolwich, Maine</h1>
<p><font face="verdana" size="+1"><em>The Woolwich Historical Society's</em>
19th Century Rural Life Museum is located at the corner of Route 1 and
```

```
Nequasset Road in Woolwich, Maine.</font></p>
<h3 align="center">Historic river-front community</h3>
<p>Woolwich is a rural community on the east shore of the Kennebec River,
opposite the historic city of Bath and approximately 12 miles from the
Atlantic Ocean. It is bordered by waterways: <i>the Sasanoa, the Sheepscot
and Merry Meeting Bay,</i> which is the confluence of five rivers. First
settled in 1600's and incorporated in 1759, the town is named for Woolwich,
England, which in like manner is situated on a large, navigable river.</p>
<p>The Kennebec brought to the territory explorers, settlers, traders and
fishermen. Indians from the hinterland used this route for summer visits to
the coast, and harried early settlers with attacks. The first settlement was
abandoned in 1600. Subsequently, the area was resettled by inhabitants whose
courage, perseverance, strength and ingenuity enabled the survival of their
town.</p>
<blockquote><i>"They lived between the dark forest and the Kennebec River
that empties into the lonely Atlantic. They did for themselves. The had to.
They left after them lilac bushes, stone walls, deeply dug wells, tall elms
now dying, old cellar holes, old things in old houses, and the Next
Generation."</i> From Carlton Day Reed Sr's Proceedings (Taken from
1760-1800 town records.)</blockquote>
<p>The Woolwich Historical Society's 19th Century Rural Life Museum affords
the visitor an opportunity to step back in time and experience life as it
was for earlier generations, while touring an eight room authentic country
farmhouse, shed and barn. On display are home furnishings, quilts, garments,
household implements and the tools and equipment of local employment:
farming, blacksmithing, dairying, brick and pottery making and
seafaring.</p>
<p>History and genealogy researchers visiting the museum will be directed to
a substantial collection of resources, among them The History of Woolwich,
Maine: a Town Remembered, which may be purchased in soft cover. </p>
<p>We also have some <a href="genealogy.html">online genealogy resources</a>
to get you started. <p>
<p>Other items for sale include a beautiful watercolor print by Betsy Bisson
(shown below), historical maps, note cards, recipe booklet, and postcards.
All items require an additional shipping and handling fee. Contact us for
more information.</p>
<img src="painting.jpg" />  ◄── **Code that was added
                               during this project**

<div align="right">
<hr />
<br />
<br />
<font color="#999999">&copy; 2000 Woolwich Historical Society</font>
</div>
</body>
</html>
```

Project Summary

The img tag enables you to add images to your Web pages. This project
gives you practice using that tag in its most basic form, before we move on
to additional formatting techniques.

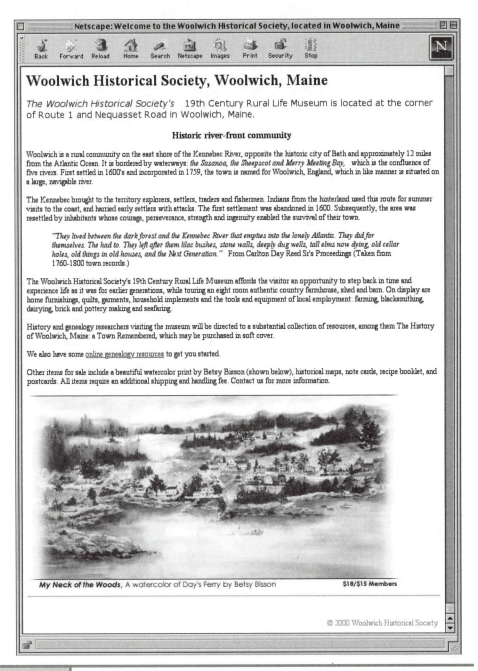

Tip

Does your image appear? If not, make sure the pathname is correct. Both the index.html and painting.jpg pages should be located in the same folder. If they aren't, you need to change the pathname to reflect the proper folder name. For more tips, see Resource C: Troubleshooting.

1-Minute Drill

● **How do you close the img tag so it is XHTML-compliant?**

● **Which attribute is used with the img tag to define the location of your image file?**

Specifying the Height and Width of Images

6

After you start adding several images to your Web pages, you may notice they sometimes cause the browser to wait a little while before displaying the page. Because they don't know the size of the image, some browsers actually wait until the images are all loaded before displaying the Web page.

Therefore, you can help speed the display of your Web pages by telling the browser the size of your images right within the img tag. You do so with the height and width attributes.

This attribute enables you to specify the width of your image	This attribute enables you to specify the height of your image

```
<img src="photo.jpg" width="391" height="274" />
```

The value of both the width and height attributes should be in pixels (not in inches or centimeters!)

● Place a space and a forward slash before the closing bracket in the img tag.

● src

If you don't know the size of your image, you can open it in a graphics editor, such as Adobe Photoshop/ImageReady or Macromedia Fireworks, to find out. Or, you can use the browser to determine the size of your images.

● **In Netscape for the Mac and PC, as well as in IE for the Mac** First, load the image by itself into the browser window (choose FILE | OPEN or FILE | OPEN PAGE and locate the image file on your computer). Then, look at the top of the browser window where the title is usually displayed. When you view an image file, Netscape prints the width and height of the image (in that order) in the title.

width and height

● **In Internet Explorer for the PC**   Load the image by itself into
the browser window (choose FILE | OPEN and locate the image file
on your computer). Then, right-click the image and choose
properties. The size is displayed as *dimensions* (width × height).

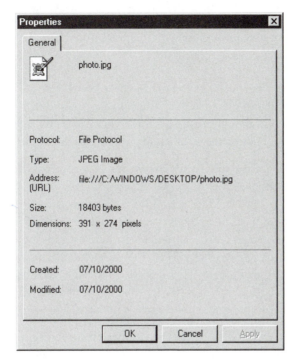

6

<hr>

─|Note ─────────────────

You can also use the height and width attributes to change the size of an
image. For example, if you were given an image that was 50 pixels high by
60 pixels wide, you could change that size by specifying a different size in
the HTML (such as 50 pixels wide by 50 pixels high). This causes the
browser to attempt to redraw the image at the newly specified size.
I don't recommend doing this, though, because it may not only slow down
the display of your pages, it may also cause the image to lose proper
proportions. Creating the image at whatever size you need it to be within
your page is best. For more tips on creating images, see Module 12.

Providing Alternative Text for Images

Some people visiting your site won't be able to see the images on your pages. A variety of reasons exist why this might be the case, but here are a few of the most common ones:

- **They have turned images off in their browsers**   Most browsers have a setting in the preferences that enable you to disable images on pages. By turning off images, visitors are able to view Web pages more quickly, and then choose which (if any) images they want to see.

- **They are using text-only browsers**   Although a minority of people using desktop computers have text-only browsers, many of those with hand-held devices do use text-only browsers on a daily basis. These hand-held devices might include Internet-ready telephones, pagers, and palm-size computers. Additionally, those who are vision-impaired often use text-only browsers with additional pieces of software that read the pages to them. In these cases, your alternate text may be the only way vision-impaired people can understand the purpose of your images.

- **The image doesn't appear**   Sometimes, even though you coded the page properly, the visitor to your site doesn't see every single image on the page. This could happen if too much traffic occurs or when visitors click the stop button in their browser before the page has fully loaded.

The good news is you can do something to help visitors to your site understand the content of your images, even if they can't see it. You can use the alt attribute of the img tag to provide alternative text for an image.

```
<img src="photo.jpg" width="391" height="274" alt="This
photo of my daughter, Corinna, was taken when she was 11
months old." />
```

The text value of the `alt` attribute displays in the box where the image should be located, if the browser cannot find the image or if it isn't set to display images (see Figure 6-3).

Another great benefit of the `alt` attribute is that even visitors who can see the image can also read the alternative text. For example, when you move your mouse over the image, the alternative text appears in a box near your pointer arrow. This process of showing informative text when

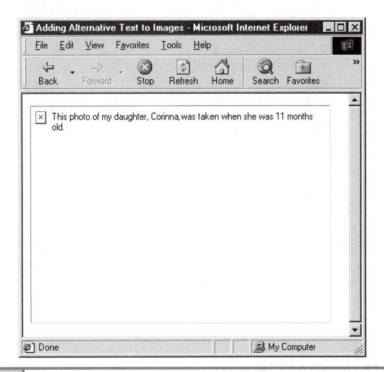

Figure 6-3 **This screen shows how the browser displays the alternative text if it cannot find the image. Without that alternative text, viewers wouldn't have any idea what they were supposed to see**

the mouse moves over an image is also called a *tool tip* in other software programs.

Note

Netscape browsers on the Macintosh don't show the alternative text when you move the mouse over an image. However, they do show the alternative text if the image doesn't display.

Linking Images

In the previous chapter, you learned how to create links to other pieces of information on the Internet. Text phrases were used to mark links and give visitors something to click. You could also use an image to label a link, with or without an additional text marker. Figure 6-4 shows an example of an image used as a link without an additional text label, while Figure 6-5's linked image does have a text label.

Figure 6-4   Here, an image alone is used as a link to another Web page

Figure 6-5   As an alternative, a text label has been added in this example to help users understand where the link will take them

Linking the Entire Image

To link an entire image, as in Figures 6-4 and 6-5, you need only to add the a tag and the `href` attribute around the image.

As with any other linked elements in a Web page, the visitor's pointer turns to a hand when she moves her mouse over the linked image (refer to Figures 6-4 and 6-5 for examples).

Linking Sections of an Image

You can also link sections of an image, creating what are called *image maps*. When only sections of an image are linked (as opposed to the entire image), the visitor's pointer only changes to the hand when he moves his mouse over one of the predefined hot spots on the image. Each *hot spot* within an image map can link to its own Web page, if wanted.

So, looking back at the photo of Corinna at 11 months, an image map could be used to link her eyes to one Web page and her mouth to a different one. Another example of an image map is an image of the United States, where each state could be designated as a hot spot, with its own link.

In this example, when you move your mouse over the state of Texas, the pointer changes to a hand telling you Texas is a link. You can see in the status bar at the bottom that the Texas hot spot links to a page called texas.html. If you were to move your mouse over to another state, such as New Mexico, you would see it is linked to newmexico.html

Two types of image maps exist: client–side and server–side.

Client-side Image Maps

Client-side image maps are called so because all the work is done on the client's (or visitor's) computer. The "work" I refer to is the computation of where the hot spot is located and to which link it corresponds. All the information about which hot spot is where and what it links to is included within the original HTML file. This makes for easy access by your visitor's Web browser because it doesn't have to look for the information elsewhere. Here's an example of what that code looks like:

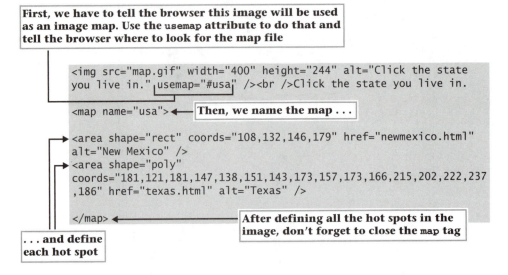

First, we have to tell the browser this image will be used as an image map. Use the `usemap` attribute to do that and tell the browser where to look for the map file

```
<img src="map.gif" width="400" height="244" alt="Click the state
you live in." usemap="#usa" /><br />Click the state you live in.

<map name="usa">
```
Then, we name the map . . .
```
<area shape="rect" coords="108,132,146,179" href="newmexico.html"
alt="New Mexico" />
<area shape="poly"
coords="181,121,181,147,138,151,143,173,157,173,166,215,202,222,237
,186" href="texas.html" alt="Texas" />

</map>
```
After defining all the hot spots in the image, don't forget to close the `map` tag

. . . and define each hot spot

You use the `usemap` attribute of the `img` tag to specify the image as a client-side image map. This attribute works similarly to something you learned in the previous chapter: links within a page. The reason for this is the map tag contains a `name` attribute that enables you to link to it.

When you use the `usemap` attribute, you reference whatever name you gave to your map in the `map` tag. So, in the previous example, the image references an image map called "usa" (`usemap="#usa"`), which is defined further down on the page by `<map name="usa">`.

Note

Remember, whenever you reference a client-side image map, you need to use the hash mark (#) before the name of the map, to tell the browser you are referencing something contained within a named section of the page.

Let's look at the code a little more closely.

```
<img src="map.gif" width="400" height="244" alt="Click the
state you live in." usemap="#usa" />
```

Here's your basic `img` tag, with the addition of the `usemap` attribute.
The value of the `usemap` attribute (in this case, *usa*) should be enclosed
in quotes and preceded by a hash mark (#).

```
<map name="usa">
```

The `map` tag surrounds all the other information defining hot spots in your
image. The opening and closing tags are both required. The `map` tag and its
enclosed information can actually be located anywhere within your HTML
page and needn't be immediately below the corresponding `img` tag. The
`name` attribute is used with the `map` tag to enable you to reference it from
anywhere else on the page (or any other page, for that matter).

```
<area shape="rect" coords="108,132,146,179"
href="newmexico.html" alt="New Mexico" />
<area shape="poly"
coords="181,121,181,147,138,151,143,173,157,173,166,215,
202,222,237,186" href="texas.html" alt="Texas" />
```

In between the opening and closing `map` tags are `area` tags for each hot
spot. The `area` tag has four basic attributes (see Table 6-1).

Note

Because the area tag doesn't have a closing tag, you need to include the
forward slash as a closing character at the end of the tag, if you want to
make your pages XHTML-compliant. If not, you can leave this slash off.

```
</map>
```

Finally, you end this section by closing the `map` tag.

Attribute	Value	Description
shape	rect, poly, or circle	Defines the shape of your hot spot: rect for rectangles, poly for polygons, and circle for circles.
cords	rect: x1,y1,x2,y2 poly: x1,y1,x2,y2,x3,y3,… circle: x,y,r	Defines the boundaries of your hot spot, where *x* and *y* are the horizontal and vertical coordinates, respectively, and *r* is the radius (for circles only). —Rectangles are defined by the upper-left and lower-right points. —Polygons are defined by each of their points, in *x,y* couples. —Circles are defined by the *x,y* coordinates of the center point and the radius.
href	filename.html	Defines the page to which you want this hot spot to link.
alt	text string	Defines the alternative text that appears for that hot spot.

Table 6-1   Attributes for the **area** Tag

Note

Very old browsers (such as the first versions of Netscape and IE) may not understand these types of image maps. However, the vast majority of your site's visitors should have no problems because all browsers since versions 2 of Netscape and IE support client-side image maps.

Finding Hot Spot Coordinates

If you need to, you can use graphics programs to find the coordinates of your hot spots. In Photoshop 5.5, which includes the Web-specific ImageReady tool, first open your file, and then choose WINDOW | SHOW INFO to display the floating Info palette. Select the marquee tool and move your mouse to the point for which you need to find the coordinates. The *x* and *y* values then appear in the Info palette.

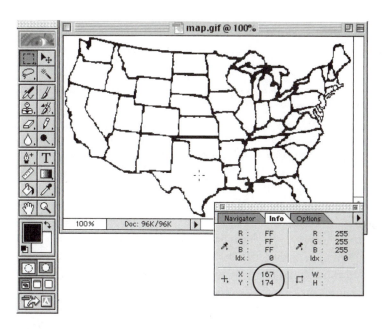

You can even use the standard Paint program that comes with Windows to find coordinates. In this program, when you use the selection tool and move your mouse to the points in question, the coordinates appear in the bottom menu bar.

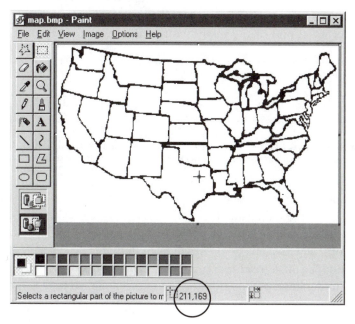

Finally, follow along the outside perimeter of your hot spot, writing down each set of coordinates. With this information, you can create the necessary code for the image map.

Note

Many other image editing tools, as well as HTML editors, have features that can help you create image maps. Check Resource *D* for links and more information about those types of programs.

Server-side Image Maps

As opposed to client-side image maps, where all the work is performed by the visitor's browser, the computation of *server-side image maps* is done on the computer hosting the Web site. This means when a visitor to your site clicks a hot spot in an image map, the browser sends a message back to the host computer seeking the corresponding link information. Then, the host computer sends the information back to the visitor's browser, showing the proper page. Even though this all happens within seconds, server-side image maps are a bit slower than client-side image maps.

Because the information for server-side image maps is stored on the host computer, you don't actually include it within your HTML page. The only portion included in the HTML page is a reference telling the browser this is an image map (`ismap` attribute) and where on the host computer it can find the necessary information (`a` tag).

> **Use the a tag and `href` attribute to tell the browser where to find the hot spots' link information for this image map**

```
<a href="usa.map"><img src="map.gif" width="400" height="244"
alt="Click the state you live in." ismap /></a>
```

> **Add this attribute to your `img` tag to designate this as a server-side image map**

> **As with all links, the a tag must be closed**

In addition, server-side image maps are not as user-friendly as client-side image maps because they don't tell you where a hot spot takes you. For example, client-side image maps show the linked page in the status bar at the bottom, whereas server-side image maps show the coordinates of the hot spot or nothing at all (refer to Figure 6-6). (This is because the browser must go back to the host computer to find out what the linked page is.)

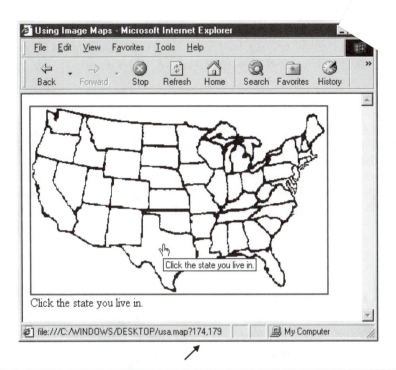

Figure 6-6   Instead of showing the link in the bottom menu bar, IE shows the
filename for the map and the coordinates of the mouse's location

After you reference the server-side image map from within the HTML
code, as previously shown, you need to create a file with the coordinates
and links for each of the hot spots. This type of file isn't done in HTML,
but it depends on the type of server on which your Web site is hosted. To
find out how to write such a file, contacting your system administrator for
the host company is best. He can give you a sample server-side image map
and make sure your site is set up to handle the files appropriately.

Here's an example server-side map file that would be appropriate for a
NCSA HTTPd server.

```
rect /aboutus/index.html 0,0,50,50
rect /contactus/index.html 50,0,100,50
rect /jobs/index.html 100,0,150,50
```

Although these map files don't use HTML, you must follow appropriate rules and guidelines. Again, check with your host company to be sure your files are created properly.

Tip

Many HTML editors and graphics programs come with image map editors. But even if you don't have one of those programs, you can download free or shareware programs that help you write both server-side and client-side image maps. A good example is Mapedit, which is available for PC, Mac, UNIX, and Linux. You can download it from **www.boutell.com/mapedit.**

Ask the Expert

Question: Why do I need to know about both client-side and server-side image maps? Would I ever need to use them both?

Answer: Many people use both client-side and server-side image maps on their sites to reach the widest possible audience of visitors. If you use both, the client-side image map first tries to run and, if it isn't understood by the browser, the server-side image map takes over.

The primary benefit of using server-side image maps is they are understood by the older browsers (such as version 2.0 and earlier), where client-side image maps aren't. However, as we update to newer browsers, it has become almost completely unnecessary to use server-side image maps at all. Ultimately, you should decide if those using early Web browsers make up a large enough percentage of your target audience to warrant using both types of image maps.

As a note, the W3C discourages the use of server-side image maps in favor of client-side image maps.

Using Borders

You might have noticed by now that all the linked images shown so far have had borders around them (refer to Figures 6-7 through 6-9). This happens because all linked images automatically have borders, just like all linked text automatically has underlines. You can customize the look of that border by adding the `border` attribute to the `img` tag.

```
<img src="map.gif" width="400" height="244" alt="Click the state
you live in." usemap="#usa" border="0" /><br />Click the state you
live in.
```

> **The border attribute enables you to
> customize the look of the image's border**

The value of the `border` attribute is expressed in pixels, where the default is 1 for linked images and 0 for nonlinked images. In this example, the value is 0. This turns the border off completely, making it invisible.

6

If you wanted to make it thicker, you would use a larger number, such as 4.

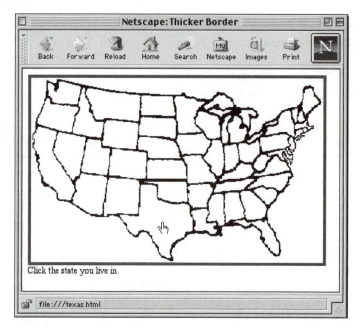

Tip

You can also use the `border` attribute to *add* a border to an image that is not linked, by specifying the value as any number greater than 0.

Aligning Images and Text

Whenever images appear within a section of text, you may want to alter the alignment. By default, the text starts wherever the image ends and flows below it.

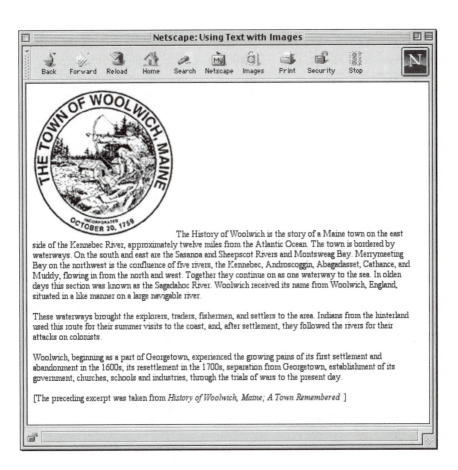

Netscape: Using Text with Images

Back   Forward   Reload   Home   Search   Netscape   Images   Print   Security   Stop

The History of Woolwich is the story of a Maine town on the east side of the Kennebec River, approximately twelve miles from the Atlantic Ocean. The town is bordered by waterways. On the south and east are the Sasanoa and Sheepscot Rivers and Montsweag Bay. Merrymeeting Bay on the northwest is the confluence of five rivers, the Kennebec, Androscoggin, Abagadasset, Cathance, and Muddy, flowing in from the north and west. Together they continue on as one waterway to the sea. In olden days this section was known as the Sagadahoc River. Woolwich received its name from Woolwich, England, situated in a like manner on a large navigable river.

These waterways brought the explorers, traders, fishermen, and settlers to the area. Indians from the hinterland used this route for their summer visits to the coast, and, after settlement, they followed the rivers for their attacks on colonists.

Woolwich, beginning as a part of Georgetown, experienced the growing pains of its first settlement and abandonment in the 1600s, its resettlement in the 1700s, separation from Georgetown, establishment of its government, churches, schools and industries, through the trials of wars to the present day.

[The preceding excerpt was taken from *History of Woolwich, Maine; A Town Remembered*]

6

As discussed in Module 4, you can use the `align` attribute with the p or `div` tag for basic alignment. The following example shows text that is centered on the screen.

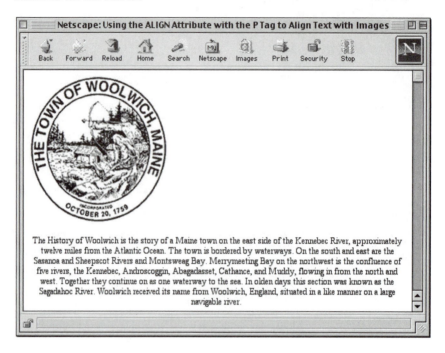

```
<img src="townseal.gif" alt="Woolwich, Maine Town Seal"
width="200" height="203" align="left" />
```

If you place the `align` attribute in the `img` tag instead, however, you can align the image, as opposed to only the text. In the following example, the value of the `align` attribute is left, thereby making the image align to the left edge of the browser; the text then flows around it to the right.

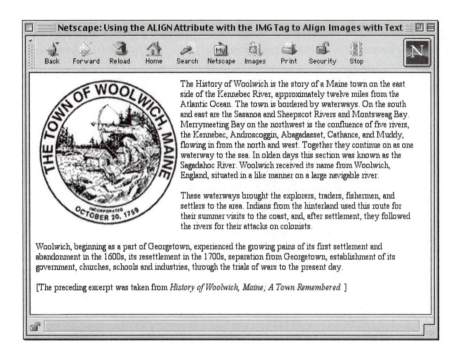

Many possible values for the align attribute can be applied to images (refer to Table 6-2).

Note that: The asterisks in Table 6-2 indicate these four types of alignment are neither part of the HTML 4.0 standard nor are they approved in XHTML 1.0. They are listed here because they were originally introduced by Netscape and, therefore, received a fair amount of use by Web developers. If you decide to use one of them, remember such alignment won't be understood by the newer XHTML browsers (when they are released).

Note

The `align` attribute for the `img` tag has been deprecated by the W3C in favor of Style Sheets, but it is still completely valid as HTML 4.0.

Type of Alignment	Value	Description	Corresponding Image in Figure 6-7
vertical	`top`	Aligns the top of the image with the top of the tallest thing on the current line.	A
vertical	`middle`	Aligns the middle of the image with the approximate middle of the text on the same line.	B
vertical	`bottom`	Aligns the bottom of the image with the bottom of the current line.	C
horizontal	`left`	Aligns the image to the left of any text following it.	n/a
horizontal	`right`	Aligns the image to the right of any text following it.	n/a
vertical	`absbottom*`	Aligns the bottom of the image with the bottom of the current line.	D
vertical	`absmiddle*`	Aligns the middle of the image to the middle of the tallest thing on the current line.	E
vertical	`baseline*`	Aligns the bottom of the image with the bottom of the current line.	F
vertical	`texttop*`	Aligns the top of the image with the top of the text on the current line.	G

Table 6-2   Options for Alignment of Images

Ending Alignment

Sometimes you may want to stop text from aligning to the right or left of an image. This might occur, for example, when you want to associate different images with each paragraph of text. Because no closing tag exists for images, you can use the `clear` attribute of the `br` tag to accomplish this task. Without one, the text continues to wrap around the image until it reaches the bottom of the image (see Figure 6-8).

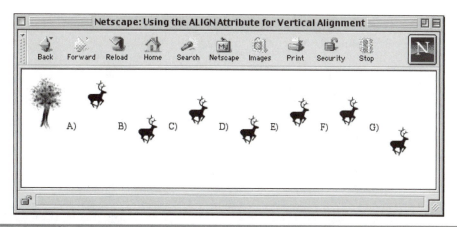

Figure 6-7   This example shows each of the vertical alignment options discussed in Table 6-2

6

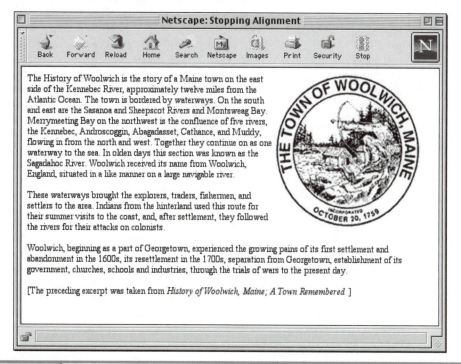

Figure 6-8   In this example, the image is aligned to the right of the text. There is no closing tag for the image, so the text continues to wrap around the image until it reaches the bottom of the image

When used with the `br` tag, the `clear` attribute has three possible values:

- `left`, which causes the text to drop down a line, below anything aligned to the left margin

- `right`, which causes the text to drop down a line, below anything aligned to the right margin

- `all`, which causes the text to drop down a line, below anything aligned to either margin

```
<img src="townseal.gif" alt="Woolwich, Maine Town Seal"
width="200" height="203" align="right" />
<p>The History of Woolwich is the story of a Maine town on
the east side of the Kennebec River, approximately twelve
miles from the Atlantic Ocean. The town is bordered by
waterways. On the south and east are the Sasanoa and
Sheepscot Rivers and Montsweag Bay. Merrymeeting Bay on the
northwest is the confluence of five rivers, the Kennebec,
Androscoggin, Abagadasset, Cathance, and Muddy, flowing in
from the north and west.  Together they continue on as one
waterway to the sea. In olden days this section was known
as the Sagadahoc River. Woolwich received its name from
Woolwich, England, situated in a like manner on a large
navigable river.</p>
<br clear="all">
```

This tag and attribute tell the browser to stop and drop down below the image before continuing

```
<p>These waterways brought the explorers, traders,
fishermen, and settlers to the area. Indians from the
hinterland used this route for their summer visits to the
coast, and, after settlement, they followed the rivers for
their attacks on colonists.</p>
<p>Woolwich, beginning as a part of Georgetown, experienced
the growing pains of its first settlement and abandonment
in the 1600s, its resettlement in the 1700s, separation
from Georgetown, establishment of its government, churches,
schools and industries, through the trials of wars to the
present day.</p>
<p> [The preceding excerpt was taken from <i>History of
Woolwich, Maine; A Town Remembered</i>]</p>
```

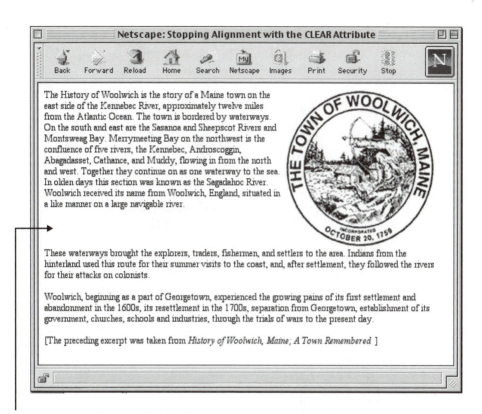

The clear attribute tells the browser to stop wrapping the text here and to drop down below the image before beginning again

Figure 6-9 By adding the **clear** attribute to the **br** tag, you can cause the text to stop wrapping around the image and not begin again until it is below the image

Adding Space Around Images

If you need to add some buffer space around an image, you can use the vspace and hspace attributes. The vspace attribute enables you to add vertical space above and below an image, while the `hspace` attributes add horizontal space to the right and left of an image. Both attributes require values in pixel dimensions.

For example, when viewed in Photoshop, you can see the actual edges of this image are quite close to the edge of the town seal. You can create a large buffer zone around this image by setting the `vspace` attribute to 50 and the `hspace` attribute to 20 in the HTML (see Figure 6-10).

```
<img src="townseal.gif" alt="Woolwich, Maine Town Seal"
width="200" height="203" align="left" hspace="20"
vspace="50" />
```

Note

The `vspace` and `hspace` attributes of the `img` tag are deprecated by the W3C in favor of Style Sheets. They are still completely valid in HTML 4.0.

This is 20 pixels of blank space

This is 50 pixels of blank space

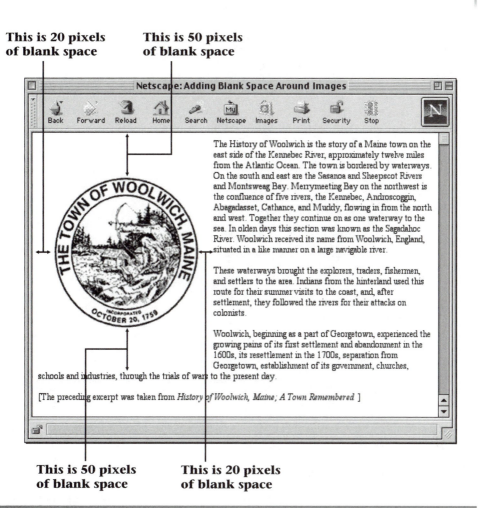

This is 50 pixels of blank space

This is 20 pixels of blank space

Figure 6-10 In this example, the **vspace** is 50 and the **hspace** is 20, creating a large buffer zone between the image and the text

6

Project 6-2: Change Image Characteristics

Returning to the index.html page, let's vary the characteristics of the image you added in the previous project. In addition, we'll add another image at the top of the page. Goals for this project include

● Specify the height and width for an image

● Provide alternative text for an image

● Link an image to another Web page

● Turn off the border for a linked image

● Align an image with the text around it

● Add some buffer space around an image

Step-by-Step

1. Open your text editor (SimpleText on the Mac or Notepad on the PC) and load the `index.html` page saved from Project 6-1.

2. Use a `p` tag and an `align` attribute to align the bottom image to the center of the screen.

3. Add the `height` and `width` attributes to that image.

4. Add alternative text to that image.

5. Add 10 pixels of vertical space around that image.

6. Link the image to "`poster.html`" and turn off the image's border.

7. Add the `townseal.gif` image to the top of the page, making sure to specify the height, width, and alternative text.

8. Align the `townseal.gif` image to the right of the text.

9. Save the file.

10. Open your Web browser and choose FILE I OPEN PAGE (or OPEN FILE or OPEN, depending on the browser you are using). Locate the file `index.html` you just saved.

11. Verify that all your changes were made as you expected. If you need to make additional changes, return to your text editor to make changes. When you finish, save the file and switch back to the browser. Choose REFRESH or RELOAD to preview the changes you just made. If you are using the Woolwich Historical Society, you can compare your files to the following code and Figure 6-11.

```
<!DOCTYPE html PUBLIC "-//W3C//DTD XHTML 1.0
Transitional//EN"
"http://www.w3.org/TR/xhtml1/DTD/transitional.dtd">
<html>
<head>
    <title>Welcome to the Woolwich Historical Society,
located in Woolwich, Maine</title>
</head>
<body bgcolor="#ffffff" text="#000000">
<h1>Woolwich Historical Society, Woolwich, Maine</h1>
<img src="townseal.gif" alt="Town Seal for Woolwich, Maine"
width="200" height="203"   ←  Code added during project
align="right" />
<p><font face="verdana" size="+1"><em>The Woolwich
Historical Society's</em> 19th Century Rural Life Museum is
located at the corner of Route 1 and Nequasset Road in
Woolwich, Maine.</font></p>
<h3 align="center">Historic river-front community</h3>
<p>Woolwich is a rural community on the east shore of the
Kennebec River, opposite the historic city of Bath and
approximately 12 miles from the Atlantic Ocean. It is
bordered by waterways: <i>the Sasanoa, the Sheepscot and
Merry Meeting Bay,</i> which is the confluence of five
rivers. First settled in 1600's and incorporated in 1759,
the town is named for Woolwich, England, which in like
manner is situated on a large, navigable river.</p>
<p>The Kennebec brought to the territory explorers,
settlers, traders and fishermen. Indians from the
hinterland used this route for summer visits to the coast,
and harried early settlers with attacks. The first
settlement was abandoned in 1600. Subsequently, the area
was resettled by inhabitants whose courage, perseverance,
strength and ingenuity enabled the survival of their
town.</p>
```

6

```
<blockquote><i>"They lived between the dark forest and the
Kennebec River that empties into the lonely Atlantic. They
did for themselves. They had to. They left after them lilac
bushes, stone walls, deeply dug wells, tall elms now dying,
old cellar holes, old things in old houses, and the Next
Generation."</i> From Carlton Day Reed Sr's Proceedings
(Taken from 1760-1800 town records.)</blockquote>
<p>The Woolwich Historical Society's 19th Century Rural
Life Museum affords the visitor an opportunity to step back
in time and experience life as it was for earlier
generations, while touring an eight room authentic country
farmhouse, shed and barn. On display are home furnishings,
quilts, garments, household implements and the tools and
equipment of local employment: farming, blacksmithing,
dairying, brick and pottery making and seafaring.</p>
<p>History and genealogy researchers visiting the museum
will be directed to a substantial collection of resources,
among them The History of Woolwich, Maine: a Town
Remembered, which may be purchased in soft cover. </p>
<p>We also have some <a href="genealogy.html">online
genealogy resources</a> to get you started.<p>
<p>Other items for sale include a beautiful watercolor
print by Betsy Bisson (shown below), historical maps, note
cards, recipe booklet, and postcards. All items require an
additional shipping and handling fee. Contact us for more
information.</p>
```

Code added during project

```
<p align="center">
<a href="poster.html"><img src="painting.jpg" width="600"
height="300" alt="A Painting by Betsy Bisson" vspace="10"
border="0" /></a>
</p>
```

```
<div align="right">
<hr />
<br />
<br />
<font color="#999999">&copy; 2000 Woolwich Historical
Society</font>
</div>
</body>
</html>
```

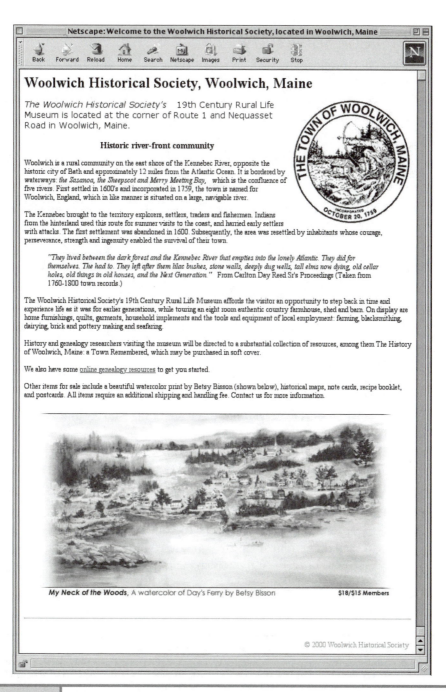

The image shows a Netscape browser window titled "Netscape: Welcome to the Woolwich Historical Society, located in Woolwich, Maine" containing a web page with the following content:

Woolwich Historical Society, Woolwich, Maine

The Woolwich Historical Society's 19th Century Rural Life Museum is located at the corner of Route 1 and Nequasset Road in Woolwich, Maine.

Historic river-front community

Woolwich is a rural community on the east shore of the Kennebec River, opposite the historic city of Bath and approximately 12 miles from the Atlantic Ocean. It is bordered by waterways: *the Sasanoa, the Sheepscot and Merry Meeting Bay,* which is the confluence of five rivers. First settled in 1600's and incorporated in 1759, the town is named for Woolwich, England, which in like manner is situated on a large, navigable river.

The Kennebec brought to the territory explorers, settlers, traders and fishermen. Indians from the hinterland used this route for summer visits to the coast, and harried early settlers with attacks. The first settlement was abandoned in 1600. Subsequently, the area was resettled by inhabitants whose courage, perseverance, strength and ingenuity enabled the survival of their town.

> *"They lived between the dark forest and the Kennebec River that empties into the lonely Atlantic. They did for themselves. The had to. They left after them lilac bushes, stone walls, deeply dug wells, tall elms now dying, old cellar holes, old things in old houses, and the Next Generation."* From Carlton Day Reed Sr's Proceedings (Taken from 1760-1800 town records.)

The Woolwich Historical Society's 19th Century Rural Life Museum affords the visitor an opportunity to step back in time and experience life as it was for earlier generations, while touring an eight room authentic country farmhouse, shed and barn. On display are home furnishings, quilts, garments, household implements and the tools and equipment of local employment: farming, blacksmithing, dairying, brick and pottery making and seafaring.

History and genealogy researchers visiting the museum will be directed to a substantial collection of resources, among them The History of Woolwich, Maine: a Town Remembered, which may be purchased in soft cover.

We also have some online genealogy resources to get you started.

Other items for sale include a beautiful watercolor print by Betsy Bisson (shown below), historical maps, note cards, recipe booklet, and postcards. All items require an additional shipping and handling fee. Contact us for more information.

My Neck of the Woods, A watercolor of Day's Ferry by Betsy Bisson $18/$15 Members

© 2000 Woolwich Historical Society

Figure 6-11 This example shows how the Woolwich Historical Society page might appear after making the changes listed in this project

Project Summary

You can customize the look and style of the images displayed in the foreground of your Web pages in many ways. This project gives you practice with many image attributes, including links, alignment, borders, and alternative text.

1-Minute Drill

● **How does an image's appearance change when you link it?**

● **Why is it important to add alternative text to images?**

Using Images in the Background

Images have another role in a Web page, which is in the background. Just as in a theatrical play, where actors may be moving in the foreground, as well as scenery in the background, two levels of design are also in a Web page (see Figure 6-12).

HTML enables you to add a single image to be used as the "scenery" in the background of your Web page. You use the `background` attribute of the `body` tag to do so.

Several benefits exist to using an image in the background as opposed to the foreground.

● You can achieve a layered look in your designs this way because an image in the foreground can actually be placed on top of the image in the background.

● Background images begin at the top of the page and run all the way to each of the four sides. By contrast, elements in the foreground are subject to borders on the top and left, similar to those that occur when you print something.

● Linked images have a border around them by default.
● Adding alternative text to images is important because cases may occur where an image does not display. In cases like this, alternative text is displayed where the image doesn't display, to assist or inform a visitor.

Figure 6-12 Here, a background image enables me to achieve a layered look because the photo in the foreground lies over the top of the image in the background

When you use a background image, you need to remember a few other things:

- **All background images tile**   *Tiling* means background images repeat in the browser window as many times as needed to cover the whole screen.

- **You can only include one image in the background**   So, if you want to use two different patterns in your background, they need to be included in a single image file.

- **Text in the foreground must be readable on top of the background**   If you are using dark colors in your background, make sure the text on your page is much lighter. Likewise, try to avoid high-contrast backgrounds because they make it extremely difficult to read any text placed on top of them.

6

● **Background images should be small in file size**   To avoid
a long download time. Take advantage of the fact that the browser
repeats a background image and cut your image down as much
as possible.

To help clarify these points, look back at Figure 6-12. If I tell you the
darker bar at the top as well as the word "Corinna" and the stars are all in
the background, can you imagine what the background image itself looks
like when it isn't tiled? Figure 6-13 gives the answer.

Because the original image was only 400 pixels tall, the browser was
forced to repeat it when the window was opened larger in Figure 6-14.

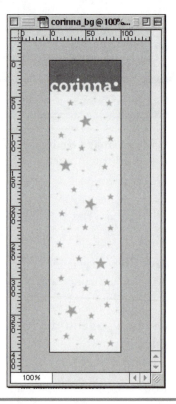

Figure 6-13   Before the image was tiled by the browser in Figure 6-12,
it looked like this

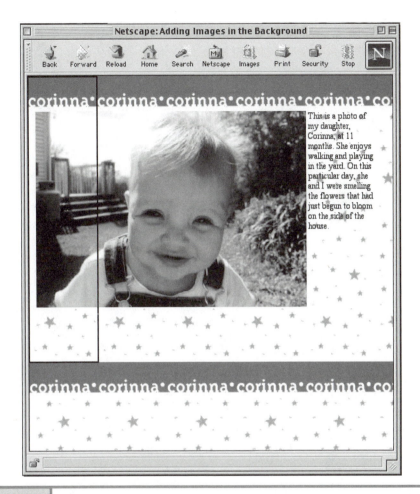

Figure 6-14 The size of the original image (100 wide by 400 high) is outlined here. Because the image is shorter than the browser window, it repeats first to the right and then down

To compensate for this, I could add additional space to my image, making it long enough to avoid tiling vertically. Testing your pages on different screen sizes is important, to ensure your background images are repeating as you expect. See Figure 6-15 for another example.

Figure 6-15 Here, I added 600 pixels to the height of the image, making it 1,000 pixels high. This helps to ensure visitors to the page won't see the darker bar and "Corinna" repeat again on the page

Can you imagine what my original image should look like if I wanted the darker colored bar to run down the left side of the screen instead of across the top. Look at Figures 6-16 and 6-17 for an idea.

Figure 6-16   When the original image was turned 90 degrees counterclockwise in a graphics program, it created a darker-colored bar down the

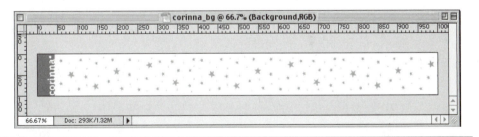

Figure 6-17   The original image used to create the background in Figure 6-16 is shown here. It is 1,000 pixels wide and 100 pixels high

---

Tip

You can find many images suitable for background tiles in the same clip-art catalogs mentioned earlier in the chapter. For more information about creating your own Web graphics like those displayed here, refer to Module 12.

Project 6-3: Add a Background Image

This final project in Module 6 gives you a chance to add a background image to your page.

Step-by-Step

1. Open your text editor (SimpleText on the Mac or Notepad on the PC) and load the `genealogy.html` page saved from Project 5-2.

2. Add one of the green leaf images (`greanleaf1.gif`) into the background of the page.

3. Save the file.

4. Open your Web browser and choose FILE | OPEN PAGE (or OPEN FILE or OPEN, depending on the browser you are using). Locate the file `genealogy.html` you just saved.

5. Preview the page to check your work. If you need to make changes, return to your text editor to make those changes. After making any changes, save the file and switch back to the browser. Choose REFRESH or RELOAD to preview the changes you just made. If you are using the Woolwich Historical Society, you can compare your files to the following code and Figure 6-18.

```
<!DOCTYPE html PUBLIC "-//W3C//DTD XHTML 1.0
Transitional//EN"
"http://www.w3.org/TR/xhtml1/DTD/transitional.dtd">
<html>
<head>
    <title>Online Genealogy Resources for Woolwich,
Maine</title>
</head>
<body bgcolor="#ffffff" text="#000000" link="#333366"
alink="#ff6633" vlink="#663399" background="greenleaf3.gif">
```

Code added during this project

```
<a name="top"></a>
<h2>Online Genealogy Resources for Woolwich, Maine</h2>
<p>We have some information about early Woolwich families
and would be glad to help you with basic searches. However,
in depth searches do need to be done in person, due to lack
of sufficient volunteer time.  Thanks for understanding! If
you have additional information to share, we would very
much appreciate receiving a copy of it - <a
href="mailto:info@woolwichhistory.org?Subject=Genealogy">em
ailed</a> or via USPS. If you can't find what you are
looking for here, you might try <a
href="http://dir.yahoo.com/Arts/Humanities/History/Genealog
y/">Yahoo's genealogy site</a>.
<p>*Note: <em>original information and comments are the
work of founding society member Roland S Bailey.</em></p>
<p><b>To begin, please choose the letter of the alphabet
that the family's last name begins with.</b></p>
<p><a href="#a">A</a> <a href="#b">B</a> <a href="#c">C</a>
D E F G H I J K L M N O P Q R S T U V W X Y Z</p>
<hr />
<a name="a"><h3>A</h3></a>
<p>AMES, JACOB E        b. abt 1756  d. March 12, 1839</p>
<p><a href="#top">Back to Top</a></p>
<a name="b"><h3>B</h3></a>
<p>BAILEY, JOSHUA SR     b. Nov 24, 1726     d. May 23,
1816 Woolwich<br />
BAILEY, JOHN (CAPT.)      b. Feb 2, 1737     d. July 29,
1813 Woolwich<br />
BLANCHARD, SAMUEL SR b. Sept 19, 1697     d. Feb 23, 1783
Woolwich<br />
BLINN, JAMES     b. abt 1725     d. Nov 13, 1813<br />
BROOKINGS, HENRY b. Mar 19, 1689 York ME     d. June 1748
killed by Indians<br />
BUCK, EPHRIAM 5th     b. Mar 6, 1761     d. Mar 13,
1821</p>
<p><a href="#top">Back to Top</a></p>

<a name="c"><h3>C</h3></a>
<p>CARD, WINCHESTER b. July 7, 1710     d. May 17, 1784<br
/>
CARLTON, JOHN SR b. July 1, 1740     d. Sept    1782</p>
<p><a href="#top">Back to Top</a></p>
</body>
</html>
```

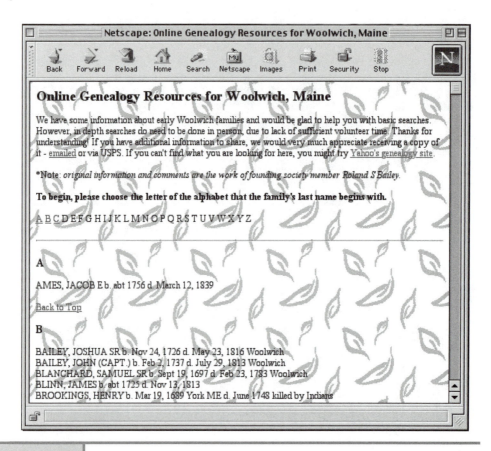

Figure 6-18 When added to the page, this green leaf image creates the look of a seamless background

Project Summary

Adding an image in the background can add depth and appeal to your Web pages, when used wisely. This activity gives you practice using the `background` attribute of the body tag to add a background image.

Tip

Having trouble getting your background to display? If so, make sure the image file is located in the same directory as your HTML file. If it isn't, you need to specify the correct file location in the `background` attribute. For more tips, see Resource C: Troubleshooting.

☑ *Mastery Check*

1. Why is providing the height and width of an image in the HTML a good idea?

_____

_____

_____

2. What are the two types of image maps?

_____

_____

_____

3. How can you make the border invisible on a linked image?

_____

_____

_____

4. How can you add some buffer space around images?

_____

_____

_____

5. How do you add an image to the background of a Web page?

_____

_____

_____

6

Module 7

Working with Multimedia

Goals

- Understand how plug-ins and ActiveX controls are used with Web browsers
- Embed different types of media into a Web page
- Link to different types of media from a Web page

181

On the Internet, the term *multimedia* is used to refer to presentations of various types of media, such as audio, video, text, graphics, or animation, which are integrated into a single file format. You may have seen multimedia presentations on news or weather sites, where they are used to display audio, video and text to viewers. Other sites use multimedia to entertain viewers, often in the form of a cartoon or an animated story.

Many forms of multimedia enable visitors to interact with the presentations. For example, a visitor might be watching an animated story, and then click the individual characters to learn more about them before continuing.

The Web itself is often considered multimedia because any Web page can contain several different types of these media files in it. By default, however, most Web browsers are only capable of understanding HTML files, graphics files such as GIF and JPEG, and plain text documents (.txt). Any other file types must be handled through a plug-in, ActiveX control, or helper application. Sometimes these types of controls come preinstalled in the browser, but other times they must be downloaded by the user.

Understanding Plug-ins, ActiveX Controls, and Helper Applications

A *helper application* is an additional piece of software that attempts to do something the browser cannot do. If you thought of yourself as the browser, then a helper might be someone who mows your lawn for you, while a plug-in is a ride-on mower that helps you do it yourself. A *plug-in* or an *ActiveX control* helps the browser do something itself, as opposed to how the helper application does it for the browser.

Hint

You might consider ActiveX to be a brand name used by Microsoft to reference its own type of technologies offering added functionality for Web browsers.

For example, if your Web browser doesn't know how to display a certain type of video file, it first looks for a plug-in capable of doing so. If your Web browser didn't find a plug-in, it might prompt you to download one or look for a helper application loaded on the computer that could display the video. If the browser cannot find a suitable plug-in or helper application, and one isn't downloaded, then it won't be able to display the file. For this reason, I do not recommend including essential information in files requiring plug-ins or helper applications, unless you also provide an alternative text-only version.

Helpers are stand-alone programs, separate from your browser, which you can purchase for your computer. By contrast, plug-ins and ActiveX controls are usually free and can be easily downloaded from the Internet. In some cases, Web browsers even come with certain plug-ins and ActiveX controls. When you download a plug-in or an ActiveX control, you should receive instructions on how to install it, if necessary.

Many times, the plug-in installs itself and you only need to close and reopen your Web browser. Other times, you are asked to place the plug-in in the appropriate folder on your computer and to restart your browser. Once you agree to download an ActiveX control, the browser downloads and installs the control usually without relaunching the browser.

Locating Plug-ins on Your Computer

You can find out which plug-ins are installed under your browser in a few different ways. For example, Netscape users can choose HELP | ABOUT PLUG-INS from the top menu in the browser to see a screen similar to the one shown in Figure 7-1.

If you are using Internet Explorer, you can navigate through your hard drive to the Plug-ins folder, which should be located in the Internet Explorer folder, to see the plug-ins that are installed (unfortunately, the view isn't as nicely arranged or easy to understand as in Figure 7-1).

Tip

PC users, try looking in C:\Program Files\Internet Explorer\Plugins.

You can tell which file extensions are linked to a particular plug-in or helper application by looking in the "suffixes" column

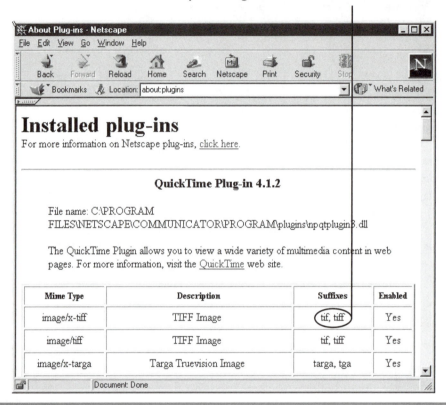

Figure 7-1 **Those using the Netscape browser can choose HELP | ABOUT PLUG-INS to see a list of all installed plug-ins**

Each browser and/or operating system keeps a list of the helper applications and/or plug-ins they are set up to handle. You access that list differently, according to the browser and operating system you have.

● **Internet Explorer for the Mac**: From within the browser, choose EDIT | PREFERENCES | RECEIVING FILES | FILE HELPERS.

- **Netscape**: From within the browser, choose EDIT | PREFERENCES | NAVIGATOR | APPLICATIONS.

- **Internet Explorer (and some other browsers) for the PC**: While viewing a folder of files on your hard drive, choose VIEW | OPTIONS | FILE TYPES (shown in Figure 7-2).

Note

While viewing these lists, you can add, edit, or delete the items on the list. Check the Help files within your browser or operating system for more information about working with helper applications and plug-ins.

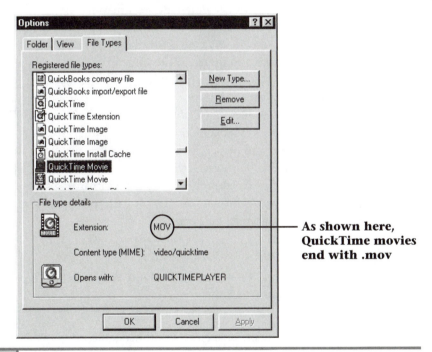

As shown here, QuickTime movies end with .mov

Figure 7-2 Windows PCs enable you to edit the file types associated with applications by choosing VIEW | OPTIONS | FILE TYPES when viewing a folder

Determining File Types, Extensions, and the Appropriate Plug-ins

You may want to link or embed many different file types in your Web pages, but Resource *E* lists some of the more popular ones. Most file types can be "played" with at least one plug-in or helper application and, quite often, with more than one. If you want to be helpful to your visitors, list the plug-in or helper application they might use to open your files. You could also provide a link to download the appropriate plug-in.

For example, Macromedia Flash, a file type requiring a plug-in, has become popular recently. You might have visited a Web site and noticed a window popup saying something about "downloading the Flash player." If you haven't noticed such a message, you may already have the plug-in installed on your computer because it's now shipping with many operating systems and browsers. In any case, Flash files are popular because they're small (which translates to quick-to-download!) and can include sound, video, interactivity, and animation. Flash files are particularly good for animations and cartoons. Another reason Flash is so popular is the plug-in used to display Flash files is available for both the Mac and the PC, and Internet Explorer and Netscape browsers.

Some plug-ins and helper applications aren't available for multiple computer systems and browsers, though. And the list of plug-ins is changing daily. To stay current on plug-ins, visit BrowserWatch's Plug-in Plaza (**browserwatch.internet.com/plug-in/plug-in-mm.html**) or Plug-in.com (**www.plug-in.com**).

Tip

Refer to Resource *E* in the back of the book for a list of file types, extensions, and descriptions.

When you're ready to include multimedia files in your HTML pages, consider how you want to include them. Do you want to *link* to them, so your visitors can choose whether to download them or view them now? Or, do you want to *embed* them within your page, so they appear right within the Web browser window? The rest of this module focuses on linking to and embedding several different types of multimedia.

Linking to Multimedia

A link to a multimedia file is essentially the same as any other link. While embedding a file can sometimes be problematic (as discussed in the next section), a link to a file can be especially useful because links are understood by all Web browsers. Figure 7-3 shows how the following code is displayed in a browser, and Figure 7-4 shows the result of clicking the video link.

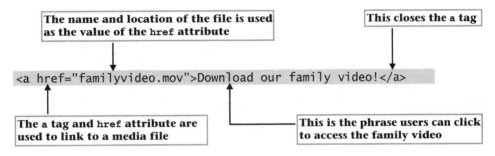

The name and location of the file is used as the value of the `href` attribute

This closes the a tag

```
<a href="familyvideo.mov">Download our family video!</a>
```

The a tag and `href` attribute are used to link to a media file

This is the phrase users can click to access the family video

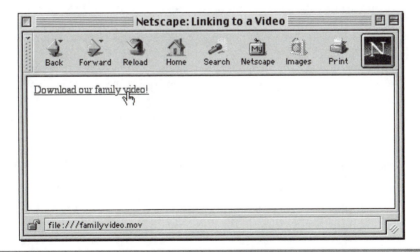

Figure 7-3   A link to a multimedia file is the same as any other link because it also uses the **a** tag and the **href** attribute

Figure 7-4 When the link is clicked, the browser may attempt to play the video itself if the QuickTime plug-in is installed

Note

Including the proper file extension for your media file is important, so the browser and operating system can understand and display it. If you are unsure as to which file extension to use, check the list in your browser or operating system (see Figures 7-1 and 7-2), or Resource *E* in this book.

Clicking the link shown in Figure 7-3 would cause one of three things to happen, depending on how the system was set up.

● It may prompt the user to download the file and save it for later (see Figure 7-5).

● It may prompt the user to download the file and view it now (see Figure 7-5).

● If the browser recognizes the file as one it is set up to display automatically, it may take over and do just that (see Figure 7-4).

Knowing that many systems may handle your multimedia files differently, try to offer your visitors as much guidance and instruction as possible. For example, list the size of the file you ask them to download,

This option enables users to download and save the file for later

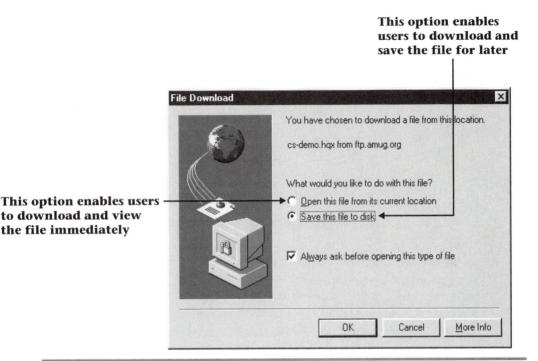

This option enables users to download and view the file immediately

Figure 7-5 When the browser doesn't recognize a file type as one it should "play" within the browser, it may prompt the user to download the file

so they can consider whether they want to wait for it to download. In addition, provide alternative ways of getting the information, included within the multimedia files wherever possible.

Embedding Multimedia

When you embed multimedia files instead of linking to them, they appear right within the context of your page. As long as the appropriate plug-in or ActiveX control is installed on the user's computer, the file will load and play along with anything else that might be on that page.

7

Two tags are currently used to embed files in HTML:

● embed—Initially developed by Netscape, this tag isn't recognized by the W3C as a standard for embedding a file. However, it's widely supported by the major browsers for embedding multimedia and Java applets other than those requiring ActiveX controls.

● object—This tag is included in the HTML 4.0 specification by the W3C as a way to embed everything from images and HTML files to multimedia and Java applets requiring ActiveX controls. At press time, it's only supported by versions 3 and newer of Internet Explorer.

When embedding multimedia files in an HTML page, you can choose to implement only one of those tags and ignore whether your page works in the other browsers. Or, you can use both tags together to try and reach the widest possible audience.

For example, if you are using an ActiveX Control to load the media, always make sure to use both the object and embed tags. That way, Internet Explorer loads the file using the appropriate ActiveX control, and Netscape loads it using a viable plug-in, thus reaching the most viewers.

Using Embed

```
<embed src="familyvideo.mov" width="160" height="120" />
```

As you can see by the preceding example, the embed tag looks similar to the img tag, in that a source is specified with the src attribute. The closing tag (</embed>) is optional. This means when you don't use the closing tag—you can use the forward slash at the end of the tag to close it in XHTML.

The embed tag has three required attributes (those shown in the previous example) and several more optional ones. All are described in Table 7-1.

Note

Some plug-ins require additional attributes aside from src, width, and height. For example, Flash also requires the pluginspage attribute. To be sure, check the documentation for whichever plug-in you're using.

Attribute	Possible Values	Description	Major Browser Support
`src="filename.ext"`	filename	Required: Tells the browser where to find the file being embedded. (Note: When using a plug-in that requires no data (such as a clock that retrieves all its information from the server), use the `type` attribute instead.)	Netscape & IC
`width="#"`	number of pixels	Required: Specifies the width of the window (video/animation) or controller (sound).	Netscape & IE
`height="#"`	number of pixels	Required: Specifies the height of the window (video/animation) or controller (sound).	Netscape & IE
The following attributes are optional			
`align="value"`	absbottom absmiddle baseline bottom left middle right texttop top	Specifies the position of the element in relation to others on the page.	Netscape & IE
`border="#"`	number of pixels	Defines the width, in pixels, of the border.	Netscape
`frameborder="value"`	yes no	Default is `yes`. When changed to `no`, the border is made invisible. (Does the same thing as `border="0"`.)	Netscape
`hidden="value"`	true false	Default is `false`. When changed to `true`, the image/controller is hidden and not displayed on the page, regardless of what was specified by the `height` and `width` attributes.	Netscape & IE (4.0+)
`hspace="#"`	number of pixels	Specifies the amount of blank space, in pixels, left on either side of the embedded file.	Netscape & IE
`name="name"`	name	Gives a name to the file.	Netscape & IE (4.0+)
`palette="value"`	foreground background	Default is `background`. When changed to `foreground`, the file being embedded takes on the palette characteristics of the foreground instead of the background.	Netscape *Windows PC only

Table 7-1   Standard Attributes for the **embed** Tag

7

Attribute	Possible Values	Description	Major Browser Support
pluginspage="location"	URL	Specifies a Web page address where users can download the plug-in needed to access the embedded file. An example would be "http://www.macromedia.com/shockwave" for Shockwave files.	Netscape
pluginurl="location"	URL	Specifies a link to a Java Archive (JAR) file if the plug-in cannot be found at the pluginspage location.	Netscape & IE (4.0+)
type="value"	MIME type (see note)	Specifies the type of file being embedded, which then defines the plug-in needed.	Netscape & IE (4.0+)
units="value"	pixels en	Default is pixels. When changed to en, the default unit of measurement for the height and width attributes becomes en (half the point size).	Netscape
vspace="#"	number of pixels	Specifies the amount, in pixels, of blank space above and below the embedded file.	Netscape & IE (4.0+)

Table 7-1   Standard Attributes for the **embed** Tag *(continued)*

Note

Multipurpose Internet Mail Extensions (MIME) is a standard system of extensions used on computer systems. This standardization makes it easy to specify a file type and to know other computers will understand it. Common MIME types for multimedia are image/png, image/gif, image/jpeg, video/mpeg, audio/x-wav, and so forth. Additional MIME types are listed in Resource *E*.

Aside from the attributes listed in Table 7-1, which are fairly standard among the browsers, many additional attributes are specific to the type of plug-in being used. In these cases, the browser ignores the attribute it doesn't recognize and passes it along to the plug-in to interpret.

For example, the loop attribute is a common one that's added to sound files. Netscape doesn't recognize it as a standard attribute of the embed tag, though. So, when Netscape sees the loop attribute, it simply ignores it and tells the plug-in playing the sound file to deal with it. As long as the plug-in understands the loop attribute, it then repeats the file for as many times as specified. Tables 7-2 through 7-5 lists some additional embed attributes specific to certain plug-ins. For more information about any of these attributes, visit the Web site of the corresponding plug-in's manufacturer.

```
<embed src="baby.wav" loop="4" width="125" height="100" />
```

Attribute	Possible Values	Description
autostart="value"	true false	Defines whether the file immediately starts playing when the page is loaded.
backgroundcolor="value"	hexadecimal code or color name	Changes the background color of the embedded file. The actual effect varies according to the plug-in being used.
center="value"	true false	Centers the embedded file in the window.
console="name"	name	Identifies this and other embedded controls by naming them.
controls="value"	all controlpanel controlpanel, statusbar controlpanel, infovolumepanel playbutton stopbutton	Specifies the style of the controller displayed in the Web page.
loop="value"	true false	Defines whether a file repeats.
nojava="value"	true false	Stops the Java Virtual Machine from running, causing your embedded file to run only with the plug-in (and not Java).
nolabels="value"	true false	Stops the presentation of label information (such as the author, copyright, and title) on the controller.
nologo="value"	true false	Prevents the RealLogo from displaying.
numloop="value"	number	Specifies the number of times a file will repeat.
shuffle="value"	true false	Plays multiple sounds in random order.

7

Table 7-2   Some Optional Attributes for Real Media

Attribute	Possible Values	Description
bgcolor="######"	hexadecimal code	Changes the background color of the embedded file. The actual effect varies according to the plug-in being used.
controls="value"	console playbutton pausebutton smallconsole stopbutton volumelever	Specifies the style of the controller displayed in the Web page.
loop="value"	true false # (number of times)	Defines how a file repeats

Table 7-3　Some Optional Attributes for Most Sound Players

Note

The plug-ins listed here aren't exhaustive, but are meant to give you an idea of some of the possibilities you have when using them.

Attribute	Possible Values	Description
base="url"	URL	Specifies the base directory all included links
play="value"	true false	Defines whether the file begins playing when the page is loaded
quality="value"	best high autohigh autolow low	Defines the quality level of embedded file.
scale="value"	showall noborder exact fit	Defines how the embedded file fits within the rest of the Web page.

Table 7-4　Some Optional Attributes for Flash

Attribute	Possible Values	Description
autoplay="value"	true false	Defines whether the file immediately starts playing when the page is loaded.
bgcolor="######"	hexadecimal code	Changes the background color of the embedded file. The actual effect varies according to the plug-in being used.
controller="value"	true false	Turns on the movie controller (When true, you need to add 16 pixels to the height of the movie.)
kioskmode="value"	true false	When true, disables the pop-up menu for the movie, so users cannot copy or save it.
loop="value"	true false	Defines whether a file repeats.
qtnextn="value"	URL	Identifies a URL for the movie to load when it finishes playing the current one.
qtsrc="value"	URL	Forces the browser to use the QuickTime plug-in to load the file instead of any other video plug-in.
scale="value"	tofit aspect #	Defines how the embedded file fits within the rest of the Web page.
volume="#"	whole number between 0 and 100	Defines the beginning volume for the movie.

Table 7-5   Some Optional Attributes for QuickTime

Tip

Whenever you embed sound within a Web page, it's always considered good practice to display at least some portion of the controls. This lets visitors turn off the sound or adjust the volume as they see fit.

Using Noembed

You can use the noembed tag to provide information to users whose browser doesn't support the embed tag (such as people using versions of Netscape prior to 2.0, which isn't that many people). In any case, using

Ask the Expert

Question: Wow! These tables are a little intimidating. Do I really need to know all this?

Answer: I completely understand. All this information is intimidating at first. But, rest assured, I only included it so when you do want to embed a specific type of file later, you can come back to this section and find the particular information that pertains to your plug-in. This information isn't here because you need to memorize every attribute. So many plug-ins are out there, that would be an impossible task!

The important thing is to understand you have these tags at your disposal and you can customize them according to your needs when the time comes.

the noembed tag is good to make sure everyone understands what's happening on your page.

```
<embed src="baby.wav" loop="4" width="125" height="100">

   <noembed>In order to listen to Corinna saying "da-da", you must first
have a web browser capable of understanding embedded multimedia. Visit <a
href="http://www.netscape.com">Netscape</a> to download a new one.</noembed>

</embed>
```

If you were to embed a Flash or Shockwave file, you could also use the noembed tag to include a regular GIF or JPEG for those who don't have the necessary plug-ins to view Flash or Shockwave files. Browsers that do understand the embed tag will simply ignore the text included in the noembed tag.

Using Object

The W3C has included the object tag in the HTML 4.01 specification as the preferred method of embedding files. A benefit of the object tag is it can handle a wider variety of file formats, including audio, video, animation, Java applets, text, ActiveX components, and images. However, its support varies widely according to the browser.

When you use the `object` tag, you must tell the browser what type of file you are embedding and where to locate that file. You use the `type` and `data` attributes to do those two things.

```
<object type="audio/wav" data="meow.wav">
```

Then, after the opening `object` tag, you add any additional attributes you want to specify using the `param` tag (short for *parameters*). This looks a bit different than the `embed` tag, where you included the attributes within the `embed` tag. The object tag enables you to specify the `height` and `width` attributes either in the `object` tag, or in `param` tags (as shown in the following), depending on the plug-in being used.

```
<param name="height" value="60" />
<param name='width" value="200" />
```

Note

Use the forward slash to make the `param` tag XHTML-compliant because it doesn't have a closing tag.

7

Finally, you close the `object` tag.

```
</object>
```

You can also use most of the attributes listed in Tables 7-1 through 7-5 here. In addition, use those listed in Table 7-6, which are specific to the `object` tag. You can find more information about any of these attributes by referring to the documentation for a specific plug-in.

Notice in Table 7-6 that Flash and Shockwave files have a few special values for certain attributes. When embedding Flash and Shockwave files, you should place the `classid` and `codebase` attributes in the `object` tag. Then, specify the actual location of the Flash or Shockwave file using the `param` tag. Here's an example of how you might embed a Shockwave file.

Attribute	Possible Values	Description
classid="value"	For Flash files: "clsid:D27CDB6E-AE6D-11cf-96B8-444553540000" For Shockwave files: "clsid:166B1BCA-3F9C-11cf-8075-444553540000" For RealMedia files: "clsid:CFCDAA03-8BE4-11cfB84B-0020AFBBCCFA"	Specifies the location of any file needed to implement the object. This can be used as an alternative to the data attribute, depending on what is being embedded in the page.
codebase="value"	For Flash files: "http://download.macromedia.com/pub/shockwave/cabs/flash/swflash.cab#version=4,0,2,0" For Shockwave files: "http://download.macromedia.com/pub/shockwave/cabs/director/sw.cab#version=7,0,0,0"	Specifies the download location of any necessary controls. When not used, the download location defaults to the current document.
codetype="value"	filename	Specifies the content type of data when the classid attribute is used.
data="value"	filename	Specifies the location of the file's data. If this is a multimedia file, this will be the actual filename (such as meow.wav).
type="value"	MIME type	Specifies the content type of the data specified by the data attribute.

Table 7-6 Additional Attributes for the **object** Tag

Tip

You can learn much more about embedding Flash and Shockwave files by visiting Macromedia's Web site: **www.macromedia.com.**

These attributes tell the browser where to find the appropriate plug-in to display the embedded file

```
<object classid="clsid:166B1BCA-3F9C-11CF-8075-444553540000"
codebase="http://download.macromedia.com/pub/shockwave/cabs/director/sw.cab#version=7,0,0,0" width="512" height="480">
     <param name="SRC" value="mymovie.dcr">
</object>
```

This tells the browser which file to embed

Similar to how the `noembed` tag works for embed, the `object` tag can contain other HTML tags and attributes, including other `object` tags. If the browser is capable of interpreting an `object` tag, it does so and ignores the HTML contained within the opening and closing `object` tags. If it doesn't understand the `object` tag, it uses the HTML included in it instead.

Using Embed and Object Together

You can also include the `embed` tag within the `object` tag, thereby taking advantage of both ways to embed files. This helps you ensure your embedded multimedia will serve the widest possible audience. Here's an example of the `embed` and `object` tags being used together to embed a Flash file.

7

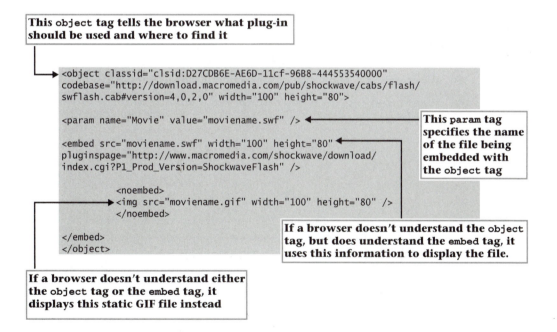

This `object` tag tells the browser what plug-in should be used and where to find it

```
<object classid="clsid:D27CDB6E-AE6D-11cf-96B8-444553540000"
codebase="http://download.macromedia.com/pub/shockwave/cabs/flash/
swflash.cab#version=4,0,2,0" width="100" height="80">

<param name="Movie" value="moviename.swf" />

<embed src="moviename.swf" width="100" height="80"
pluginspage="http://www.macromedia.com/shockwave/download/
index.cgi?P1_Prod_Version=ShockwaveFlash" />

        <noembed>
        <img src="moviename.gif" width="100" height="80" />
        </noembed>

</embed>
</object>
```

This `param` tag specifies the name of the file being embedded with the `object` tag

If a browser doesn't understand the `object` tag, but does understand the `embed` tag, it uses this information to display the file.

If a browser doesn't understand either the `object` tag or the `embed` tag, it displays this static GIF file instead

Both the `object` and `embed` tags need to be closed, from inside out (the last tag to be opened is closed first …).

Ask the Expert

Question: I've heard you can include background sounds. Why haven't you mentioned that?

Answer Yes, a bgsound tag enables you to specify a background sound in a Web page. The tag looks like this: `<bgsound src="music.wav" loop="4" />` and should be placed in the head section of the Web page (between the opening and closing head tags, not within the body section).

The reason I haven't included this tag here is it's only supported by Internet Explorer and isn't part of the HTML specification. The embed tag is a more useful way of including a sound in a Web page because it's supported by both Netscape and Internet Explorer. You can use the autostart attribute to make the tag play as soon as the page loads.

1-Minute Drill

● **What are two ways you can reference a multimedia file?**

● **What two tags can be used to embed a multimedia file within a Web page?**

Java Applets

You can also use the object tag to embed Java applets in your Web page. *Java applets* are miniapplications (which is where we get the term *applet*) written in the Java programming language that can run within your browser window. Web developers use these miniapplications to do things that aren't easily accomplished through HTML or other means.

● **Link to the file or embed it**
● **embed and object**

Java applets can be used to add functionality to your Web pages, whether through a real-time clock, a mortgage calculator, a stock ticker, or an interactive game.

Tip

Visit **dir.yahoo.com/Computers_and_Internet/Programming_Languages/Java/Applets/** for links to all things related to Java applets.

Here's an example of how to embed these applets using the `object` tag.

> **This attribute of the `object` tag tells the browser which applet to embed and where it is located**

```
<object classid="applet.class">
Here is my stock ticker.
</object>
```

> **This is the alternative text that's displayed when the browser cannot show the applet**

You might be able to use many different types of attributes to customize the look of your applet but, for the most part, the attributes will depend on the type of applet you're using. Don't worry—if you search for free or shareware applets online, the developer will usually give you detailed instructions on how to embed the file. If you're writing your own applets, you can tailor the look of your applet within the Java code.

Project 7-1: Embed sound in a Web page

Now you're going to create a page to be used by the Woolwich Historical Society Timeline. This page includes a photo and an embedded sound file used as narration.

7

Note that all the files needed to complete the projects in this book for the Woolwich Historical Society can be downloaded from **www.osborne.com** or **www.willardesigns.com/htmlbook/**. In addition, you can view my version of the Web site anytime by visiting **www.woolwichhistory.org.** Those of you not using the Woolwich Historical Society can tailor the project to your particular needs.

Step-by-Step

1. Open your text editor (SimpleText on the Mac or Notepad on the PC) and create a new file entitled `ice.html`.

2. Type all the HTML tags needed for a basic Web page.

3. Specify a white background color.

4. Place the image `icephoto.jpg` in the page.

5. Use the `embed` tag and the `object` tag to include the WAVE file called `narration.wav` in the Web page.

6. Specify that the console should be used as the `control` type.

7. Set the autoplay to `true`.

8. Specify the file should not loop.

9. Include alternative text in case the browser cannot understand the `embed` tag or the `object` tag. Use the following:

```
NARRATION: Worrall Prescott remembers how his grandfather, Worrall
Reed, was in the ice harvesting business for many years during the
late 1800s and early 1900s. <i>To hear this narration, you must have a
browser capable of embedding multimedia. You can download one from
<a href="http://www.netscape.com">Netscape</a> or <a
href="http://www.microsoft.com">Microsoft</a>.</i>
```

10. Use "Ice Harvesting in Woolwich, Maine" as a level 1 headline above the photo and sound console.

11. Use `div` tag to align the headline, console, and photo to the center of the page.

12. Save the file.

13. Open your Web browser and choose FILE I OPEN PAGE (or OPEN FILE or OPEN, depending on the browser you are using). Locate the file `ice.html` you just saved. Make sure the sound file plays.

14. If you need to make changes, return to your text editor to make changes. After making any changes, save the file and switch back to the browser. Choose REFRESH or RELOAD to preview the changes you just made. If you are using the Woolwich Historical Society, you can compare your files to Figure 7-6 and the following code.

```
<!DOCTYPE html PUBLIC "-//W3C//DTD XHTML 1.0 Transitional//EN"
"http://www.w3.org/TR/xhtml1/DTD/transitional.dtd">
<html>
<head>
    <title>Ice Harvesting in Woolwich, Maine</title>
</head>
<body bgcolor="#ffffff" text="#000000">
<div align="center">
<h1>Ice Harvesting in Woolwich, Maine</h1>
<img src="icephoto.jpg" alt="Ice Harvesting on the Kennebec River"
width="600" height="328">
<br />
<object type="audio/wav" data="narration.wav" height="60" width="200"
autostart="true" controls="console">
    <embed src="narration.wav" loop="0" width="200" height="60"
autostart="true" controls="console">
    <noembed>In this narration, Worrall Prescott remembers how his
grandfather, Worrall Reed, was in the ice harvesting business for many
years during the late 1800s and early 1900s. To listen, you must have
a browser capable of understanding embedded multimedia. You might try
downloading an updated browser from <a
href="http://www.netscape.com">Netscape</a> or <a
href="http://www.microsoft.com">Microsoft</a>.</noembed>
</embed>
</object>
</div>
</body>
</html>
```

7

Figure 7-6   Those using the Woolwich Historical Society can compare their files to this example

Summary

The object and embed tags can be used together to enable you to reach the widest audience. This project gave you a chance to practice using those two tags together to embed a sound file in a Web page.

Tip

Does your sound file play? If not, first make sure the pathname is correct. Both the ice.html and narration.wav files should be located in the same folder. If they aren't, you need to change the path name to reflect the proper folder name. Next, make sure your speakers are attached to your computer. (If you are using a PC, you also need to make sure you have a sound card installed.) Finally, make sure the volume is turned up on your speakers and the sound isn't muted. For more tips, see Resource C: Troubleshooting.

Note

For extra practice, try embedding any of the additional multimedia files in the Module7 folder into some Web pages.

7

✓ *Mastery Check*

1. What's the difference between a plug-in and a helper application?

2. What's the simplest and most widely supported way of referencing multimedia in your Web pages?

3. When you want to embed multimedia within a Web page, which tag is recommended by the W3C?

4. What can you do for visitors whose browser doesn't support the `object` tag?

5. What is a Java applet?

Module **8**

Creating Lists

Goals

- Differentiate between the different types of lists available in HTML
- Use each type of list in a Web page
- Combine and nest two or more types of lists in a Web page

Lists are everywhere—on your refrigerator, in school books, next to the telephone, on bills, and in all sorts of other documents. That's why there's a special set of tags just for creating lists. This module focuses on the three different types of lists possible in HTML:

- Ordered lists

- Unordered lists

- Definition lists

Lists are especially useful in Web pages to draw attention to short pieces of information. Keep that in mind when you create your lists and try to include short phrases, instead of long sentences, in each list item.

Using Ordered Lists

An *ordered list* is one in which each item is preceded by a number or letter. For example:

My favorite fruits are

1. raspberries

2. strawberries

3. apples

If you want to create the previous list on a Web page, you should use an ordered list. Here's what the HTML code would look like:

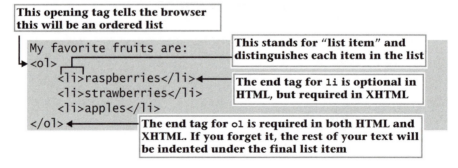

Note

While it's not required, I indent the list items to make seeing the structure of the list easier.

Notice I didn't include any numbers in my list. This is because I used the `ol` tag to tell the browser this is an ordered list. When browsers see ordered lists, they know to place a number in front of each list item.

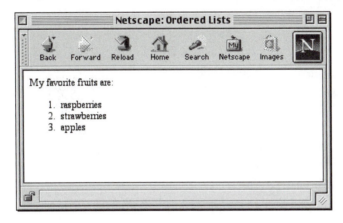

The default type of ordered list uses Arabic numbers, but you can use the `type` attribute to change that. Table 8-1 identifies the different types of ordered lists you can create with the `type` attribute.

To change the type of ordered list, add the `type` attribute and its value to the opening `ol` tag.

```
<ol type="I">
    <li>Introduction</li>
    <li>Understanding the Medium</li>
    <li>Basic Page Structure</li>
</ol>
```

8

Type Attribute Value	Numbering Style	
1	Arabic numbers	1,2,3,…
a	Lowercase alphabet	a,b,c,…
A	Uppercase alphabet	A,B,C,…
i	Lowercase Roman numerals	i,ii,iii,…
I	Uppercase Roman numerals	I, II, III,…

Table 8-1   Ordered List Types

Note

The `type` and `start` attributes are deprecated by the W3C, which prefers you to use Style Sheets to customize the look of your lists, but they are still widely supported by the browsers.

Here, I changed the type to "I", which tells the browser to place uppercase Roman numerals in front of each list item. So the previous code would create a list like this:

I. Introduction

II. Understanding the Medium

III. Basic Page Structure

You can also specify the starting number or letter for an ordered list with the `start` attribute. The default for the starting number is 1. To change this, add the `start` attribute to your `ol` tag.

```
<ol type="a" start="3">
    <li>Color</li>
    <li>Working with Text</li>
    <li>Working with Links</li>
</ol>
```

Even though the value of the `type` attribute may be something other than Arabic numerals, the value of the `start` attribute is always an integer. So, in the previous example, `start="3"` actually tells the browser to start the list with the third letter because `type="a"`.

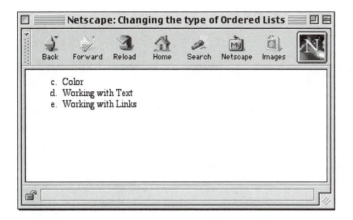

If you want to change an individual value, for example, if you want to make the third item in the list use the letter *g,* you can add the `value` attribute to the specific `li tag`.

```
<ol type="a" start="3">
    <li>Color</li>
    <li>Working with Text</li>
    <li value="7">Working with Links</li>
</ol>
```

As with the start attribute, the `value` attribute is always an integer. The browser looks at the value of the third list item, and changes it to *g* because the type is *a.*

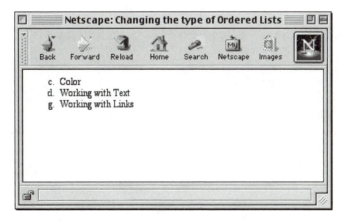

8

Ask the Expert

Question: When I use these tags to create a list, a blank line always appears above my list. Can I make the list appear directly below the text that precedes it?

Answer: You're correct—all lists in HTML are separated from the text above them by a blank line. Some people have found that by using the li tags without the ol tags, you can delete this extra blank line. But, be aware, this is considered illegal in HTML standards and can cause unpredictable results in some browsers. If you must make your lists rest flush against the text above them, use Style Sheets, as discussed in Module 15, to do so.

Using Unordered Lists

The second type of list is similar to the first, except *unordered lists* don't use numbers or letters. As the name suggests, unordered lists don't rely on order for importance. These lists use bullets to precede each list item. Here's an example of an unordered list:

- red

- green

- blue

You still use the li tag to identify each item in the list but, instead of beginning with the ol tag, unordered lists begin with the ul tag.

```
<ul>
    <li>red</li>
    <li>green</li>
    <li>blue</li>
</ul>
```

Aside from that, the code used to create the first two types of lists is almost identical. In fact, you can even use the `type` attribute here to change the style of the bullets. Three possible options exist for bullet style:

- "`disc`"—usually displayed as a small, filled-in circle

- "`circle`" —usually displayed as an open circle

- "`square`" —usually displayed as an open square

Initially, all unordered lists default to the disc style, which is usually represented as a small, filled-in circle. However, if you nest unordered lists, that is, if you include an unordered list in another unordered list, the default value changes. This is discussed later in the module.

Project 8-1: Use Lists on Your Web Page

The Woolwich Historical Society relies in part on membership dues to run its museum. In this project, you create a Web page listing membership benefits and fees. Goals for this project include

- Use an ordered list in a Web page

- Use an unordered list in a Web page

Note that: All the files needed to complete the projects in this book for the Woolwich Historical Society can be downloaded from **www.osborne.com** or **www.willardesigns.com/htmlbook/**. In addition, you can view my version of the Web site anytime by visiting **www.woolwichhistory.org**. Those who aren't using the Woolwich Historical Society can tailor the project to their particular needs.

Step-by-Step

1. Open your text editor (SimpleText on the Mac or Notepad on the PC) and create a new file entitled `membership.html`.

8

2. Type all the HTML tags needed for a basic Web page.

3. Specify a white background color.

4. Type the content listed in the section (following these steps) titled *Text to Add* (or copy it from the files in the Module 8 folder of the .zip file) and format it appropriately, so what is italicized in the text becomes italicized in the Web page, and so forth.

5. Format the top headline as a Level 1 header.

6. Format the list of membership benefits as an unordered list.

7. Format the cost of membership list as an alphabetical ordered list.

8. Link the word "store" in the list of membership benefits to "store.html".

9. Link the words "e-mail us" in the last paragraph to the e-mail address: info@woolwichhistory.org.

10. Save the file.

11. Open your Web browser and choose FILE | OPEN PAGE (or OPEN FILE or OPEN, depending on the browser you are using). Locate the file membership.html you just saved. Make sure the file appears as you intended.

12. If you need to make changes, return to your text editor to make changes. After making any changes, save the file and switch back to the browser. Choose REFRESH or RELOAD to preview the changes you just made. If you are using the Woolwich Historical Society, you can compare your files to the following code and Figure 8-1.

```
<!DOCTYPE html PUBLIC "-//W3C//DTD XHTML 1.0 Transitional//EN"
"http://www.w3.org/TR/xhtml1/DTD/transitional.dtd">
<html>
<head>
    <title>Woolwich Historical Society Membership
Information</title>
</head>
<body bgcolor="#ffffff" text="#000000">
<h1>Woolwich Historical Society Membership Information</h1>
```

```
<p>As a relatively small group of people interested in preserving
the history of Woolwich, Maine - we need money to fund expenses of
maintaining and running our Museum, paying for speakers for our
general meetings, and publishing our newsletter. The various
categories give one the choice of a support level.</p>

<p>We also maintain a Memorial Fund which we borrow from when major
expenses need to be made (new furnace; publish book).  The names of
those in whose memory donations have been made are read at the
Annual meeting each October - thereby keeping them alive in many
minds.</p>

<p>Membership in the Woolwich Historical Society offers the
following benefits:
<ul>
    <li>receipt of the <i>Woolwich Times</i> newsletter 4 times per
year, containing interesting articles, business items, and a
genealogy section</li>
    <li>discounts on some <a href="store.html">store</a> items</li>
    <li>free visitation of the Museum</li>
    <li>unlimited use of genealogy materials</li>
    <li>opportunities to volunteer with events such as Woolwich
Day</li>
</ul>
</p>

<p>The cost of membership varies according to the level of
involvement.
<ol type="A">
    <li>Individuals ($10/yr)</li>
    <li>Families ($15/yr)</li>
    <li>Supporting ($25/yr)</li>
    <li>Patron ($50/yr)</li>
    <li>Life ($300)</li>
</ol>
</p>

<p><b>If you are interested in becoming a member, please <a
href="mailto:info@woolwichhistory.org">email us</a> or mail your
tax deductible check to P.O.Box 98, Woolwich, ME 04579.</b></p>

</body>
</html>
```

8

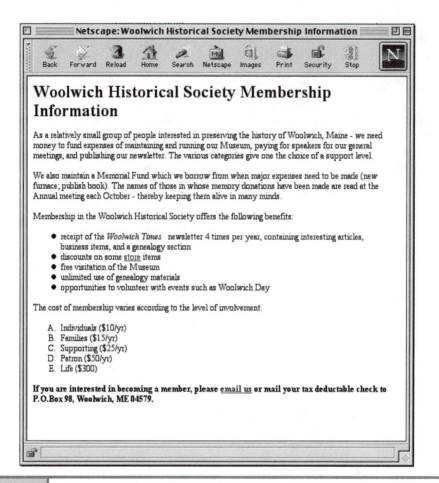

Figure 8-1 Those using the Woolwich Historical Society should have a page that looks similar to this

Text to Add

The following paragraphs (mentioned previously in Step 4) should be added to your Web page. The text is also included in the .zip file available from the Osborne Web site.

Woolwich Historical Society Membership Information

As a relatively small group of people interested in preserving the history of Woolwich, Maine - we need money to fund expenses of maintaining and

running our Museum, paying for speakers for our general meetings, and publishing our newsletter. The various categories give one the choice of a support level.

We also maintain a Memorial Fund which we borrow from when major expenses need to be made (new furnace; publish book). The names of those in whose memory donations have been made are read at the Annual meeting each October – thereby keeping them alive in many minds.

Membership in the Woolwich Historical Society offers the following benefits:

- receipt of the *Woolwich Times* newsletter 4 times per year, containing interesting articles, business items, and a genealogy section

- discounts on some <u>store</u> items

- free visitation of the Museum

- unlimited use of genealogy materials

- opportunities to volunteer with events such as Woolwich Day

The cost of membership varies according to the level of involvement.

A. Individuals ($10/yr)

B. Families ($15/yr)

C. Supporting ($25/yr)

D. Patron ($50/yr)

E. Life ($300)

If you are interested in becoming a member, please <u>email us</u> or mail your tax deductible check to P.O.Box 98, Woolwich, ME 04579.

Summary

Ordered and unordered lists can be great ways to draw attention to important information on your page. This project gave you practice using each type of list, in preparation for using them on your own Web pages.

Tip

Is the text after your list indented? If so, check to make sure you closed your lists with the proper ending tag (`</ol>` or `</ul>`). For more tips, see Resource C: Troubleshooting.

Using Definition Lists

The third type of list you can create in HTML is called a *definition list*. As its name suggests, you might use a definition list to shown terms and their definitions. For example, in the following list, the term is listed on the first line, and then the definition is on the line below the term.

W3C

 The World Wide Web Consortium was created in 1994 to develop standards and protocols for the World Wide Web.

HTML

 Hypertext Markup Language is the authoring language used to create documents for the World Wide Web.

A definition list works just like this one, where you use HTML tags to identify the terms and definitions for each of the list items. The code looks like this:

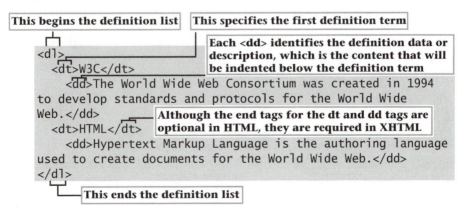

This begins the definition list

This specifies the first definition term

Each `<dd>` identifies the definition data or description, which is the content that will be indented below the definition term

```
<dl>
    <dt>W3C</dt>
        <dd>The World Wide Web Consortium was created in 1994
to develop standards and protocols for the World Wide
Web.</dd>
    <dt>HTML</dt>
        <dd>Hypertext Markup Language is the authoring language
used to create documents for the World Wide Web.</dd>
</dl>
```

Although the end tags for the dt and dd tags are optional in HTML, they are required in XHTML

This ends the definition list

You can use more than one dd for each dt if you need to, and the browser then simply indents each line below the dt. This might be useful if you want to make your own bullets. For example, you could place a reference to an image at the beginning of each <dd> and create your own style of bullets.

```
<dl>
  <dt>W3C</dt>
    <dd><img src="star.gif" width="12" height="12" alt="star">
The World Wide Web Consortium was created in 1994</dd>
    <dd><img src="star.gif" width="12" height="12" alt="star">
It develops standards and protocols for the World Wide
Web.</dd>
  <dt>HTML</dt>
    <dd>Hypertext Markup Language is the authoring language
used to create documents for the World Wide Web.</dd>
</dl>
```

> **In this example, I used a graphic of a small star at the beginning of each dd**

When viewed in a browser, the previous code would create a page similar to the following:

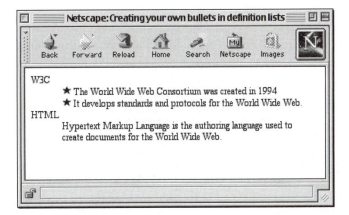

Note

Although it can be quite useful to use the dd tag outside a definition list as a way to indent text, this isn't valid HTML, and it can produce unpredictable results in some browsers. Because indenting text with the dd tag does the same thing as the blockquote tag, you might as well use that tag to indent a block of text.

Nesting Lists

You can also use another list inside itself or even one type of list inside another type of list. Each time you use a list inside another list, you are *nesting* lists. Perhaps the best example for nested lists is an outline like those created for a term paper.

I. Introduction

II. Part 1

    A. Description

    B. Examples

        1. Reference One

        2. Reference Two

III. Part 2

IV. Summary

Can you imagine what the HTML code would look like for the previous outline? The best solution would be to use a series of nested ordered lists as shown in the following code and Figure 8-2.

```
<ol type="I">          ← This opens the first ordered list and sets
<li>Introduction</li>     the type to capital Roman numerals
<li>Part I</li>
    <ol type="A">      ← This opens the second ordered list
                          and sets the type to capital letters
        <li>Description</li>
        <li>Examples</li>      This opens the third ordered
        <ol type="1">   ←     list and sets the type to Arabic
                              numerals (this is also the default)
            <li>Reference One</li>
            <li>Reference Two</li>
        </ol>   ←         This closes the third ordered list because
    </ol>                 it was the last one to be opened
    <li>Part 2</li>
    <li>Summary</li>
</ol>   ←          This closes the first and original ordered list
```

This closes the second ordered list

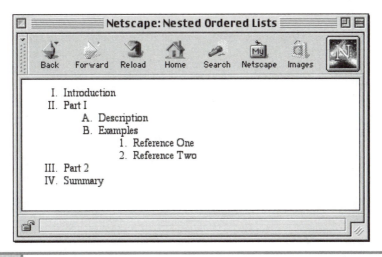

Figure 8-2   Three ordered lists are used to create this outline

As I mentioned before, you can also nest one type of list inside another type of list. For example, you could include a bulleted list inside a definition list to give further clarification to a definition description. Look at the following code and Figure 8-3 to see what I mean.

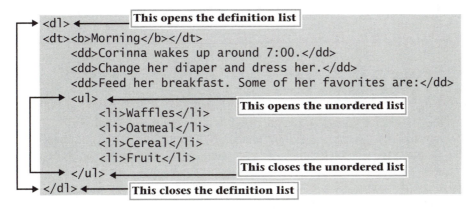

```
<dl>                                   This opens the definition list
<dt><b>Morning</b></dt>
    <dd>Corinna wakes up around 7:00.</dd>
    <dd>Change her diaper and dress her.</dd>
    <dd>Feed her breakfast. Some of her favorites are:</dd>
    <ul>                               This opens the unordered list
        <li>Waffles</li>
        <li>Oatmeal</li>
        <li>Cereal</li>
        <li>Fruit</li>
    </ul>                              This closes the unordered list
</dl>          This closes the definition list
```

8

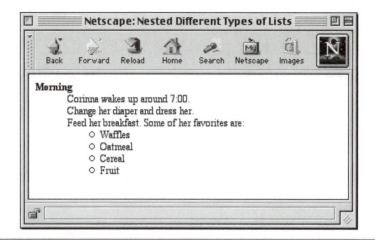

Figure 8-3 A definition list and an unordered list were used to create this set of instructions

Tip

The most important thing to remember when nesting lists is always to confirm that you have closed each list. If you notice a section of your nested list is indented more than it should be or continues within the list above it, try drawing semicircles from each of the list's opening and closing tags. If any of the circles cross or don't have an ending spot, you may need to recheck your work for errors.

Project 8-2: Use Two Different Types of Lists Within Your Web Page

The Woolwich Historical Society also has a museum store that sells various items to support the organization. Although they aren't initially planning to have an online store complete with credit-card processing, they want to list the products available in case a viewer wants to call and order something. In this project, we create a Web page listing these items for sale. Goals for this project include

● Use a definition list in a Web page

● Use a combination of two different types of lists, nested within a Web page

Step-by-Step

1. Open your text editor (SimpleText on the Mac or Notepad on the PC) and create a new file entitled `store.html`.

2. Type all the HTML tags needed for a basic Web page.

3. Specify a white background color.

4. Type the content in the section (following these steps) titled *Text to Add* (or copy it from the files in the Module 8 folder of the .zip file) and format it appropriately, so what is bold in the following becomes bold in the Web page, and so forth.

5. Place each of the notes at the bottom in an ordered list.

6. Separate the notes from the rest of the content with a horizontal rule.

7. Format the list of items for sale with a definition list, so each item is the definition term and the information about the item (such as pricing) is the definition description.

8. Make the top headline a Level 1 header.

9. Format the second headline (just above the list of items) as a Level 2 header.

10. Use an unordered list for each of the four different types of maps available. This list should be nested with the definition list.

11. Link the words "e-mail us" in the second paragraph to the e-mail address: info@woolwichhistory.org.

12. Link the phrase "Print by Betsy Bisson" to a photo of the print, called `painting.jpg`.

13. Link the words "membership page" in the second note to the `membership.html` page you created in Project 8-1.

14. Save the file.

15. Open your Web browser and choose FILE I OPEN PAGE (or OPEN FILE or OPEN, depending on the browser you are using). Locate the file `store.html` you just saved. Make sure the file appears as you intended.

8

16. If you need to make changes, return to your text editor to do so. After making any changes, save the file and switch back to the browser. Choose REFRESH or RELOAD to preview the changes you just made. If you are using the Woolwich Historical Society, you can compare your files to the following code and Figure 8-4.

```
<!DOCTYPE html PUBLIC "-//W3C//DTD XHTML 1.0
Transitional//EN"
"http://www.w3.org/TR/xhtml1/DTD/transitional.dtd">
<html>
<head>
    <title>Woolwich Historical Society Museum Store</title>
</head>
<body bgcolor="#ffffff" text="#000000">
<h1>Woolwich Historical Society Museum Store</h1>

<p>Our Museum store is small, consisting primarily of items
which relate to the Town of Woolwich and which visitors
have requested. Lack of space does not permit a large
variety - so most items are of a printed nature: the
<i>History of Woolwich</i> and <i>Nequasset Cemetery</i>
books, the Bisson print, various maps, booklets, notecards,
& postcards.  We also have magnets.</p>

<p><b>If you are interested in any of the items below,
please <a href="mailto:info@woolwichhistory.org">email
us</a> or send a check or money order to P.O.Box 98,
Woolwich, ME 04579.</b></p>

<h2>A selections of items from our store</h2>
<dl>
<dt><b><i>History of Woolwich</i></b></dt>
    <dd>Soft cover book; $20 + $1.10 sales tax; p/h -
$4.30</dd>
<dt><b><i>My Neck of the Woods</i></b></dt>
    <dd><a href="painting.jpg">Print by Betsy Bisson</a>;
$18 (members $15); p/h $3.20</dd>
<dt><b>Maps</b></dt>
```

```
    <dd>$3.50 (members  $3.00); p/h $3.20 (for up to 10
rolled maps sent to one address)</dd>
    <dd>Specify:</dd>
    <ul>
        <li>1858 Woolwich Map</li>
        <li>1740 Johnson Plan - vertical or horizontal
version</li>
        <li>2nd Division Plan (Joseph Frie/Frye Plan)</li>
        <li>Gilmore Survey</li>
    </ul>
<dt><b>Note Cards</b></dt>
    <dd>$3.50 (members $3.00); p/h $1.25</dd>
<dt><b><i>Sweet Receipts</i> Recipe booklet</b></dt>
    <dd>$2.00; p/h $1.25</dd>
<dt><b><i>Bump Jumpers</i> booklet</b></dt>
    <dd>$2.00; p/h $1.25</dd>
<dt><b>Postcards (reproductions)</b></dt>
    <dd>Each: .40 (members .30); p/h $.35/3 cards</dd>
    <dd>Any 10 cards: 3.00; p/h $1.00</dd>
    <dd>Set of all 22 cards: 6.00; p/h $2.00</dd>
</dl>
<hr />
<p>
NOTES:
<ol>
    <li>p/h = postage and handling, for U.S. addresses
only. Call for foreign postage rates.</li>
    <li>Some items have a discount for members. (See the <a
href="membership.html">membership page</a> for more
information)</li>
    <li>Some items are in limited supply.</li>
    <li>Sales tax applies to some items for residents of
Maine.</li>
    <li>All prices are in U.S. dollars.</li>
</ol>
</p>
</body>
</html>
```

8

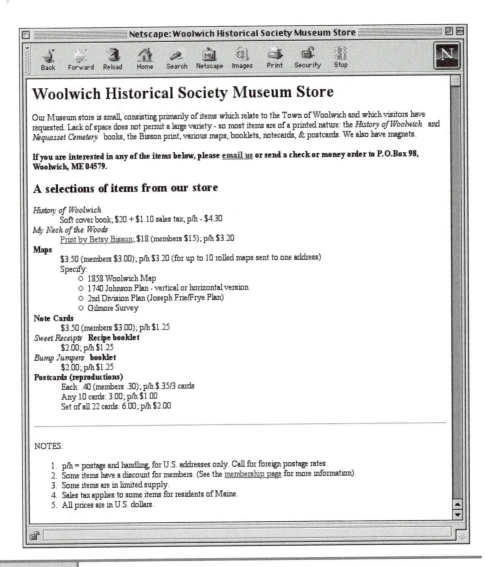

Figure 8-4 If you are the Woolwich Historical Society, your page might look like this

Text to Add

The following paragraphs (mentioned previously in Step 4) should be added to your Web page. The text is also included in the .zip file available from the Osborne Web site.

Woolwich Historical Society Museum Store

Our Museum store is small, consisting primarily of items which relate to the Town of Woolwich and which visitors have requested. Lack of space does not permit a large variety - so most items are of a printed nature: *the History of Woolwich* and *Nequasset Cemetery* books, the Bisson print, various maps, booklets, notecards, & postcards. We also have magnets.

If you are interested in any of the items below, please <u>email us</u> or send a check or money order to P.O.Box 98, Woolwich, ME 04579.

A selection of items from our store

History of Woolwich
Soft cover book; $20 + $1.10 sales tax; p/h - $4.30

My Neck of the Woods
<u>Print by Betsy Bisson</u>; $18 (members $15); p/h $3.20

Maps
$3.50 (members $3.00); p/h $3.20 (for up to 10 rolled maps sent to one address)

Specify:
1858 Woolwich Map
1740 Johnson Plan - vertical or horizontal version
2nd Division Plan (Joseph Frie/Frye Plan)
Gilmore Survey

Note Cards
$3.50 (members $3.00); p/h $1.25
Sweet Receipts Recipe booklet
$2.00; p/h $1.25

8

Bump Jumpers booklet
$2.00; p/h $1.25

Postcards (reproductions)
Each: .40 (members .30); p/h $.35/3 cards
Any 10 cards: 3.00; p/h $1.00
Set of all 22 cards: 6.00; p/h $2.00

NOTES:

1. p/h = postage and handling, for U.S. addresses only. Call for foreign postage rates.

2. Some items have a discount for members. (See the <u>membership page</u> for more information)

3. Some items are in limited supply.

4. Sales tax applies to some items for residents of Maine.

5. All prices are in U.S. dollars.

Summary

Many times, you can use a combination of ordered, unordered, or definition lists to organize the information on a Web page. This project gave you practice working with each of these types of lists on a single page.

Tip

Is the text after your list indented? If so, check to make sure you have closed your lists with the proper ending tag (`</ol>` or `</ul>`). For more tips, see Resource C: Troubleshooting.

Mastery Check

1. What are three types of lists in HTML?

2. What tag is used to denote list items in ordered and unordered lists?

3. What term is used to describe the process of including one type of list inside another type of list?

4. The definition description tag (<dd>) is used after which other tag in a definition list?

5. How can you change an ordered list from using Arabic numbers to capital Roman numerals?

8

Module 9

Using Tables

Goals

- Understand the concept and uses of tables in Web pages
- Create a basic table structure using text and images
- Format tables within Web pages
- Format content within table cells
- Use seamless and nested tables for page layout

At this point in the book, you've made it through the majority of the basic tags used to create Web pages. The next few chapters deal with content that can seem a bit more complicated than what you just learned. Don't worry, though, because even the pros struggle with these concepts when they first start (myself included).

Understanding Tables

Even though you might not recognize the terminology, you have undoubtedly seen tables in other printed or electronic documents. In fact, throughout the course of this book, I've used tables to give order to certain sections that might otherwise be confusing. Quite simply, a *table* is a section of information, broken up into columns and/or rows of blocks, called *cells*.

Those of you who use Microsoft Word may be familiar with a menu item in that program called "Table" that enables you to create tables just like those used in Web pages. Microsoft's word processor isn't the only one with tables. Most word processors are capable of letting you format content in tables.

Another form of a table, either printed or electronic, is the spreadsheet. Along these lines, you might think about a table as a large piece of grid paper, where you get to decide the size of the cells that will hold the information.

To make decisions about how large or small your cells and table should be, you need to do a little planning. Even though HTML tables are created in digital documents, the best way to plan out tables is to use a pencil and paper when you're first learning. As you become more familiar with the structure of a table, you may be able to plan it in your head, without first drawing it.

Let's first consider what a table would look like for a simple tic-tac-toe game.

● Draw a large box on your piece of paper.

- Divide that box into three columns and three rows.

- Place an *X* or an *O* in each of the boxes, leaving no boxes empty.

Following these steps will probably get you a piece of paper with a drawing similar to mine.

O	X	O
X	O	X
X	O	X

Now, imagine you want to translate this tic-tac-toe game into a Web page. How would you do that? You've already learned that in HTML, you cannot simply tab over to the next column and type an *X* as you might in a spreadsheet application. You can, however, use a table to lay out the tic-tac-toe game's structure.

Creating a Basic Table

First, decide how large you want your table or, in this case, how large you want your tic-tac-toe game. Remember, pixels are the units of measure on the screen, and inches or centimeters won't get you far in HTML. In the beginning, it'll probably be useful for you to write out your measurements on your drawings. Don't worry–nothing you're doing now is set in stone, and you can make changes later as needed.

9

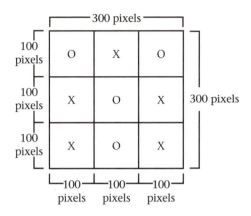

After planning out the dimensions of the table, it's time to get started working on the table structure in HTML.

Table Structure

You need to know about four basic table tags, as described in the following table:

`<table>` `</table>`	The `table` tag is a container for every other tag used to create a table in HTML. The opening and closing `table` tags should be placed at the beginning and the end of your table.
`<tr>` `</tr>`	The `tr` tag stands for *table row*. The opening and closing `tr` tags surround the cells for that row.
`<th>` `</th>`	The `th` tag stands for table header. An optional tag used instead of the `td` tag, this tag defines a cell containing header information. By default, the content in header cells is bolded and centered.
`<td>` `</td>`	The `td` tag stands for table data and holds the actual content for the cell. There's an opening and closing `td` tag for each cell in each row.

With these tags in mind, you can create both basic and complex table structures according to your needs. If you want to create a basic table structure, such as the following one.

Popular Girls' Names	Popular Boys' Names
Emily	Jacob
Sarah	Michael

Your code might look like this:

```
<table>
<tr>
    <th>Popular Girls' Names</th>
    <th>Popular Boys' Names</th>
</tr>
<tr>
    <td>Emily</td>
    <td>Jacob</td>
</tr>
<tr>
    <td>Sarah</td>
    <td>Michael</td>
</tr>
</table>
```

Note

While you're not required to indent your `td` or `th` tags, I did so here to help you differentiate between table rows and cells.

9

Opening and closing `table` tags surround the entire section of code. This tells the browser everything inside these tags belongs in the table. And there are opening and closing `tr` tags for each row in the table. These surround `td` or `th` tags, which, in turn, contain the actual content to be displayed by the browser.

Cell Content

You can include nearly any type of content in a table cell that you might include elsewhere on a Web page. This content should be typed in between the opening and closing td tags for the appropriate cell. All tags used to format that content should also be included in between the td tags.

Tip

Want to include a blank cell with no content? Type the code for a nonbreaking space ( ) between the opening and closing td tags, and your cell will appear blank.

If we return to our tic-tac-toe game, here is the code for that table.

```
<table>
<tr>
    <td>O</td>
    <td>X</td>
    <td>O</td>
</tr>
<tr>
    <td>X</td>
    <td>O</td>
    <td>X</td>
</tr>
<tr>
    <td>X</td>
    <td>O</td>
    <td>X</td>
</tr>
</table>
```

If you were to create a basic HTML page with this code, save it, and preview it in your browser, you'd see something like this.

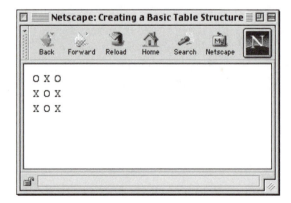

By default, the size of each cell is only as large or as small as the content of the cell. If you typed three *X*s or *O*s in each cell and added a sentence in the center cell, the table would change to look like this:

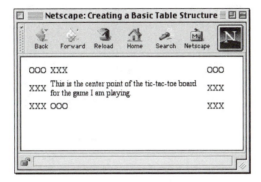

After a certain number of characters, the browser may *wrap* the content. This means it stops printing on that line and continues on the next line. This usually doesn't occur until the table runs up against another element within the page or the edge of the window. The default point at which the content wraps varies according to the browser.

Text

You can customize the text within each cell with the tags you learned in previous modules. For example, you can add the b tag to make the text within a cell bold.

```
<table>
<tr>
    <td>OOO</td>
    <td>XXX</td>
    <td>OOO</td>
</tr>
<tr>
    <td>XXX</td>
    <td>This is the center point of the <b>tic-tac-toe board</b>
for the game I am playing.</td>

<td>XXX</td>
</tr>
<tr>
    <td>XXX</td>
    <td>OOO</td>
```

This text is made bold, by using the b tag in the cell

9

```
    <td>XXX</td>
</tr>
</table>
```

Enclosing the words "tic-tac-toe board" in the center cell with the opening and closing versions of the b tag tells the browser to make that text bold.

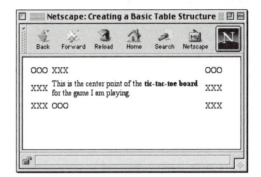

If you want to make all the text in every cell take on the same characteristics, there isn't an easy way to do this yet. For example, if you want to change the font of the text within the table, you could add a font tag with the appropriate directions above the table tag, like this:

```
<font name="verdana" size="-1">
<table>
<tr>
```

This would, indeed, change all the text inside the table to be displayed in Verdana, one size smaller than the current size, but it would only work in versions of Internet Explorer. Netscape requires you to place such information inside every single cell you want it to affect. This means to change the font size and face of all the text in this table, I would have to add the font tag to each cell, like this:

```
<table>
<tr>
    <td><font face="verdana" size="-1">000</font></td>
    <td><font face="verdana" size="-1">XXX</font></td>
    <td><font face="verdana" size="-1">000</font></td>
```

```
</tr>
<tr>
    <td><font face="verdana" size="-1">XXX</font></td>
    <td><font face="verdana" size="-1">This is the center
point of the <b>tic-tac-toe board</b> for the game I am
playing. </font></td>
    <td><font face="verdana" size="-1">XXX</font></td>
</tr>
<tr>
    <td><font face="verdana" size="-1">XXX</font></td>
    <td><font face="verdana" size="-1">000</font></td>
    <td><font face="verdana" size="-1">XXX</font></td>
</tr>
</table>
```

Tip

The text in the center cell of this table is a bit long. If I want to force it to break at a certain point, I could add the `br` tag at that spot.

You can see how this might get extremely tedious and add to the size of your HTML file (slowing it down for your users). However, this is the technically correct and the most widely supported way of changing the text attributes inside a table because both Netscape and Internet Explorer understand it.

Another way to customize the text inside a table is to use CSS style sheets. You learn about CSS style sheets in detail in Module 15, where I give you tips on how to affect the text inside of your tables more easily. The biggest drawback about using CSS style sheets is they aren't yet supported the same way in each of the popular browsers.

This means, when all is said and done, you must be flexible in the way your tables are rendered in the browsers. The most important thing is the text content is easily read and understood by visitors to the Web site, regardless of the font face or size in which it's displayed.

Images

You can also add images to any of the cells in your HTML tables. To do so, add the image reference (using the `img` tag) inside the cell in which you want it to appear. In the following example, I used a graphic of an *O* instead of text, wherever the *O* appeared in the game board.

9

```
<table>
<tr>
    <td><img src="images/o.gif" alt="O" width="19" height="19" /></td>

<td>XXX</td>
    <td><img src="images/o.gif" alt="O" width="19" height="19" /></td>
</tr>
<tr>
    <td>XXX</td>
    <td><img src="images/o.gif" alt="O" width="19" height="19" /></td>
    <td>XXX</td>
</tr>
<tr>
    <td>XXX</td>
    <td><img src="images/o.gif" alt="O" width="19" height="19"></td>
    <td>XXX</td>
</tr>
</table>
```

> **This image reference is contained in between the opening and closing td tags of this cell. Because no other content is in this cell, the image appears by itself**

When viewed in the browser, the image Os appear where the text Os used to appear:

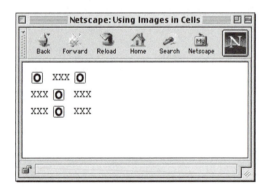

You can also combine text, images, and other types of media (such as animation, sound, and video) within table cells by drawing on many of the tags discussed in previous modules. The key is determining which elements go in which cells.

Formatting Tables

You may have noticed by now that all the text in a table appears aligned to the left side of each cell. This, and may other features of a table, can be easily customized with a few table attributes.

Borders

Tables, by nature of their design, have internal and external borders. By default, most recent browsers set the border size to zero, making them invisible. However, borders can be quite useful for tables of statistical information, for example, where it's necessary to see the columns to understand the data better. The key is understanding the three attributes related to the use of these borders.

Tip

When a table with borders is viewed in a text-based browser, the borders are represented as dashes for the horizontal borders and as pipes (|) for the vertical borders.

The Border Attribute

Even if you ultimately want your table borders to be invisible, a great way to see how your table is shaping up while you're building it is to turn on all the table borders temporarily. You can do so by adding the `border` attribute to the `table` tag and specifying a whole number greater than zero.

```
<table border="3">
```

Changing the border size to "3" for my tic-tac-toe table lets you see more clearly where each cell begins and ends because it turns on all the internal and external borders. The larger the number you specify, the thicker the borders become.

9

Note

If you don't want your borders to appear, it's best to specify border="0" in the table tag. That way, you are sure your borders will be invisible, even if the browser defaults to something else.

The Frame Attribute

A new attribute in HTML 4.0, the `frame` attribute, specifies which of the external borders surrounding the table will be displayed. Several possible values exist for this attribute, as described in the following table.

Note

At press time, this attribute was only supported by Internet Explorer. It's expected to be supported by future versions of Netscape.

Value	Description
void	Turns off all four sides. (Same as `border="0"`.)
above	Turns on the top border only.
below	Turns on the bottom border only.
hsides	Turns on the horizontal border (left and right) only.
vsides	Turns on the vertical borders (top and bottom) only.
lhs	Turns on the left-hand side border only.
rhs	Turns on the right-hand side border only.
box	Turns on all four sides. (Same as `border="n"`.)
border	Turns on all four sides. (Same as `border="n"`.)

You can use this attribute multiple times in a single table, so you could, for example, turn on only the top and left-hand side borders. The code to do this might look like the following.

```
<table border="2" frame="lhs" frame="above">
```

Remember, to use the `frame` attributes, the `border` attribute must be set to a whole number greater than zero

The Rules Attribute

Another new attribute in HTML 4.0 is the `rules` attribute, which can be used to specify those internal borders of a table that should be displayed. As with the `frame` attribute, this attribute only works if you have specified a border size greater than zero. When the `rules` attribute and the `border` attribute are both specified, the `rules` attribute takes precedence in browsers that support it.

Note

At press time, this attribute was only supported by Internet Explorer. It's expected to be supported by future versions of Netscape.

```
<table border="1" rules="cols">
```

A value of `cols` tells the browser only to display the vertical internal borders that lie between the columns

9

Several possible values exist for the `rules` attributes, as listed in the following table.

Value	Description
none	Turns off all internal borders.
groups	Turns on the vertical internal borders between groups of columns and/or rows.*
rows	Turns on the internal borders between rows only (horizontal).
cols	Turns on the internal borders between columns only (vertical).
all	Turns on all internal borders.

*You learn how to designate groups of columns and rows later in this module.

The next two illustrations show the same page viewed in Netscape 4.06 and Internet Explorer 5. Because Netscape doesn't understand the `rules` or `frame` attributes, it displays the table with all internal and external borders.

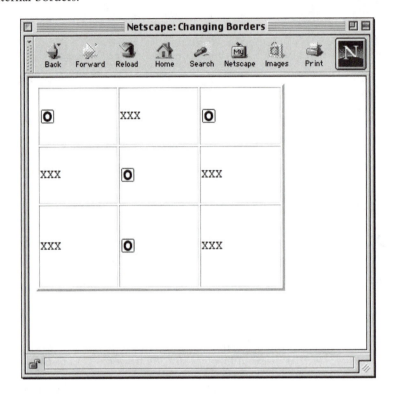

Internet Explorer recognizes the rules are set to "none" and the frame is set to "box" and renders the page accordingly.

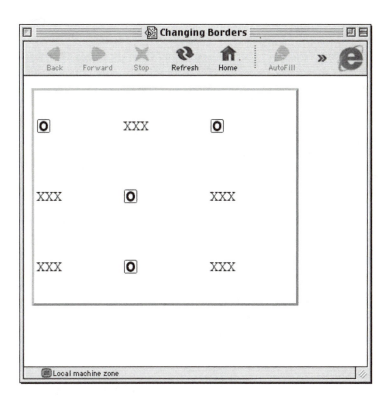

The opening `table` tag for this page is shown here.

```
<table border="3" width="80%" height="80%" frame="box"
rules="none">
```

9

Note

Internet Explorer also supports three additional attributes related to table borders (as shown in the following table). The three attributes only work in Internet Explorer, and they are ignored in Netscape and most other browsers. To use any of these attributes, the `border` attribute must be set to a whole number greater than zero. The value of these attributes must be either a hexadecimal color or a supported color name.

Attribute	Description
bordercolor="value"	Sets the color of the border drawn around the table
bordercolorlight="value"	Sets the lighter color in a 3-D table border
bordercolordark="value"	Sets the darker color in a 3-D table border

Cell Padding & Spacing

When the borders are visible for a table, it's easier to see how much space is around the content and in between the cells. Two attributes can be added to the table tag, so you can control those types of spaces.

● cellpadding—space between the content within the cell and the edges of that cell

● cellspacing—space in between each of the individual cells

First, cellpadding affects the amount of space between the content and the edge of the cell. When the borders are visible, increasing the cell padding can give extra *buffer space* around the text, so it doesn't run into the borders.

Second, cellspacing affects the amount of space between each of the cells in the table. While not located inside of the actual cells, this space can be increased to allow for a *gutter* between multiple cells, similar to the blank space between columns in a newspaper.

Tip

The default value for each one may vary according to the browser, so it may take some experimentation before you achieve the result you want.

The values for both of these attributes should be expressed in pixels, as a whole number greater than 0. A value of 0, in effect, turns off the cell padding or cell spacing, causing the cells to butt up against one another.

Hint

You use 0 values for cellpadding and cellspacing when creating seamless tables, which is discussed at the end of this module.

The following illustration shows two examples of different
`cellpadding` and `cellspacing` values.

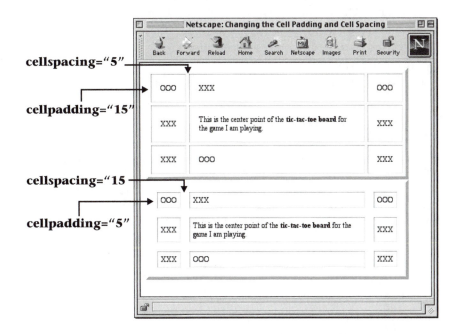

In the first table, the `border` is 5 pixels wide, the `cellpadding` is
15 pixels wide and the `cellspacing` is 5 pixels wide. This creates a
rather large buffer zone around the cell content, but a small amount of
space in between each of the cells.

```
<table border="5" cellpadding="15" cellspacing="5">
```

When those values are reversed in the second table, so the
`cellpadding` is 5 pixels wide and the `cellspacing` is 15 pixels
wide, the space between the cells is increased while the space around the
text in each cell is reduced.

```
<table border="5" cellpadding="5" cellspacing="15">
```

Width & Height

When I first introduced tables, I mentioned planning out the size of your tables ahead of time. This is particularly important if the table you are creating needs to fit within a predetermined amount of space on your page. You can use the `height` and `width` attributes independently of each other. If you don't specify them in your HTML, the browser chooses the size based on the amount of content within each cell and the amount of available space in the window.

Note

Although the `width` attribute of the `table` tag is included in the HTML 4.0 specification, the `height` attribute isn't included. While the `height` attribute is supported in most browsers, the way in which it is supported may vary. As with any Web page, it's best to test your page in multiple browsers to be sure you're achieving the desired result.

Let's say I want to include that tic-tac-toe game in my Web page, but I only had an available space on my page that measured 200 pixels wide by 200 pixels high. Because tables have a tendency to "grow" according to the amount of content in them, I might want to restrict the height and width of my table, to avoid it growing out of that 200 × 200–pixel area I designated for it. I could do so by adding the `height` and `width` attributes to my table tag.

```
<table border="3" height="200" width="200">
```

In this case, I would specify an *absolute size* for my table, one that shouldn't change if the browser window were larger or smaller.

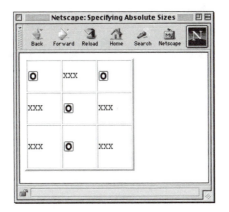

On the other hand, if I didn't care about the exact measurements of my table, but I only wanted it to take up 50 percent of the window and no more, I could use a percentage in the value of those attributes.

```
<table border="3" height="50%" width="50%">
```

This is called *relative sizing* because I'm not specifying absolute pixel dimensions but, instead, sizes that are relative to the browser window opening. Compare the next two illustrations, to see how, with relative sizing, the table size varies according to the window size.

9

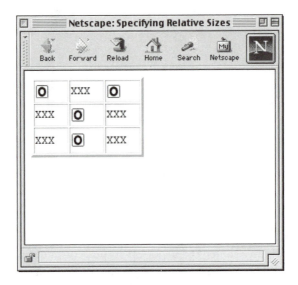

It's best not to mix absolute sizes with relative sizes when you use the `height` and `width` attributes together. This can sometimes cause unpredictable results when the page is viewed by different browsers.

Ask the Expert

Question: Which should I use—pixel dimensions or percentages when I create tables for my Web pages?

Answer: This is a great question, one that's receiving much debate among Web developers. The benefit of using pixel dimensions (absolute sizes) is, unlike percentages (relative sizes), they won't change and you can be certain your tables will look the same on the majority of browsers. However, percentages offer a benefit because relative tables can resize themselves according to the visitor's window size. It all comes down to this: who are your designing for?

As was discussed in Module 1, knowing your target audience is important. This also means knowing what screen size the majority of those people are using, by conducting research both online and offline. Look at Figures 9-1 and 9-2. These figures show a page designed for a screen resolution of 640 × 480, the smallest screen size users of desktop computers can usually access the Internet with. This page uses tables to lay out the entire page, meaning each element on the page is contained within a central table. In this case, the table width is specified as 600 pixels.

In Figure 9-1, the screen resolution is, indeed, 640 × 480, and the table fills the screen horizontally. However, in Figure 9-2, the screen resolution is 800 × 600, which is the next size up for desktop computers. Although 640 × 480 used to be the screen resolution of the vast majority of users, 800 × 600 is disputably the current standard for desktop computers. (I keep referring to desktop computers specifically, because there are so many other devices, such as Web-ready pagers and cell phones, that don't follow these standards.) As you can see, when the page is viewed at a higher resolution (Figure 9-2), blank space may appear on either side of the table.

This is a trade off, because this blank space does appear on larger resolutions, but it doesn't cause the page to be unreadable. One can argue that if you were to force your table widths to be 800 pixels, you would cause portions of your pages to be unreadable for viewers using a 640 × 480 resolution because they would have to scroll horizontally.

By contrast, relative table sizes do allow the table to resize itself according to the window size. Look at Figures 9-3 and 9-4 to see an example of a page laid out with a relative table, where the table width is set to 100 percent. In Figure 9-3, the resolution of the screen is 640 × 480. Figure 9-4 shows the page again with the screen resolution at 800 × 600. The table resizes to fill the space available, and more of the content is displayed without scrolling.

9

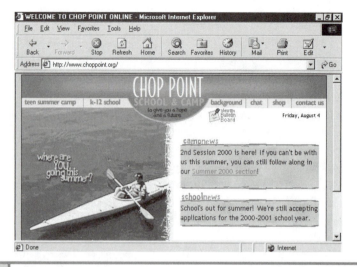

Figure 9-1 This page uses a large, 600-pixel wide table to lay out the various elements. When viewed in a 640 × 480 screen resolution, it fills the screen

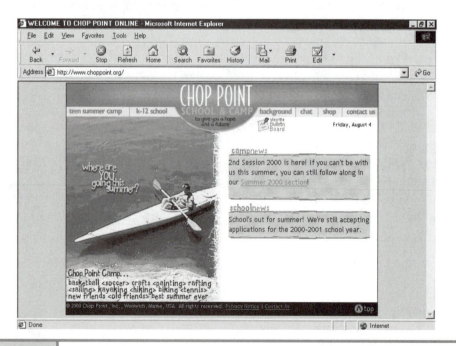

Figure 9-2 This page uses a large, 600-pixel wide table to lay out the various elements. When viewed in an 800 × 600 screen resolution, blank space is visible around the table

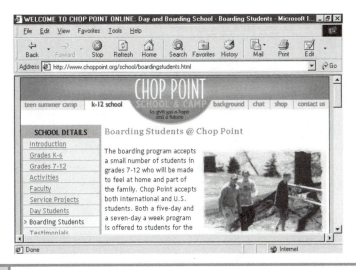

Figure 9-3   This page uses a relative sized table to lay out the various elements. When viewed in a 640 × 480 screen resolution, it fills the screen

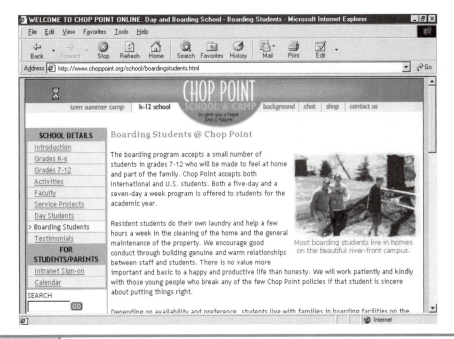

9

Figure 9-4   This page uses a relative sized table to lay out the various elements. When viewed in an 800 × 600 screen resolution, it also fills the screen

Ask the Expert

Question: Are you telling me to use relative sizes as opposed to absolute sizes?

Answer: I prefer using relative sized tables wherever possible, but these types of tables are much more difficult to use in some cases and might not be technically possible.

In some cases, you can actually use both—where a table with absolute sizes is nested inside a relative sized table. (More details about nesting tables can be found at the end of this module.)

For this reason, I want to give you descriptions of both to help you make more informed decisions when the time comes. Whatever you decide, remember to test your pages in multiple browsers, as well as on a variety of computer systems and monitors to make sure you are achieving the results you want.

Alignment

In Figure 9-2, you might have noticed the blank space appeared on both sides of the table. This occurred because the table included an `align` attribute that had a value of "center."

```
<table width="600" align="center">
```

Had that table not been aligned to the center of the screen, it would have appeared flush against the left side of the window by default. Centered tables with an absolute width can sometimes appear more balanced within the browser window.

Note

The W3C has deprecated the `align` attribute in favor of Style Sheets. The `align` attribute is currently supported by all the major browsers, though, and it's a valid attribute in HTML 4.0.

Additional values of the `align` attribute are "left" and "right." When either of these two is used, content outside the table flows around it. For example, the following illustration shows a table aligned to the right of the window, with text flowing around it on the left.

As discussed in Module 4, you could also place your entire table within a `div` tag using the `align` attribute to achieve the same result as `<table align="center">`.

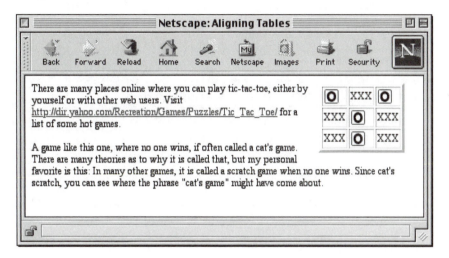

Colors

You can add the `bgcolor` attribute to the `table` tag to change the background color of the whole table. As with other instances of the `bgcolor` attribute, the value should be either a hexadecimal color or a predefined color name.

```
<table bgcolor="#999999">
```

Note

The W3C has deprecated the `bgcolor` attribute in favor of Style Sheets. The `bgcolor` attribute is currently supported by all the major browsers, though, and it's a valid attribute in HTML 4.0.

9

Depending on which browser renders the table, the background color you specify may or may not appear within the borders. Be sure to test your pages in multiple browsers to be sure.

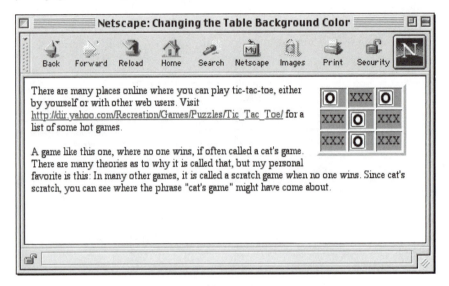

Background Images

Netscape 4.0+ and Internet Explorer 3.0+ (as well as several other browsers) enable you to add a background image to your table. This is accomplished by adding the `background` attribute to the `table` tag, similar to how you use the `background` attribute in the `body` tag to add a background image to your entire Web page.

```
<table background="images/clouds.jpg">
```

The problem with using this attribute in the `table` tag is it isn't included in the HTML 4.0 specifications. This means its present support varies according to the browser, and future support is questionable. Use caution when relying on a table's background image to provide important information to your Web page visitors, and always test your pages thoroughly to avoid having them be unreadable in another browser type.

Captions

The optional `caption` tag enables you to specify captions for your tables.
This isn't an attribute of the `table` tag; it's a stand-alone element used after
the `table` tag, but before the first table row.

```
<table border="3" align="right" bgcolor="#999999">
<caption align="bottom"><b>This is a game of
tic-tac-toe.</b></caption>
<tr>
    <td><img src="images/o.gif" alt="0" width="19"
height="19"></td>
    <td>XXX</td>
    <td><img src="images/o.gif" alt="0" width="19"
height="19"></td>
</tr>
```

Opening and closing `caption` tags surround the actual text you want to
display as a caption for the table. You can use the `align` attribute to specify
whether the caption should be located above ("top") or below ("bottom") the
table. By default, the caption is aligned at the "top" of the table.

You can also use additional formatting tags to draw more attention to
a caption. The following illustration shows how the browser might render
the previous code to display a bolded caption below the table.

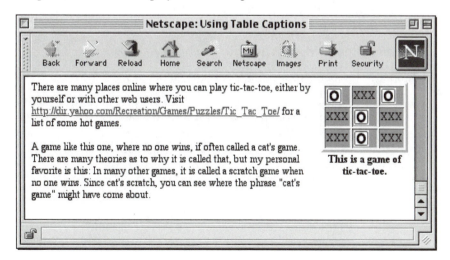

9

Project 9-1: Create a Basic Table

The Woolwich Historical Society maintains a historical timeline of events related to Woolwich history. We use a table to begin laying out this timeline. Goals for this project include

● Create a basic table structure

● Add text content to the table structure

● Format the table

Reminder

All the files needed to complete the projects in this book for the Woolwich Historical Society can be downloaded from **www.osborne.com** or **www.willardesigns.com/htmlbook**. In addition, you can view my version of the Web site anytime by visiting **www.woolwichhistory.org**. Those of you who aren't using the Woolwich Historical Society can tailor the project to your particular needs.

Step-by-Step

1. Open your text editor (SimpleText on the Mac or Notepad on the PC) and create a new file entitled `timeline.html`.

2. Type all the HTML tags needed for a basic Web page.

3. Specify the background, text, and link colors of your choice.

4. Create a table on the page, using the following table as a guideline. The following four columns correspond to the years 1639, 1651, 1654, and 1658 in the timeline, with the year alternating in location between Row 1 and Row 2. These are the first four columns in the timeline.

1639	--Birth of William Phips, son of James and Mary, who was a shipbuilder, discoverer of sunken treasure, knighted by King James II of England, involved with war with French and Indians, Governor of Massachusetts.		1654	--Nequasset sawmill was established by Major Clark and Captain Lake.
--Deed to Nequasset territory conveyed to John Browne and Edward Bateman by Indian Chief Mowhotiwormet. The Browne family were Nequasset settlers for seven years. --James Phips established his plantation by the Sheepscot River and Hockomaock Bay.	**1651**	--Edward Bateman sold Nequasset area to James Cold, who sold to Thomas Clark and Thomas Lake in 1658. --A settler acquired land from proprietors by building a house, owning oxen and tilling the acreage for five years. --Court of Menymeeting - organization of laws by a committee of 15 pioneers of the territory to govern the settlers along the Kennebec.	**1658**	

5. Specify a border size of 1, so you can see the outlines of the table and better understand its structure.

6. Make each of the cells contains a date and a header cell, so the date is bolded and centered in the cell.

7. Add the following Level 1 headline above the table: Woolwich, Maine, Historical Timeline 1639–Present*.

8. Add the following note at the bottom of the page: *prior to 1639, there were no permanent settlements, but a number of temporary ones.

9

9. Save the file.

10. Open your Web browser and choose FILE I OPEN PAGE (or OPEN FILE or OPEN, depending on the browser you are using). Locate the file `timeline.html` you just saved. Make sure the file appears as you want.

11. If you need to make changes, return to your text editor. After making any changes, save the file and switch back to the browser. Choose REFRESH or RELOAD to preview the changes you just made. If you are using the Woolwich Historical Society, you can compare your files to the following code and Figure 9-5.

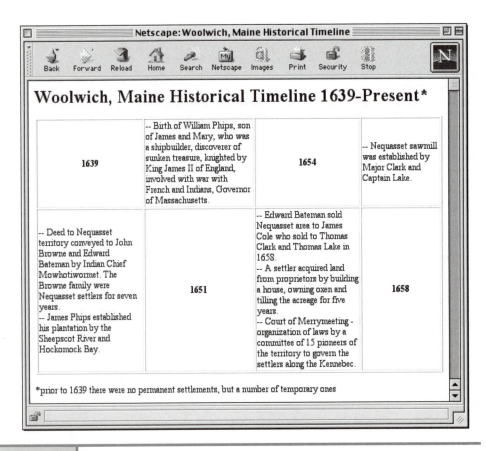

Figure 9-5 Those using the Woolwich Historical Society may see a page similar to this one

Tip

Is your table missing when you try to view the page? If so, check to make sure you have closed your `table` tag (`</table>`). For more tips, see Resource C: Troubleshooting.

```
<!DOCTYPE html PUBLIC "-//W3C//DTD XHTML 1.0
Transitional//EN"
"http://www.w3.org/TR/xhtml1/DTD/transitional.dtd">
<html>
<head>
    <title>Woolwich, Maine Historical Timeline</title>
</head>
<body bgcolor="#ffffff" text="#000000">

<h1>Woolwich, Maine Historical Timeline 1639-Present*</h1>
<table border="1">
<tr>
    <th>1639</th>
    <td>-- Birth of William Phips, son of James and Mary,
who was a shipbuilder, discoverer of sunken treasure,
knighted by King James II of England, involved with war
with French and Indians, Governor of Massachusetts.</td>
    <th>1654</th>
    <td>-- Nequasset sawmill was established by Major Clark
and Captain Lake.</td>
</tr>
<tr>
    <td>-- Deed to Nequasset territory conveyed to John
Browne and Edward Bateman by Indian Chief Mowhotiwormet.
The Browne family were Nequasset settlers for seven years.
<br />--  James Phips established his plantation by the
Sheepscot River and Hockomock Bay.</td>
    <th>1651</th>
    <td>-- Edward Bateman sold Nequasset area to James Cole
who sold to Thomas Clark and Thomas Lake in 1658. <br />--
A settler acquired land from proprietors by building a
house, owning oxen and tilling the acreage for five years.
<br />-- Court of Merrymeeting - organization of laws by a
committee of 15 pioneers of the territory to govern the
settlers along the Kennebec.</td>
    <th>1658</th>
</tr>
</table>
```

9

```
<p>*prior to 1639 there were no permanent settlements, but
a number of temporary ones</p>
</body>
</html>
```

Summary

Tables are used in a wide variety of ways throughout the digital and print industries. This project gave you practice creating a basic table structure, using the beginning of a timeline for the Woolwich Historical Society.

1-Minute Drill

- **What tag is used to designate a new table row?**
- **What tag encloses the content in a particular cell?**

Formatting Content in Table Cells

Just as you can format the entire table, you can format each of the individual cells within the table. This means changing the alignment, width, height, and background colors, as well as restricting line breaks and spanning content across multiple columns or rows.

Note

The align, width, height, and nowrap attributes are deprecated by the W3C in favor of Style Sheets, but remain valid in HTML 4.0.

Alignment

If you refer to the table you created in Project 9-1, or to Figure 9-5, you may notice the alignment appears differently for some of the cells depending on how wide the browser window is open. For example, in Figure 9-5, the

- `<tr>`
- `<td>`

second cell across in the first row is filled with text content, while the first cell in that same row is a header cell that is aligned to the center horizontally and vertically.

To change vertical and horizontal alignment, you can add the `align` attribute for horizontal alignment or the `valign` attribute for vertical alignment to the `tr`, `th`, or `td` tags. The following table lists the possible values for these two attributes.

1. `tr`—Adding the `align` or `valign` attribute to the `tr` tag causes the alignment you specify to take effect for all the cells in that row.

2. `td`, `th`—Adding the `align` or `valign` attribute to the `td` or `th` tag causes the alignment you specify to take effect for only that cell.

Attribute	Possible Values
align	left
	right
	center
valign	top
	bottom
	middle

Tip

The default values for the `align` and `valign` attributes are left and middle, respectively. For header cells (using the `th` tag), however, the horizontal alignment defaults to center instead of left.

9

Returning to the tic-tac-toe table, I can add `align` and `valign` attributes to some of the cells to give you a better idea of how each one works. For a visual representation of this code in the browser, see Figure 9-6.

```
<table width="100%" height="100%" border="1">
<tr>
    <th>Tic</th>
    <th>Tac</th>
    <th>Toe</th>
</tr>
<tr valign="top">
```

Adding this `valign` attribute to the `tr` tag causes all three cells in this row to be vertically aligned to the top

```
    <td align="left">000</td>
    <td align="center">XXX</td>
    <td align="right">000</td>
</tr>
<tr valign="middle">
    <td align="left">XXX</td>
    <td align="center">000</td>  ◄
    <td align="right">XXX</td>
</tr>
<tr valign="bottom">
    <td valign="top" align="left">XXX</td>  ◄┐
    <td align="center">000</td>
    <td align="right">XXX</td>
</tr>
</table>
```

> **Adding this `align` attribute to the `td` tag causes this cell to be horizontally aligned to the center**

> **In this case, a `valign` attribute is in that row's `tr` tag as well as in the individual cell's `td` tag. When this happens, attributes in the `td` tag take precedence over those in the `tr` tag for that row**

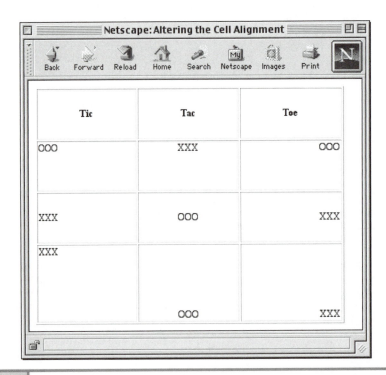

Figure 9-6 Each of the values for the **align** and **valign** attributes cause the browser to align the content differently

Width & Height

Earlier in the module, you added the `width` and `height` attributes to the table tag to identify the size of the table. You can also specify the size of individual cells by adding the `width` and/or `height` attribute(s) to your `td` or `th` tags.

Tip

This can be particularly useful if you want to have columns that are the same size because most browsers won't make columns the same size when the width is left unspecified.

You may remember the value of these two attributes can be either a pixel value or a percentage. This is the same whether you are using these attributes in the `table` tag or in the `td` or `th` tags. And I'll give you the same advice I gave before: mixing pixel values with percentages isn't wise because you might get unpredictable results in different browsers.

Look at the table in the following example. Although the `table` tag has a `width` attribute to make it 100 percent of the window opening in width, none of the cells have `width` attributes. This leaves the decision about how wide each cell should be up to the browser.

This column is smaller than the other two, because the content in this column is shorter

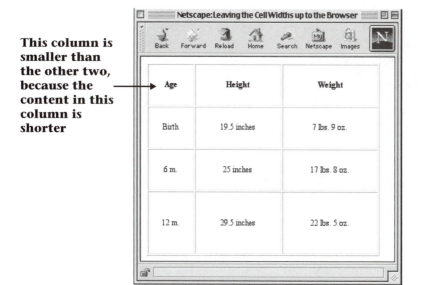

9

If I want to make all three of the columns the same width, regardless of what size the browser window is, I could add the width attribute and a value of 33 percent to the first cell in each of the columns.

```
<tr>
    <th width="33%">Age</th>
    <th width="33%">Height</th>
    <th width="33%">Weight</th>
</tr>
```

Then, each of the following cells in that column will have the same width (and/or height). An exception to this rule might be when one cell contains an extremely long string of text without spaces, such as "abcdefghijklmnopqrstuvwxyz". In this case, the browser may have to make that cell larger, as necessary, to accommodate the long string of text. It isn't necessary to place width attributes in every cell in a column—only the first one. Again, I recommend testing your pages in multiple browsers to verify the table appears as you want.

This column is now the same size as the other two because they all three have a width of 33 percent of the table

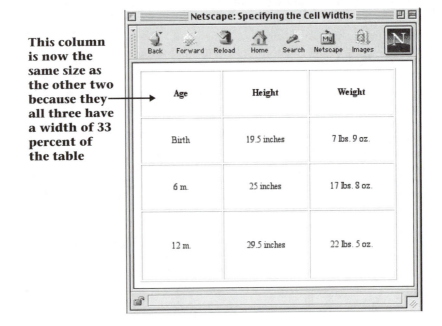

─┤Note ───────────────

Although the `height` attribute is not in the HTML 4.0 specification for the `table` tag, it is in the specification for the `td` and `th` tags. This means when you add the `height` attribute to your `td` and `th` tags, you see results that are a bit more uniform across different browsers than when you use the `height` attribute with the `table` tag.

Colors

While adding the `bgcolor` attribute to the `table` tag lets you change the color for the entire table, using the `bgcolor` attribute with the `tr`, `td`, or `th` tags lets you specify the color of a single row or cell.

   You can include a background color for the entire table, as well as colors for individual cells. When you include both and the page is viewed in Netscape (see Figure 9-7), the background color of the table only shows through in any cells that don't have their own color. When you include both and the page is viewed in Internet Explorer (see Figure 9-8),

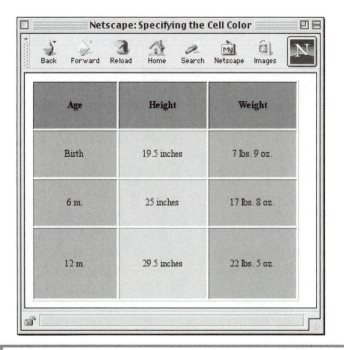

| **Figure 9-7** | Because all these cells have their own background color, the table's background color doesn't show through when the page is viewed in Netscape |

9

Because this row has a background color in the `tr` tag, the color runs across the entire row, even in the borders in between the cells. This currently occurs only in Internet Explorer

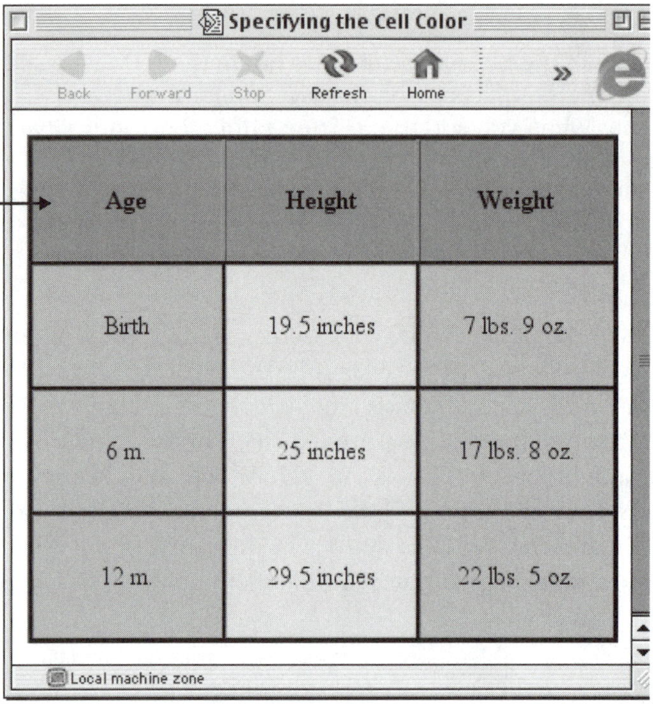

Specifying the Cell Color
Back
Forward
Stop
Refresh
Home
Age
Height
Weight
Birth
19.5 inches
7 lbs. 9 oz.
6 m.
25 inches
17 lbs. 8 oz.
12 m.
29.5 inches
22 lbs. 5 oz.
Local machine zone

Figure 9-8 **Internet Explorer shows the table's background color in the borders between the cells, even when each individual cell has its own background color**

however, the background color of the table may also show through in between the cells (in the border).

Unfortunately, this is a big issue for Web developers because the two most popular browsers render background colors in tables so differently. My best advice to you on this topic is to test your pages in a wide number of settings to make sure you're happy with how they look under each different browser.

Tip

When you're working with a table whose borders are invisible, you can also try setting the `cellspacing` to "0" to avoid having the table's background color show through.

Ask the Expert

Question: I noticed when you type your table tags, you run each of the opening and closing `td` tags right up against the content of the cell, like this:

```
<td>This is my cell content</td>
```

Is that required? Is there any reason why I couldn't type this instead?

```
<td>
This is my cell content
</td>
```

Answer: This varies according to the browser but, most of the time, these extra spaces in between the opening and closing `td` tags impact the look of your tables. I know this goes against what I told you in earlier modules because I said it wouldn't matter if you typed RETURN or ENTER in between your tags—the browser doesn't understand those.

Things are a bit different with tables, though. In this case, the browser does recognize spaces in between the opening and closing `td` tags as content for that cell. These extra spaces may cause your cells to be taller, wider, or just generally bigger than you intended. In addition, if you leave spaces before or after an image reference in a cell, that image may, indeed, have extra spaces around it when its rendered by the browser.

This becomes important when creating seamless tables, where all the cells are supposed to run up against each other, without any borders in between. Figure 9-9 shows the table initially created by the following code.

```
<table align="center" border="0" bgcolor="000000">
<tr>
    <td><img src="images/biggero.gif" width="100" height="100" alt="0" /></td>
    <td><img src="images/biggero.gif" width="100" height="100" alt="0" /></td>
    <td><img src="images/biggero.gif" width="100" height="100" alt="0" /></td>
</tr>
<tr>
    <td><img src="images/biggerx.gif" width="100" height="100" alt="x" /></td>
    <td><img src="images/biggero.gif" width="100" height="100" alt="0" /></td>
    <td><img src="images/biggerx.gif" width="100" height="100" alt="x" /></td>
</tr>
<tr>
    <td><img src="images/biggerx.gif" width="100" height="100" alt="x" /></td>
    <td><img src="images/biggerx.gif" width="100" height="100" alt="x" /></td>
    <td><img src="images/biggero.gif" width="100" height="100" alt="0" /></td>
</tr>
</table>
```

9

When the RETURN or ENTER key is pressed after the `img` tag in the top, middle cell, Figure 9-10 shows what happens. To avoid situations like this, try not to use the ENTER or RETURN key inside of a cell unless you have tested the page in several different browsers and are happy with the results.

In general, the only place where extra spaces cause problems is in between the opening and closing `td` and `th` tags. Extra spaces in between other table tags (such as `tr`) usually don't cause problems.

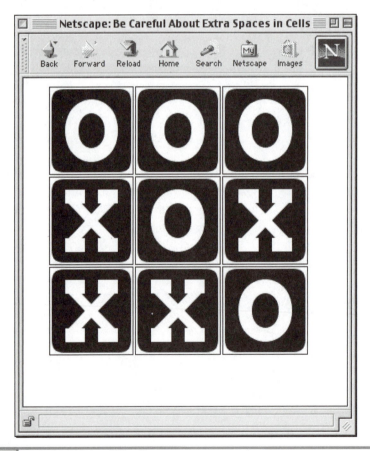

Figure 9-9 Without any extra spaces in between the opening and closing `td` tags, all the images in this table line up perfectly

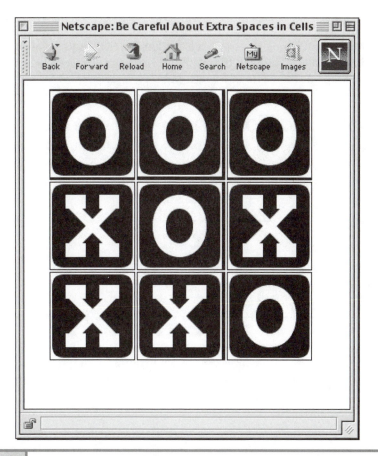

| **Figure 9-10** | Here, extra space is evident around some of the cells because the RETURN key was pressed after the **img** tag in the top, middle cell |

Prohibiting Line Breaks

At times, you might have content in a cell that needs to be kept on a single line. In cases like this, you can add the nowrap attribute to your td or th tag, which tells the browser to try and keep all the content in that cell on a single line if at all possible. (This might not be possible if the browser window is so small that the content cannot be rendered across a single line.)

```
<tr>
    <td nowrap>This cell's content should not wrap.</td>
</tr>
```

Note

While this attribute doesn't have a value, XHTML requires all attributes to have values. To make this attribute XHTML-compliant, you can use "nowrap" as the value of the attribute: `nowrap="nowrap"`.

Spanning Columns

So far in this module, you have only worked with tables in a grid-like fashion where an equal number of cells are in each row and column. While this is the default, you can add an attribute to a `td` or `th` tag to cause it to merge with another cell below it (see the next illustration).

These two cells have been merged so the content from the first cell flows into the second.		3
4	5	6

To accomplish this, use the `colspan` attribute. By default, each cell is set to *span*, or to go across, only one column. Using the `colspan` attribute enables you to change that, so a cell spans two or more columns. The following HTML shows how you might code the previous table.

```
<table border="1">
<tr>
    <td colspan="2">These two cells have been merged, so
that the content from the first cell flows into the
second.</td>
    <td>3</td>
</tr>
<tr>
    <td>4</td>
    <td>5</td>
    <td>6</td>
</tr>
</table>
```

Notice only two td tags are here for this first row, even though a total of three columns are in the table. That is because the first td tag contains the colspan attribute, telling it to span across the first two columns

Spanning Rows

Just as you can merge cells across two or more columns, you can merge cells across two or more rows. The attribute used to do so is `rowspan`.

If you take the table used in the previous section and merge the two cells on the right (#3 and #6) into one, the table might look like this one.

These two cells have been merged so the content from the first cell flows into the second.		These two cells have been merged so the content from the top one flows into the bottom one.
4	5	

Here you have two cells in the first row merged, and the third cell from the first row merged with the third cell from the second row. The HTML used to create this table is shown in the following.

```
<table border="1">
<tr>
    <td colspan="2">These two cells have been merged, so
that the content from the first cell flows into the
second.</td>
    <td rowspan="2">These two cells have been merged so
that the content from the top one flows into the bottom
one.</td>
</tr>
<tr>
    <td>4</td>
    <td>5</td>
</tr>
</table>
```

Notice only two td tags are here for this second row, even though a total of three columns are in the table. That is because the third cell was merged with the one above it, which contains the rowspan attribute

The rowspan attribute can be used by itself in a td tag to cause a cell to merge with the cell below it, or it can be combined with the colspan attribute to cause a cell to merge with both the cell below it and the one next to it.

Although the colspan and rowspan attributes give Web developers a lot of power to build creative table structures, they add a degree of complexity to tables that's often difficult to grasp. Don't worry—everyone struggles with these concepts at first. If you have trouble, go back to using your pencil and paper to plan out your table structure before you type a single key.

9

Tip

If you have a picture in your mind of the final output of your table, draw that first. Then, go back and add the table or grid structure around the picture, placing each piece into a cell or a group of cells. This is also one of the places where a WYSIWYG HTML editor may come in handy because it enables you to *see* the table while you're creating it.

Project 9-2: Format Cell Content

Returning to the `timeline.html` page you began in Project 9-1, let's format some of the individual cells and add a horizontal rule that spans the entire width of the table. Goals for this project include

● Change the alignment of content within table cells.

● Cause a cell to span across multiple columns.

Note

All the files needed to complete the projects in this book for the Woolwich Historical Society can be downloaded from **www.osborne.com** or **www.willardesigns.com/htmlbook**. In addition, you can view my version of the Web site anytime by visiting **www.woolwichhistory.org**. Those of you who aren't using the Woolwich Historical Society can tailor the project to your particular needs.

Step-by-Step

1. Open your text editor (SimpleText on the Mac or Notepad on the PC) and open the file `timeline.html` created in Project 9-1.

2. Format all the cells in the first row so they're vertically aligned to the bottom.

3. Format all the cells in the second row so they're vertically aligned to the top.

4. Add a new row in between the two existing rows.

5. Add a cell to the new row that spans across all four columns.

6. Place a horizontal rule in the new cell, giving it a width of 100 percent. (This will act as the actual "timeline" in our table.)

7. Turn off the borders for the table.

8. Save the file.

9. Open your Web browser and choose FILE I OPEN PAGE (or OPEN FILE or OPEN, depending on the browser you're using). Locate the file `timeline.html` you just saved. Make sure the file appears as you intended it.

Note

Feel free to experiment with other types of formatting, such as adding background colors to individual table cells.

10. If you need to make changes, return to your text editor to do so. After making any changes, save the file and switch back to the browser. Choose REFRESH or RELOAD to preview the changes you just made. If you are using the Woolwich Historical Society, you can compare your files to the following code and Figure 9-11.

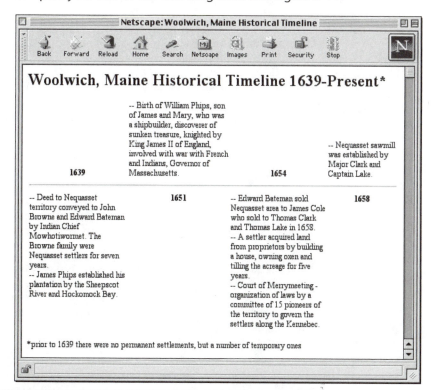

9

Figure 9-11 If you are using the Woolwich Historical Society, your page may look like this

Tip

Does the cell containing the horizontal rule span across all four columns? If not, make sure you have placed a `colspan="4"` attribute in that cell's opening `td` tag. For more tips, see Resource C: Troubleshooting.

```
<!DOCTYPE html PUBLIC "-//W3C//DTD XHTML 1.0
Transitional//EN"
"http://www.w3.org/TR/xhtml1/DTD/transitional.dtd">
<html>
<head>
     <title>Woolwich, Maine Historical Timeline</title>
</head>
<body bgcolor="#ffffff" text="#000000">
<h1>Woolwich, Maine Historical Timeline 1639-Present*</h1>

<table border="0">
<tr valign="bottom">
```

code that was added in this project

```
<th>1639</th>
     <td>-- Birth of William Phips, son of James and Mary,
who was a shipbuilder, discoverer of sunken treasure,
knighted by King James II of England, involved with war
with French and Indians, Governor of Massachusetts.</td>
     <th>1654</th>
     <td>-- Nequasset sawmill was established by Major Clark
and Captain Lake.</td>
</tr>
```

code that was added in this project

```
<tr>
     <td colspan="4"><hr width="100%"></td>
</tr>
```

code that was added in this project

```
<tr valign="top">
```

```
     <td>-- Deed to Nequasset territory conveyed to John
Browne and Edward Bateman by Indian Chief Mowhotiwormet.
The Browne family were Nequasset settlers for seven years.
<br />--  James Phips established his plantation by the
Sheepscot River and Hockomock Bay.</td>
     <th>1651</th>
     <td>-- Edward Bateman sold Nequasset area to James Cole
who sold to Thomas Clark and Thomas Lake in 1658. <br />--
A settler acquired land from proprietors by building a
```

```
house, owning oxen and tilling the acreage for five years.
<br />-- Court of Merrymeeting - organization of laws by a
committee of 15 pioneers of the territory to govern the
settlers along the Kennebec.</td>
    <th>1658</th>
</tr>
</table>

<p>*prior to 1639 there were no permanent settlements, but
a number of temporary ones</p>
</body>
</html>
```

Summary

Although somewhat complex in nature, the `colspan` and `rowspan` attributes enable you to build more creative tables than might otherwise have been possible. In addition, formatting techniques such as adjusting alignment, colors, and sizes are ways to draw attention to cell content. This project gave you practice working with many of these features.

1-Minute Drill

● **What attribute can you use to prohibit a line break in a cell?**
● **Which attribute is used to merge cells across multiple columns?**

9

Using Additional Formatting Techniques

HTML 4.0 has introduced some new tags geared toward helping Web developers build more user-friendly tables. These tags and attributes enable you to group rows and/or columns so the browser more clearly understand the purposes of each element.

● **nowrap**
● **colspan**

Grouping and Aligning Rows

Three tags in particular are used to group rows within tables.

1. thead—table header

2. tfoot—table footer

3. tbody—table body

When you use these tags, the browser is able to differentiate between the header and footer information, and the main content of the page. The benefit here is, when a user views a page containing a long table, the header information is repeated at the top of each page or screen view of the table, even if the table is printed. This helps users avoid wondering what column three was supposed to hold, when they are looking at page four, and the title of column three was only listed on page one.

Note

The only downside of these tags is they're currently not widely supported by the browsers. However, as new browsers become available and users upgrade, tags like this will become essential.

While these three tags are never required, when they are used, each must contain at least one table row, as defined by the tr tag. In addition, if you include a thead and/or a tfoot, you must also include at least one tbody. So, a table layout using these three tags might look like this:

```
<table width="100%" height="100%" border="1"
bgcolor="#000000">
<thead>    ◄
<tr bgcolor="#666666">
    <th width="33%">Age</th>
    <th width="33%">Height</th>
```

> **When used, the thead always comes before the tfoot or any tbody tags, and must be closed with </thead>**

```
    <th width="33%">Weight</th>
  </tr>
</thead>
<tfoot> ◄─────────────────────
<tr bgcolor="#666666">
    <td colspan="3">Data taken from the Corinna Research
Society</td>
  </tr>
</tfoot>
<tbody> ◄────────────────────────
<tr align="center">
    <td bgcolor="#999999">Birth</td>
    <td bgcolor="#cccccc">19.5 inches</td>
    <td bgcolor="#999999">7 lbs. 9 oz.</td>
</tr>
<tr align="center">
    <td bgcolor="#999999">6 m.</td>
    <td bgcolor="#cccccc">25 inches</td>
    <td bgcolor="#999999">17 lbs. 8 oz.</td>
</tr>
<tr align="center">
    <td bgcolor="#999999">12 m.</td>
    <td bgcolor="#cccccc">29.5 inches</td>
    <td bgcolor="#999999">22 lbs. 5 oz.</td>
</tr>
</tbody> ◄─────────────────
</table>
```

> **When used, the tfoot always comes after the thead or before any tbody tags, and must be closed with </tfoot>**

> **When used, any tbody tags always come after any tfoot and thead tags**

> **Although HTML 4.0 doesn't require </tbody> to be closed, XHTML does**

9

Figure 9-12 shows how the previous code would be viewed in a browser that understands these three tags, in this case Internet Explorer 5.0 for the Macintosh. However, Figure 9-13 shows what happens when a browser (such as Netscape 4) that doesn't understand these tags renders the page. It simply ignores the thead, tfoot, and tbody tags, and renders each tr tag one row after the other. This means the tfoot section is displayed at the top, just under the header, instead of at the bottom of the table.

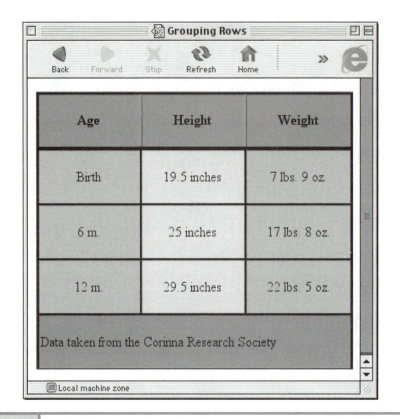

Age	Height	Weight
Birth	19.5 inches	7 lbs. 9 oz.
6 m.	25 inches	17 lbs. 8 oz.
12 m.	29.5 inches	22 lbs. 5 oz.
Data taken from the Corinna Research Society		

Figure 9-12 The **thead, tfoot,** and **tbody** tags are only understood by HTML 4.0-complient browsers. Netscape 4.0 isn't one of them

If this is acceptable for your page and doesn't confuse your user, then you can leave it. If not, you could discontinue using the `tfoot` tag until it's more widely supported by the browsers. The `thead` and `tbody` tags don't cause any problems because the information is still displayed in the proper order, regardless of whether each tag's other characteristics are understood.

You can also add the `align` and `valign` attributes to these tags to change the alignment of each of the cells contained within them.

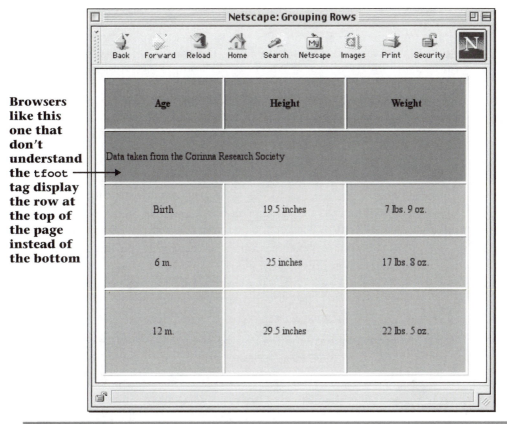

Browsers
like this
one that
don't
understand
the `tfoot`
tag display
the row at
the top of
the page
instead of
the bottom

Figure 9-13 The **thead**, **tfoot**, and **tbody** tags are only understood by
HTML 4.0-compliant browsers, such as Internet Explorer 5.0 for
the Macintosh

Grouping and Aligning Columns

Along the same lines, you can group columns together with the `col` and
`colgroup` elements. Browsers that understand these tags can then render
the table incrementally, instead of all at once. This causes long tables to load
more quickly than they might otherwise. In addition, using `colgroups`
enables you to apply styles and characteristics to entire sections of columns,
as opposed to individually.

Tip

Unlike the `thead`, `tfoot`, and `tbody` tags, the `colgroup` and `col` tags don't contain `tr` or `td` tags for the table. This means browsers that don't understand the `colgroup` and `col` tags will simply ignore them and the page display won't be affected. Simply stated, the `colgroup` and `col` tags are ways to pass information about structure and style on to the browser in the beginning of the table, to help in rendering it.

The opening and closing `colgroup` tags enclose one or more columns in the group, and can dictate how those columns should be rendered. This means you can add the `align` or `valign` attributes to the opening `colgroup` tag, to align all the columns in that group the same way.

You can also add the `span` attribute and the `width` attribute to this tag, to tell the browser how many columns should be included in the group and how wide each of those columns should be, respectively.

Tip

If you had both colgroups and theads, the colgroups would be placed before the theads in your table structure.

In this example, the first `colgroup` contains five columns, each 20 pixels in width. The second `colgroup` contains two columns, each 50 pixels in width. You can see the `colgroup` tags are placed at the top of the table, before all the table rows and table cells.

```
<table border="1">
<colgroup width="20" span="5"></colgroup>
<colgroup width="50" span="2"></colgroup>
<tr>
    <td>
```

If you specify any of these attributes in the `colgroup` tag, they take effect for all the columns in that group. If you need to alter the width or alignment of specific columns in the group, you can use the `col` tag within the opening and closing `colgroup` tags to do so. In this example, the first ten columns in this group are 20 pixels wide, while the last four columns in the group are 10 pixels wide.

```
<table border=1>
<colgroup align="center">
    <col width="20" span="10">
    <col width="10" span="4">
</colgroup>
<tr>
    <td>
```

Whether used in the colgroup or the col tag, the value of the width attribute can be specified in one of three possible ways, as demonstrated in the following table.

Value	Description	Example
pixels	Sets the width of each column in pixel dimensions	`<colgroup width="50">` `<col width="10">`
percentages	Sets the width of each column in percentages, relative to the size of the entire table	`<colgroup width="50%">` `<col width="10%">`
relative length	When used in the colgroup tag, 0* tells the browser to render each column only as wide as the content requires it to be, making the table as small as possible. Any other number followed by an asterisk tells the relative length of the column in proportion to the other column.	`<colgroup width="0*">` `<col width="1*">`

9

Hint

If three columns are in a table that is 200 pixels wide and the first two are set to "1*", while the third is set to "2*", then the entire width of the table is divided by 4 (1+1+2=4). In this case, 1=50 (4/200). So the first two columns would be 50 pixels wide and the last column would be 100 pixels wide.

*Relative length is not yet supported by a major browser.

Using Tables for Page Layout

So far in this module, I've used examples that *look* like tables. In other words, a tic-tac-toe game already fits easily into a grid, so it *looks* like a table. Now let's talk about using tables to lay out an entire page, regardless of whether it looks like it would fit into a grid or a table structure.

One of the best ways to learn about using tables for page layout is to dissect actual Web pages to see how others have done it. With that in mind, look at Figure 9-14. This is a screen shot of a page from the Chop Point Web site. If I told you that all the elements on the page were contained within a table, could you figure out where the individual cells were located?

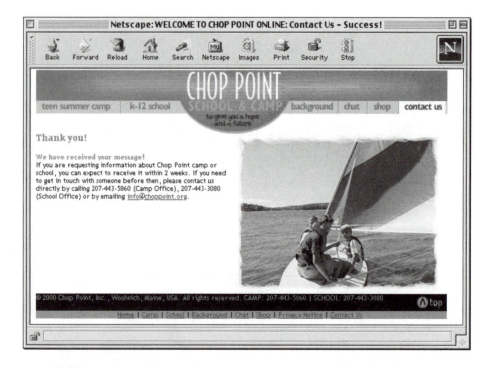

Figure 9-14 All the elements on this page are contained within a table

One way to find out is to view the HTML code for the page, using the VIEW SOURCE command in the browser. You can even save a copy of this source to your computer and turn on the table borders to see how the page was created. (You also need to download the images used on the page or change their reference so they include the complete link address. If you don't do either of these, the page will still work, but none of the images will appear when you view the page from your computer.)

```
Netscape: Source of: http://www.choppoint.org/contactus/contact_test.html

<table width="100%" cellpadding="0" cellspacing="0" border="3" align="center
<tr>
        <td bgcolor="#6666FF" align="center"><a href="/index.html"><img src="/i
</tr>

<tr bgcolor="#ffcc33" align="center">
        <td nowrap="nowrap"><a href="/camp/index.html" onmouseover="chgImg('camp
</tr>

<tr valign="top" align="center">
        <td><img src="/images/int_center.gif" alt="" width="595" height="28" bo
</tr>

<tr valign="top">
        <td bgcolor="#ffffff"><font face="trebuchet ms, trebuchet, arial, helveti
<img src="/images/camp_sunfish.jpg" width=309 height=226 align=right alt="Campe
<h2>Thank you!</h2>
<b>We have received your message!</b><br>
If you are requesting information about Chop Point camp or school, you can expect to
</tr>

<tr>
        <td bgcolor="#000000"><a href="#top"><img src="/images/link_top.gif" alt
</tr>

<tr>
        <td bgcolor="#999999" align="center"><a href="/index.html">Home</a> | <
</tr>
</table>

</body>
</html>
```

When the borders are turned on (by changing the value from 0 to 3) in the table from Figure 9-14, you can see the structure of the table, as well as what elements are in each cell.

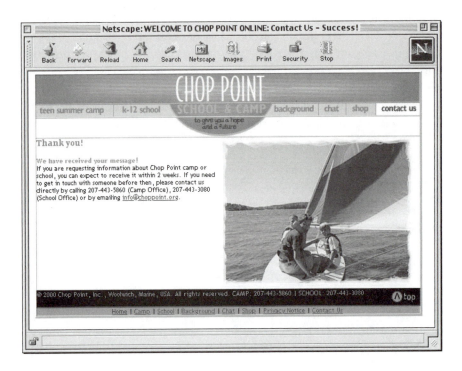

Even though the page might not have appeared to be conducive to a table layout, the actual table structure is quite simple. Six rows span the entire length of the table. The first row contains the long header graphic.

The second row contains seven smaller graphics, five of which are linked to other sections of the Web site. The other two graphics in this cell are the center semicircle and the "Contact Us" graphic designating this section as the *active* section, or the one you are currently viewing. Here, you can see more easily how these graphics are broken into pieces to make them easier to link and replace.

The third row contains a graphic that finishes off the semicircle from the two rows above, while the fourth row contains the main content of the screen, consisting of a headline, a paragraph of text, and a photograph.

The final two rows at the bottom of the screen contain the copyright information, a link back to the top of the page, and text links to other sections of the site.

Seamless Tables

The table we just dissected certainly didn't look like the typical table when we first viewed it. One of the reasons is this is a *seamless* table, or one in which the cells are flush up against one another, without borders to separate them. To turn a regular table into a seamless table, you must set several attributes in the `table` tag to 0, to eliminate any extra space around the table cells.

If I set the `border` value to 0, that gets us started. As you can tell in the following illustration, however, some small spaces are still between the cells.

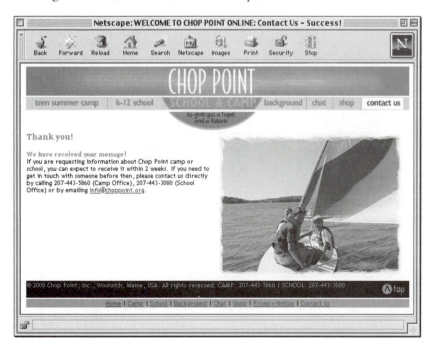

To eliminate all the spaces in between each of the cells, you can also change the `cellpadding` and `cellspacing` (discussed in the beginning of this module) to 0.

```
<table border="0" cellspacing="0" cellpadding="0">
```

The only problem with turning off all the spaces in between the cells is any text in those cells may butt up against another cell. If you run into this problem with your seamless tables, experiment with increasing the `cellpadding` a bit to see if that helps. Another possible solution is to use a nested table.

Nested Tables

A *nested* table is one contained within the cell of another table. This can be useful when you need to create a completely different table structure in one portion of a page, which cannot be incorporated into the structure of the rest of the page. For example, in the summer camp section of the Chop Point Web site, a navigation bar runs down the left side of the page that lets you navigate within the camp section. This navigation bar is its own table structure because it didn't fit in with the rest of the page's table structure.

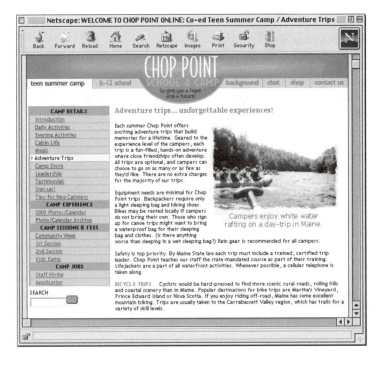

Hint

The most common cause for broken pages when using nested tables is that one of the tables isn't closed. If you try to view a page, but it appears blank, go back to your HTML and make sure every table is closed with a `</table>`.

A nested table structure might look like this.

```
<table border="1">          ◄——————  This tag opens table #1
<tr>
    <td colspan="3">Top Banner</td>
</tr>
<tr>
    <td colspan="3" align="center"><table border="3">
        <tr>
        <td>Link 1</td>            This tag opens table #2
        <td>Link 2</td>
        <td>Link 3</td>
        <td>Link 4</td>
        <td>Link 5</td>
        </tr>
        </table></td>
</tr>                            This tag closes table #2
<tr>
    <td width="100" height="100">Text Column 1</td>
    <td width="100" height="100">Text Column 2</td>
    <td width="100" height="100">Text Column 3</td>
</tr>
</table>   ◄————————————————  This tag closes table #1
```

Because the borders are turned on in both tables, you can more easily see the table structures when the page is viewed in the browser.

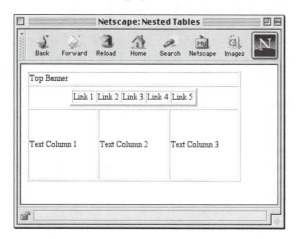

9

—|—*Tip*————————————————
If you are having trouble with your pages when you view them in Netscape, try choosing VIEW | PAGE SOURCE from the top menu. Netscape will try to show you where the problem is by blinking any offending code in your page.

While no special tags are used to nest tables, it does take some practice trying to determine which table you are in at any given time. I recommend working with the table borders turned on, just until you can get your table structure set. Once you complete all the tables on a page, you can turn off the borders for seamless, nested tables.

Nested tables can be quite useful when you need to create complex page layouts, but they can cause the download time of the page to become slower if the browser has to calculate the size of every single table and its cells. To help minimize the number of calculations the browser has to make, specify the size (using the `width` attribute) of your tables and cells wherever possible.

Project 9-3: Using Seamless and Nested Tables

The timeline developed in the first two projects in this module ultimately will be quite lengthy, taking visitors from 1639 to the present day in Woolwich history. Many of the dates on the timeline have multiple entries and some may have photos or other supplementary information. So far, we've separated these multiple entries with only a line break and two dashes. Another option might be to use nested tables in these cells, whereby each entry is enclosed in a different colored table cell. In addition, we'll add an icon to each entry, designating whether it's in the category of settlers, industry, government, or births. The goal for this project is to add a seamless, nested table to an existing table structure.

┤*Reminder*

All the files needed to complete the projects in this book for the Woolwich Historical Society can be downloaded from **www.osborne.com** or **www.willardesigns.com/htmlbook**. In addition, you can view my version of the Web site anytime by visiting **www.woolwichhistory.org.** Those of you who aren't using the Woolwich Historical Society can tailor the project to your particular needs.

Step-by-Step

1. Open your text editor (SimpleText on the Mac or Notepad on the PC) and open the file `timeline.html` saved from Project 9-2. Using Figure 9-15 as your guide, make the following changes to the table.

2. Add a seamless, nested table to each cell that contains historical information for the timeline.

3. Alternate the background colors of the cells, so if there's more than one entry for a particular date, the entries don't have the same background colors.

4. Add one of four graphical icons to each of the entries, according to whether it relates to settlers (flag.gif), business and industry (money.gif), births (bottle.gif), or government (star.gif).

5. Save the file.

6. Open your Web browser and choose FILE | OPEN PAGE (or OPEN FILE or OPEN, depending on the browser you are using). Locate the file `timeline.html` you just saved. Make sure the file appears as you intended it.

7. If you need to make changes, return to your text editor to make changes. After making any changes, save the file and switch back to the browser. Choose REFRESH or RELOAD to preview the changes you just made. If you are using the Woolwich Historical Society, you can compare your files to the following code and Figures 9-15 and 9-16.

9

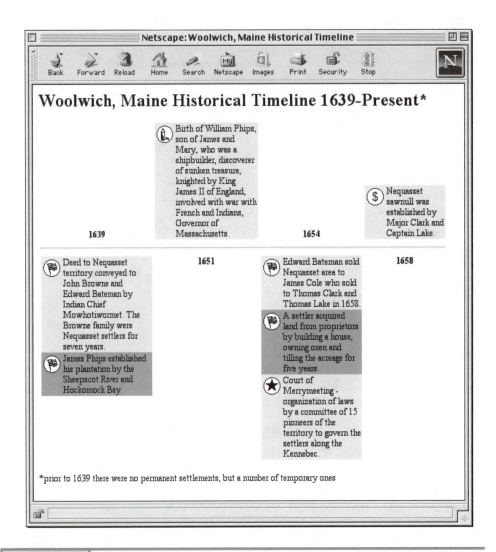

Figure 9-15 Those using the Woolwich Historical Society should use this page as a guide when adding the seamless, nested tables to the existing content

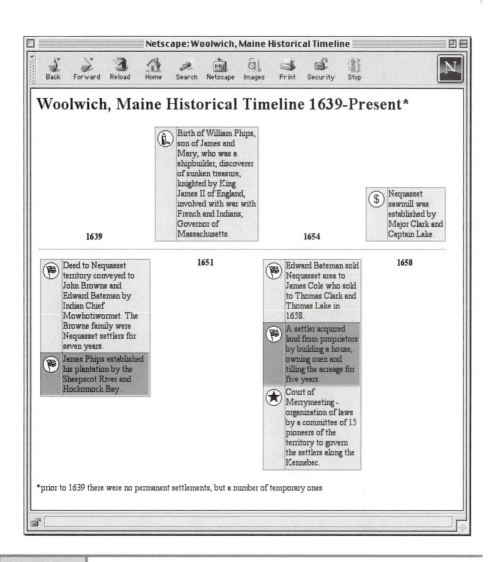

Figure 9-16   Those using the Woolwich Historical Society might see a page similar to this one when the borders of the nested tables are turned on

9

Tip

Confused about the structure of the nested tables? Figure 9-16 shows the finished page with the borders turned on, so you can see how it was created. For more tips, see Resource C: Troubleshooting.

```
<!DOCTYPE html PUBLIC "-//W3C//DTD XHTML 1.0
Transitional//EN"
"http://www.w3.org/TR/xhtml1/DTD/transitional.dtd">
<html>
<head>
     <title>Woolwich, Maine Historical Timeline</title>
</head>
<body bgcolor="#ffffff" text="#000000">

<h1>Woolwich, Maine Historical Timeline 1639-Present*</h1>

<table border="0">
<tr valign="bottom">
    <th>1639</th>
    <td><table border="0" cellspacing="0"><tr
bgcolor="#cccccc" valign="top"><td><img
src="images/bottle.gif" width="27"
height="28"></td><td>Birth of William Phips, son of James
and Mary, who was a shipbuilder, discoverer of sunken
treasure, knighted by King James II of England, involved
with war with French and Indians, Governor of
Massachusetts.</td></tr></table></td>
    <th>1654</th>
    <td><table border="0" cellspacing="0"><tr
bgcolor="#cccccc" valign="top"><td><img
src="images/money.gif" width="27"
height="28"></td><td>Nequasset sawmill was established by
Major Clark and Captain Lake.</td></tr></table></td>
</tr>

<tr>
    <td colspan="4"><hr width="100%"></td>
</tr>

<tr valign="top">
    <td><table border="0" cellspacing="0"><tr
```

```
bgcolor="#cccccc" valign="top"><td><img
src="images/flag.gif" width="27" height="28"></td><td>Deed
to Nequasset territory conveyed to John Browne and Edward
Bateman by Indian Chief Mowhotiwormet.  The Browne family
were Nequasset settlers for seven years.</td></tr><tr
bgcolor="#999999" valign="top"><td><img
src="images/flag.gif" width="27" height="28"></td><td>James
Phips established his plantation by the Sheepscot River and
Hockomock Bay.</td></tr></table></td>
    <th>1651</th>
    <td><table border="0" cellspacing="0"><tr
bgcolor="#cccccc"
valign="top"><td><imgsrc="images/flag.gif" width="27"
height="28"></td><td>Edward Bateman sold Nequasset area to
James Cole who sold to Thomas Clark and Thomas Lake in
1658.</td></tr><tr bgcolor="#999999" valign="top"><td><img
src="images/flag.gif" width="27" height="28"></td><td>A
settler acquired land from proprietors by building a house,
owning oxen and tilling the acreage for five
years.</td></tr><tr bgcolor="#cccccc" valign="top"><td><img
src="images/star.gif" width="27" height="28"></td><td>Court
of Merrymeeting - organization of laws by a committee of 15
pioneers of the territory to govern the settlers along the
Kennebec.</td></tr></table></td>
    <th>1658</th>
</tr>
</table>

<p>*prior to 1639 there were no permanent settlements, but
a number of temporary ones</p>
</body>
</html>
```

9

Summary

Many additional formatting techniques were discussed in the final section of this module. This project gave you practice using the most popular of those techniques—seamless, nested tables for page layout.

☑ *Mastery Check*

1. Identify what's wrong with this table structure.

```
<table>
    <td>Cell 1</td>
    <td>Cell 2</td>
</table>
```

2. Which attribute is used to alter the amount of space between the content within a cell and the cell's edges?

3. What term is used to refer to a table completely contained within another table?

4. What tags are used to group and align table rows?

5. Because tables are often rendered differently by the various browsers, what's the best way to verify that your tables work properly?

Module 10

Developing Frames

Goals

- Understand the concept and uses of frames in Web pages
- Create a basic frameset
- Format frames within a frameset
- Create links between frames
- Nest framesets
- Use inline frames
- Accommodate non-frames-capable browsers

Have you ever visited a Web site, clicked a link within that site, and noticed after doing so that only a portion of the page changed? This type of Web site was probably created using frames and lets you see two different Web pages at the same time. Module 10 walks you through understanding what frames are and how they can be used in a Web site, as well as how to format frames for your needs.

Understanding Frames

The use of frames on a Web site is similar to a television set with picture-in-picture. While picture-in-picture enables you to watch two television programs at one time, frames in a Web site enable you to view two (or more) separate HTML pages at the same time.

You, as the Web developer, can specify where the additional pages appear on the screen—in columns, rows, or a combination of each. For example, you might choose to load your site's links in a column on the left side of the screen, and then load the actual page's of content in another frame on the right side of the screen. This group of frames is called a *frameset*.

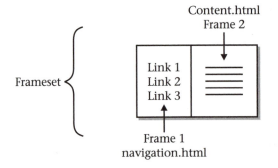

Tip

Just as with tables, I find it useful to map out my frames on paper before beginning.

Each frame in the frameset displays a different HTML page, just as each picture on the television displays a different channel. What can sometimes become confusing is the process of keeping track of which page is displayed in which frame, as well as updating each of those pages . . . sort of like trying to watch two television programs at the same time. Throughout this module, I give tips on streamlining this process and keeping track of your frames.

In addition, this module addresses two different types of frames:

● standard (anchored) frames

● inline (floating) frames

Whenever you see a reference to the term *frames*, you can assume I am talking about standard frames. When I delve into *inline frames* toward the end of the module, I always call them by that name to avoid confusion.

Browser Support for Frames

Just as certain types of television sets are capable of displaying picture-in-picture, certain browsers can handle frames. Netscape 2.0 was the first to introduce and support frames, but Microsoft quickly added support in its Internet Explorer 3.0 browser. But frames didn't become an official part of the W3C's HTML specifications until version 4.0, which means not many other browsers supported frames until recently. In fact, some still don't.

If you use frames on your site, remember to provide alternative versions of your Web site for those people visiting with a non-frames-capable browser. You learn how to do that at the end of this module.

10

Creating a Basic Frameset

There's a special type of HTML file for a frameset. Unlike the pages discussed so far in this book, a frameset page doesn't have a body tag. This is because a frameset HTML file contains a set of instructions for the browser regarding how the browser window is broken up and which pages are loaded into each frame, or section, of the window. Here's an example of what a typical frameset looks like.

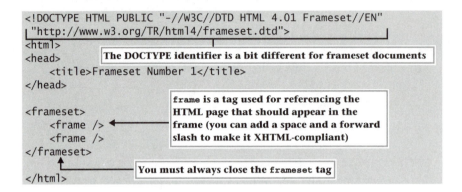

Instead of a body tag, frameset documents have opening and closing frameset tags that enclose the rest of the tags on the page. The difference is frameset tags don't enclose text, images, or other types of content like the body tag does. frameset tags only contain references to the individual parts that make up the frameset, using frame tags.

Several attributes are used with the frameset and frame tags that enable you to identify the content for the frames and customize the look of them.

Columns and Rows

You add the cols and rows attributes to the opening frameset tag to specify the size and location of each of the frames. Depending on the layout you intend to create, you might use the cols attributes only (for vertical frames), the rows attribute only (for horizontal frames), or both the cols and rows attributes for a mixed layout.

Tip

You cannot test your framesets without specifying pages to load in each frame. If you're not ready to load real pages yet and only want to experiment with your columns and rows, create a blank HTML page called blank.html and use that as the content for each frame during testing.

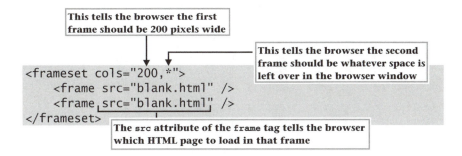

Regardless of whether you are using the cols or rows attribute, the value of each is specified by a pixel value, a percentage, or as a variable (*). The first size (in this case, 200) corresponds to the first frame tag, the second size (in this case, *) corresponds to the second frame tag, and so on.

When you use the asterisk to represent a variable frame size, the browser considers the total width of the browser window before subtracting any absolute frame sizes (which are expressed by pixels) to determine the variable frame's size.

Hint

As with tables, relative sizing (using percentages or variables) is preferred over absolute sizing if you are trying to create a layout that expands to fill a variety of window sizes. Not all the frames need to be variable in size, though. You can accomplish this by using one or more columns of fixed size and one set variable (*), so it expands and contracts to fill the available space.

In the previous example, the first frame is set to an absolute size of 200 pixels wide and the second frame is variable (as denoted by the asterisk). If the browser window was open to 600 pixels wide, the size of that variable frame would be 400 pixels ($600 - 200 = 400$).

Columns Only

Using the `cols` attribute without the `rows` attribute will achieve a frames setup with columns, like this one.

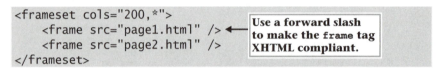

```
<frameset cols="200,*">
    <frame src="page1.html" />
    <frame src="page2.html" />
</frameset>
```

Use a forward slash to make the `frame` tag XHTML compliant.

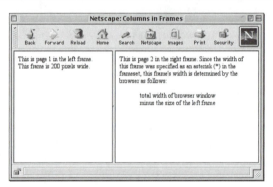

You can easily see the outline of each frame in this example because a border separates the two, framed columns. To add a third column to this frameset, you must add another width to the `cols` value in the `frameset` tag.

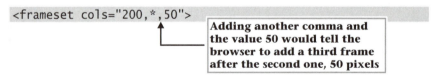

```
<frameset cols="200,*,50">
```

Adding another comma and the value 50 would tell the browser to add a third frame after the second one, 50 pixels

Rows Only

Using the rows attribute without the `cols` attribute will achieve a frames setup with horizontal rows, like this one.

```
<frameset rows="75,*">
    <frame src="page3.html" />
    <frame src="page4.html" />
</frameset>
```

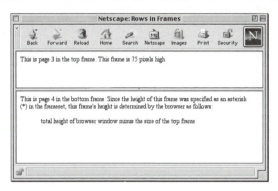

To add another row, the process is the same as adding another column. Commas separate the sizes of the columns and/or rows, and there is one size for each column or row.

A layout with four equal-sized rows might be expressed like this:

```
<frameset rows="*,*,*,*">
```

or like this:

```
<frameset rows="25%,25%,25%,25%">
```

In both cases, the window is separated into four equal horizontal frames.

10

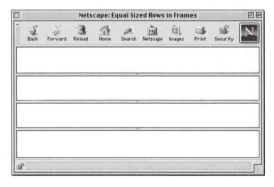

Mixed Layouts

You can use both the `cols` and `rows` attribute in a single frameset to combine a horizontal and vertical layout. The structure of a mixed layout can become tricky, but always remember you begin at the top and move from left to right, top to bottom, creating a grid of frames. Here's an example with four frames, created from two rows and two columns:

Note

When you mix columns and rows in a frameset, you are limited to the same number of columns as rows. If you want to have a different number of columns than rows in your layout, you must nest `framesets`, as discussed later in this module.

```
<frameset rows="*,*" cols="*,*">
    <frame src="blank.html" />
    <frame src="blank.html" />
    <frame src="blank.html" />
    <frame src="blank.html" />
</frameset>
```

Because all the rows and columns are variable (denoted by an asterisk as the size), the frames in Figure 10-1 are all the same size.

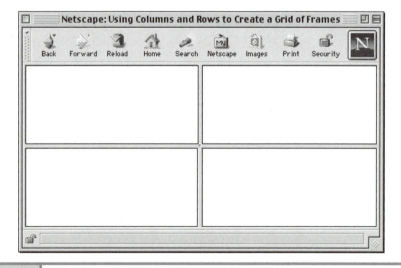

Figure 10-1 This layout uses both the **cols** and **rows** attributes to accomplish a grid-like structure of frames

Identifying Frame Content

Once you have the structure of your frameset identified, you need to tell the browser which pages to load in each of the frames. You use the `src` attribute in the `frame` tag to do so but, remember, the top, left frame must be defined before moving to the right and down the page.

In this example, I took the mixed layout from Figure 10-1 and reproduced it in an illustration to help determine which frames correspond to which HTML pages.

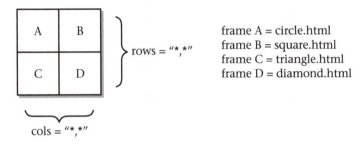

This type of preparation can help when I code the frameset, working top-to-bottom, left-to–right.

```
<frameset rows="*,*" cols="*,*">
    <frame src="circle.html" />
    <frame src="square.html" />
    <frame src="triangle.html" />
    <frame src="diamond.html" />
</frameset>
```

10

The final output, shown in Figure 10-2, has each of the HTML pages appearing in the appropriate frame of the window, based on my illustration.

Tip

To view the source of a specific frame, first click inside the frame you are interested in, and then choose VIEW I PAGE SOURCE. (Netscape) or VIEW I SOURCE (Internet Explorer).

When you look at this page in the browser, whose filename is `frameset_shapes.html`, it's easy to forget this screen (Figure 10-2) was created with five different HTML files (one for the frameset and four

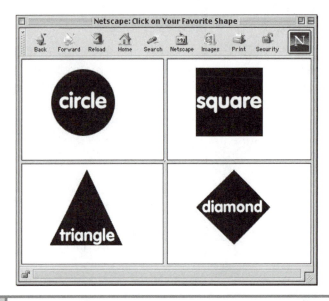

| **Figure 10-2** | This frameset includes two rows and two columns, creating a grid of four frames. Each one contains a different HTML page |

for the individual pages). If you need to make a change to any of these pages, however, you must:

- Open the specific HTML file in question.

- Make your change(s) and save the file.

- Return to the browser and click RELOAD or REFRESH. If the change you made isn't readily apparent, try choosing FILE | OPEN (Internet Explorer) or FILE | OPEN PAGE (Netscape) instead of RELOAD or REFRESH.

Formatting Frames

Now that you know how to define the structure of a frameset and identify the page content for each frame, let's discuss how you can customize the look of the frames using several attributes of the `frameset` or `frame` tags.

Naming

The first attribute I discuss enables you to identify your frames with a name. This is important so, later, when you need to add a link to a page in one of the frames, you can tell the browser in which frame to load that link.

To name your frames, add the name attribute to each of your frame tags and specify a name that relates to the content of the frame. For example, if you used the left frame in a two-column frameset for all your links, you might name that frame "links."

```
<frameset cols="150,*">
   <frame src="links.html" name="links" />
```

Then, if the right frame contains an introduction about your company, you might call that frame the "intro."

```
   <frame src="intro.html" name="intro" />
</frameset>
```

The concept used here is the same as when you link to sections within the same Web page (discussed in Module 5). Before you can set up any links to it, you must first give the place you're linking to a name. The process of creating links to these frames is discussed toward the end of this module.

Borders

If you refer to Figures 10-1 or 10-2, you can see, by default, the browser separates each frame in a frameset with a gray border. At times, making those borders invisible might be necessary, giving the appearance of borderless or seamless frames. Turning the borders of frames off is similar to getting bifocal glasses that don't have a line in between the two different types of glass—the frames are still there, but you can no longer see the edges.

HTML 4.0 includes the frameborder attribute to alter the borders between frames. Setting this attribute to 0 tells the browser not to display the borders between the frames. The default value is 1, which tells the browser to go ahead and display the borders between the frame in question and any adjoining frames.

10

```
<frameset cols="150,*">
    <frame src="links.html" name="links" frameborder="0" />
    <frame src="intro.html" name="intro" frameborder="0" />
</frameset>
```

Note

Internet Explorer also recognizes the `bordercolor` attribute when used in the `frame` tag to change the color of the frame borders. However, this attribute isn't part of the official HTML 4.0 specifications and is ignored by Netscape.

The problem with this attribute is, at press time, many browsers don't fully recognize it. For example, Figure 10-3 shows how the code in the previous example is rendered in version 4 of Netscape. You can see that although the `frameborder="0"` attribute turned off the three-dimensional look of the border, it left a gray space in between the two frames that is unacceptable.

To eliminate the three-dimensional borders, as well as that leftover space (as shown in Figure 10-4), use the `border` attribute with a value of

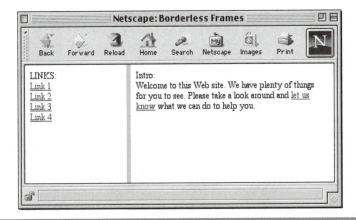

Figure 10-3 Using only the **frameborder** attribute doesn't completely turn off the space between the frames

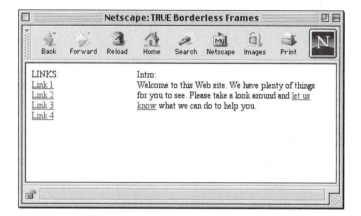

Figure 10-4 | **The best way to turn off the space completely in between the frame is to set both the `border` and `frameborder` attributes to 0**

0 in your `frameset` tag. Keeping the `frameborder` attribute in your `frame` tags helps to ensure your frames are border-free in the largest number of browsers.

```
<frameset cols="150,*" border="0">
    <frame src="links.html" name="links" frameborder="0" />
    <frame src="intro.html" name="intro" frameborder="0" />
</frameset>
```

Note

While the `frameborder` attribute is only supposed to be used in the `frame` tag (as shown in the previous example), Netscape and Internet Explorer also recognize it when used in the `frameset` tag. This means you could use it once in the `frameset` tag, instead of having to use it twice in each `frame` tag. Remember, other browsers may not understand this attribute in the `frameset` tag because it isn't part of the official HTML 4.0 specifications.

10

Margin Height and Width

In the previous module, you learned how to adjust the space in between content in table cells and the edges of those cells using the `cellpadding` attribute. You can use the `marginheight` and `marginwidth` attributes of the `frame` tag to do something similar.

- `marginheight` adjusts the space between the content of a frame and the top and bottom edges of that frame

- `marginwidth` adjusts the space between the content of a frame and the left and right edges of that frame

Because both Netscape and Internet Explorer use a default margin size of about 8 pixels, the text in each frame is indented that much from the edges of the browser. To see what I mean, compare any of the previous figures in this module with Figure 10-5, in which I changed the sizes of both the height and width of the frame margins. The code used to create Figure 10-5 is included here.

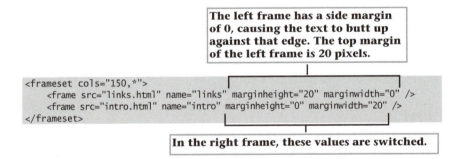

The left frame has a side margin of 0, causing the text to butt up against that edge. The top margin of the left frame is 20 pixels.

```
<frameset cols="150,*">
    <frame src="links.html" name="links" marginheight="20" marginwidth="0" />
    <frame src="intro.html" name="intro" marginheight="0" marginwidth="20" />
</frameset>
```

In the right frame, these values are switched.

Scrolling

Whenever a page contains information that is longer than the current window, the browser includes a vertical scroll bar along the right side of the screen. Likewise, when information is wider than can be displayed, the browser includes a horizontal scroll bar across the bottom of the screen.

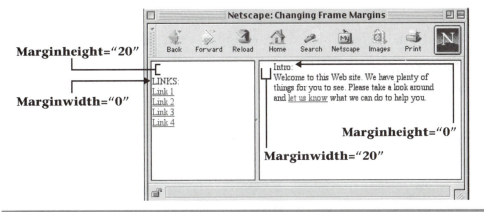

Marginheight="20"

Marginwidth="0"

Marginheight="0"

Marginwidth="20"

Figure 10-5 | The `marginheight` and `marginwidth` attributes can be used to change the amount of indent in each of the frames

Ask the Expert

Question: You mentioned several times that frames aren't understood by all browsers and they aren't interpreted the same by browsers that do understand them. Does this mean frames aren't a viable layout technique for Web developers?

Answer: Many people have a love/hate relationship with frames. While they might love the possibilities frames offer, they hate the inequalities among Web browsers, as well as some of the poorer uses of frames present on the Web.

That said, good and bad ways exist to use frames. For example, a good use of frames might be one that saves users from having to click several times to reach important information. A bad use of frames might be one that uses frames only to use the latest technology and doesn't offer any benefits to users. In fact, bad uses of frames often cause more problems for users than they give benefits.

As with any newer technology like frames, I recommend you consider whether you could accomplish the same task without the new technology. If you could, then consider if the use of the new technology offers your users an added benefit. If it does offer an added benefit, you are probably justified in using the technology. If it doesn't, though, perhaps you should reconsider the use of such technology.

10

Question: Should I be aware of any other problems?

Answer: Yes. First, each frame within the frameset operates separately when a user uses the back button. This can be confusing if a user is trying to back up several pages because he will have to click the back button more times than expected and may simply give up.

Second, some browsers make it difficult for users to bookmark pages within framesets. So when a user clicks a button in the browser to add a page to the list of bookmarks or favorites, she may or may not actually be bookmarking the right page. For example, she may find later she bookmarked the navigation frame instead of the frame with the actual page content. This can also cause confusion for users.

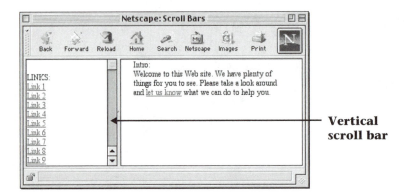

Vertical scroll bar

Tip

The scroll bar takes up between 10 and 15 pixels in width, depending on the browser. Remember to allow room for scroll bars when allotting sizes for frames.

Using the `scrolling` attribute in the `frame` tag, you can force the browser to display or not display the scroll bars for each frame. Table 10-1 lists the possible choices for this attribute.

Attribute and Value	Description
scrolling="yes"	Tells the browser to display the scroll bars for the frame.
scrolling="no"	Tells the browser never to display the scroll bars for the frame.
scrolling="auto"	Tells the browser only to provide the scroll bars when necessary, based on the content of the frame. (This is the default for each frame.)

Table 10-1 | Values of the **scrolling** Attribute

Resizing

By default, browsers give users the capability to resize variable or relative sized frames as needed. This is accomplished by clicking-and-dragging on a visible border in between the frames.

⊣Note

Users cannot resize frames where the border is turned off or on those that have absolute sizes.

This visual marker in Netscape lets you know this frame border can be moved to the left or the right. Internet Explorer displays borders without this marker

10

You can click-and-drag the border to the left and right (if it's a vertical border) or up and down (if it's a horizontal border). When doing so, the mouse cursor changes to look like two little arrows pulling away from each other.

While this is a useful technique for many Web sites, at times, you might want to restrict users from being able to resize your frames. To do so, add the `noresize` attribute to the `frame` tag.

Tip

Because the `noresize` attribute doesn't have an official value, use `noresize="noresize"` to make your page XHTML-compliant.

```
<frame src="links.html" name="links" marginheight="20"
marginwidth="0" noresize="noresize" />
```

1-Minute Drill

● **Which attribute is added to the `frameset` tag to set up a frame structure with frames in columns?**

● **What character is used to denote the size of a frame is variable?**

● cols
● *

Linking Between Frames

Whenever you use frames on a Web site, you have to deal with the issue of linking between them. By default, whenever a user clicks a link within a frame, the page loads within that same frame. Sometimes it becomes necessary to load a linked page within *another* frame.

Before you can link to another frame, it must have a name. Earlier in this module, you learned how to use the `name` attribute with the `frame` tag to identify a frame by name. Once the frame has been given a name, you only need to add the `target` attribute to the link.

Targets

Imagine you have a frameset with two columns called frameset_cols.html. The frames in this structure are called "links" on the left and "intro" on the right. When a user clicks the words "About Us" in the left frame, you want the "About Us" page to load in the right frame.

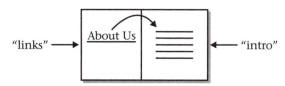

Accomplishing this task requires two steps.

1. Identify the frame with the `name` attribute.

2. Use the `target` attribute in the `a` tag of the link to specify in which frame the link should load.

Note

This is different from all the other attributes discussed so far in this module because this requires editing the HTML pages *within* the frames, as opposed to the HTML page for the frameset.

10

To change the target window of the "About Us" link, you have to edit the HTML page containing that link. In this case, the page you edit is saved as links.html.

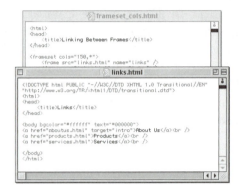

As shown in the illustration, add target="*value*" where *value* is the name you gave to the frame in which you want the link to load.

```
<a href="aboutus.html" target="intro">About Us</a>
```

This attribute would then cause the aboutus.html page to appear in the *intro* frame (the one on the right) instead of in the *links* frame.

Base Targets

If you want all the links on this page to load in the intro frame, you can use the base tag to simplify things.

```
<head>
    <title>Links</title>
    <base target="intro">
</head>
```

The base tag goes in between the opening and closing head tags, usually below the title tags, as shown in the previous example. By using the target attribute in the base tag instead of the individual links, you can avoid typing `target="intro"` (or whatever the name of your frame was) after every single link on your page.

If you did want one link to load in a frame other than the one specified in your `base` tag, just add the `target` attribute to that individual link. A `target` tag in the `a` tag overrides any in the `base` tag.

Nesting Frames

In the beginning of this module, I mentioned that with a single frameset, an equal number of columns and rows must exist. If you want to create a frame structure with an irregular structure of columns and rows, you need to nest two or more framesets.

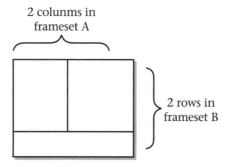

For example, in this case, you need to create two framesets. Frameset A contains two vertical columns, while frameset B contains two horizontal rows. While, initially, it may appear these could be contained in a single frameset, this isn't possible because both of the columns (in Frameset A) are located within a single row of frameset B. This cannot be accomplished with a single frameset.

The actual HTML for nested frames takes on the same structure as any other nested tags. First, think about the overall structure of the frameset and decide which one contains the other. In this case, we already established that frameset B—specifically, the first row in that frameset—contains frameset A. The HTML is coded as such (see Figure 10-6 for a visual representation).

10

Figure 10-6 You can use a nested frameset to create irregularly shaped frames structures

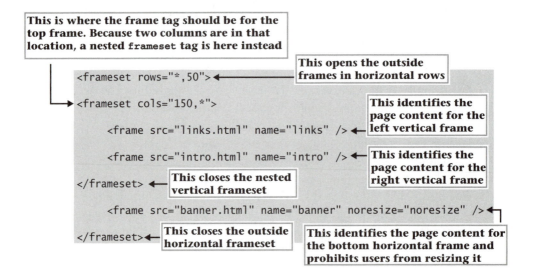

You can easily become confused when you nest any tags, but it's particularly confusing with frames. The most recently opened table must be closed first, so you work from the inside out. (Remember the semicircles that didn't touch in Module 2?)

Another way to deal with irregularly shaped frames structures avoids nesting. In this technique, you reference another HTML file with frames, instead of embedding those frames in the current HTML file. For example, here's how the previous code might be changed to avoid using nested framesets.

> **Instead of embedding another frameset here, as in the previous example, that frameset is contained in its own HTML file and simply referenced here as a single frame**

```
<frameset rows="*,50">
    <frame src="frameset-A.html" name="columns" />
    <frame src="banner.html" name="banner" noresize="noresize" />    ]  Frameset-B.html
</frameset>
```

If you used this HTML code instead of the nested frameset example, you also must create frameset-A.html to contain the frameset with columns.

```
<frameset cols="150,*">
    <frame src="links.html" name="links" />    ]  Frameset-A.html
    <frame src="intro.html" name="intro" />
</frameset>
```

1-Minute Drill

- **What must you do before you can load links into another frame?**
- **Which tag and attribute are used to change the target frame for all links within a page?**

- Use the `name` attribute to identify that frame
- `<base target="`*frame*`">`

Creating Inline Frames

Sometimes you may want to include an entire Web page within another one. While you can use the `object` tag to do this (discussed in Module 7), HTML 4.0 also enables you to use the `iframe` tag for the same purpose. Originally introduced by Microsoft to compete with Netscape's standard frames, *inline* or *floating frames* are only supported by versions 3.0 and later of Internet Explorer. At press time, Netscape doesn't support these inline versions of frames.

The biggest advantage of inline frames is their flexibility because they can be included anywhere on a Web page similar to an image or multimedia component. For example, Figure 10-7 shows a Web page with an inline frame. Each of the links in the paragraph next to the inline frame is loaded into that frame. The following shows the HTML used to create this page.

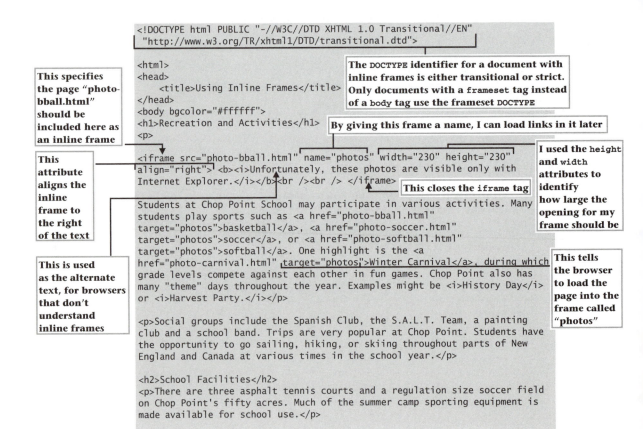

```
<!DOCTYPE html PUBLIC "-//W3C//DTD XHTML 1.0 Transitional//EN"
 "http://www.w3.org/TR/xhtml1/DTD/transitional.dtd">

<html>
<head>
    <title>Using Inline Frames</title>
</head>
<body bgcolor="#ffffff">
<h1>Recreation and Activities</h1>
<p>

<iframe src="photo-bball.html" name="photos" width="230" height="230"
align="right"> <b><i>Unfortunately, these photos are visible only with
Internet Explorer.</i></b><br /><br /> </iframe>

Students at Chop Point School may participate in various activities. Many
students play sports such as <a href="photo-bball.html"
target="photos">basketball</a>, <a href="photo-soccer.html"
target="photos">soccer</a>, or <a href="photo-softball.html"
target="photos">softball</a>. One highlight is the <a
href="photo-carnival.html" target="photos">Winter Carnival</a>, during which
grade levels compete against each other in fun games. Chop Point also has
many "theme" days throughout the year. Examples might be <i>History Day</i>
or <i>Harvest Party.</i></p>

<p>Social groups include the Spanish Club, the S.A.L.T. Team, a painting
club and a school band. Trips are very popular at Chop Point. Students have
the opportunity to go sailing, hiking, or skiing throughout parts of New
England and Canada at various times in the school year.</p>

<h2>School Facilities</h2>
<p>There are three asphalt tennis courts and a regulation size soccer field
on Chop Point's fifty acres. Much of the summer camp sporting equipment is
made available for school use.</p>
```

This specifies the page "photo-bball.html" should be included here as an inline frame

This attribute aligns the inline frame to the right of the text

This is used as the alternate text, for browsers that don't understand inline frames

The DOCTYPE identifier for a document with inline frames is either transitional or strict. Only documents with a frameset tag instead of a body tag use the frameset DOCTYPE

By giving this frame a name, I can load links in it later

This closes the iframe tag

I used the height and width attributes to identify how large the opening for my frame should be

This tells the browser to load the page into the frame called "photos"

```
<p>The waterfront equipment includes Sunfish sailboats, wind surfers, motor
boats, canoes, kayaks, a 23-foot sloop and a 42-foot ketch. Fully-equipped
computer and science labs are available to students at all grade levels.</p>

</body>
</html>
```

Remember these additional things because only Internet Explorer displays inline frames.

- Include alternative text in between the opening and closing `iframe` tags for browsers not supporting inline frames.

- Browsers other than Internet Explorer may launch a new browser window when loading the links that were supposed to load in the inline frame. This happens because that frame was given a name that doesn't exist for browsers not supporting inline frames. When trying to load a link within a named frame it cannot find, the browser usually launches a new browser window, giving it that name.

- Attributes that can be used in the `iframe` tag include those listed in Table 10-2.

Hint

Most HTML tags can be used within that alternative text, but be wary of using the `p` tag there. In my testing, this tag caused the alternative text to be visible in Internet Explorer, appearing next to the inline frame.

10

Attribute & Value(s)	Description
`src="filename.html"`	Identifies the HTML page to be included.
`name="frame name"`	Gives the frame a name, so links can be loaded into it.
`width="#"`	Specifies a width for the frame in pixel dimensions.
`height="#"`	Specifies a height for the frame in pixel dimensions
`align="direction"`	Aligns the frame on the page. Possible values are left, right, or center. (This attribute is deprecated in favor of style sheets.)
`marginwidth="#"`	Specifies the amount of blank space between the frame's content and its horizontal borders

Table 10-2   Attributes for the **iframe** tag

Attribute & Value(s)	Description
`marginheight="#"`	Specifies the amount of blank space between the frame's content and its vertical borders.
`scrolling="value"`	Defines whether scroll bars are visible for the frame. Possible values are yes, no, or auto.
`frameborder="#"`	Specifies whether the frame has a visible border. Possible values are 0 (turns the border off) and 1 (turns the border on).

Table 10-2   Attributes for the `iframe` tag *(continued)*

Creating Content for Non-Frames-Capable Browsers

You need one final piece of information before you create HTML frames. Because some browsers don't support frames, you need to include alternative content for those unable to see the content of your frames. This is accomplished through the use of the `noframes` tag.

Note

If you don't include the `noframes` tag, those who visit your page using a non-frames-capable browser will see only a blank page.

The `noframes` tag—placed in the HTML document after the frame tags, but before the closing `frameset` tag—is best used to link visitors to your individual HTML pages outside the frameset. For example, in the following code, the `noframes` tag provides visitors with a link to an alternative HTML page containing all the important information from the frame documents.

```
<frameset cols="50%,50%">
    <frame src="links.html" name="links" />
    <frame src="intro.html" name="intro" />
    <noframes>◄
<p>This site uses frames to display its content but, unfortunately
your Web browser is not capable of displaying frames. We have
created an <a href="noframes.html">alternative page</a> with all
the same content for you.
    </noframes>
</frameset> ◄
```

> **This opening noframes tag tells the browser to display only the following content in browsers that don't understand frames**

> **Remember to close the noframes tag**

You can also add the `noframes` tag to regular HTML pages, particularly the ones you plan to load within a frames structure. The content of the `noframes` tag would then only be displayed when the page was not viewed within the context of a frameset.

Note

This is especially important for those coming to your Web site from a search engine because most search engines index the pages referenced by the frames, as well as the frames document.

For example, if you have a Web site where the links for the site were included in a second frame, visitors who viewed the content pages outside the frame wouldn't see the links. By including those links within a `noframes` tag on every page of your Web site, you can be assured all viewers will have access to the links, even if they view the pages without the frames.

10

Project 10-1: Creating a Basic Frameset

So far, you have created pages for the Woolwich Historical Society without any links to other pages in the site. In this project, you place those pages into a frame structure so the links are always present in a frame at the bottom of the screen. This is called a *navigation bar* because it contains all the links visitors can use to navigate the pages of the site. Goals for this project include

● Create a basic frameset

● Format the frames within the frameset

Reminder

All the files needed to complete the projects in this book for the Woolwich Historical Society can be downloaded from **www.osborne.com** or **www.willardesigns.com/htmlbook**. In addition, you can view my version of the Web site anytime by visiting **www.woolwichhistory.org.** Those of you who aren't using the Woolwich Historical Society can tailor the project to your particular needs.

Step-by-Step

1. Open your text editor (SimpleText on the Mac or Notepad on the PC) and create a new file entitled `frameset.html`.

2. Type all the HTML tags needed for a basic frameset page containing two horizontal rows.

3. Format the top frame to be variable in size and the second frame to be 50 pixels tall.

4. Name the top frame "content" and the bottom frame "navigation."

5. Turn off the borders so the frames appear seamless and borderless.

6. Set the margin height and width of the bottom frame each to have a value of 2.

7. Use `index.html` (last edited in Project 6–2) as the source for the top frame.

8. Create a new page for the source of the bottom frame, called `navigation.html`.

● Include all the HTML tags needed for a basic HTML page, as well as a table similar to the one in the following table.

Home	Historical Timeline	Genealogy	Membership	Items for Sale

● Format the links in the table so they are loaded into the top frame.

● Each one should link to a page you have already created: Home > `index.html`; Historical Timeline > `timeline.html`; Genealogy > `genealogy.html`; Membership > `membership.html`; Items for Sale > `store.html`.

● Give this page the background color of your choice, making sure your link color stands out against the background.

9. Include alternative text in the `noframes` tag of `frameset.html`, to link to the `index.html` page for non-frames-capable browsers.

10. Save the files.

11. Open your Web browser and choose FILE | OPEN PAGE (or OPEN FILE or OPEN, depending on the browser you're using). Locate the file `frameset.html` you just saved. Make sure the file appears as you intended.

12. If you need to make changes, return to your text editor to do so. After making any changes, save the file, and then switch back to the browser. Choose REFRESH or RELOAD to preview the changes you just made.

Tip

10

Does your screen appear blank? If so, check to make sure you closed your `frameset` tag (`</frameset>`). For more tips, see Resource C: Troubleshooting.

13. If you're using the Woolwich Historical Society, you can compare your files to the following code and Figure 10-7.

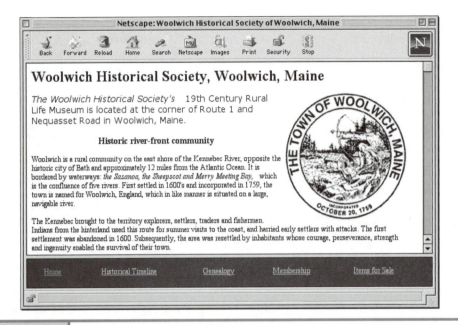

Figure 10-7 If you're using the Woolwich Historical Society, you might see a screen similar to this one

frameset.html

```
<!DOCTYPE HTML PUBLIC "-//W3C//DTD HTML 4.01 Frameset//EN"
 "http://www.w3.org/TR/html4/frameset.dtd">
<html>
<head>
    <title>Woolwich Historical Society of Woolwich, Maine</title>
</head>

<frameset rows="*,50">
    <frame src="index.html" name="content" />
    <frame src="navigation.html" name="navigation" noresize="noresize" />
    <noframes>Since your browser does not understand Web documents created
with frames, please use our <a href="index.html">page without
frames</a>.</noframes>
</frameset>
</html>
```

navigation.html

```
<!DOCTYPE html PUBLIC "-//W3C//DTD XHTML 1.0 Transitional//EN"
 "http://www.w3.org/TR/xhtml1/DTD/transitional.dtd">
<html>
<head>
    <title>Woolwich Historical Society Navigation</title>
    <base target="content">
</head>
<body bgcolor="#333333" text="#ffffff" link="#cccccc" vlink="#999999"
alink="#ffffff">

<table width="100%">
<tr align="center">
    <td><a href="index.html">Home</a></td>
    <td><a href="timeline.html">Historical Timeline</a></td>
    <td><a href="genealogy.html">Genealogy</a></td>
    <td><a href="membership.html">Membership</a></td>
    <td><a href="store.html">Items for Sale</a></td>
</tr>
</table>
</body>
</html>
```

Summary

Frames can offer many additional formatting and layout possibilities to
Web developers when used properly and with the Web site user in mind.
This project gave you practice creating a basic frameset for a navigation
bar, which is a typical use of frames on the Web.

Note

10

For extra practice, try adding `noframes` tags to all the pages you've
created. Include the links listed in this `navigation.html`, so anyone
viewing those pages outside the frames structure can navigate the Web site.

✓ Mastery Check

1. What's wrong with the following HTML code?

```
<frame rows="200,*">
    <frameset src="links.html" />
    <frameset src="intro.html" />
</frame>
```

2. What could you add to `<frameset>` to create three columns of equal width?

3. Fix the mistakes in the following line of HTML code:

```
<frame name="links.html" src="links" />
```

4. Fill in the blanks in the following XHTML-compliant HTML code.

```
<_____ rows="20%,80%">
<_____ _____="links.html" noresize="_____" __>
    <_____ _____="intro.html" __>
<_____>
```

5. When nesting frames, which `frameset` tag should be closed first?

6. Which tag is used to include content for non-frames-capable browsers?

Module 11

Employing Forms

Goals

- Understand the concept and uses of forms in Web pages
- Create a basic form
- Provide a way for your form to be processed
- Understand formatting techniques for forms

One of the best features of the Web is its capability to enable new forms of communication with each other in new ways. Online forms are popular ways of facilitating such communications. For example, forms allow Web site visitors to comment on a site, order a product, add a post to a bulletin board, sign a guest book, and register for a service. This module discusses how to create forms such as these and use them effectively on your Web site.

Understanding Forms

The most basic purpose of any form is to collect information. When you register to vote, you fill out a form specifying your name, address, birth date, and political party affiliation. The form is collected and processed. The same basic concept holds true with online forms—they are filled out, collected, and processed.

For example, Figure 11-1 shows a page from the Chop Point Web site with a form for parents and friends to send a message to a camper at the summer camp.

Just as paper forms must have once been written, typed, or otherwise created, online forms need to be coded. This can be accomplished with HTML alone or by combining HTML with other technologies. For the purposes of this module, we use HTML to create our forms.

Creating a Basic Form

Even the most basic forms have the same structure. This includes opening and closing `form` tags, input controls, and processing methods. The `form` tags surround the entire form, just as `html` tags surround the entire HTML document.

```
<form>
 ... content goes here ...
</form>
```

First, let's discuss *input controls*, or ways for users to enter data. For example, for you to enter your name on a form, there must be a space for you to do so. This space is what I'm referring to when I use the phrase input control or simply "control." Figure 11-1 contains some input controls that are labeled for you.

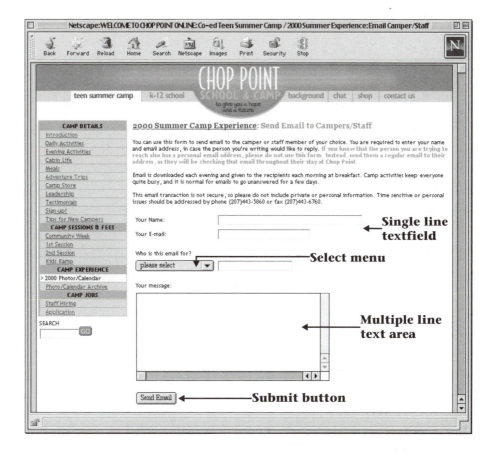

Figure 11-1   Online forms can be used for a variety of reasons, from sending
messages to searching for keywords

Note

You can also use the `object` tag (discussed in Module 7) to embed
objects within forms. These are called *object controls*.

- text inputs
- check boxes
- radio buttons

- select menus

- file selects

- buttons (submit buttons, reset buttons, and push buttons)

- hidden controls

Because the majority of these controls are created with an `input` tag, the actual description of which control you want to include is made through the `type` attribute, as in the following example:

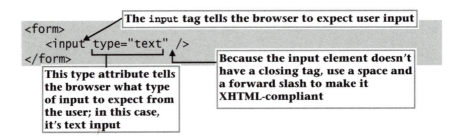

The next sections explain the specific types of controls created with the `input` tag, as well as a few others that aren't created by it.

Text Input

Two types of text input are afforded in HTML: single-line text boxes (called *textfields*) and multiple-line text areas.

Single-Line Textfields

The most basic type of input control is the single-line textfield. This control is a space, looking like a box, that can contain a single line of text.

Usually, textfields are preceded by descriptive text telling the user what to enter in the box. For example:

```
<form>
   Please enter your first name: <input type="text" /><br />
   Please enter your last name: <input type="text" />
</form>
```

As the following illustration shows, textfields are single-line, white spaces that appear slightly indented into the page. Unless you specify otherwise with the `size` attribute, textfields are usually 20 characters in length.

┼Note

The sizes of textfields are specified in characters. However, it ultimately depends on the default font size in the viewer's browser. This means even though you might specify a textfield to be 25 characters in length, it may appear larger or smaller on someone else's system, depending on how that person's browser is set up.

Attribute	Value(s)	Description
name	*name*	Identifies the control so it's correctly handled when the form is processed. This information isn't displayed when the form is viewed through a browser.
size	*number*	Specifies the length of the textfield in characters.
maxlength	*number*	Specifies the maximum number of characters that can be entered in the textfield by the user.
value	*value*	Defines what text, if any, should be present within the textfield when it's initially displayed on the page.

Table 11-1   **Attributes for Textfields**

Any of the attributes listed in Table 11-1 can be added to this `input` tag to customize the textfield.

Of all the attributes listed in Table 11-1, perhaps the most important one is `name`. To process all the controls in your form, each one must be identified with a name. For example, when the form is processed, you could tell it to take whatever the user entered in the control you named "FirstName", and print that text at the top of an e-mail message.

Tip

Blank spaces in between words in the value of some attributes can cause problems in HTML and other coding methods. To avoid such problems when using the `name` attribute, many developers like to run any phrases together, capitalizing the first letter in each word. For example, instead of using "Middle Initial" as the value of your `name` attribute, use "MiddleInitial". Just remember, these values are case-sensitive, which means whenever you reference that control later, you must also capitalize the first letters of each word. In addition, be sure to use unique names to avoid confusion when the form is processed.

```
<form>
   Please enter your first name: <input type="text" name="FirstName" /><br />
   Please enter your last name: <input type="text" name="LastName" />
</form>
```

The other three attributes, `size`, `maxlength`, and `value` are optional. You can use the `size` attribute to specify the length of the textfield in characters, while the `maxlength` attribute enables you to limit the number of characters that can be entered in that box. For example, if you created a textfield where users can enter their birthdays in the following format: mm-dd-yy, you could specify a `maxlength` of eight characters.

Every control has an initial value and a current value. An *initial value* is an optional value you specify for a control when you code the form, while a *current value* is whatever the user entered that is then processed with the form. For example, instead of giving directions in the space before a textfield, you might use the `value` attribute to place the directions within the textfield. If you do, and the user doesn't enter any data, then the initial value you entered is sent along when the form is processed.

```
<form>
 <input type="text" name="FirstName" value="Enter First Name" /><br />
 <input type="text" name="LastName" value="Enter Last Name" size="20" />
</form>
```

When the page is viewed, however, users may have to erase the phrase before entering their information.

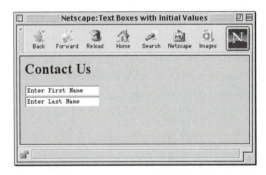

Textfields for Passwords

HTML enables you to create two types of textfields: one for regular text (as you just learned) and a second for passwords. The main difference between the two is password textfields show text that's entered as bullets instead of straight text.

11

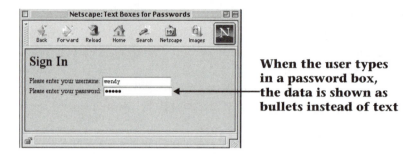

When the user types
in a password box,
the data is shown as
bullets instead of text

You use `password` as the value of the `type` attribute in your
`input` tag to create this type of control. Here's an example of the code
for the previous illustration:

```
<form>
    Please enter your username: <input type="text" name="UserName"><br />
    Please enter your password: <input type="password" name="Password">
</form>
```

Although this may seem as if it adds a level of security to your page,
it's merely a way to prevent those looking over the user's shoulder from
seeing a password. The actual password is not encrypted in any way when
the form is processed and, therefore, this control shouldn't be implemented
as the only means of security for pages with passwords.

Multiple-Line Text Areas

When it's necessary to allow your Web site visitors to enter more than a
single link of text, use a text area instead of a textfield. Unlike most other
form input controls, a *text area* uses the `textarea` tag instead of the
input tag.

```
<form>
    We welcome your thoughts and opinions about our products.<br />
    <textarea name="Comments"></textarea>
</form>
```

The closing `textarea` tag is required

To specify the size of the text area, use the `cols` and `rows` attributes.

● The `cols` attribute identifies the visible width of the text area, based
   on an average character width.

● The `rows` attribute identifies the visible height of the text area,
   based on the number of text lines.

Because the sizes of the `rows` and `cols` attributes relate to the character width in the browser, the actual size of the text area may differ, depending on the user's settings. Scroll bars may appear when users attempt to enter more data than can be displayed in the visible text area.

You don't use the `value` attribute in this tag to create an initial value that prints within the text area. Instead, include any text you want to print within the text area between the opening and closing `textarea` tags. Figure 11-2 shows how the following code might be displayed in a browser.

```
<form>
    We welcome your thoughts and opinions about our products.<br />
    <textarea name="Comments" cols="30" rows="5">Type your comments here.</textarea>
</form>
```

Another attribute is quite useful when creating text areas because it causes the text in the text area to stop when it reaches the edge of the text area and to drop down to the next line before continuing. This process is called text *wrapping,* and allows all the text the user is typing to be visible without having to scroll horizontally. The values for the `wrap` attribute are listed in Table 11-2. You can see an example where the `wrap` attribute is set to "`virtual`" in Figure 11-3.

Although the `wrap` attribute isn't included in the official HTML 4.0 specification, it is supported by versions 3.0 and above of both Netscape

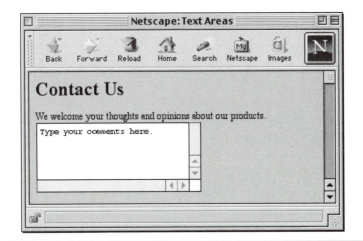

11

| **Figure 11-2** | Text areas enable users to enter more than a single line of text. Any text you enter between the opening and closing **textarea** tags is used as the initial value of the text area |

and Internet Explorer. Because the wrap attribute doesn't cause any known problems for browsers that don't support it, but it does add benefit for users of Netscape and Internet Explorer, I recommend using it.

Radio Buttons

Radio buttons are small, round buttons that enable users to select a single option from a list of choices. This is accomplished with the input tag and a value of "radio" in the type attribute. You might use radio buttons to allow those interested in receiving more information the option of choosing to do so via e-mail, phone, fax, or regular mail. When the user selects one of the options by pressing the radio button, the circle is filled in with a black dot.

Tip

Radio buttons are particularly useful for questions requiring a yes or no answer.

How would you like to receive more information about our company?
- ○ e-mail
- ● phone
- ○ fax
- ○ regular mail

Attribute & Value	Description
wrap="off"	This is the default value and causes the text lines to be processed exactly as they are typed without any wrapping.
wrap="hard" wrap="physical"	Both these values cause the text to be wrapped when it's typed in the browser. The text is then processed with the wrapping, and long lines are cut off when sent to the server.
wrap="soft" wrap="virtual"	Both of these values cause the text to be wrapped when it's typed in the browser. The text is processed as long lines, however, and not wrapped when sent to the server.

Table 11-2 Values of the **wrap** Attribute

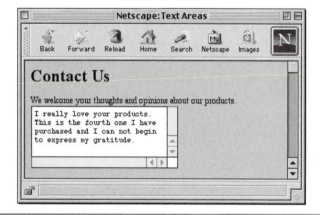

Figure 11-3 The **wrap** attribute can prohibit text in a text area from being continued across long lines out of the visible window

11

The `name` and `value` attributes are especially important to radio buttons because they help to make sure the data is processed correctly. Consider the following HTML code used to create the previous illustration:

```
<form>
    How would you like to receive more information about our company?<br />
    <input type="radio" name="ContactMe" value="e-mail"> e-mail<br />
    <input type="radio" name="ContactMe" value="phone"> phone<br />
    <input type="radio" name="ContactMe" value="fax"> fax<br />
    <input type="radio" name="ContactMe" value="mail"> regular mail<br />
</form>
```

Notice the `name` attributes contain the same value for all four options. This ensures these four controls are linked together when the form is processed. Because the type of control is "radio," the browser knows only one option can be selected.

When the form is processed, it locates the selected option (meaning it looks for whichever radio button the user pressed) and transmits that option's `value` along with its `name`. If I pressed the radio button next to the word "fax," the appropriate name and value would be transmitted: ContactMe - fax. You can see how using words and phrases that actually mean something can be important.

If you want to set one of the radio buttons to be selected by default when the page is initially loaded, use the checked attribute in the `input` tag. Users can select a different option if they want.

```
<input type="radio" name="ContactMe" value="fax" checked="checked"> fax<br />
```

Because this attribute doesn't have an official value, use "checked" as its value to make it XHTML-compliant

Check boxes

Check boxes are similar to radio buttons because they don't let users enter any data, but can only be clicked on or off. However, check boxes let the user select more than one choice from a list of options. For example, you might use check boxes to give users the option to select for which services they want receive more information. When a check box is pressed, a small *x* or a check mark typically appears in the box, depending on the browser.

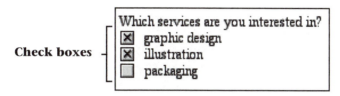

Check boxes

To include a check box in your online form, use the `input` tag and `type` attribute with a value of `checkbox` (note that check box is one word when used as an HTML value). Just as with radio buttons, the values of the `name` attributes for all the options should be the same. Use the `value` attribute to identify what is different about each option, as in the following example:

```
<form>
   Which services are you interested in?<br />
   <input type="checkbox" name="Services" value="graphic design"> graphic design<br />
   <input type="checkbox" name="Services" value="illustration"> illustration<br />
   <input type="checkbox" name="Services" value="packaging"> packaging
</form>
```

When the form is processed, the values of any check boxes pressed by the user will be transmitted to the server along with the value of the `name` attribute. So, in the previous example, if I pressed the check boxes next to "graphic design" and "illustration," the appropriate name and values would be transmitted: Services - graphic design, illustration.

Use the `checked` attribute any time you want a check box to be selected by default when the page is loaded. Users can uncheck that box if they want.

```
<input type="checkbox" name="Services" value="packaging" checked="checked"> packaging
```

Because this attribute doesn't have an official value, use "checked" as its value to make it XHTML-compliant

11

Select Menus

Whenever you want to let users select from a long list of options, you might consider using a select menu instead of check boxes or radio buttons. Select menus are lists that have been compressed into one or more visible options, similar to those menus you find at the top of other software applications.

Note

Menus may appear differently depending on which browser or computer system is used. These examples show menus from both Macintosh and Windows systems.

Also called *drop-down menus,* this type of menu enables users to click an option initially visible, and then pull down to reveal additional options. Unless a number greater than 1 is specified in the size attribute, only a single option is visible when the page loads. This option is accompanied by a small arrow signifying the menu expands.

This is how Internet Explorer typically displays a drop-down menu on a PC

Please choose your favorite color: blue ▼

Please choose your favorite color: blue ▼

When a user clicks the triangle to the right of the first option, the menu expands. This menu is from Netscape on a Mac

When the size attribute is 2 or more, that number of choices is visible in a scrollable list.

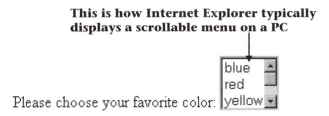

This is how Internet Explorer typically displays a scrollable menu on a PC

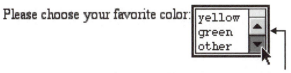

Users can click the arrows in the scroll bar to view additional menu options. This menu is from Netscape on a Mac.

The select element is used to create the menu initially, while option tags surround each item in the menu. A menu asking users to choose their favorite color might be coded like the following:

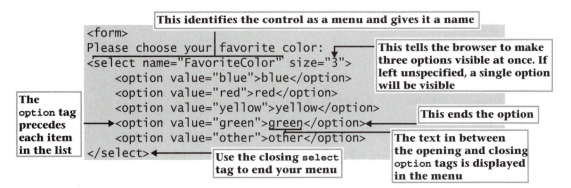

This identifies the control as a menu and gives it a name

```
<form>
Please choose your favorite color:
<select name="FavoriteColor" size="3">
    <option value="blue">blue</option>
    <option value="red">red</option>
    <option value="yellow">yellow</option>
    <option value="green">green</option>
    <option value="other">other</option>
</select>
```

This tells the browser to make three options visible at once. If left unspecified, a single option will be visible

The option tag precedes each item in the list

This ends the option

Use the closing select tag to end your menu

The text in between the opening and closing option tags is displayed in the menu

11

Note

It isn't required that you use the `value` attribute with each `option` tag. If you don't, the text displayed in the menu will be transmitted as the option's value when the form is processed. Based on my experience, I recommend using the `value` attribute whenever possible to avoid confusion when the form is processed.

By default, users can select one item from the list. If you'd like them to be able to choose more than one option, add the `multiple` attribute to your opening `select` tag. The way users select more than one menu item depends on their computer system. For example, Macintosh users hold down the COMMAND key when clicking, while Windows users hold down the SHIFT key, or the CONTROL key, to select noncontiguous choices in the list, and click.

```
<select name="FavoriteColors" size="3" multiple="multiple">
```

Because no official value exists for the `multiple` attribute, use `multiple="multiple"` to make it XHTML-compliant

In addition, you can specify any item to be already selected when the page is loaded by adding the `selected` attribute to that item's opening `option` tag. Users can select a different menu item if they choose.

Note

Don't specify more than one item as `selected`, unless you also let users choose more than one option by adding the `multiple` attribute to the `select` tag.

```
<option value="red" selected="selected">red</option>
```

Because no official value exists for the `selected` attribute, use `selected="selected"` to make it XHTML-compliant

Submenus

HTML 4.0 allows for a tag to create more user-friendly menus. The `optgroup` element is used to divide long menus into categories of submenus. The `label` attribute is used along with the `optgroup` element to give the submenu a name. Here's an example of how to create submenus with `optgroup` tags.

Note

Although the current version of HTML doesn't allow nesting `optgroup` tags, the next version is expected to allow them.

```
<form>
Please choose the time and day that is best to reach you.
<select name="TimeDay">
<optgroup label="Monday">
    <option value="Monday AM">Monday AM</option>
    <option value="Monday PM">Monday PM</option>
</optgroup>
<optgroup label="Tuesday">
    <option value="Tuesday AM">Tuesday AM</option>
    <option value="Tuesday PM">Tuesday PM</option>
</optgroup>
</select>
</form>
```

Unfortunately, neither Netscape nor Internet Explorer supports the `optgroup` tag at press time. When graphical browsers do support submenus, the result will probably look something like this.

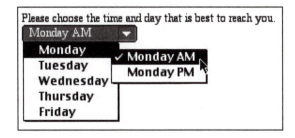

11

File Uploads

Some online forms might require a file be transmitted along with any data from the form. For example, you might provide the option for potential employees to submit a photo along with a job application being filled out online. This can be accomplished by using `type="file"` with the `input` tag.

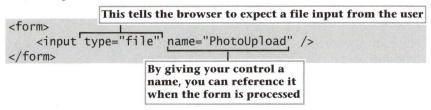

```
                        This tells the browser to expect a file input from the user
<form>
    <input type="file" name="PhotoUpload" />
</form>
                        By giving your control a
                        name, you can reference it
                        when the form is processed
```

For document uploads, most browsers display a textfield followed by a button typically labeled *Browse...* By clicking the button, users can locate the file they want to send with the form on their computers (see Figure 11-4). After doing so, the browser prints the location and name of the file in the textfield provided (see Figure 11-5).

You can increase the size of the textfield by adding the size attribute to the input tag. Because many file locations may be long, you might want to specify a size of 30–40 characters.

```
<input type="file" name="PhotoUpload" size="40" />
```

Hidden Fields

Depending on the type of form you are creating, you may need to include a hidden field. For example, many teachers create several versions of a test to avoid having students look over their classmate's shoulder and cheat. In cases like this, you might make a special mark on the test to identify to which answer key it belongs. On Web forms, these special marks are called *hidden fields*.

A hidden field is data attached to and processed with a form that cannot be seen or changed by the user. You can use as many hidden fields in your form as you'd like, using `input` tags with `type` attributes set to `hidden`.

```
<input type="hidden" name="TestVersion" value="3" />
<input type="hidden" name="Creator" value="Wendy Willard" />
```

Tip

This is also how you pass information from one form to the next when you start to build multipage forms.

Buttons

Buttons enable users to interact with a form. For example, to tell the browser you're finished filling out a form and are ready to process it, you might click a button labeled *Submit*. You can create three types of buttons with HTML 4.0:

- submit buttons—used to process a form

- reset buttons—used to reset a form

- other buttons—serving any alternative needs for buttons in a form

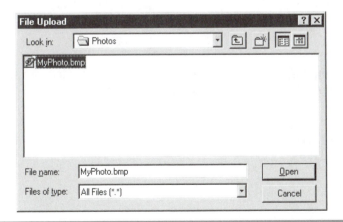

Figure 11-4 | Users can locate the file they want to upload on their computers after clicking the button labeled *Browse...*

11

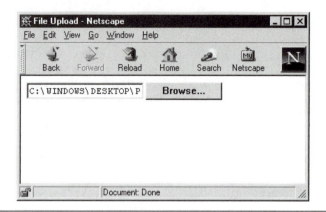

Figure 11-5 After locating the file to be uploaded, the browser prints its name and location in the textfield provided

You can use the `input` or `button` tag to create any of these tags. Although the `input` tag is supported by both Internet Explorer and Netscape as a way to add buttons to your page, at press time, the `button` tag is only supported by versions 4 and higher of I nternet Explorer.

In either case, add the `type` attribute and appropriate `value` to identify which button you are creating (see Table 11-3).

Note

On the PC, these buttons are displayed as rectangles with squared off edges. On the Mac, these buttons have rounded edges.

Type of Button	Description	HTML	Browser View
submit	When pressed, this button processes the form.	`<input type="submit" value="Submit" />` `<button type="submit" />Submit</button>`	Submit
reset	When pressed this button resets all the form's fields back to their initial values.	`<input type="reset" value="Reset" />` `<button type="reset" >Reset</button>`	Reset
button	When pressed, an action or event is triggered, based on a predefined script or function.*	`<input type="button" value="Verify Data" />` `<button type="button value="Verify Data" />Verify Data</button>`	Verify Data

* This usually involves some scripting language such as JavaScript. For more information, see Module 14.

Table 11-3	**Types of Buttons**

┼Note

Because Netscape doesn't support the `button` tag, I don't recommend creating buttons with it unless you know your target audience consists of only Internet Explorer users. If you do use the `button` tag and users visit your page with Netscape, they'll see the text without the clickable button.

Formatting with the Button Tag

While the `input` and `button` tags both create a basic gray button with text inside, the `button` tag has additional formatting possibilities. You

11

may have noticed in Table 11-3 that, unlike the `input` tag, which doesn't have a closing version, the `button` element has both opening and closing tags. This enables you to enter text, images, and other HTML that will be placed on the button when viewed in the browser.

For example, if I include an `img` tag in between the opening and closing `button` tags, that image would be displayed in the center of the button when viewed in the browser.

```
<button type="submit" name="Submit" value="Submit">
<img src="sendmessage.gif" width="100" height="68"
alt="Send Message">
</button>
```

When viewed in a browser supporting the `button` tag, such as Internet Explorer 5.0, that button might look like this.

Tip

Remember, all buttons have gray background colors by default. If you want your images to appear seamlessly on the button, use that same gray as your image's background color or make the image's background transparent. For more tips on creating Web graphics, see Module 12.

Graphical Buttons with the Input Tag

You can also use an image as a button with the `input` tag, by changing the type to `image`, as in the following example.

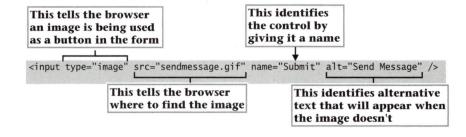

Graphical buttons created with the `input` tag are different from those created with the `button` tag because they aren't placed on a button in the browser. Instead, they're surrounded by a border, just like what's around any other linked image by default.

To turn off the border, add `border="0"` to the input tag →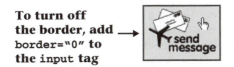

Project 11-1: Creating a Basic Form

All Web sites should contain some way for visitors to contact the business or organization. Otherwise, it's like having an advertisement in the phone book that doesn't list your phone number! This could be accomplished through a simple e-mail link, a listed phone number, or even a *Contact Us* form. In this project, you create a *Contact Us* form for the Woolwich Historical Society. The goals for this project include

● Create a basic form

● Use several different input controls in the form

● Create submit and reset buttons

─┤*Reminder*──────────────

All the files needed to complete the projects in this book for the Woolwich Historical Society can be downloaded from **www.osborne.com** or **www.willardesigns.com/htmlbook**. In addition, you can view my version of the Web site anytime by visiting **www.woolwichhistory.org**. Those of you who aren't using the Woolwich Historical Society can tailor the project to your particular needs.

11

Step-by-Step

1. Open your text editor (SimpleText on the Mac or Notepad on the PC) and create a new file entitled `contactus.html`.

2. Type all the HTML tags needed for a basic HTML page.

3. Type opening and closing `form` tags.

4. Using Figure 11-6 as your guide, type the HTML tags needed to create the form.

5. Save the file.

6. Open your Web browser and choose FILE I OPEN PAGE (or OPEN FILE or OPEN, depending on the browser you're using). Locate the file `contactus.html` you just saved. Make sure the file appears as you intended it. Note: nothing will happen when you try to "submit" your form, but don't worry—we address processing forms in the next section. For now, we're focusing on creating the form itself.

7. If you need to make changes, return to your text editor to make changes. After making any changes, save the file and switch back to the browser. Choose REFRESH or RELOAD to preview the changes you just made.

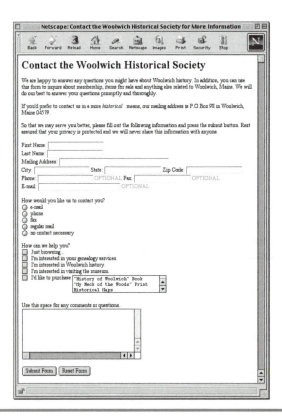

| **Figure 11-6** | Using this as your guide, create a form allowing visitors to contact the Woolwich Historical Society for more information |

Tip

Do your textfields, select menus, and other controls appear? If not, check to make sure you closed your `form` tag (`</form>`). For more tips, see Resource *C:* Troubleshooting.

---

8. If you are using the Woolwich Historical Society, you can compare your files to the following code and Figure 11-6.

```
<!DOCTYPE html PUBLIC "-//W3C//DTD XHTML 1.0 Transitional//EN"
 "http://www.w3.org/TR/xhtml1/DTD/transitional.dtd">
<html>
<head>
    <title>Contact the Woolwich Historical Society for More
 Information</title>
</head>
<body bgcolor="#ffffff" text="#000000">

<h1>Contact the Woolwich Historical Society</h1>
<p>We are happy to answer any questions you might have about Woolwich
 history. In addition, you can use this form to inquire about membership,
 items for sale and anything else related to Woolwich, Maine. We will do our
 best to answer your questions promptly and thoroughly.</p>
<p>If you'd prefer to contact us in a more <i>historical</i> means, our
 mailing address is P.O.Box 98 in Woolwich, Maine 04579.</p>

<form>
<p>So that we may serve you better, please fill out the following
 information and press the submit button. Rest assured that your privacy is
 protected and we will never share this information with anyone.</p>

<p>First Name: <input type="text" name="FirstName"><br />
Last Name: <input type="text" name="LastName"><br />
Mailing Address: <input type="text" name="Address" size="40"><br />
City: <input type="text" name="City">
State: <input type="text" name="State"> Zip Code: <input type="text"
 name="ZipCode"><br />
Phone: <input type="text" name="Phone"> <font
 color="#999999">OPTIONAL</font>
Fax: <input type="text name="Fax"> <font color="#999999">OPTIONAL</font><br
 />
E-mail: <input type="text name="Email" size="30"> <font
color="#999999">OPTIONAL</font></p>

<p>How would you like us to contact you?<br />
<input type="radio" name="ContactMe" value="e-mail"> e-mail<br />
<input type="radio" name="ContactMe" value="phone"> phone<br />
<input type="radio" name="ContactMe" value="fax"> fax<br />
<input type="radio" name="ContactMe" value="mail"> regular mail<br />
<input type="radio" name="ContactMe" value="no"> no contact necessary</p>

<p>How can we help you?<br />
<input type="checkbox" name="Interests" value="just browsing..."> Just
 browsing...<br />
```

11

```
<input type="checkbox" name="Interests" value="genealogy"> I'm interested in
 your genealogy services.<br />
<input type="checkbox" name="Interests" value="packaging"> I'm interested in
 Woolwich history.<br />
<input type="checkbox" name="Interests" value="packaging"> I'm interested in
 visiting the museum.<br />
<input type="checkbox" name="Interests" value="purchase"> I'd like to
 purchase <select name="Purchase" multiple="multiple" size="3">
   <option value="History of Woolwich Book">"History of Woolwich"
Book</option>
   <option value="My Neck of the Woods Print">"My Neck of the Woods"
Print</option>
   <option value="Maps">Historical Maps</option>
   <option value="Note Cards">Note Cards</option>
   <option value="Recipe Booklet">"Sweet Receipts" Recipe Booklet</option>
   <option value="Bump Jumpers Booklet">"Bump Jumpers" Booklet</option>
   <option value="Postcards">Postcards</option>
</select></p>

<p>Use this space for any comments or questions.<br />
<textarea cols="40" rows="7" name="Comments"></textarea></p>

<input type="submit" name="submit" value="Submit Form">
<input type="reset" name="reset" value="Reset Form">
</form>
</body>
</html>
```

Summary

Online forms are a great way to get customer feedback. In addition, forms make it easy for your visitors to ask questions about products and services. This project gave you practice working on a basic form.

1-Minute Drill

● **What tag is used to create spaces where users can enter multiple lines of text?**

● **Radio buttons enable users to select how many choices?**

● <textarea>

● 1

Processing Forms

The phrase *processing method* refers to what happens to the form after the user enters all the data and presses the Submit button. Is it e-mailed to the site's administrator or stored in a database? Or, perhaps it's written to another Web page on the site, such as occurs with a guest book or bulletin board? Many possibilities exist, which ultimately depend on the purpose of the form.

Inside the opening `form` tag, you need to tell the browser how to process your form. This is accomplished through the `action` attribute (which is required) and the `method` and `enctype` attributes (which are optional).

Action Attribute

The `action` attribute gives the location where the form's information should be sent. This can either be in the form of an e-mail address

```
<form action="mailto:name@emailaddress.com">
```

or the URL of a CGI script.

```
<form action="../cgi-bin/form.cgi">
```

While the easiest way to process a form is to have the data sent to an e-mail address, I don't recommend this method. Because no official specification exists for using e-mail to process forms in HTML, the results achieved with this method vary according to the browser. In fact, many browsers don't support this method at all. Perhaps the best use of this might be testing your forms before implementing a CGI script.

11

Tip

You might think of a CGI program as being similar to the mail carrier for your post office. This person picks up your mail and transports it to and from the post office. Some mail carriers drive trucks, while others drive cars or walk. Regardless of how they get there, they all take mail to the post office and bring mail back to you. In like manner, CGI scripts, regardless of which language they are written in, transfer information to and from the server.

CGI stands for *Common Gateway Interface* and refers to a program that sends information to and from the server. This program, also called a *script*, can be written in several different computer languages such as Visual Basic, C++, and Java. The most common of these languages is Perl, because of its ease of use and the large number of people able to write it.

CGI scripts must reside on your server (the computer hosting your Web pages for everyone on the Web to access) in directories with special settings allowing them to be *executed* or run. For this reason, using a CGI script requires you to talk to the company that hosts your Web site about whether it supports CGI scripts and, if it does, how to implement them. Most hosting companies receive questions about CGI scripts quite often and have pages of information on their Web sites dedicated to this subject. When in doubt, visit your host company's Web site or call to see what your next step should be.

Note

One reason some hosting providers don't allow CGI scripts on their servers is they can infringe on the site's security. If your hosting provider doesn't let you use a CGI script, don't worry. Several services are set up to host these scripts and process your forms for you. Check with your own hosting provider for referrals, or visit **dir.yahoo.com/ Computers_and_Internet/Internet/World_Wide_Web/ Programming/Forms/** for a list of companies providing these types of services.

What Does a CGI Script Look Like?

Just because a CGI script cannot be written in HTML doesn't mean you can't learn how to write one. As I mentioned before, I don't consider myself a computer programmer and I didn't study computer science in school. I can understand and write basic Perl scripts to process my HTML forms, though.

While creating CGI scripts (whether in Perl or another language) is beyond the scope of this book, Figure 11-7 shows what a CGI script written in Perl looks like. By showing this, I hope to give you an idea of what happens to the form data after a user clicks the Submit button.

Where Can I Get a CGI Script?

Literally thousands of free CGI scripts are available on the Web, and thousands of others are available for small fees. First, check with your hosting provider for referrals. Your provider might even have some scripts on hand for you to use, which are already set up to work on their systems.

If you need to find your own scripts, try looking at some of these sites:

- Matt's Script Archive (**www.worldwidemart.com/scripts**)

- GetScripts.com (**www.scripts.com**)

- ZDNet Developer Script Library
  (**www.zdnet.com/devhead/resources/scriptlibrary/**)

- The CGI Resource Index (**www.cgi-resources.com/**)

Pay attention to the documentation offered with each script because it should tell you how to customize the script for your needs and how to install it on your server.

11

Method and Enctype Attributes

The two other attributes you'll probably use in the opening `form` tag are `method` and `enctype`. The `method` attribute tells the browser how to send the data to the server. There are two possible values for this attribute: `get` and `post`.

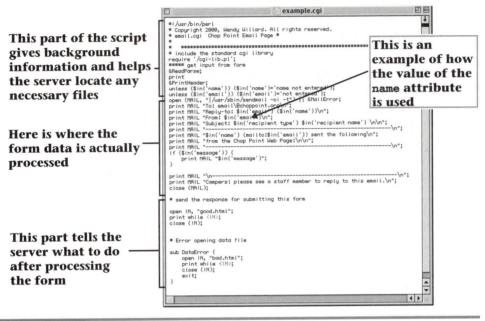

This part of the script gives background information and helps the server locate any necessary files

Here is where the form data is actually processed

This part tells the server what to do after processing the form

This is an example of how the value of the name attribute is used

Figure 11-7 This CGI script, written in Perl, is used to process a form that lets parents and friends e-mail kids at camp

Tip

For help deciding which method or enctype to use, consult your hosting provider or the creator of your CGI script.

The get method takes all the data submitted with the form and sends it to the server attached to the end of the URL. For example, say the script location is http://www.yoursite.com/cgi-bin/form.cgi, and the only data from the form is the user's name (in this case, we'll use wendy). If the method was set to get, here's what would be sent to the server when the user clicked the Submit button.

```
http://www.yoursite.com/cgi-form.cgi?name=wendy
```

This method works best for searches, where a small amount of information must be transferred to the server, such as the keywords you are searching for. For more comprehensive forms, the post method can be used. Instead of attaching the information to the URL of the script, the information is sent directly to the location of the script file.

The `enctype` attribute, short for *encoding type,* tells the browser how to format the data when the `method` attribute is set to `post`. The default value is `application/x-www-form-urlencoded`. Because this should work for most of your forms, you needn't include the `enctype` attribute in your `form` tag unless you want to change the value.

For example, if you are allowing users to upload files with your form, you need to change the `enctype` to `multipart/form-data`, as in the following example.

```
<form action="myscript.cgi" method="post" enctype="multipart/form-data">
```

Additional Formatting Techniques

You can use many of the formatting techniques discussed in previous modules to format your forms. For example, to make the label of a textfield bold, simply add the b tags around the text.

```
<b>First Name:</b> <input type="text" name="FirstName">
```

If you refer to Figure 11-6, you'll notice the textfields are scattered through the page. If, instead, you want to have all the textfields lined up in a column, you could use a table to format your form.

Tables

11

When using a table to lay out a form, you will probably place each individual element in its own table cell. Perhaps the labels for the form (telling people what information to enter) might be placed in cells in the first column, while the input controls (textfields, and so forth) might be placed in the second column.

```
<form action="..." method="post">
<table>
```

```
<tr>
    <td>First Name</td>
    <td><input type="text" name="FirstName" /></td>
</tr>
```

> This text label is in a cell by itself in the first column

> This cell in the second column contains only the input control for the user's first name

```
<tr>
    <td>Last Name</td>
    <td><input type="text" name="LastName" /></td>
</tr>
<tr>
    <td>Mailing Address</td>
    <td><input type="text" name="AddressLine1" /></td>
</tr>
<tr>
    <td> </td>
    <td><input type="text" name="AddressLine2" /></td>
</tr>
```

> This textfield is a second line for users to enter their mailing addresses

> This cell is empty

> The two columns are merged for this row to allow the Submit and Reset buttons to flow freely at the bottom of the table

```
<tr>
    <td colspan="2"><input type="submit" value="Send Form"
 /><input type="reset" value="Start Over" /></td>
</tr>
</table>
</form>
```

Using a table like this enables you to achieve a more uniform look in your forms. Notice in the following illustration how each of the textfields line up vertically, regardless of how long or short the preceding text is.

Tip

Because determining where each text label and input control should be placed can initially be confusing, I recommend you first create the form itself before placing it into a table. As with any table, it may help to plan the form on paper before coding.

Tab Order and Keyboard Shortcuts

Module 5 discussed changing the tab order and adding keyboard shortcuts for links using the `tabindex` and `accesskey` attributes. You can also use these attributes to format input controls in a form.

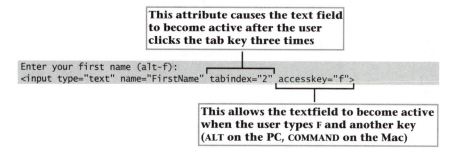

This attribute causes the text field to become active after the user clicks the tab key three times

```
Enter your first name (alt-f):
<input type="text" name="FirstName" tabindex="2" accesskey="f">
```

This allows the textfield to become active when the user types F and another key (ALT on the PC, COMMAND on the Mac)

Refer to Module 5 for details on using either of these two attributes. Although present in the HTML 4.0 specification, neither of these attributes is fully supported by the major browsers at press time.

Labels

Whenever you include descriptive text before an input control, you are labeling it for users, helping them to understand what type of information they should enter. To link the label and the associating control formally, you can use the `label` tag and the `id` attribute. Each `label` can only be attached to one control.

11

This gives the label a name so it can be referenced by the input control

```
<label for="birthday">When is your birthday? (MM/DD/YY)</label>
<input type="text" name="BirthDate" id="birthday" size="8"
/>
```

This references the previous appropriate label

Ask the Expert

Question: I used a table to lay out my Web page and placed a form for searching in one cell. However, when I did so, I noticed a lot of extra space in that cell, which I can't seem to delete by adjusting the `cellpadding` or `cellspacing`. What's going on?

Answer: Unfortunately, this is a common problem. The root of the problem lies in understanding what kind of tag the `form` tag is. Tags in HTML usually fall into one of two categories: block elements or inline elements. *Block elements,* like the `form` tag and the `table` tag, are used for structure and layout on a page, while inline elements are used to alter the appearance of `text`. For example, the `b` tag, an inline element, is used to make text bold, but it doesn't alter the location of the text.

Block elements do alter the location of text or other items on a page, and, by default, many of them force a line break within the page. This means wherever you place the `form` tag, a blank line is also inserted.

Question: Yes, but isn't there any way around that?

Answer: Well . . . no. Believe me, I feel your pain on this one. You can try to fudge things by moving your `form` tag to another location where the space is less obvious but, remember, you cannot nest forms. So, if you have more than one form on your page, each of their opening and closing tags must not overlap.

Note

At press time, the use of either the `label` tag or the `id` attribute doesn't change the way the page appears in a graphical browser.

This formal labeling process is new to HTML 4.0 and, at press time, isn't supported by either Netscape or Internet Explorer. When it is supported, however, it'll be an important technique for linking labels and controls, particularly when tables are used for layout. The reason for this is, when tables are used, controls and their labels are often separated across table cells. This can be especially troublesome for nonvisual browsers when they try to link controls with the appropriate label.

```
<form action="..." method="post">
<table>
<tr>
    <td><label for="fname">First Name</label></td>
    <td><input type="text" name="FirstName" id="fname" /></td>
</tr>
<tr>
    <td><label for="lname">Last Name</label></td>
    <td><input type="text" name="LastName" id="lname" /></td>
</tr>
</table>
</form>
```

Groups

While the `label` attribute is used to attach names to controls formally, the `fieldset` attribute enables you to group sets of labels and controls. For example, if you had an employee application form with three distinct sections, such as Schooling, Work Experience, and Skills, you could use the `fieldset` attribute to group all the labels and controls under these headings. The `legend` attribute then gives a caption to the group, if you want to include one.

11

```
<form action="..." method="post">
<fieldset>
  <legend>Schooling</legend>
  <p>
  High School: <input type="text" name="HighSchool" /><br />
  College: <input type="text" name="College" />
  </p>
</fieldset>
<fieldset>
  <legend>Work Experience</legend>
  <p>
  Current Job: <input type="text" name="CurrentJob" /><br />
  Previous Job: <input type="text" name="PreviousJob1" /><br />
  Previous Job: <input type="text" name="PreviousJob2" />
  </p>
</fieldset>
<fieldset>
  <legend>Skills</legend>
  <p>
  Skill 1: <input type="text" name="Skill1" /><br />
  Skill 2: <input type="text" name="Skill2" /><br />
  Skill 3: <input type="text" name="Skill3" />
  </p>
</fieldset>
</form>
```

Internet Explorer 5.0 displays boxes around each group identified by the `fieldset` tag and places the caption from the `legend` tag in the outline of the box as a headline.

Netscape doesn't support these tags at press time. So the same code that caused Internet Explorer to draw boxes around the groups is ignored in Netscape.

While the use of these tags is completely optional, it may become the standard when they are uniformly supported by the browsers. Until then, remember to test your pages in a variety of browsers to ensure you have achieved the desired results.

Disabling Form Elements

When you want to restrict a user's input for a specific element, you might use one of two attributes:

- `readonly`
- `disabled`

11

Note

At press time, these two attributes are not yet supported by Netscape.

The `readonly` attribute can be added to input controls so users cannot change the values. For example, in the following code, the phrase `ww1234` is displayed in the textfield, but cannot be changed by the user. If you try to type in a textfield that has been set to `readonly`, an alert is displayed or heard but, otherwise, no change exists in the appearance of the box.

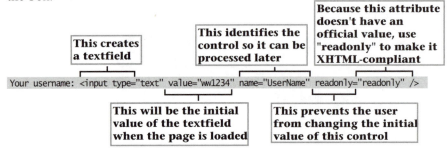

The `disabled` attribute works essentially the same way, except input controls that are disabled also appear in gray or faded text to reduce their importance in the form. You cannot click in a textfield that has been set to `disabled`.

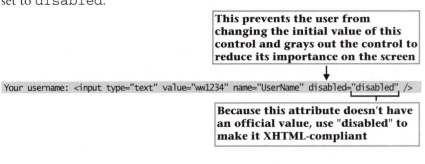

Project 11-2: Formatting the Form

Returning to the Contact Us page created in Project 11-1, use additional formatting techniques to achieve a more uniform appearance of the labels and controls. Goals for this project include

- Use a table to lay out a form

- Set the tab order for the elements on a form

- Group form elements with the `fieldset` and `legend` tags

- Reference a CGI script in the `action` attribute of the `form` tag

┤Reminder

All the files needed to complete the projects in this book for the Woolwich Historical Society can be downloaded from **www.osborne.com** or **www.willardesigns.com/htmlbook**. In addition, you can view my version of the Web site anytime by visiting **www.woolwichhistory.org.** Those of you who aren't using the Woolwich Historical Society can tailor the project to your particular needs.

Step-by-Step

1. Open your text editor (SimpleText on the Mac or Notepad on the PC) and open the file entitled `contactus.html` from Project 11-1.

2. Using Figures 11-8 and 11-9 as a guide, use a table to lay out the form.

3. Set the tab order for all the controls on the form.

4. Group all the controls under the "How can we help you?" headline using a `fieldset` tag.

11

5. Add the `action` and `method` attributes to the opening `form` tag. For testing purposes, you can have the results mailed to your e-mail address or simply use a fake address for a CGI script. Set the `method` to `post`.

6. Save the file.

7. Open your Web browser and choose FILE | OPEN PAGE (or OPEN FILE or OPEN, depending on the browser you're using). Locate the file `contact us.html` you just saved. Make sure the file appears as you intended it.

8. If you need to make changes, return to your text editor to make changes. After making any changes, save the file and switch back to the browser. Choose REFRESH or RELOAD to preview the changes you just made.

9. If you are using the Woolwich Historical Society, you can compare your files to the following code and Figures 11-8 through 11-10.

```
<!DOCTYPE html PUBLIC "-//W3C//DTD XHTML 1.0 Transitional//EN"
"http://www.w3.org/TR/xhtml1/DTD/transitional.dtd">
<html>
<head>
    <title>Contact the Woolwich Historical Society for More
Information</title>
</head>
<body bgcolor="#ffffff" text="#000000">
<h1>Contact the Woolwich Historical Society</h1>
<p>We are happy to answer any questions you might have about Woolwich
history. In addition, you can use this form to inquire about membership,
items for sale and anything else related to Woolwich, Maine. We will do our
best to answer your questions promptly and thoroughly.</p>
<p>If you'd prefer to contact us in a more <i>historical</i> means, our
mailing address is P.O.Box 98 in Woolwich, Maine 04579.</p>
<form action="form.cgi" method="post">
<p>So that we may serve you better, please fill out the following
information and press the submit button. Rest assured that your privacy is
protected and we will never share this information with anyone.</p>
<p>

<fieldset>
<legend><h2>Contact Information</h2></legend>
<table>
<tr>
  <td>First Name:</td>
  <td><input type="text" name="FirstName"></td>
</tr>
<tr>
    <td>Last Name:</td>
    <td><input type="text" name="LastName"></td>
```

```
</tr>
<tr>
   <td>Mailing Address:</td>
   <td><input type="text" name="Address" size="40"></td>
</tr>
<tr>
   <td>City:</td>
   <td><input type="text" name="City"></td>
</tr>
<tr>
   <td>State:</td>
   <td><input type="text" name="State"></td>
</tr>
<tr>
   <td>Zip Code:</td>
   <td><input type="text" name="ZipCode"></td>
</tr>
<tr>
    <td>Phone:</td>
    <td><input type="text" name="Phone">
<font color="#999999">OPTIONAL</font></td>
</tr>
<tr>
    <td>Fax:</td>
    <td><input type="text name="Fax">
<font color="#999999">OPTIONAL</font></td>
</tr>
<tr>
    <td>E-mail:</td>
    <td><input type="text name="Email" size="30">
<font color="#999999">OPTIONAL</font></td>
</tr>
<tr>
    <td colspan="2">How would you like us to contact you?</td>
</tr>
<tr>
    <td><input type="radio" name="ContactMe" value="e-mail"> e-mail</td>
    <td><input type="radio" name="ContactMe" value="phone"> phone</td>
</tr>
<tr>
    <td><input type="radio" name="ContactMe" value="fax"> fax</td>
    <td><input type="radio" name="ContactMe" value="mail"> regular mail</td>
</tr>
<tr>
    <td><input type="radio" name="ContactMe" value="no"> no contact
 necessary</td>
</tr>
</table>
</fieldset>

<fieldset>
<legend><h2>How can we help you?</h2></legend>
<table>
<tr>
    <td><input type="checkbox" name="Interests" value="just browsing...">
 Just browsing...</td>
   <td><input type="checkbox" name="Interests" value="genealogy"> I'm
```

11

```
 interested in your genealogy services.</td>
</tr>
<tr>
    <td><input type="checkbox" name="Interests" value="packaging"> I'm
 interested in Woolwich history.</td>
    <td><input type="checkbox" name="Interests" value="packaging"> I'm
 interested in visiting the museum.</td>
</tr>
<tr valign="top">
    <td><input type="checkbox" name="Interests" value="purchase"> I'm
 interested in learning more about:</td>
    <td><select name="Purchase" multiple="multiple" size="3">
    <option value="History of Woolwich Book">"History of Woolwich"
Book</option>
    <option value="My Neck of the Woods Print">"My Neck of the Woods"
Print</option>
    <option value="Maps">Historical Maps</option>
    <option value="Note Cards">Note Cards</option>
    <option value="Recipe Booklet">"Sweet Receipts" Recipe Booklet</option>
    <option value="Bump Jumpers Booklet">"Bump Jumpers" Booklet</option>
    <option value="Postcards">Postcards</option></select></td>
</tr>
<tr>
    <td colspan="2">Use this space for any comments or questions.<br
 /><textarea cols="40" rows="7" name="Comments"></textarea></td>
</tr>
</table>
</fieldset>
<input type="submit" name="submit" value="Submit Form">
<input type="reset" name="reset" value="Reset Form">
</form>
</body>
</html>
```

Summary

Many of the additional formatting techniques used with forms help to make them more efficient and accessible. This project gave you practice using some of those techniques to make an existing form more user-friendly.

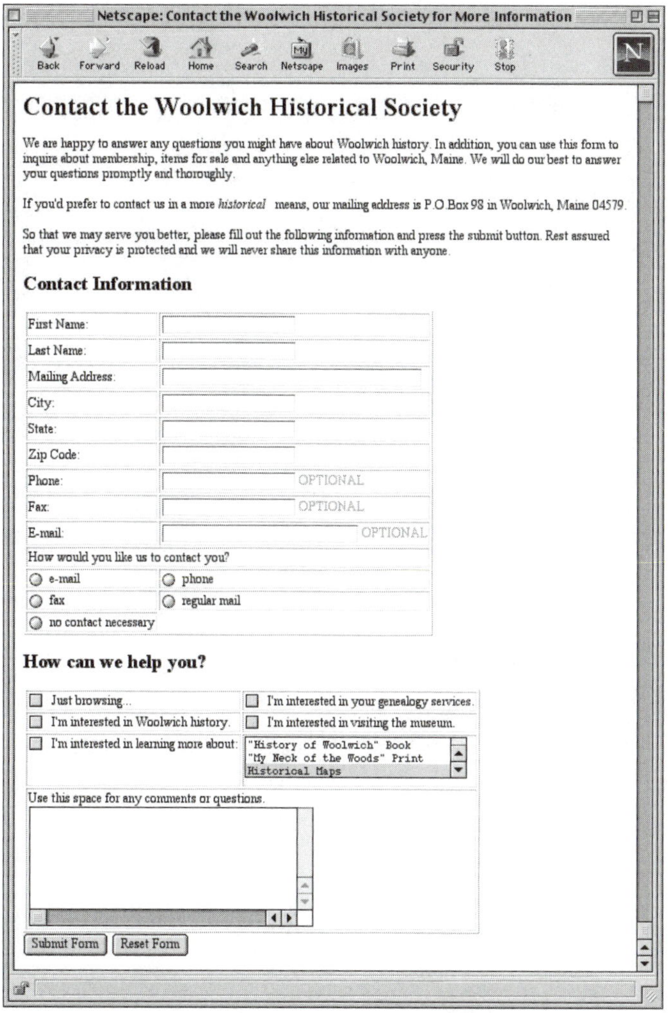

Figure 11-8 Those using the Woolwich Historical Society can use this as a guide for laying out a form with a table. To show you where each cell lies, the table borders are set to 1 in this example

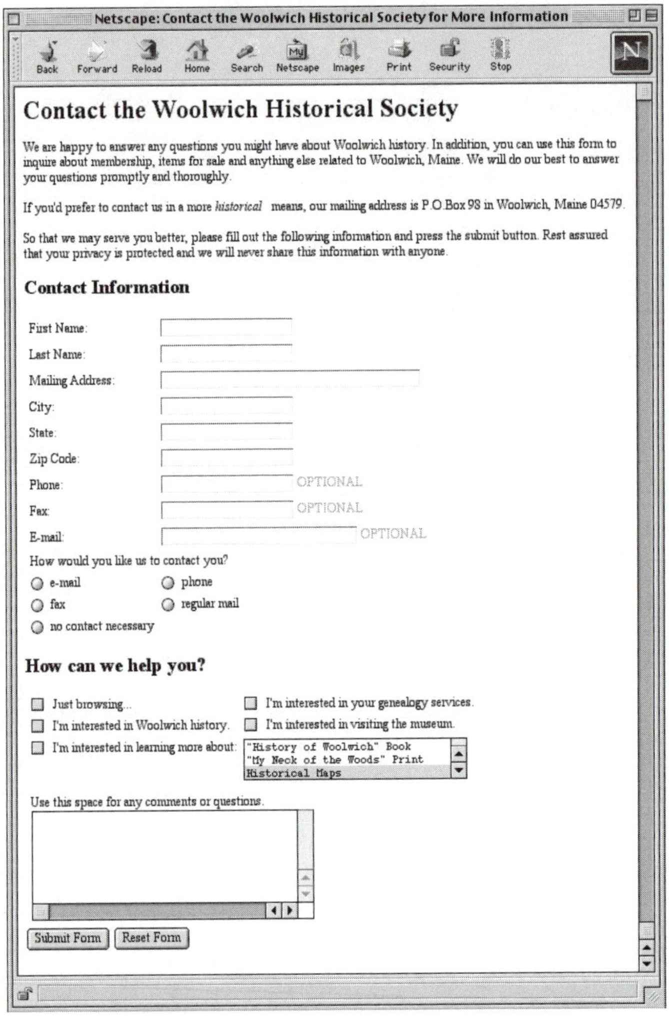

Figure 11-9 When the borders are turned off, you can see how a table adds a sense of structure to a form

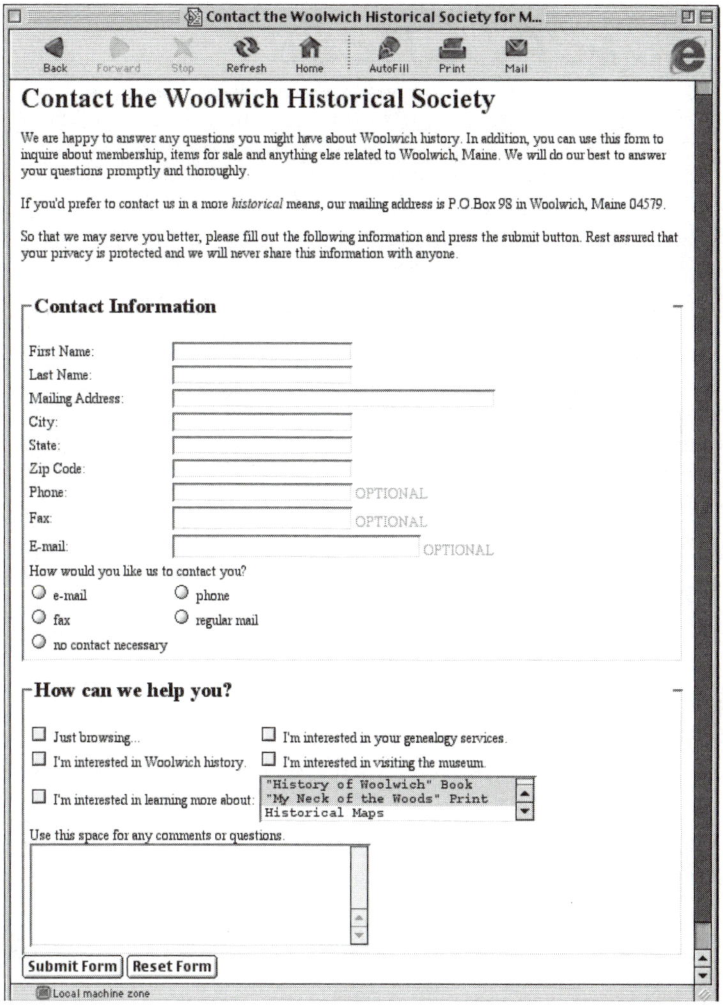

Contact the Woolwich Historical Society for M...

Back   Forward   Stop   Refresh   Home   AutoFill   Print   Mail

Contact the Woolwich Historical Society

We are happy to answer any questions you might have about Woolwich history. In addition, you can use this form to inquire about membership, items for sale and anything else related to Woolwich, Maine. We will do our best to answer your questions promptly and thoroughly.

If you'd prefer to contact us in a more *historical* means, our mailing address is P.O.Box 98 in Woolwich, Maine 04579.

So that we may serve you better, please fill out the following information and press the submit button. Rest assured that your privacy is protected and we will never share this information with anyone.

Contact Information

First Name:

Last Name:

Mailing Address:

City:

State:

Zip Code:

Phone: OPTIONAL

Fax: OPTIONAL

E-mail: OPTIONAL

How would you like us to contact you?

○ e-mail   ○ phone

○ fax   ○ regular mail

○ no contact necessary

How can we help you?

☐ Just browsing...   ☐ I'm interested in your genealogy services.

☐ I'm interested in Woolwich history.   ☐ I'm interested in visiting the museum.

☐ I'm interested in learning more about: "History of Woolwich" Book
                                           "My Neck of the Woods" Print
                                           Historical Maps

Use this space for any comments or questions.

[Submit Form] [Reset Form]

Local machine zone

Figure 11-10   The page looks a bit different when viewed in Internet Explorer 5.0 because this browser understands the **fieldset** tag and displays the page accordingly

☑ *Mastery Check*

- To process forms, what attribute is required in the `form` tag?

- Name two optional attributes used in the `form` tag to customize how the form is processed.

- What attribute is used to set the keyboard shortcut for a control?

- What two attributes let you restrict form elements from being altered by the user?

- What tag is used to group form elements?

Part 2

Beyond HTML

Module 12

Creating Your Own Web Graphics

Goals

- Become familiar with graphics software

- Understand issues that impact design decisions

- Recognize graphic file formats for the Web

Creating graphic images for a Web site can be an enjoyable experience for anyone, regardless of artistic experience. Success in this area requires a bit of determination and creativity. This module gives a brief introduction to the issues involved in creating your own Web graphics.

Graphics Software

If you walk down the software aisles of your local computer store, you might be surprised by the sheer volume of graphics-related software available. You can buy clip art and photography, fonts, scanning utilities, animation titles, photo editing programs, desktop publishing applications, drawing tools, and so forth.

Tip

You'll hear the term *layers* used a lot when discussing graphics software. You might think of using layers in a graphics program as similar to making a bed. You place sheets, blankets, and pillows over the mattress, but you can change any of those items freely if you decide you dislike one. The same is true with layers—you can paint on a layer, and then delete it later if you don't like it. Layers offer much flexibility in graphics programs.

For the purposes of this module, I focus on those software titles offering you the best tools for creating Web graphics. Two main categories of software titles exist: vector and bitmap.

Bitmap applications, also called *raster,* create graphics using tiny dots called *bits.* These types of images are more difficult to resize because you must change each individual dot, but they have been around longer and enjoy more support from file formats. GIFs and JPEGs are bitmap images.

Vector applications, also called *object-oriented,* are based on mathematically calculated lines and curves that are easily changed and updated. Images created with vectors tend to be smaller in file size and, for that reason, are increasing in popularity on the Internet.

Note

Can't decide which graphics program to purchase? All the products listed here have trial or demo versions available free. Visit each company's Web site for details.

The programs discussed in the following are by no means the only products available for creating Web graphics. Given the scope of this book, though, I thought it best to limit the discussion to the most popular programs. If none of these tools suit your needs, try searching in Yahoo! (**www.yahoo.com**) or CNET's download center (**download.cnet.com**) for "Web graphics" and, perhaps, you'll find one more suitable to your purposes.

Adobe

Adobe is the world leader in graphics and imaging software. It offers such renowned titles as Photoshop and Illustrator that have been used in the printing and design industry for years. When designers started being asked to create graphics for the Web, Photoshop was used mostly because it was what everyone had. Adobe quickly began working on a Web-specific software title, called ImageReady.

Tip

Adobe's products are available for Windows and Macintosh systems. For more information, visit **www.adobe.com.**

Photoshop aficionados wanted the Web features of ImageReady to be added to Photoshop and, with version 5.5, Adobe conceded. ImageReady is now bundled and shipped with versions 5.5 and 6 of Photoshop, offering users a superb suite of tools for graphic design for print and the Web.

Photoshop is a bitmap program, best known for image manipulation, using layers to allow for virtually limitless flexibility in design. In fact, if you've recently bought a new scanner, you might have acquired a scaled-back version of Photoshop with it. Illustrator, on the other hand, is a vector tool, more suited for freehand drawing and illustration. Both products can save and open Web file formats.

12

In many design circles, Adobe's Photoshop is *the* product to use. For the typical home user, however, the price for the full version is a bit steep (around $600). If you're familiar with Adobe's products and enjoy them, I recommend sticking with Photoshop. Likewise, if you're interested in creating Web graphics as well as editing images for printed publications, Photoshop is your best bet.

If you don't fall into either of those categories, you might be interested in Photoshop LE (the scaled-back version), which costs under $100. While this version doesn't have all the high-powered image editing tools used by the professionals, it's more than capable of handling the needs of someone just starting. Photoshop LE, available for both the Mac and the PC, is a superb gateway graphics program for the typical home user.

Macromedia

Macromedia was once best known for its animation title, Director. With the advent of the Web, Macromedia has become a major player in the graphics industry. Fireworks is Macromedia's Web-specific tool for creating Web graphics. I use the term *Web-specific* because, unlike many other graphics software titles, Fireworks was created specifically for the Web.

Tip

Macromedia's products are available for Windows and Macintosh. For more information, visit **www.macromedia.com.**

Fireworks offers such features as Web animation, file optimization, image slicing, rollover creation, and Web previewing. It also seamlessly integrates with Dreamweaver, Macromedia's top-rated WYSIWYG tool for Web authoring and page layout, making the two software titles a highly regarded and powerful Web development suite.

Fireworks has a particularly strong following among Web designers who never got hooked on Adobe's products. Although its learning curve is a bit steeper than that of Jasc's Paint Shop Pro (discussed at the end of this section), at $200–300 it remains a viable alternative for cost-conscious home users.

Macromedia also develops Flash, which is worth mentioning, even though it doesn't directly compete with any of the other products listed here. Flash is a vector application specifically designed for creating animations and interactive presentations on the Web. When you combine Flash with

Fireworks and Dreamweaver, Macromedia really shines as a leader in Web development software.

Jasc's Paint Shop Pro

The least expensive of these programs is Jasc's Paint Shop Pro. Retailing for about $100, the latest version of this title offers much for that price. Features include animation, direct digital camera support, layers, filters, watermarks, special effects, and advanced text tools, such as text on a path.

Tip

Paint Shop Pro is available for Windows 95, 98, and NT. For more information, visit **www.jasc.com.**

Those of you who are interested in creating Web graphics will be pleased to know that version 7 includes image slicing, support for rollovers, and previewing capabilities in up to three Web browsers. Image map tools and support for the PNG file format also put this title on the forefront of Web graphics.

For the cost-conscious home user trying to create some Web graphics, I recommend starting out with Paint Shop Pro. You may even decide you don't need anything else.

Issues That Impact Design Decisions

Consider a printed magazine. Regardless of where the magazine is purchased, the images displayed inside look the same. In fact, only those who are color-blind or vision-impaired will encounter differences in printed graphics. This isn't the case with Web graphics because each person viewing a Web site is doing so with a different set of experiences, affected by his or her computer, browser, monitor, lighting, and modem to name a few.

When creating your own Web graphics, several issues directly affect the outcome and must be considered. These issues include

- platforms
- target audience demographics

12

- HTML

- browsers

- color

- bandwidth

While entire books are written on some of these topics, the next few sections give you a basic understanding of what to consider. At the end of this module is a section entitled "Learning More" that gives you a list of places to go for more in-depth discussion on any of these topics.

Platforms

A person's Web experience is affected by his or her platform, or the type of device being used to access the Web. While obvious differences exist between computers and telephones, both are used to view Web pages. Furthermore, many differences exist between the types of computers used; for example, consider the differences among hand-held computers, laptop computers, and desktop computers.

And among those different types of computers, Windows, Macintosh, UNIX, Linux, and many other operating systems are running. WebTV even enables you to surf the Web from your television. Undoubtedly, many more such devices are to come.

The most important thing to consider about platforms is the one you're working on probably won't be the only one your visitors will use. Here are a few general things to remember when you're designing for more than one platform.

- Graphics generally look darker on a PC than they do on a Mac, but PC gamma can vary widely. A graphic that appears fine on one PC might look much darker on another PC with different settings.

- Software (such as browsers, plug-ins, and ActiveX controls) available for your platform might not be available for others.

- The size and settings of the viewing device (be it a 15" monitor, a 27" TV, or a 2" hand-held screen) used by your visitors will alter the appearance of your graphics.

The moral of this section is you need to be aware of these differences and plan accordingly. In addition, test your Web graphics on a variety on platforms to be sure you are achieving the results you want.

Target Audience Demographics

Module 1 contained a brief section on planning for Web sites. This included identifying the target audience as a key step in the planning stages of Web development. One reason identifying the target audience is so important is because it directly affects how the graphics should be created.

Tip

Some online surveys about audience demographics might be of help to you in this category. Visit **dir.yahoo.com/Computers_and_Internet/ Internet/Statistics_and_Demographics/** for links to these resources.

For example, if you are creating a site for your company's private network, wherein the people on that network only use Windows PCs, you can safely rule out the need to test your pages on Macintosh computers. Likewise, if you know that everyone on your network uses 17" monitors, you can design at that size.

While these scenarios might not be the norm, knowing your target audience can also help in identifying the style to develop for. Consider that a site geared for 12–18-year-olds might use different colors than one geared toward those over age 63. In addition, a site for young children should use a color palette and graphics style different than one for teenagers.

Designing for a Specific Size

Module 9 discussed using tables for page layout in Web pages. In that module, I mentioned that, whenever possible, it's best to create tables that grow or shrink in proportion to the size of the browser window.

Even if you do design your pages to grow or shrink according to window size, remember, the smallest screen resolution for desktop and laptop computers is 640 by 480 pixels. If you take into consideration the scroll bars and edges of the browser window, that leaves you with about 600 pixels across for your graphics.

12

Vertically, you have to deal with the many buttons and toolbars in the browser. Depending on how many toolbars are visible at any given time, you may lose 100–200 pixels in height from the top of the screen and about 25 pixels at the bottom for the status bar. (Windows users who have their Start menu at the bottom of the screen may lose another 50–100 pixels.)

So, if you want your pages to fit, even in the smallest of window sizes, make sure your graphics are no longer than 600 pixels in width. In addition, the most important information on your page should be located within the top 300 pixels, to ensure all viewers see the information when the page is initially loaded. Figure 12-1 is an example of a viewable portion of the Web page.

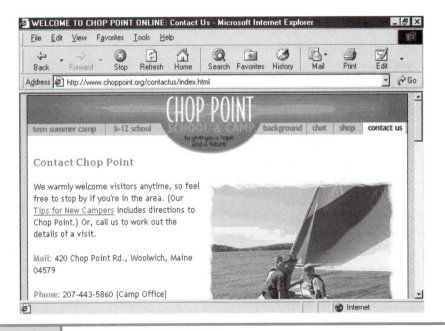

Figure 12-1   When this page is viewed at a 640 by 480 resolution, the viewable portion of the Web page is about 600 by 300 pixels

HTML

As you've probably noticed by now, HTML has some restrictions and limitations that can affect the way graphics are used on a Web page. For example, all graphics in a Web page must be contained in a rectangular box, even if that box isn't readily apparent to viewers. Any text flowing around a graphic must either follow the rectangular shape of the box or be contained within the graphic.

Without understanding these limitations, it's hard to create Web graphics that will work in an HTML page. This is especially true because graphics editors enable you to mix text and graphics. A layout like this one is entirely possible in a graphics editor.

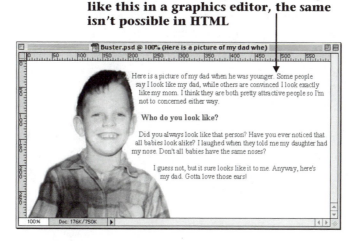

Those with HTML experience recognize this layout isn't possible in HTML, unless the text itself is contained within that graphic. A more suitable layout using the same text and graphic might be the following.

12

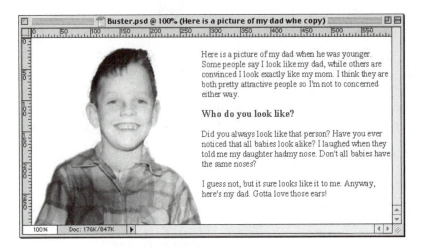

Whenever you create your own Web graphics, it's important to remember the limitations and possibilities of HTML presented in this book.

Browsers

While the most popular browsers may be Netscape and Internet Explorer, many other browsers are in use by Web surfers. Web sites like CNET's **browsers.com** call these others *Rebel Browsers*, and include browsers like Opera, NetCaptor, NetPositive, Lynx, iCab, and NeoPlanet in that category. All told, **browsers.com** lists over 200 different versions of browsers, the vast majority of which are free to download.

What does this mean to you as a Web developer? That depends. As I mentioned, knowing your audience affects more than just the marketing plan. It affects which browsers you build the site for and why. Because it's ultimately the browser creator's decision on which tags to support, you might find some browsers display your pages much differently than others.

In fact, some of the rebel browsers are text-only browsers, for systems incapable of displaying graphics. Anyone using these browsers won't be able to see the graphics you include on your Web pages. Because of this, remember, if the most important information on your site is shown in graphics, alternative text-only versions should also be made available. Figure 12-2 shows different ways of handling cases where the page is viewed without the graphics.

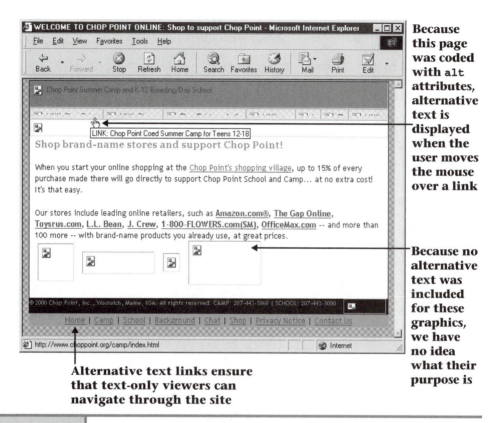

Because this page was coded with `alt` attributes, alternative text is displayed when the user moves the mouse over a link

Because no alternative text was included for these graphics, we have no idea what their purpose is

Alternative text links ensure that text-only viewers can navigate through the site

Figure 12-2 When this page is viewed with graphics turned off in Internet Explorer, boxes appear where the graphics should have. Whenever alternative text is included using the **alt** attribute, users have an idea what the graphic shows

Here are a few things to remember when designing Web graphics for different browsers...

1. Use standard HTML 4.0 tags. Throughout this book, I mentioned many tags that were either introduced by Netscape or Internet Explorer and aren't supported by other browsers. While in some cases, using these proprietary tags might be considered acceptable, you shouldn't do so if you are trying to reach the widest possible audience. Try to stick

12

with standard HTML tags recognized by the W3C (**www.w3c.org**) and you'll be better suited to reach the most people.

2. **Provide alternatives.** Whether this means coding your pages with the `alt` attributes for those who can't view images or including different ways of accessing the information, providing alternative means of navigating and viewing your site is important.

3. **Test, test, test.** Don't settle for viewing your pages in Netscape and Internet Explorer on your personal computer. Go to your neighbor's house or your office computer and view the pages there. You'll undoubtedly find differences you may or may not appreciate.

For additional resources on browser differences, visit any of the following Web sites.

- **www.browsers.com**

- **browserwatch.internet.com**

- **dir.yahoo.com/Computers_and_Internet/Software/Internet/ World_Wide_Web/Browsers/**

Color

A big consideration for those developing Web graphics is color. While graphics created for the printed page look relatively the same to all who view them, Web graphics may look vastly different from one computer to the next.

As discussed in Module 3, in the section "Using Web-safe Colors," this variation in color can be caused by differences in system color palettes, as well as lighting and gamma issues related to the user's monitor. Whenever you need to render a specific color that needs to look the same on as many systems as possible, stick with a Web-safe color.

Tip
You can find a color version of the Web-safe palette on the inside of the front cover.

You can create a Web-safe color in any graphics editor by altering the red, green, and blue values. To make things easier, you can also load premade Web-safe color swatches into most graphics editors. These color swatches (see Figure 12-3) are often called *CLUTS,* short for *color lookup tables*. You can find several different CLUTS for use in many graphics programs on Lynda Weinman's Web site: **www.lynda.com/ downloads/CLUTS/.**

Bandwidth

Another big difference between graphics created for the Web and those created for virtually any other medium is bandwidth. The term *bandwidth* refers to the speed at which Web users access the Internet. Telephone modem users offer access at speeds of 28.8K to 56K, while cable modem or network users' speeds are double or triple that amount. Because people visiting your Web site will probably be doing so from many different access speeds, you must design your graphics accordingly.

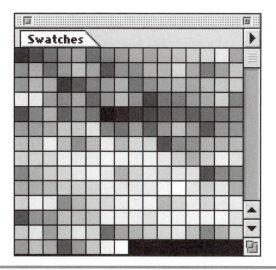

Figure 12-3 | This is how a Web-safe CLUT is displayed in Photoshop

12

The biggest issue related to bandwidth is file size. If the graphics on your Web pages are large in file size, they'll take longer to download. Whenever I ask my friends or family how long they're willing to wait for pages to download on the Internet, they usually give their answer in seconds as opposed to minutes. It's true that most of us are quick to click that mouse button and zoom off to a new Web site if the current one takes more than a few seconds to capture our interest. This means the graphics on your Web pages need to be quite small in file size.

Determining File Size

So, exactly how small is small? Let's use a 56 Kbps (the Kbps stands for kilobits per second) modem connection as our example. A 56 Kbps modem will download about 7000 keystrokes of information per second. That translates to about 2.5 single-spaced typewritten pages of text or about 6–7 kilobytes (K) of Web content per second.

As you know, Web pages are comprised of text and images. To estimate the size of a Web page, you have to add together the sizes of the text (the HTML file) and the images (the GIFs and JPEGs). Using the previous approximation, a page totaling 30K in content might take five seconds to download on a 56 Kbps modem. Table 12-1 shows the best download speeds per second for the most common connection types.

If you're creating Web pages for the general public, a good rule of thumb is to limit your pages to no more than 20–30K in total size. HTML files usually weigh in at about 1–3K, so that leaves a mere 17–29K for other content such as graphics. In fact, this amount is quite tiny and can often restrict you to using the most important and necessary graphics on a page.

Connection Type	Best Download Per Second
T1 Network	200K
Cable Modem	180K
56 Kbps Modem	6–7K
33.6 Kbps Modem	4–5K
28.8 Kbps Modem	3–4K

Table 12-1   Best Download Speeds for Popular Connection Types

Tip

To put things into perspective, consider that a floppy disc holds 1.4MB or about 1,400,000K of data.

You can determine the actual file size of an image in several ways. Many graphics editors display the file size and approximate download speed right within the program. For example, Figure 12-4 shows how the size of a Web graphic is displayed within Photoshop's SAVE FOR WEB feature.

With all this talk about best download speeds, I must warn you that many things might cause a connection to be slower at any given time. Just as detours can happen when you drive somewhere, detours can also occur in the route taken from your computer to the one housing a particular Web site. So while you can use the numbers in Table 12-1 to give you

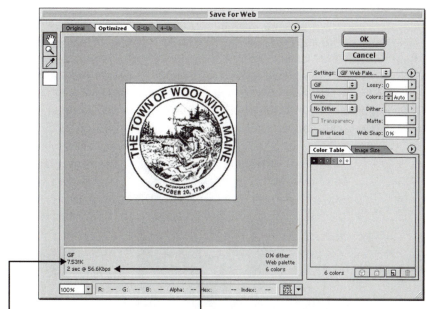

When saved with these settings, this file will be 7.531K in size

At this file size, it takes approximately two seconds to load the graphic on a 56 Kbps modem connection

Figure 12-4   In Photoshop's SAVE FOR WEB features, you can see the file's size and approximate download time

12

an idea of how fast your page *might* download; remember, it could be significantly slower for some users.

Ways to Reduce File Sizes of Images

Two basic rules exist in reducing the file sizes of your images.

- Reduce the actual height and width.

- Compress the image.

When you reduce the height or width of an image, you make it smaller in physical size and in file size. This can be accomplished by shrinking the entire image or by cropping it to show only a portion of the original.

Note

Another way to reduce your overall page size is to remove images altogether. In some cases, you may find a text solution works just as well, if not better.

Consider if the following photograph was used in a Web page. At 275 by 350 pixels, this illustration is about 27K.

By simply cropping in on the most important part, I can cut the file size down to less than 5K.

If the file needed to remain at its original size, I could try compressing it instead. *File compression* refers to the way in which data is stored or packed. Just as different people can stuff more or less clothing into a single suitcase, different compression types can pack more or less data into a file.

Specific compression methods—GIFs and JPEGs—work best for Web graphics. The next few sections of this module discuss GIFs and JPEGs, and their compression methods in further detail.

1-Minute Drill

● **How can a user's platform affect how she views a Web page?**

● **What are two ways to reduce a graphic's file size?**

File Formats

If you try to load a Windows Bitmap file (.bmp) or a Macintosh Picture File (PICT) into your Web page, users will see a broken image symbol. This occurs because graphics in Web pages must be in a format understood by the Web browser. The most popular graphics file formats recognized by Web browsers are GIF and JPEG. A newer file format called PNG is also gaining popularity because it's supported by the latest versions of Netscape and Internet Explorer.

12

● **Graphics generally look darker on a PC than they do on a Mac. Software available for your platform might not be available for others. The size and settings of the viewing device used by your visitors will alter the appearance of your graphics**

● **Reduce the actual height or width, and compress the image**

Terminology

Before you dive into the actual file types, you need to learn a few terms that relate to Web file formats.

Compression Methods

Web graphic file formats take your original image and compress it, to make it smaller for Web and e-mail delivery. Two types of compression methods are used for Web graphics.

- lossy
- lossless

Lossy compression requires data to be removed from the image to compress the file and make it smaller. The compression method attempts to remove the least important data first, to avoid making files unreadable. *Lossless* compression is the opposite of *lossy*, in that no data is lost when the file is compressed. In these cases, the actual data looks the same whether it's compressed or uncompressed.

Resolution

In a previous module, you learned about monitor resolution, but in this case I'm referring specifically to file resolution. Whenever you create or edit a file in a graphics editor, you need to specify a file resolution (see Figure 12-5). The standard file resolution for Web graphics is 72 *dots per inch* (*dpi*).

Transparency

When you view an image and are able to *see through* parts of it, that image is said to have *transparency*. Some graphics editors show this transparency by displaying a gray and white checkerboard behind the image. Figure 12-6 shows an example of this in Paint Shop Pro.

When a Web graphic contains transparency, the page's background color or background tile shows through in the transparent areas.

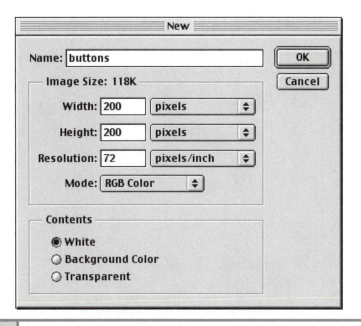

Figure 12-5 **When working with Web graphics, use a file resolution of 72 dpi**

File types that support transparency fall into two categories: binary and variable. *Binary transparency* means any given pixel is either transparent or opaque. *Variable transparency*, also known as *alpha channel,* allows pixels to be partially transparent or partially opaque and, therefore, is capable of creating subtle gradations.

Certain file types don't support transparency. If the image shown in Figure 12-6 were to be saved in a file format not supporting transparency, the areas shown in a checkerboard would be filled in with a solid color.

12

Figure 12-6 When a file with transparency is displayed in Paint Shop Pro, you can see a gray and white checkerboard in the transparent areas of the image

Interlacing

Have you ever viewed a Web page and noticed that a Web graphic first appeared blocky or fuzzy before becoming less blocky and crisp? *Interlacing* is a process where the graphic is displayed at multiple levels of clarity, from blurry to clear.

When an interlaced JPEG is loaded in the browser, it first appears blotchy and blurry

Once it is fully loaded, the blurriness disappears

Noninterlaced images must be fully loaded before the browser displays them on a page. If you have a large image on a page, users may see only blank space if the graphic takes a while to download. If it takes too long, users may leave.

Because interlaced graphics appear more quickly, even if they appear fuzzy, users might be more willing to wait for the page to download fully. Ultimately, the choice in using interlaced or noninterlaced graphics depends on the size and style of the graphics on your page. I generally use interlacing for larger graphics that take up more space on the screen, as opposed to small buttons or icons that load quickly anyway.

Animation

Some Web file formats support animation as well as still images. These animation files contain two or more individual files called *animation frames*. The following illustration shows three frames of an animation. Notice the position of the rattle changes slightly from frame to frame.

12

When the file is played back through the browser, viewers watch the various frames of the animation appear, one after the other. The rate at which the frames change can vary between a speedy filmstrip and a slowly blinking button. In the preceding example, the rattle appears to shake.

GIF

GIF is the acronym for *graphic interchange format*. Originally designed for online use in the 1980s, GIF uses a compression method that is well suited to certain types of Web graphics. This method, called *LZW compression,* is lossless and doesn't cause a loss of file data. However, several characteristics of GIFs restrict the type of files capable of being saved as GIFs. Table 12-2 lists these and other characteristics of the GIF file type.

Note

According to its creator, GIF is officially pronounced with a soft *g*. Because the word is an acronym, though, many people pronounce it with a hard *g*.

Because of these characteristics, the following types of images lend themselves to being saved as GIFs. Notice all of these are limited in colors.

Characteristic	Description
Color Mode	Restricted to no more than 256 exact colors (8-bit)
Comprehension Method	Lossless
Animation	Supported
Transparency	Supported (binary only)
Interlacing	Supported

Table 12-2   **GIF File Format Characteristics**

Tip

The *g* in GIF gives you a hint about what types of images are best saved as GIFs: graphics.

- text

- line drawings

- cartoons

- flat–color graphics

Ask the Expert

Question: I noticed photographs aren't on this list. I've seen plenty of photographs used on Web pages—can't they be saved as GIFs?

Answer: Images with photographic content shouldn't usually be saved as GIFs, unless they're part of an animation or require transparency. Other file types are more capable of compressing photographs. In fact, the JPEG file format was created specifically for photographs and shouldn't be used for other types of images like flat-color graphics and text.

12

Saving a GIF

When you save a file as a GIF in a graphics program, look for it to be called GIF, GIF87, GIF89, GIF89a, or even CompuServe GIF. In most cases, any of these options will work. If your file includes transparency or animation, use GIF89 or GIF89a.

You have the option of saving your image with or without dithering. GIF color palettes only have a limited number of colors and, the fewer colors present, the smaller the file size. When you want to reduce the number of colors in the palette, the program must know what to do with the areas in your image that contain the colors you're removing.

Note

You may recall the term "dithering" from Module 3, where it was discussed in reference to Web-safe colors.

If you tell the program to use dithering (you can specify an amount of dithering between 0 and 100 percent), it may use multiple colors in a checkerboard pattern in those areas to give the appearance of the color you removed. If no dithering is used, the removed colors are replaced with another solid color (see Figure 12-7). Dithering can be useful to give the appearance of gradations or subtle color shifts but, be forewarned, it adds to the file size.

Hint

Few images actually need all 256 colors available in a GIF color palette. Try reducing the number of colors all the way down to 8 or 16, and work your way back up as high as you need to go to make the image look acceptable. This assures that you reach the minimum colors more easily than if you try to work from the most colors on down. Remember, the fewer colors in the palette, the smaller the file size.

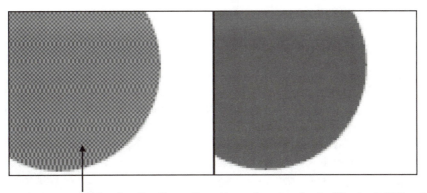

This checkerboard pattern is a typical effect of dithering

| **Figure 12-7** | In this example, the graphic on the left is dithered, while the graphic on the right is not |

JPEG

The *JPEG* file format (pronounced *jay-peg*) was created by the *Joint Photographers Expert Group*, seeking to create a format more suitable for compressing photographic imagery. After reading Table 12-3, review Table 12-2 to compare JPEG's characteristics with those of GIFs.

Characteristic	**Description**
Color Mode	Displayed in 24-bit color, also called *millions of colors*. If the user's monitor isn't set to view 24-bit color, the file is displayed with as many colors as are available
Compression Method	Lossy
Animation	Not Supported
Transparency	Not Supported
Interlacing	Supported as *Progressive* JPEGs

| **Table 12-3** | **JPEG File Format Characteristics** |

12

One major difference between GIFs and JPEGs is JPEGs don't contain an exact set of colors. When you save a photograph as a JPEG, you might consider all the colors in the file to be *recommended*, because the lossy compression might require some colors to be altered. In addition, all Web JPEG files must be in the RGB (Red, Green, Blue) color mode, as opposed to the print standard—CMYK (Cyan, Magenta, Yellow, Black).

Saving a JPEG

When you save an image as a JPEG, you choose between several different quality levels. The highest quality JPEG has the least amount of compression and, therefore, the least amount of data removed. The lowest quality JPEG has the most amount of data removed and often looks blotchy, blurry, and rough. I usually save JPEG images with a medium quality. The decision is made based on how low in quality you can go without compromising the integrity of the file: the lower the quality level, the lower the file size.

Tip

Don't bother making your JPEGs Web-safe. Not only will they look terrible but, because you can't specify exact colors in the JPEG file format, the Web-safe colors will quickly become un-Web-safe.

PNG

PNG, which stands for *Portable Network Graphics* and is pronounced *ping*, is the newest and most flexible of these three graphics file formats. After looking at the list of characteristics for PNG in Table 12-4, you might think of PNG as being the best of both the GIF and JPEG formats.

Characteristic	Description
Color Mode	Can be stored in 8-bit, 24-bit, or 32-bit
Comprehension Method	Lossless
Animation	Not supported
Transparency	Supported (Variable/Alpha)
Interlacing	Supported (Two-dimensional)

Table 12-4 PNG File Format Characteristics

Tip

32-bit color is similar to 24-bit color because it also has millions of colors. However, 32-bit color also has a masking channel, which can be used for alpha transparency.

Note

You can check to see which browsers currently support PNG graphics at **www.libpng.org/pub/png/pngapbr.html.**

An additional benefit of PNG is its gamma correction. The PNG file format has the capability to correct for differences in how computers and monitors interpret color values. While all these characteristics make PNG well suited for almost any type of Web graphic, only some of the newest browsers support it. Unfortunately, this means users of older browsers must download a plug-in to view Web graphics saved in the PNG format.

Saving a PNG

When saving a file as a PNG, you must first choose how many colors to include in its palette. Saving as a PNG-8 uses an exact palette of 256 colors or less. Transparency and dithering are available in the PNG-8 setting. PNG-24 and PNG-32 offer 24-bit (millions) and 32-bit (millions, plus an alpha channel) color modes, respectively.

Choosing the Best File Format for the Job

Now that you know a little about the different Web graphics file formats, you're probably wondering how you might select the best format for the job. While I wish I could give you a foolproof method, the answer, ultimately, lies in your own testing.

Luckily, many of the popular graphics programs make this testing easy. For example, Photoshop and Fireworks enable you to compare how a single image might look when saved in any of these file formats.

12

Tip

If the graphics program you're using doesn't allow you to compare and preview file types, save several different versions of the same file and preview each one in a browser. Compare their file size (download speed) and appearance to determine which file type and settings are the best.

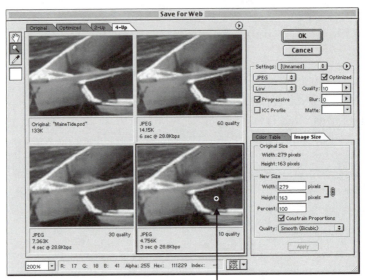

When magnified to 200 percent, you can better see how the lower quality affects the image

In the preceding example, I used Photoshop's Save for Web feature to compare three different quality levels for the JPEG file format. The settings and file sizes are printed below each example to help decide which would work the best.

Choosing the best file format is like shopping—you are looking for the file format that looks the best, but costs the least. In this case, the cost comes in download time for Web page visitors.

Project 12-1: Saving Web Graphics

Designers often receive images for Web pages on disc, via e-mail, or even in printed format. On receipt of these files, you need to put them in a Web-ready format by saving them as GIFs, JPEGs, or PNGs.

If you have a graphics program, this project gives you a chance to practice saving different types of images in the appropriate Web file format. If you don't already have a graphics program, you might visit the Web sites listed in the beginning of this module to download trial copies or demo versions. Goals for this project include

● Save a photograph in an appropriate Web file format

● Save an illustration in an appropriate Web file format

Note, all the files needed to complete the projects in this book for the Woolwich Historical Society can be downloaded from the Osborne Web site (**www.osborne.com**). In addition, you can view my version of the Web site anytime by visiting **www.woolwichhistory.org.** Those of you who aren't using the Woolwich Historical Society can tailor the project to your particular needs.

Step-by-Step

1. Open your graphics editor and load the file called `spinning.tif` from the Module 12 folder.

2. Determine which file format is the most appropriate for this image, using any of the following techniques. If needed, keep track of your progress by entering each file's setting in the following table. The first two rows give examples of how the table might be used.

● Review the guidelines in this module.

● If available, use the program's preview and compare features.

● Save multiple versions of the file, using different settings in each one, and view them in a Web browser.

3. Repeat this process for `1775events.tif`, also found in the Module 12 folder.

12

File Name	File Type	Colors	Interlaced	Dithered	Quality	File Size
spinning.gif	GIF	128	Yes	100%	--	53kB
spinning.jpg	JPEG	--	Yes	--	Medium (50%)	16kB

4. Open your Web browser and choose FILE | OPEN PAGE (or OPEN FILE or OPEN, depending on the browser you're using). Locate the graphics you just saved. Make sure the image appears as you intended.

5. If you need to make changes, return to your graphics editor to make changes. After making any changes, save the file and switch back to the browser. Choose REFRESH or RELOAD to preview the changes you just made.

Tip

Do you see broken image symbols instead of your images? Make sure the filenames end in a three-letter extension (such as .gif or .jpg). If they don't, go back to your graphics editor and resave or reexport the file as a GIF, JPEG, or PNG. For more tips, see Resource C: Troubleshooting.

Summary

Creating your own Web graphics can be a great way to add your own personal style to your Web pages. This project gave you a chance to practice saving files in formats viewable on the Web.

Note

For extra practice, try processing any of the additional files found in the Module 12 folder and including them in a Web page. Then, embed the graphics you just saved into any of the Woolwich Historical Society pages you already created.

☑ *Mastery Check*

1. Fill in the blank: Colors usually appear _____ on a PC than on a Mac.

2. When designing for 640 by 480 screen resolutions, what is the largest width the page's graphics should be?

3. How many colors can a GIF contain?

4. What term is used to classify the type of compression JPEG uses?

5. Fill in the blank: Selecting the best file format for an image is a balance between aesthetics (how good the file looks) and _____.

Learning More

This module barely touched the surface of creating your own Web graphics. If you found this is something you are interested in, I encourage you to consider any of the following sources of additional information.

- **Lynda Weinman.**   Lynda was my teacher at Art Center College of Design, where she also became my friend and respected colleague. She is a renowned expert on the subject of Web graphics, having written many excellent books on the subject. Lynda produces training videos and an informational Web site, in addition to running her own courses on the subject in Ojai, California. Visit **www.lynda.com** for more information on any of Lynda's endeavors.

- **Jakob Nielsen.**   Mr. Nielsen is an expert in Web site usability, particularly helping developers create Web sites that work. His book, *Designing Web Site Usability: The Practice of Simplicity*, is a must-read for

12

anyone creating Web sites. His Web site, **www.useit.com**, offers additional information about creating useable information technology.

● **WebReview.** This online magazine, located at **www.webreview.com**, is chock full of tips, techniques, and advice for Web developers. Topics include Web Authoring (HTML, JavaScript, and so forth), Design (Graphics, Fonts, and so forth), Developing (Databases, Perl, and so forth), E-Commerce, Multimedia, and Backend (Networks, Security, and so forth).

● **iGeneration.** This company's mission is to "close the Internet skills' gap by empowering a new generation to dream, architect, and build the Internet era." What this means to you is it will asses your skills, and then help you find training, get certified, and land a job working in the Internet industry. Visit **www.igeneration.com** to begin the process or to learn more.

● For an updated list of resources, visit my Web site: **www.willardesigns.com/resources**.

Module 13

Web Content

Goals

- Understand ways to ensure onscreen readability of text
- Recognize effective links
- Understand the issues involved in offering printer-friendly pages

Because the bulk of the information available on the Internet is in text format, you must take care to ensure users can locate and view this information in the quickest and most efficient manner possible. This module takes an introductory look at ways to do just that.

Ensuring Onscreen Readability

Reading extensive amounts of text on a screen is not only difficult on the eyes, it's also tiresome and inconvenient. Even so, many people use the same text content written for the printed page on their Web sites. This repurposing of content detracts from a company's overall identify and can make reading the Web site content quite difficult.

To make things easier on Web readers, try following these guidelines.

Tip

In an article entitled "Writing for the Web," usability expert Jakob Nielsen instructs, "write no more than 50 percent of the text you would have used in a hardcopy publication" (**www.useit.com/alertbox/9703b.html**).

1. **Keep it short and concise.** Chances are good that most Web readers won't last through more than a few screens of text on a Web page. If you have a long article that needs to be made available to Web surfers, try breaking it in to several pages to avoid the super-long-page-scroll. Remember, you only have a few seconds to grab a user's attention, and long-winded "speeches" (even if they're on the Web) rarely work.

2. **Separate paragraphs with blank lines.** On the printed page, paragraphs are designated by an indent of the first sentence in each paragraph. On the screen, such paragraphs seem to run together. For easier onscreen reading, use paragraph tags (<p>) to leave a blank line in between paragraphs.

3. **Limit column widths.** Ever wonder why newspaper columns are so short? One reason is it eases and speeds reading for the viewer. The same is true online, so be wary of 500-pixel wide columns. I like to stay between 200–400 pixels.

4. Avoid underlining. On the Web, underlined text signifies a link. When you use the u tag to give nonlinked text an underline, it's confusing to users.

5. When centering text, use moderation. Avoid centering a whole section or paragraph of text because more than a line or two of centered text is difficult to follow.

6. Do place emphasis on important text, but don't overemphasize. While the b and i tags draw attention to important text, you can easily overdo it by bolding too much.

7. Avoid using all capital letters. Consider which is used more on street and highway signs: all caps or a mix of lowercase and capital letters. You rarely see all caps used on street signs because it's much easier to read words with a mix of uppercase and lowercase letters. In addition, the use of all capital letters is considered "screaming" in online communication.

8. Use lists and group related information. Lists improve the "scannablity" of your page, making them easier to scan quickly in search of particular information. Headlines can also help differentiate between sections and offer users quick insight on the section's content.

9. Place the most important information at the top of the page. If users have to scroll for it, you may lose them. Avoid pages that are too busy by limiting paragraphs to one main idea and pages to no more than seven main options or thoughts.

10. Make information easy to find. Most studies show users don't click more than three times on a Web site to try to find the information they want. Avoid burying content more than three levels deep, if you expect anyone to find it. And, if you have a search engine on your site (which you should have if your site contains more than 100 pages), take care to ensure the titles of each page are descriptive.

Overall, remember most people scan Web pages, as opposed to read them. When you create a Web page, put it away for a day or two and then look at it from a user's standpoint. If you had no idea what the purpose of the page was because you just stumbled on it, would you be

13

able to pick out the main point(s) within ten seconds? If not, you might want to rework the content.

Or, ask a friend to look at the page and identify the first, second, and third things that pop out. If those three things aren't the most important things on the page, perhaps you need to reevaluate the page.

Creating Effective Links

The Web is all about links. If users cannot find the links on your page and successfully use them, that linked content might as well be deleted. One of the problems with so many Web pages is what's commonly referred to as the "click here syndrome."

Discussed briefly in Module 5, this occurs when the phrase *click here* is used as a link's label text. Consider the following example:

Woolwich is a rural community on the east shore of the Kennebec River, opposite the historic city of Bath and approximately 12 miles from the Atlantic Ocean. First settled in the 1600s and incorporated in 1759, the town is named for Woolwich, England, which in like manner is situated on a large, navigable river. (Click here for information about Woolwich, England.)

The words *click here* were underlined in the preceding example, but don't shed any light on exactly what you would find if you clicked that link. A better example might be:

Woolwich is a rural community on the east shore of the Kennebec River, opposite the historic city of Bath and approximately 12 miles from the Atlantic Ocean. First settled in the 1600s and incorporated in 1759, the town is named for Woolwich, England, which in like manner is situated on a large, navigable river.

Now, when you scan the paragraph, the words *Woolwich, England* jump out and you know more information about that place can be found by clicking the linked words.

Another common pitfall is using entire sentences as link labels. Compare the two links in the next paragraph. The shorter link at the end is easier to spot because you have to read the entire first sentence to understand the content of the link.

Woolwich is a rural community on the <u>east shore of the Kennebec River, opposite the historic city of Bath and approximately 12 miles from the Atlantic Ocean</u>. First settled in the 1600s and incorporated in 1759, the town is named for Woolwich, England, which in like manner is situated on a <u>large, navigable river</u>.

If you needed to place multiple links within a paragraph of text, it might be better to convert the paragraph into a list, where each link is at the beginning of the list item.

Woolwich is a rural Maine community on the east shore of the Kennebec River.

- <u>Historic Bath</u> is located opposite Woolwich
- <u>Atlantic Ocean</u> is approximately 12 miles down river
- <u>First settled</u> in the 1600s
- <u>Incorporated</u> in 1759
- <u>Woolwich, England</u>, gives the town its name

To summarize, it's important to scan over your Web pages from the user's prospective to determine if your links are easy to spot and use. Short, meaningful words and phrases work better than lengthy marketing jargon.

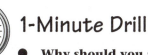

1-Minute Drill

- **Why should you avoid underlining text in a Web page?**
- **Using lists can help the _____ of your pages.**

- **Because users may confuse it with linked text**
- **Scannability**

Offering Printer-friendly Pages

Even though many people use electronic documents to avoid having reams of paper on their desks, plenty of us still print lots of pages from the Web. The fact of the matter is we are more likely to read long articles of text if it's printed. The problem with this is most Web pages were not created to be printed and, as such, don't print well.

A solution to this problem is to enable users to download postscript versions of the documents. A *postscript* file, in contrast to an HTML file, was created with a printer in mind and contains specific instructions on how the file should be printed. Different types of postscript files can be created from all kinds of software titles, regardless of the computer platform.

For example, Adobe's *Portable Document Format* (*PDF*) enables you to take any file from another program (such as Microsoft Publisher or Adobe PageMaker) and save it in a universally recognizable file format, characterized by the .pdf file extension. Adobe PDF has become a standard in electronic document delivery because of its ease of use, reliability, and stability.

Unlike HTML pages, which look different depending on the browser and computer system, PDF files look the same across different platforms, even when printed. This makes it easy to distribute documents, such as your company's annual report or newsletter.

Tip

Some programs are automatically able to save as PDF. Check with your page layout or publishing program's manual before purchasing Adobe Acrobat.

To save files in the PDF format, you must have the Adobe Acrobat software loaded on your system. Once you do, it's only a matter of selecting a few menu items before the file is converted to the PDF format.

To view PDF files, you must have the Adobe Acrobat Reader installed on your system. This free utility is available from Adobe's Web site. Even if you've never downloaded the Reader, you may already have it because it's included with many other software titles and computer systems. If you do include a link to a PDF file on your Web page, remember also to tell users what is needed to view the file and where to download the Reader.

Note

Visit **www.adobe.com/products/acrobat/readermain.html** to download the free Acrobat Reader.

Because users must have the reader to view a PDF, avoid using PDFs as the only means for electronically delivering important information. Whenever possible, it's good to have both an HTML version—for online viewing—and a PDF version—for printing—of important documents.

Whenever you create pages that will be printed, remember these things:

- **Page Size.** Whereas Web pages are designed for screen format (landscape, 640 × 480 pixels, and so forth), printed pages should be designed for the paper on which they will be printed. Most users in the U.S. will probably print in portrait format on standard letter-size paper (8.5" by 11"). Be sure to leave at least a 1/2" margin on all sides.

- **Color.** Avoid dark background colors on printed pages. Many browsers don't print background colors anyway, so someone might end up with light-colored text on white paper and have trouble reading anything. Remember, many people have black and white printers as opposed to color, so printed documents should be readable in both formats.

- **Reference.** Always include the Web page address (URL) on a printed page, so users can return to the page for more information as needed.

Project 13-1: Optimizing Text Content

Every Web page can use an edit or two to verify the content is optimized for online reading (or scanning). This project asks you to perform such an edit on the home page created for the Woolwich Historical Society. The goal for this project is

- Edit a page of text content for online readability

13

Note: All the files needed to complete the projects in this book for the Woolwich Historical Society can be downloaded from **www.osborne.com** or **www.willardesigns.com/htmlbook**. In addition, you can view my version of the Web site anytime by visiting **www.woolwichhistory.org.** Those of you who aren't using the Woolwich Historical Society can tailor the project to your particular needs.

Step-by-Step

1. Open your text editor (SimpleText on the Mac or Notepad on the PC) and load the home page used in previous projects entitled `index.html`.

2. Using the guidelines from this module, edit the page for online readability. To begin, scan the page from a user's standpoint to determine the most important information and how it is portrayed.

3. Check to make sure any links are clear and concise.

4. Feel free to delete repetitive information or to move content to any of other pages you created as you see fit.

5. Save the file.

6. Open your Web browser and choose FILE I OPEN PAGE (or OPEN FILE or OPEN, depending on the browser you are using). Locate the file `index.html` you just saved. Quickly scan the page as a Web surfer would do make sure the file appears as you intended it.

7. If you need to make changes, return to your text editor to make changes. After making any changes, save the file and switch back to the browser. Choose REFRESH or RELOAD to preview the changes you just made.

8. Compare your pages with Figures 13-1 and 13-2 to see how a thorough edit for Web-readability can make a big difference.

Summary

Given how little time most of us spend viewing many Web sites, editing text content for online readability is an important skill for anyone maintaining a Web site. This project gave you a chance to work on this skill using a page of unedited content from the Woolwich Historical Society.

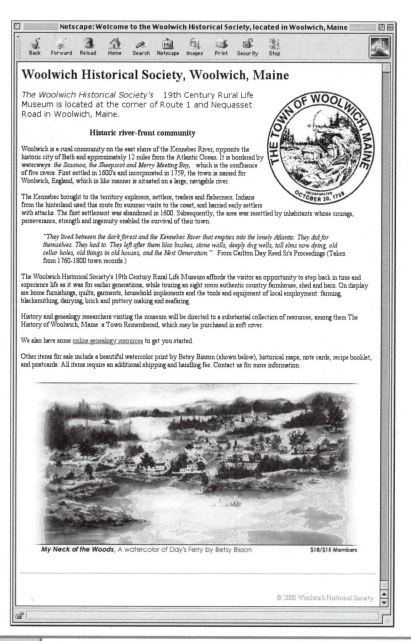

The image contains a Netscape browser window with the title bar: "Netscape: Welcome to the Woolwich Historical Society, located in Woolwich, Maine"

Browser toolbar buttons: Back, Forward, Reload, Home, Search, Netscape, Images, Print, Security, Stop

Woolwich Historical Society, Woolwich, Maine

The Woolwich Historical Society's 19th Century Rural Life Museum is located at the corner of Route 1 and Nequasset Road in Woolwich, Maine.

Historic river-front community

Woolwich is a rural community on the east shore of the Kennebec River, opposite the historic city of Bath and approximately 12 miles from the Atlantic Ocean. It is bordered by waterways: *the Sasanoa, the Sheepscot and Merry Meeting Bay,* which is the confluence of five rivers. First settled in 1600's and incorporated in 1759, the town is named for Woolwich, England, which in like manner is situated on a large, navigable river.

The Kennebec brought to the territory explorers, settlers, traders and fishermen. Indians from the hinterland used this route for summer visits to the coast, and harried early settlers with attacks. The first settlement was abandoned in 1600. Subsequently, the area was resettled by inhabitants whose courage, perseverance, strength and ingenuity enabled the survival of their town.

"They lived between the dark forest and the Kennebec River that empties into the lonely Atlantic. They did for themselves. They had to. They left after them lilac bushes, stone walls, deeply dug wells, tall elms now dying, old cellar holes, old things in old houses, and the Next Generation." From Carlton Day Reed Sr's Proceedings (Taken from 1760-1800 town records.)

The Woolwich Historical Society's 19th Century Rural Life Museum affords the visitor an opportunity to step back in time and experience life as it was for earlier generations, while touring an eight room authentic country farmhouse, shed and barn. On display are home furnishings, quilts, garments, household implements and the tools and equipment of local employment: farming, blacksmithing, dairying, brick and pottery making and seafaring.

History and genealogy researchers visiting the museum will be directed to a substantial collection of resources, among them The History of Woolwich, Maine: a Town Remembered, which may be purchased in soft cover.

We also have some online genealogy resources to get you started.

Other items for sale include a beautiful watercolor print by Betsy Bisson (shown below), historical maps, note cards, recipe booklet, and postcards. All items require an additional shipping and handling fee. Contact us for more information.

My Neck of the Woods, A watercolor of Day's Ferry by Betsy Bisson $18/$15 Members

© 2000 Woolwich Historical Society

13

Figure 13-1   This screen shows the index.html page before I edited it

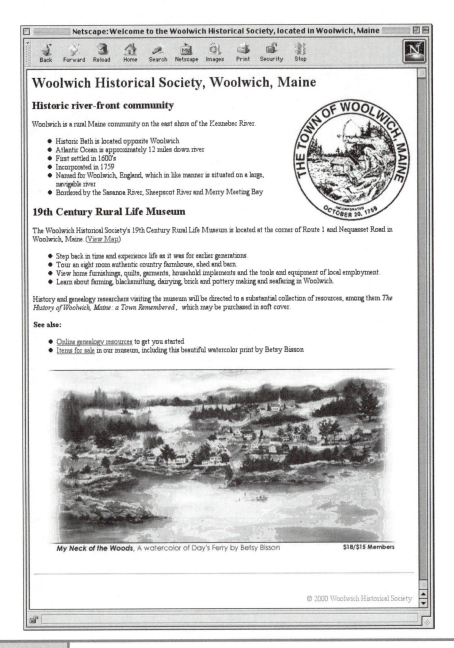

Netscape: Welcome to the Woolwich Historical Society, located in Woolwich, Maine

Woolwich Historical Society, Woolwich, Maine

Historic river-front community

Woolwich is a rural Maine community on the east shore of the Kennebec River.

- Historic Bath is located opposite Woolwich
- Atlantic Ocean is approximately 12 miles down river
- First settled in 1600's
- Incorporated in 1759
- Named for Woolwich, England, which in like manner is situated on a large, navigable river
- Bordered by the Sasanoa River, Sheepscot River and Merry Meeting Bay

19th Century Rural Life Museum

The Woolwich Historical Society's 19th Century Rural Life Museum is located at the corner of Route 1 and Nequasset Road in Woolwich, Maine. (View Map)

- Step back in time and experience life as it was for earlier generations.
- Tour an eight room authentic country farmhouse, shed and barn.
- View home furnishings, quilts, garments, household implements and the tools and equipment of local employment.
- Learn about farming, blacksmithing, dairying, brick and pottery making and seafaring in Woolwich.

History and genealogy researchers visiting the museum will be directed to a substantial collection of resources, among them *The History of Woolwich, Maine: a Town Remembered*, which may be purchased in soft cover.

See also:

- Online genealogy resources to get you started
- Items for sale in our museum, including this beautiful watercolor print by Betsy Bisson

My Neck of the Woods, A watercolor of Day's Ferry by Betsy Bisson $18/$15 Members

© 2000 Woolwich Historical Society

Figure 13-2   After an edit for Web–readability, the page can more easily be scanned by busy Web surfers

☑ Mastery Check

1. How do most people "read" Web pages?

2. Where should the most important information on a Web page be?

3. Give two characteristics of effective and usable link labels.

4. Fill in the blank: A postscript file is one that contains instructions for _____ the file.

5. Name three things to consider when designing a printable version of a Web page.

Learning More

This module introduced you to the topic of writing for the Web, which has recently become a hot subject. Whole courses have sprung up at colleges and universities on this topic. If you've found this is something you're interested in, I encourage you to consider any of the following sources of additional information.

- **Jakob Nielsen.** Mr. Nielsen is an expert in Web site usability, particularly in helping developers create Web sites that work. His book, *Designing Web Site Usability: The Practice of Simplicity*, is a must-read for anyone creating Web sites. Mr. Nielsen's Web site, **www.useit.com,** offers additional information about creating useable information technology.

- **usableweb.com.** This Web site is a collection of links about human factors, user interface issues, and usable design specific to the Web. In particular, visit **usableweb.com/topics/001310-0-0.html** for links to articles about writing content for the Web.

- For an updated list of resources, visit my Web site at **www.willardesigns.com/resources**

13

Module 14

JavaScript

Goals

- Understand the concept and uses of JavaScript in Web pages
- Use and modify an example JavaScript in a Web page

While HTML enables you to create static, or unchanging Web pages, JavaScript extends the capabilities of HTML, enabling you to create dynamic pages, which either change or react to users' input. This module is not meant to teach you to be a JavaScript programmer, but rather to help you use it in simple formats in your pages.

To that end, this module gives a brief introduction into the how and why of JavaScript, and then focuses on the presentation of four typical examples of using JavaScript in a Web page. If this whets your appetite for JavaScript and you what to learn more, don't miss the great additional resources listed at the end of the module.

Understanding JavaScript

Contrary to what its name implies, JavaScript is not the same as Java. Sun Microsystems created the Java programming language, while Netscape developed JavaScript. Unlike Java, which can run on its own as a mini application, *JavaScript* is built into Web browsers and cannot stand on its own. Essentially, it's just a set of statements, or scripts, that are instructions for the browser.

Note

JavaScript is not supported by all Web browsers. In addition, users can turn off support for JavaScript from within their personal browser. This means you should use caution when relying on JavaScript to transfer important information to users.

When you write JavaScript, it's actually placed right within the HTML on your page. This means you can learn JavaScript from your favorite Web sites, just like you can with HTML, by viewing the HTML source from within the browser.

But, before you can do that, you have to know what JavaScript *looks* like and where to look for it. Here's a basic example:

This is JavaScript code

```
<html>
<head>
    <title>My Web Page</title>
<script language="JavaScript" type="text/javascript">
    document.write("I can write JavaScript!");
</script>
</head>
<body>
```

These attributes and values tell the browser everything inside this tag is JavaScript.

This closing tag is required, so the browser knows when to stop treating the code as JavaScript and to return to HTML

Most scripts fall between the opening and closing **head** tags

A semicolon is used to designate the end of a command or statement

The opening and closing `script` tags are HTML, while everything in between them is written in JavaScript. This is an important distinction because JavaScript is quite different than HTML in several ways:

1. JavaScript is case-sensitive; HTML is not.

2. In JavaScript, quotes are required; in HTML quotes are optional.

3. JavaScript has a distinct format that must be adhered to; HTML is forgiving about spacing and formatting.

Tip

These JavaScript restrictions might remind you of XHTML, which is also case-sensitive, requires quotes, and does adhere to more of a format than HTML.

Given those restrictions, troubleshooting JavaScript can be a bit tricky. Whenever you copy a script from a Web site or a book, be sure to copy it exactly as it is written, unless otherwise specified. For example, placing a line break in the middle of the previous example could produce an error when the page is viewed in a browser.

```
<script language="JavaScript" type="text/javascript">
    document.write("I can write JavaScript!
");
</script>
```

This misplaced line break can cause browsers to display an error when the page is viewed

14

Troubleshooting JavaScript

Netscape offers a great way to troubleshoot your JavaScript. Type `javascript:` into the GO TO: location box in the browser and a console pops up with error information (if any errors exist).

You can use this console to view errors on your pages or even to test strings of code. For example, in Figure 14-1, you can see how I typed a string of JavaScript into the console that was producing an error when viewed in the browser. After I clicked the Enter or Return button on my keyboard, the browser displayed the exact error in the frame above. In this case, it pointed to the first quotation mark to remind me that I started a quotation, but never ended it.

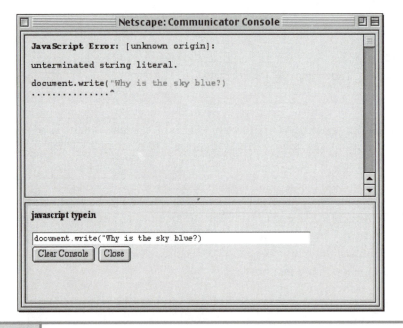

Figure 14-1   Netscape's Console helps you troubleshoot JavaScript errors

Likewise, when a page displays with errors in Internet Explorer, you should see a statement such as the following at the bottom of the browser window.

⚠ Done, but with errors on page.

Clicking the icon to the left of the statement causes a smaller window to open, which contains information about the error(s).

Hiding Scripts

If you look at a few JavaScripts on the Web, you may notice many look like they are actually commented out in the HTML.

| This is the HTML code used to begin a comment |

```
<script language="JavaScript" type="text/javascript">
<!-- This hides the script from older browsers
    document.write("I can write JavaScript!");
// This stops hiding the script from older browsers -->
</script>
```

| This is JavaScript's way of adding a comment. Without these double slashes before the closing HTML comment code (-->), the browser may become confused |

| This is the HTML code used to end a comment |

This is done so older browsers that aren't capable of understanding JavaScript will simply skip over the script and not produce any errors.

Terminology

You should learn several new terms before you use any JavaScript. Here are the most common.

Note

Many Web sites and books contain the official JavaScript specifications. Refer to the "Learning More" section at the end of this module for details.

14

Objects & Methods

To understand these terms, let's first look back at the previous example and identify the pieces.

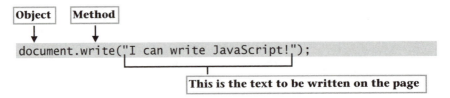

In this example, `document` is acting a JavaScript object. Quite simply, an *object* is any thing that can be manipulated or changed by the script. In this case, the object `document` tells the browser the code directly following it is referring to the HTML document itself.

Objects can have *methods*, which are actual things that happen to the objects (in this case, a document is written to). Methods are followed by a set of parentheses, containing any specific instructions on how to accomplish the method. In the previous example, the text inside the parentheses is written within the current document.

Properties

Just as an object, such as a car, has features (tires, brakes, and so forth) in the real world, JavaScript objects can have *properties*. This is useful if, for example, you want to manipulate a specific section of a document. Objects and properties are separated by periods. When you want to specify the *value* of a property, such as the color of the background, you add the value after the property, as in the following example.

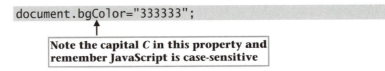

Note

An object can even have a property that is, in itself, another object. For example, `document.location.href` includes a `document` object, its `location` (an object itself and a property of `document`), and an `href` (property of `location`).

Variables, Operators, & Functions

In JavaScript, a *variable* is something you specify for your own needs. You might think of variables as labels for changeable values used within a single script. To define a variable, type `var`, followed by the one-word name of the variable.

Tip

Remember, JavaScript is case-sensitive. If you capitalize a letter when you first define a variable, you must also capitalize that letter every time you refer to it.

```
var VotingAge;
```

An *operator* does something, such as a calculation or a comparison between two or more variables. The symbols used to do this (listed in Table 14-1) should look familiar because they are also used in simple mathematics. One place you can use operators is in defining values of variables, as in the following example:

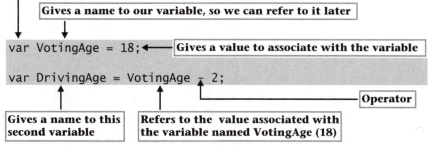

Tells the browser we are defining a variable

Gives a name to our variable, so we can refer to it later

```
var VotingAge = 18;
```
Gives a value to associate with the variable

```
var DrivingAge = VotingAge - 2;
```
Operator

Gives a name to this second variable

Refers to the value associated with the variable named VotingAge (18)

Likewise, a *function* is a group of commands to which you give a name, so you can refer to the group later in the page. To create a function, type `function`, followed by the function name and a set of parentheses. Then, type the commands that are part of the function below the name and enclosed in curly brackets. This is shown in the following example.

```
function functionName()
    { commands go here
}
```

14

Operator	Description	Operator	Description
+	Adds	-	Subtracts
*	Multiplies	/	Divides
++	Adds one	--	Subtracts one
=	Sets value	==	Is equal to
<	Less than	>	Greater than
<=	Less than or equal to	>=	Greater than or equal to
!=	Is not equal to	||	Or
&&	And		

Table 14-1 **JavaScript Operators**

You can't use just any name for a variable or a function because there's a list of reserved words that have a special meaning in either JavaScript or Java. If you use one of these words (shown in Table 14-2) as a function or a variable, users may encounter errors when viewing your pages.

abstract	break	boolean	byte
case	char	comment	continue
default	delete	do	double
else	export	false	final
float	for	function	goto
if	implements	import	instanceOf
in	int	interface	label
long	native	new	null
package	private	protected	public
return	switch	this	typeof
synchronized	this	throws	transient
true	typeof	var	void
while	with		

Table 14-2 **Reserved JavaScript Words**

Event Handlers

Different from other terms discussed here, *event handlers* needn't be placed within the opening and closing `script` tags. These pieces of JavaScript can actually be embedded within HTML to respond to a user's interaction and make a page dynamic. For example, placing the event handler `onClick` within an `a` tag causes the event to occur when the user clicks the link. So, if I wanted to change the page's background color when a link was clicked, I could use the following code.

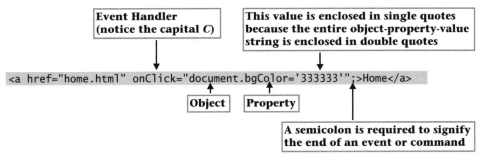

Table 14-3 lists popular event handlers, but more information can be found in the resources listed at the end of this module.

JavaScript Logic

Given that scripts are essentially a set of instructions to the browser, you can often read them logically as a series of commands. For example, in the following script, I am telling the browser to write one thing if the user has Netscape and something else if the user doesn't have Netscape.

> **This part of the script tells the browser to see if the browser's name is Netscape. Notice two equals signs are there**

> **This is what the browser is supposed to do if the user's browser IS Netscape**

```
<script language="JavaScript" type="text/javascript">
<!-- Begin hiding script from older browsers
if (navigator.appName == "Netscape") {
    document.write("The Magic 8-ball says: Your browser is Netscape Navigator.");
}
else {
    document.write("The Magic 8-ball says: Your browser is not Netscape Navigator.");
}
// End hiding script from older browsers -->
</script>
```

> **This is what the browser is supposed to do if the user's browser IS NOT Netscape**

14

Event Handler	Specifies Action to Occur...
onAbort	...when the user stops loading the current page.
onBlur	...when the user moves away from an object (such as a browser window).
onChange	...when the user changes an object.
onClick	...when the user clicks an object
onFocus	...when the user brings an object (such as a browser window) to the foreground.
onLoad	...when an object is fully loaded.
onMouseDown	...when the user presses the mouse button down over an object.
onMouseOver	...when the user moves the cursor over an object (such as an image or text).
onMouseOut	...when the user moves the mouse away from an object (such as an image or text).
onMouseUp	...when the user releases the mouse button after clicking an object.
onSelect	...when the user selects an object (such as a check box or another form field).
OnSubmit	...when the user submits a form.

Table 14-3   Common Event Handlers in JavaScript

These types of *if...then* statements are called *conditionals* and tell the browser to do one thing if *x* is true, and to do something else if *x* is false. Notice the actual instructions on what to do are included within curly brackets {}. The spacing here is important because the opening curly bracket should be on the same line as the `if` or `else`. The closing curly bracket is on a line by itself, after the instructions end. In addition, all statements (instructions) end with semicolons. Here's a simple example of the layout.

```
if (something) {
    do this;
}
else {
    do this;
}
```

It could also appear below, which, although less common, easily splits the conditions from each other.

```
if (something)
{
    do this;
}
else
{
    do this;
}
```

Sample Scripts

The next few sections include sample scripts for you to try in your Web pages. Remember, these are provided as examples only. They might not work in every situation. Because it's beyond the scope of this book to teach you JavaScript at the same level you've learned HTML, please refer to the additional resources at the end of this module for more help.

Adding the Current Date and Time

The most basic way to add the current date and time to a Web page is shown in the following script. Once you learn more about JavaScript, you can customize this script. For example, you might tell the browser to only print the month and day, or to print the month, day, and year in 00/00/00 format.

Place this script within the body of your Web page wherever you want the date to appear.

```
<script language="JavaScript" type="text/javascript">
<!--
    document.write(Date());
// -->
</script>
```

14

Making Required Form Fields

To avoid receiving unusable form responses, you can use JavaScript to make certain form fields required. For example, if your page included a form for posting on a bulletin board, you might want to make the comments field required so no one accidentally posts a blank message. Likewise, if you want to be able to respond to users via e-mail, you might want to make the field asking for their e-mail addresses required.

If you use this script and users don't enter any text in the required fields, the browser brings up an alert message telling them to do so before they can submit the form.

Instructions & Script

Place the JavaScript code enclosed by the `<script>` and `</script>` tags in the header of the HTML page (not in the body). Then, place the appropriate event handler in the `form` tag within the body of your HTML page. The bolded text highlights pieces of the script you should customize.

Note

Thanks to Christian DeLoach for writing this script. Christian is the Creative Director for Fishnet NewMedia (**www.ahoy.com**), one of the first Internet design, production, and software development companies to provide Web-centric new media solutions and productions. Christian joined Fishnet NewMedia in 1999, and he's primarily responsible for overseeing the design and production of client sites. Christian received a BFA degree in Illustration and Design from Syracuse University.

This names the function, so we can refer to it later

This should be the name of your form, as specified in the name attribute of the opening form tag

```
<script language="JavaScript" type="text/javascript">
<!-- Start hiding script from older browsers
function checkInput(formName) {

if (formName.yourName.value == "") {
        alert("Please enter your name");
        formName.yourName.focus();
        return false;
```

This is the text the user will see if the required field is left empty

This should be the name of the field you want to require, as specified in the input control's name attribute

This prevents the form from being submitted

```
}
// End hiding script -->
</script>
```

This `onSubmit` event handler needs to go in the opening `form` tag, and then the form needs to be named with the `name` attribute, like this:

```
<form onSubmit="return checkInput(this);" name="formName" action="processForm.cgi">
```

Then continue with the rest of the form, making sure to name each form field appropriately:

```
Your Name: <input type="text" size="20" name="yourName" /><br />
<input type="submit" value="submit" />
</form>
```

Changing Page Elements When the User Points to Them

If you've done any amount of surfing on the Web, you've probably noticed page elements sometimes change when you move the cursor over them. For example, have you ever moved your mouse over a link and found it changed color or style? Or, have you noticed a message appearing in the status bar at the bottom of the page when your mouse is pointed toward a certain image or text? These things can be accomplished using event handlers in JavaScript.

Adding a Label in the Status Window

Normally, when a user moves the mouse over a link, the link's location or URL appears in the status bar at the bottom of the browser window.

You can use JavaScript to replace that URL with a more descriptive link label if needed. Or, because some people like to use the URL to aid in the navigation of a site, you could add a link label to the URL instead of replacing it. You can see an example of this in Figure 14-2.

14

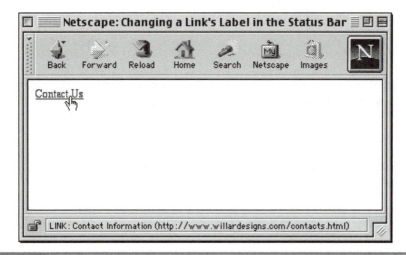

Using JavaScript, you can change the information displayed in the browser's status bar when a user moves the mouse over the link

Instructions & Script   Place the JavaScript code right within the a tag for the link. No other script is necessary to make this easy technique work. The bolded text highlights pieces of the script you should customize.

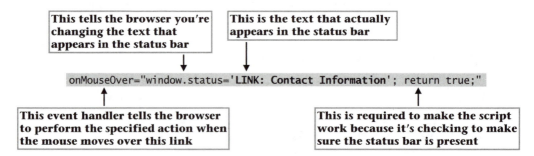

And here's an example of how the JavaScript code is placed within an a tag.

─┤Note ──────────────

If you want to have any apostrophes or quotes appear in the status bar label, you must differentiate them from the other quotes used in JavaScript by preceding them with a backslash: Here\'s a list of our favorite links!

```
<A HREF="contacts.html" onMouseOver="window.status='LINK: Contact Information';
return true;">Contact Us</A>
```

Replacing an Image

You can also use the `onMouseOver` event handler to replace an image when the mouse is moved over an image. This handler is placed within the a tag, so you can only replace an image when the user rolls over a link (either the image itself or a text link).

Because this script is a bit more involved than just changing a link's status bar label, it requires additional JavaScript in the header of the HTML page. Both the code at the top of the page and the code in the a tag must be present for the image swap to work.

You also need two versions of each image you want to change: one that's present when the page is first viewed and another for when the mouse is rolled over the image or link—and both of those versions should be the same size. Name your images so you can recognize which one should be used when. For example, the original link to a section called "camp," might be referred to as *campOff*, while the version appearing when the user rolls over it might be called *campOver*.

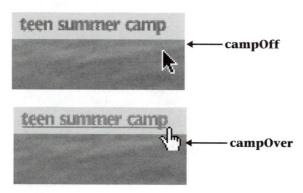

Instructions & Script Place this script in the header of your page (in between the opening and closing head tags). The bolded text highlights pieces of the script you should customize.

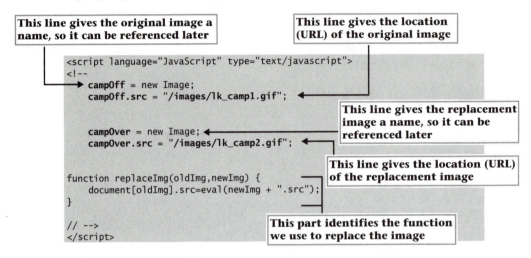

This line gives the original image a name, so it can be referenced later

This line gives the location (URL) of the original image

This line gives the replacement image a name, so it can be referenced later

This line gives the location (URL) of the replacement image

This part identifies the function we use to replace the image

```
<script language="JavaScript" type="text/javascript">
<!--
    campOff = new Image;
    campOff.src = "/images/lk_camp1.gif";


    campOver = new Image;
    campOver.src = "/images/lk_camp2.gif";

function replaceImg(oldImg,newImg) {
    document[oldImg].src=eval(newImg + ".src");
}

// -->
</script>
```

Place the onMouseOver and onMouseOut event handlers in the a tag of the link for the image that should be changed. Place the name attribute in the img tag, to identify the image to be changed.

Here's an example of how the script looks when placed within an a tag for an image:

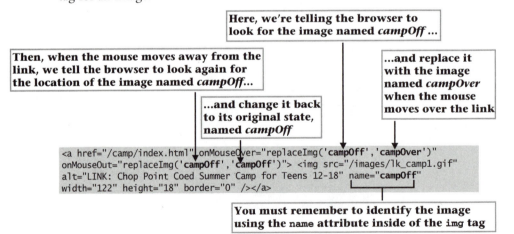

Here, we're telling the browser to look for the image named *campOff*...

Then, when the mouse moves away from the link, we tell the browser to look again for the location of the image named *campOff*...

...and replace it with the image named *campOver* when the mouse moves over the link

...and change it back to its original state, named *campOff*

```
<a href="/camp/index.html" onMouseOver="replaceImg('campOff','campOver')"
onMouseOut="replaceImg('campOff','campOff')"> <img src="/images/lk_camp1.gif"
alt="LINK: Chop Point Coed Summer Camp for Teens 12-18" name="campOff"
width="122" height="18" border="0" /></a>
```

You must remember to identify the image using the name attribute inside of the img tag

Formatting a New Window

While you learned in previous modules that you could use the target attribute to load links into another browser window, you cannot control the size and style of that browser window with HTML. Instead, you can use JavaScript to specify settings such as how large or small that window should be and whether the scroll bars are present (see Figure 14-3).

Some of the characteristics you can specify include

- `toolbar=yes` or `no` (turns the browser tool bar—Back, Stop, Reload, and so on—on or off in the new window)

- `location=yes` or `no` (turns the browser location bar on or off in the new window)

- `status=yes` or `no` (turns the browser status bar on or off in the new window)

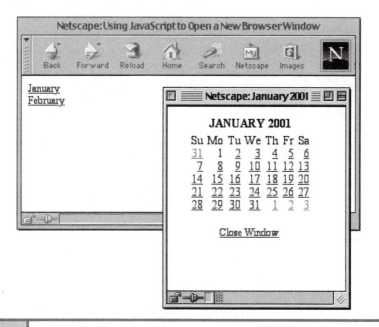

Figure 14-3   You can use JavaScript to force a link to load into a new browser window

- `menubar=yes` or `no` (turns the browser menus—File, Edit, View, and so on—on or off in the new window)

- `resizeable=yes` or `no` (specifies whether users can resize the new window)

- `scrolling=yes`, `no` or `auto` (allows or prevents scrolling, or leaves it up to the browser to decide as needed)

- `width=#` (specifies width of new window in pixels)

- `height=#` (specifies height of new window in pixels)

Instructions & Script

Place this script in the header of your page (in between the opening and closing `head` tags). The bolded text highlights pieces of the script you should customize.

> **This part identifies the function we use to open the new window, so we can reference it later**

```
<script language="JavaScript" type="text/javascript">
<!--
function NewWindow(link) {

var MonthWindow = window.open(link, 'Month', 'toolbar=no,location=no,
status=yes,menubar=no,resizable=yes,scrollbars=yes,width=200,height=200');

MonthWindow.focus();

}
// -->
</script>
```

> **This defines the characteristics of the new window. When typed in your text editor, these should be contained on a single line without any breaks**

> **This part brings the window named `MonthWindow` to the front of the screen**

Then, in the body of your page, reference the function created in the previous script from within the appropriate link. You can use the following code to load other links in the `NewWindow`, simply by changing the URL listed in the parentheses.

```
<a href="javascript:NewWindow('january.html')">January</a><br />
```

> **This tells the browser to perform the function called `NewWindow`**

> **This gives the location of the page to load in the new window**

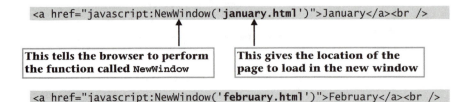

```
<a href="javascript:NewWindow('february.html')">February</a><br />
```

If you want to give users the option of closing the window easily, you can add the following code to the bottom of the page that's loaded into the new window. So, in this case, the code was added to the `january.html` and `february.html` pages. Refer to Figure 14-3 for an example.

```
<a href="javascript:window.close()">Close Window</a>
```

Project 14-1: Using JavaScript to Launch a New Browser Window

JavaScript can add much to a Web site, which wouldn't otherwise be possible with HTML. Many of the popular JavaScript techniques used on the Web make a site seem more dynamic. In this project, we use JavaScript to launch a new browser window from a link on the Woolwich, Maine Timeline. The goal for this project is to use JavaScript to launch and control a new browser window.

Note

All the files needed to complete the projects in this book for the Woolwich Historical Society can be downloaded from **www.osborne.com** or **www.willardesigns.com/htmlbook**. In addition, you can view my version of the Web site anytime by visiting **www.woolwichhistory.org**. Those of you who aren't using the Woolwich Historical Society can tailor the project to your particular needs.

Step-by-Step

1. Open the file `timeline.html` saved from Module 9 in your text editor (SimpleText on the Mac or Notepad on the PC).

2. Add the necessary JavaScript to the header of the page to set up a function for launching a new browser window.

3. Name the window `DetailsWindow`.

4. Title it '`Details`'.

5. Turn the menu bar, the status bar, the tool bar, and the location off in the new window.

6. Set the scrolling to `auto`.

14

7. Format the new window to be 300 by 300 pixels in size.

8. Create a link from the phrase *Court of Merrymeeting* in the year 1654. Using JavaScript, specify the text should link to a page called `1654-May23.html` and should open in the `DetailsWindow`.

Note

`1654-May23.html` was created for you and is located in the Module14 folder for this book on the Osborne Web site.

9. Save the file.

10. Open your Web browser and choose FILE | OPEN PAGE (or OPEN FILE or OPEN, depending on the browser you're using). Locate the file `timeline.html` you just saved. Click the link labeled *Court of Merrymeeting* to verify the linked page opens in a new browser window with the appropriate customizations.

11. If you need to make changes, return to your text editor to make changes. After making any changes, save the file and switch back to the browser. Choose REFRESH or RELOAD to preview the changes you just made.

Tip

Do you get an error or see nothing in the new browser window? Make sure the 1654-May23.html page is located in the same folder as the timeline.html page. If you receive other errors, verify your script against the following one or try using your browser's JavaScript console for troubleshooting.

```
<!DOCTYPE html PUBLIC "-//W3C//DTD XHTML 1.0 Transitional//EN"
"http://www.w3.org/TR/xhtml1/DTD/transitional.dtd">
<html>
<head>
    <title>Woolwich, Maine Historical Timeline</title>
<script language="JavaScript" type="text/javascript">
<!--
function NewWindow(link) {
    var DetailsWindow = window.open(link, 'Details', 'toolbar=no,location=no,
status=no,menubar=no,resizable=yes,scrollbars=yes,
width=300,height=300');
```

This should be one line

```
   DetailsWindow.focus();
   }
// -->
</script>
</head>
<body bgcolor="#ffffff" text="#000000">
<h1>Woolwich, Maine Historical Timeline 1639-Present*</h1>
```

. . . The code in between these two sections remains unchanged.

```
<td><a href="javascript:NewWindow('1654-May23.html')">Court of Merrymeeting</a>
- organization of laws by a committee of 15 pioneers of the territory to govern
the settlers along the Kennebec.</td>
```

. . . The rest of the page remains unchanged.

Summary

Although JavaScript isn't the same as HTML, the two can be used together to make Web pages more dynamic in nature. This project gave you a chance to practice one JavaScript technique—controlling browser windows.

Mastery Check

1. What are two ways JavaScript differs from HTML?

2. What can you type into Netscape's location bar to bring up the JavaScript troubleshooting console?

3. What's one way you can tell a JavaScript method apart from an object?

4. Fill in the blank: JavaScript is case-_____.

5. Give an example of a JavaScript event handler.

Learning More

While I didn't expect this module would teach you everything you need to know about JavaScript, I hope it gave you a basic understanding of what types of things JavaScript can do. If you'd like to learn more, many sources of additional information are available on this topic. Here are some of the most popular.

Online References & Scripts

- **Doc JavaScript—www.webreference.com/js/.** This Web site includes tutorials, tips, and reviews of tools.

- **Joe Burns' JavaScript Primer—htmlgoodies.earthweb.com/ primers/jsp/.** This site is packed with 30 tutorials on JavaScript, starting with the basics.

- **javascripts.com—**You can find thousands of free scripts and information about how to use them.

- **ZDNet's Developer Script Library for JavaScript— www.zdnet.com/devhead/resources/scriptlibrary/javascript/.** This site has thousands of free scripts you can download and customize.

Books

- *JavaScript for the World Wide Web* (Visual Quickstart Guide), by Tom Negrino and Dori Smith, is a good place for beginners to start.

- *JavaScript: The Definitive Guide,* by David Flanagan, offers more advanced information for users with a bit of previous programming experience.

- *JavaScript Goodies,* by Joe Burns, is the companion to his popular Web site and a great resource for HTML developers who want to add some JavaScript to their Web sites.

- *Designing with JavaScript,* by Nick Heinle, is another good book for beginners.

Module 15

Cascading Style Sheets

Goals

- Understand the concept and uses of cascading style sheets in Web pages

- Differentiate between external, internal and inline CSS style sheets

- Understand formatting techniques for Web pages using CSS styles

Throughout the course of this book, you learned some ways to format text and other page elements with HTML, but these ways are limited because HTML was never intended to become a page layout program. The advent of the *cascading style sheets* (*CSS*) specification by the W3C provided new formatting techniques for many frustrated Web developers and designers.

This module gives you an introductory look at how CSS style sheets work and what you might accomplish with them.

Note

While saying "CSS style sheets," might sound redundant, this terminology actually is the recommendation of the W3C. In the course of this module, the discussion is always about CSS style sheets.

Understanding CSS

Although CSS isn't part of HTML, it does work with HTML to give you more control over the layout and presentation of Web pages. For example, if you want to make all the Level 2 headlines (h2) display in 14-point size, using the Verdana font face, as well as appear blue and italicized, you have to use three HTML tags and three attributes in every location where the company's name appears.

With CSS, whose style declarations are also referred to as *styles*, you can give the browser instructions to render all h2 tags in a particular way, thereby making the coding of the page much cleaner and simpler. In fact, you can even specify that all h2 tags on all pages in the site should be rendered the same way, definitely cutting down on the amount of work you'd have to do, as well as making the maintenance of the pages easier.

The biggest drawback to CSS is its lack of complete support among browsers. While Internet Explorer has been quick in adapting most of the CSS specifications, Netscape didn't support any of the CSS specification until it released the fourth version of its browser. Even today, versions of both browsers support only certain aspects of CSS. This all makes coding CSS somewhat difficult for Web developers, especially when you're trying to anticipate how the page will appear in each browser.

With some forethought, however, developers can use quite a bit of the more important CSS styles effectively in all browsers. This is, in part, because even when browsers don't render all styles correctly, they often ignore the styles altogether. This means you're often dealing with pages that usually still work in older browsers, but look a bit less "pretty," particularly if you're using CSS style sheets to affect the font and background characteristics of your pages. Remember this when coding your HTML, and be sure to test your pages in several browsers.

Tip

For an excellent online resource listing all the aspects of CSS and the browsers that support them, see **webreview.com/wr/pub/guides/ style/mastergrid.html**.

To understand how style sheets work, let's look at some of the terminology and concepts involved.

CSS1 Versus CSS2

As you can probably tell by now, nothing on the Internet ever stands still and CSS is no exception. About two years after creating the CSS1 specification in 1996, the W3C added a new level to CSS that, in 1998, formally became part of the specification now referred to as *CSS2*. New features in CSS2 include the following:

- printer management—giving you control over how a Web page prints

- additional device control—enabling you to provide instructions for displaying your page on devices other than computers and monitors

- dynamic content—enabling you to customize text within a page for the end user

- better positioning—providing you with tools capable of placing an element almost anywhere on a page

Browser developers are now working to support a newer round of CSS that is finally gaining acceptance among mainstream audiences. And

15

while this is going on, the W3C is working on a third level of CSS, referred to as *CSS3*. While I encourage you to learn about these new features, be forewarned that, at press time, few browsers supported them.

Hint

The official CSS2 specification can be found at **www.w3.org/TR/ REC-CSS2/.**

Wherever necessary, I point out any differences by referring to the original specifications as CSS1 and the newer additions as CSS2. When making general comments about style sheets, I use CSS.

Selectors

To define a style, you first must identify which tag you want to affect. This tag is then called a *selector* in CSS. So, if you wanted to specify the style of all the Level 2 headlines (`<h2>`) on a page, you would use h2 as your selector.

```
h2
```

In fact, the selector is essentially the tag without the brackets. With that in mind, can you guess what the selector for `<p>` would be?

```
p
```

Note

Many different types of selectors are introduced in CSS1 and CSS2. Additional information can be found in the resources listed at the end of this module.

Properties

Once you have a selector, you can define its properties. Similar to how attributes work in HTML, CSS *properties* alter specific attributes of a selector. With attributes, the browser determines how to render a particular page element, but with CSS properties, you decide how the element should be rendered. (Note, in the end, the browser still wins because it may or may not support styles at all.)

Returning to the previous example, if you want to change the style of the Level 2 headlines on your page to 14-point Verdana, italic, and blue, you can use the following properties:

```
font-family
font-style
font-size
color
```

You can use many other properties to customize your pages, but I get to those in a few minutes.

Declarations & Rulesets

When you specify values for properties, you are creating a *declaration* for that selector. The declaration and selector together is then referred to as a set of *rules*, or a *ruleset*. In the typical ruleset, the declaration is enclosed in curly brackets after the selector.

So here are the pieces of our ruleset:

```
                    selector
h2  ←
font-family ←          property
verdana ←                        value
{font-family: verdana} ←
                          declaration
```

And here is the final ruleset:

```
h2 {font-family: verdana}
```

Universal Classes

Sometimes you might not want to cause all the h2 tags on your page to be rendered in the same way. Maybe you'd rather break them down into two categories instead. Using *universal classes*, you could specify that the h2 tags in the first half of the page were 12-point Verdana, italic, and blue, while the h2 tags in the second half were 12-point Verdana, italic, and red.

15

Universal classes are defined by placing a period before the class name instead of using an HTML tag as a selector, as in the following examples:

```
.blue {font-family: verdana;
       color: blue;
       font-style: italic;
       font-size: 12pt}
.red  {font-family: verdana;
       color: red}
       font-style: italic;
       font-size: 12pt}
```

Note, the class name is something you define, almost as if you were naming your own selector. The period tells the browser this "selector" isn't a *real* tag.

You then reference the class by adding the `class` attribute to your h2 tag wherever you want it to appear. Notice the period doesn't appear in the name of the class.

```
<h2 class="red">This headline is red.</h2>
<h2 class="blue">This headline is blue.</h2>
```

Having done this, I could now apply the red class to an entire paragraph by giving that paragraph's p tag the `class` attribute.

```
<p class="red">This paragraph is red.</p>
```

Note

When you apply classes to the p tag, closing the p tag to avoid having the rest of your page appear in that style is especially important.

Another way to apply classes is to use the ID attribute. The basic concept is the same but, instead of using a period to identify the class in the style sheet, you use a hash mark (#).

```
#red {color: red}
```

Then, when you reference the class in your HTML, use the `ID` attribute instead of the `class` attribute.

```
<p ID="red">This paragraph is red.</p>
```

Note

The biggest difference between using the `class` attribute or the `ID` attribute is the `ID` attribute can only appear once within a page, whereas the `class` attribute can appear as many times as you want. The only common use of the `ID` attribute is for absolutely positioned elements in CSS and some JavaScript.

Ask the Expert

Question: How do I assign styles to whole sections of a Web page as opposed to individual paragraphs?

Answer: You can use the `div` tag as a selector, and then surround the section you want to style with `<div>` and `</div>`. If you need to have multiple sections in a page, each with its own set of styles, you can add classes to each `div` tag, such as `<div class="section1">` and `<div class="section2">`. Then, assign those classes in your style sheet by placing a period before the class name:

```
.section1 {style information}
.section2 {style information}
```

A second option is to use the `span` tag. You use the `span` tag in essentially the same way as the `div` tag, placing the opening and closing tags around the section you want to affect, and defining the class(es) in the CSS style sheet. The benefit of the `span` tag is it has no other meaning in HTML, which causes older browsers simply to ignore it and leave the page unchanged.

Another difference between the `span` and `div` tags is the `div` tag—being a block level element—causes blank lines to appear before and after its use, whereas the `span` tag does not.

15

Value Types

As with attributes in HTML, properties have values. Most values can be specified either in terms of color, keyword, length, percentage, or URL. Length and percentage units can also be made positive or negative by adding a plus (+) or minus (-) sign in front of the value.

Color

When specifying color in a value, you can do so in one of three ways:

- hexadecimal code, such as #000000

- RGB values, such as rgb(0,0,0) or rgb(0%,0%,0%)

- one of the 16 predefined keywords, which are aqua, black, blue, fuchsia, gray, green, lime, maroon, navy, olive, purple, red, silver, teal, white, and yellow

Keyword

A *keyword* is a word defined in CSS that's translated into a numerical value by the browser. For this reason, keywords are often considered relative because, ultimately, it's up to the browser to decide how to render the content. An example of a keyword is small.

Length

In HTML, most units are defined in pixels. In CSS, however, you have the option of using many other types of units. For example, when specifying text sizes with the font-size property, you can use any of the following. (Abbreviations are shown in parenthesis.)

- points (pt)—72 points in an inch

- picas (pc)—12 points in a pica

- pixels (px)—a dot on the screen

- ems (em)—refers to the height of the font in general

- exs (ex)—refers to the height of an *x* in a particular font

- inches (in)

- millimeters (mm)

- centimeters (cm)

Percentage

Just as with HTML table sizing, relative percentages can be useful in CSS when used to position elements on a page. This is because percentages allow elements to move around, depending on how large the screen and window size is. When used in CSS, a percentage sign (%) following a numerical value, such as 100%, indicates a relationship between the surrounding elements.

URL

When you reference an absolute URL in CSS, use the following form:

```
url(http://www.osborne.com)
```

Similarly, relative URLs are referenced in the following manner:

```
url(home.html)
```

Structure

Now that you know a little about the individual parts of CSS, let's put them together to create a few styles. The organization of these pieces depends a bit on which type of style sheet you are creating: inline, internal, or external.

Inline

Inline styles are created right within the HTML of the page, hence, the name. In the previous examples, a declaration was surrounded by curly quotes, but inline declarations are enclosed in straight quotes using the `style` attribute.

```
<h2 style="font-family: verdana">
```

You can separate multiple rules by semicolons, but the entire declaration should be included within quotes.

```
<h2 style="font-family: verdana;color: #003366">
```

Inline styles are best for making quick changes to a page, but they aren't suited for changes to an entire document or Web site. The reason for this is when styles are added to a tag, they occur only for that individual tag and not for all similar tags on the page.

Tip

Inline styles overrule internal and external styles when multiple types of style sheets are found on the same page. For more on this topic, see the section in "Advanced Concepts" called "The Cascade."

Internal

When you want to change the style of all the h2 tags on a page, you can use an *internal*, or *embedded*, style sheet. Instead of adding the style attribute to a tag, use the style tag to contain all the instructions for the page. The style tag is placed in the header of the page, in between the opening and closing head tags. Here's an example of what an internal style sheet might look like.

```
<head>
    <title>CSS Example</title>
<style type="text/css">
<!--
h2 {font-family: verdana; color: blue}
.red {font-family: verdana; color: red}
-->
</style>
</head>
```

Enclosing your styles in HTML comments can help older browsers ignore the styles and avoid errors

As the previous example shows, the selector is placed before the declaration, which is enclosed in curly brackets. This entire ruleset can be contained on a single line or broken up into multiple lines, as in the following example.

```
h2
{font-family: verdana;
color: blue}
```

You can write styles in several ways, and the following example is just as valid as the previous one.

```
h2 {font-family: verdana;
    color: blue}
```

In addition, you can use certain shorthand properties to reduce the amount of coding necessary. For example, instead of specifying both font family: Verdana and font size: 12 point, you could type the following because both properties begin with font.

```
h2 {font: verdana 12pt}
```

External

An *external* style sheet is essentially the same information as an internal one, except an external style sheet is contained in its own text file, and then referenced from within the Web page. So an external style sheet might look like this:

Notice that external style sheets don't use the style tag or attribute, but simply include a list of rulesets as instructions for the browser. Once you create your external style sheet, save it as a text file, with the .css file extension.

Then, return to your HTML file and add the link tag to the page header to reference the external style sheet, as in the following example.

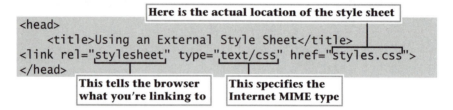

Note

External style sheets can be overruled by internal and inline style sheets.

Advanced Concepts

While this module is intended as an introduction into style sheets, I also want to give you a brief explanation of two of the more advanced concepts. For more information about these and any other CSS principles, see the "Learning More" section at the end of this module.

The Cascade

The word *cascading* refers to the way CSS sorts out which styles take precedence. For example, in a large company where you might have many departments managing their own portions of the corporate Web site, maintaining a consistent look and feel across all sections of the Web site can be difficult.

With CSS, the Web development team can set up a series of style sheets that cascade in importance, causing the main corporate style sheet to be imported into any department style sheet and, ultimately, take precedence.

In a nutshell, CSS styles apply from general to specific. This means a ruleset in the head tag of a document overrides a linked style sheet, while a ruleset in the body of a document overrides one in the head tag. HTML styles (using font tags) inside an inline ruleset overrides that. In addition, more local styles only override the parent attributes where overlap occurs.

The Inheritance

Just as children can inherit certain traits from their parents in family life, so can page elements inherit the characteristics of those that contain them. For example, if you create a set of rules specifying that everything contained within p tags on your page is rendered in green, bold text, those rules even apply to the italicized text within that paragraph.

Similarly, most elements on a page are contained within the body tag and take on any styles defined in it (such as font color and size). You could override the inherited styles of the body tag by applying other styles to specific selectors within the page.

Formatting Pages

Now that you know a little about CSS, let's look at some of the actual properties you can use to format the following aspects of your Web pages when they're viewed in a browser on a typical computer monitor:

- text display
- backgrounds
- tables
- lists
- controlling white space
- borders
- positioning
- printing

Hint

The properties in each of the following tables are listed first according to whether they are part of CSS1 or CSS2, and then in alphabetical order.

Because this is meant to be an introduction to CSS, I cover some topics briefly and don't include others I consider more advanced. For more information about any of these and other topics related to CSS, consult the additional resources at the end of this module.

Note

In the following tables, the content in the first column (Sample Property and Value) should be on a single line when typed in a text editor.

Text Display

Sample Property and Value	Description	Possible Values	Notes
`color: black`	Changes the text color. Similar to using <font color=""> in HTML.	Can use hexadecimal code: #000000, RGB values: `rgb (0,0,0)`, or color names: `black`	n/a
`font-family: verdana, arial, sans-serif`	Changes the font face of the text. Similar to using `<font face="">` in HTML.	Can specify font families, a list of individual font faces, or a combination of both (such as in the previous example). Generic font families include `serif`, `sans-serif`, `cursive`, `monospace`, and `fantasy`.	With specific font faces and families, users must have specified font installed.
`font-size: 14pt`	Changes the size of the text. Similar to using `<font size=#>` in HTML.	Can use absolute or relative sizes. Absolute sizes can be specified with a numeric value and a unit (such as `12pt`) or a keyword (`xx-small`, `x-small`, `small`, `medium`, `large`, `x-large`, `xx-large`). Relative keywords are `larger` and `smaller`.	The default is usually `medium`, but the size ultimately depends on the user's browser and platform.
`font-style: italic`	Changes the style of the text causing it to appear vertical or slightly slanted. Similar to using `<i>` in HTML.	Can be `normal`, `italic`, or `oblique`.	`italic` and `oblique` appear the same in most cases.
`font-variant: small caps`	Lets you specify text as small capitals.	Can use `normal` or `small-caps`.	n/a

Sample Property and Value	Description	Possible Values	Notes
`font-weight: bold`	Changes how heavy or thick the font appears. Similar to using `<b>` in HTML.	Can use keywords (`normal`, `bold`, `bolder`, `lighter`) or numbers (`100, 200, 300...900`). `normal` is 400, `bold` is 700; `bolder` and `lighter` cause the weight to be one step lighter or darker that the rest of the text.	Many browsers only understand `normal` and `bold`.
`letter-spacing: 10em`	Changes the spacing between the letters. Similar to kerning in other programs and print methods.	Can be specified by a length value (such as `5em`) or the keyword `normal`.	Negative values provide for a tighter, more condensed display, where letters run together.
`line-height:2`	Changes the spacing between lines. Similar to leading in other programs and print methods.	Can be specified as a percentage of the font size (such as `200%` to achieve a "double-spaced" look), multiples of the font size (`1.5` or `2`), lengths (`72px`) or with the keyword `normal`.	n/a
`text-align: left`	Changes the alignment of the text.	Can be `left`, `right`, `center`, or `justify`.	n/a
`text-decoration: overline`	Lets you alter the appearance of the text in a variety of ways.	Can use `none`, `underline`, `overline`, `line-through`, or `blink`.	Non-linked text defaults to `none`, while linked text defaults to `underline`.
`text-indent: 20px`	Lets you indent the first line of a section of text, such as a paragraph.	Can use percentages or lengths to specify an amount of indent.	n/a
`text-transform: uppercase`	Changes the case of the text.	Can use `none`, `capitalize` (capitalizes all words), `uppercase` (makes all letters uppercase), or `lowercase` (makes all letters lowercase).	n/a

Sample Property and Value	Description	Possible Values	Notes
`vertical-align: text-bottom`	Allows text to be aligned vertically, without the use of tables.	Can be specified by relative keywords (`baseline`, `middle`, `sub`, `super`, `text-top`, `text-bottom`, `top`, `bottom`) or percentages.	Negative percentages result in text below the baseline.
`word-spacing: 20em`	Changes the spacing between words. Similar to tracking in other programs or print methods.	Can be specified by a length value (such as `20em`) or the keyword `normal`.	Negative values provide for a tighter, more condensed display where words run together. This property is only reliable in the latest versions of Internet Explorer.
`direction: rtl`	Changes the direction in which the text is rendered across the screen.	Can be `rtl` (right-to-left) or `ltr` (left-to-right).	CSS2 (minimal browser support at press time)
`font-size-adjust: 1.5`	Adjusts the font size, according to which font is actually used to display the page, in cases where several fonts of different sizes are specified in the font-family property.	Can be `none` or a decimal value. `none` specifies no size adjusting should take place. When size adjusting is needed, specify the amount of change necessary using a decimal value (such as `.75`).	CSS2 (minimal browser support at press time)
`font-stretch: wider`	Lets you expand and condense characters in fonts.	Can be absolute keywords (`ultra-condensed`, `extra-condensed`, `condensed`, `semi-condensed`, `normal`, `semi-expanded`, `expanded`, `extra-expanded`, `ultra-expanded`) or relative keywords (`wider` and `narrower`).	CSS2 (minimal browser support at press time)

Sample Property and Value	Description	Possible Values	Notes
`text-shadow: 10 px, 20px, 5px, blue`	Allows for text to have shadow effect.	Can specify a length value each for the top and left side of the shadow, as well as a color and optional color blur radius. (Commas separate these values.)	CSS2 (minimal browser support at press time)

Backgrounds

Sample Property and Value	Description	Possible Values	Notes
`background-attachment: scroll`	Allows the background in a page to remain stationary, or to move when the page is scrolled.	Can be `scroll` or `fixed`.	Works best with page backgrounds. Recognized only by Internet Explorer, at press time.
`background-color: #336699`	Changes the background color of a page or element.	Can use hexadecimal code: #000000, RGB values: `-rgb(0, 0, 0)`, or color names: `black`	Can be used with many types of elements.
`background-image: url("image.gif")`	Lets you specify a background image for the page or an individual element.	Specify the location of the image (URL).	Can be used with many types of elements.
`background-position: 50%, 50%`	Lets you specify the position of a background image.	Can use pairs of percentages, lengths, or keywords (such as `top`, `left`, `center`, `right`, `bottom`)	Can be used with many types of elements. Recognized only by Internet Explorer at press time.
`background-repeat: repeat-y`	Specifies whether the background image is repeated and, if so, how it repeats.	Can be `repeat`, `repeat-x` (horizontally only), `repeat-y` (vertically only), or `no-repeat`.	Can be used with many types of elements. Recognized only by Internet Explorer at press time.

15

Ask the Expert

Question: With all these different specifications, how do I make sure my pages actually work in the browsers?

Answer: The most important thing to remember about style sheets is testing, testing, testing. In an ideal world, everything recommended in the W3C specifications for CSS2 would be supported by both Netscape and Internet Explorer on both Macs and PCs. After a few years of hands-on use, I can assure you various discrepancies exist in support of many features of CSS, even the most common features. So here are a few tips:

- Avoid shorthand, especially relating to fonts because Netscape's (version 4.*x*) support for shorthand is sketchy. This means you'd use `{font-family: verdana; font-size: 10px; color: #009900}` instead of `{font: verdana, 10px, #009900}`.

- Be careful when assigning properties to the `body` tag because Netscape (4.x) may ignore them. This is because of a bug that causes styles (whether they're HTML or CSS) not to be inherited in tables. So, when you do use styles in the `body` tag, you may be required to duplicate them for the appropriate tags within the page's tables.

- Never use underlines or other special characters in naming your classes in a style sheet, and don't start the names with a number. Netscape (4.*x*) ignores all that class information and may interpret the rest of your style sheet information in an interesting manner because of it. In addition, remember, class definitions must be preceded by a period.

- If you're using style sheets to set the size of fonts, remember pixel sizes are absolute, but point sizes vary from one platform to another.

- Turning off the underlines for links (`text-decoration: none`) doesn't work uniformly in all browsers, so be sure to test carefully. This process isn't recommended because it takes away the user's way to identify a link quickly and clearly.

Ask the Expert Bio   This expert advice was provided by Kelley Green, who has been involved on the design technology side of the Web for the past five years. Kelley is currently the manager of a design technology department for a design firm in San Francisco. When she's not cranking out code for various e-commerce clients, Kelley enjoys cooking, gardening, and hanging out with her partner Sam Foster.

Tables

Sample Property and Value	Description	Possibe Values	Notes
border-collapse: separate	Specifies whether the borders of each cell merge together to form one thicker border, or separate to form two thinner borders.	Use collapse (one border) or separate (individual borders).	CSS2 (minimal browser support at press time)
column-span: 3	Specifies the number of columns a cell spans.	Use an integer.	CSS2 (minimal browser support at press time); can only be used with elements designated as table cells or captions.
row-span: 4	Specifies the number or rows a cell spans.	Use an integer.	CSS2 (minimal browser support at press time); can only be used with elements designated as table cells or captions.
table-layout: auto	Specifies whether the table is allowed to grow or shrink according to the table content.	Can be auto (resizes the table according to the size of the content) or fixed (renders the table in a specific size, regardless of the content).	CSS2 (minimal browser support at press time)

15

Lists

Sample Property and Value	Description	Possible Values	Notes
`list-style-image: url(bullet.gif)`	Changes the appearance of the bullet by replacing it with an image.	Specify the location of the image (URL).	Use only with elements designated as list items. Recognized only by Internet Explorer at press time.
`list-style-position: inside`	Identifies the indentation of additional lines in list items.	Can be `inside` (lines after the first on are not indented) or `outside` (all lines in the item are indented).	Use only with elements designated as list items. Recognized only by Internet Explorer at press time.
`list-style-type: decimal`	Changes the appearance of the bullet or characters at the beginnings of each list item.	Can be none (no bullets), `disc`, `circle`, `square`, `decimal` (numbers), `lower-roman` (lowecase Roman numerals), `upper-roman` (uppercase Roman numerals), `lower-alpha` (lowercase letters), `upper-alpha` (uppercase letters).	Use only with elements designated as list items.

Controlling White Space

Sample Property and Value	Description	Possible Values	Notes
`margin-bottom: 80%` `margin-left: 20px` `margin-right: auto` `margin-top: 4in`	Controls white space around an element.	Use a percentage or length unit, or the keyword `auto`.	n/a
`padding-bottom: 30px` `padding-left: 72cm` `padding-right: 25%` `padding top: auto`	Controls white space within an element.	Use a percentage or length unit, or the keyword `auto`.	Cannot be set to a negative number.
`white-space`	Changes whether the browser displays white space entered in the HTML. Using the value `pre` is similar to using the `pre` tag in HTML.	Can be normal (ignore white space in the code), `pre` (render the text exactly as it's typed, or `no-wrap` (render the text on a single line, unless a ` ` is present).	Applies only to block level elements.

Borders

Tip

All these values are tricky to use in Netscape, which has terrible support for these properties. My advice is to test early, before a design is set in stone, so you can design around the properties that won't work reliably.

Sample Property and Value	Description	Possible Values	Notes
border-bottom-width: thick border-left-width: 4px border-right-width: 6px border-top-width: thin border-width: medium	Controls sizes of an element's borders, individually or as a whole.	Can use length units or keywords (thin, medium, or thick).	Minimal browser suppport.
border-color: #ffffff, #cccccc, #999999, #666666	Specifies the border's color.	Can use between one and four color values.	n/a
border-style: double	Specifies the border's style.	Can use none, dotted, dashed, solid, double, groove, ridge, inset, or outset.	Minimal browser support.

Positioning & Page Layout

In CSS, *positioning* refers to where elements are placed on the page. While HTML only permits rudimentary positioning such as align left or center, CSS enables you to position items according to specific coordinates, just as you might do with a traditional page layout program. There are four flavors of positioning.

● Absolute—The item is placed without regard to other elements on the page.

● Fixed—The item is placed without regard to other elements on the page and maintains its position when the page is scrolled.

- Relative—The item is placed relative to other elements on the page.

- Static—The item flows according to how the elements around it are placed. (This is the default and the same as using HTML.)

You identify which flavor is being used with the position property, and then follow with additional properties and length values to specify the element's location, as in the following example:

```
.logo {position: fixed;
       width: auto;
       height: auto;
       top: 10px;
       right: 0;
       bottom: 100px;
       left: 10em}
```

This example just scratches the surface of CSS positioning, as it quickly becomes rather complex. For more information, consult the resources at the end of this module.

Formatting for Other Media

CSS2 enables you to give instructions on how your pages should be displayed in other types of media, such as the printed page or handheld devices. Although many browsers don't yet support these newer features of CSS, they're expected to gain widespread support soon.

Most of these instructions are given through the @media rule. When you use this rule, you must also specify for what media the instructions are given.

- all
- aural (speech synthesizers)
- braille (braille tactile feedback devices)
- embossed (paged braille printers)
- handheld (typically small screen, monochrome, limited bandwidth)
- print

- `projection`

- `screen` (color computer screens)

- `tty` (media using a fixed-pitch character grid, such as teletypes or terminals)

- `tv` (typically low resolution, color, limited scrollability)

After you identify the type of media the instructions are for, you can continue by identifying the actual instructions, just as you would in a typical style sheet. Notice in the following example that the selector, `body`, and its declaration are enclosed in a set of curly brackets, distinguishing them as instructions for this specific media type.

```
@media print {
    body {font-size: 10pt}
}
```

Project 15-1: Create a Style Sheet

To practice creating a style sheet, let's use the most recent copy of the `index.html` page for our Web site. (The last time you worked on it was probably in Module 13.) We need to create an external style sheet that could be used throughout the site to standardize the look of the text. Goals for this project include

- Create an external CSS style sheet.

- Reference the external CSS style sheet from within a Web page.

Note

All the files needed to complete the projects in this book for the Woolwich Historical Society can be downloaded from **www.osborne.com** or **www.willardesigns.com/htmlbook**. In addition, you can view my version of the Web site anytime by visiting **www.woolwichhistory.org**. Those of you who aren't using the Woolwich Historical Society can tailor the project to your particular needs.

15

Step-by-Step

1. Open your text editor (SimpleText on the Mac or Notepad on the PC) and create a new file entitled `styles.css`.

2. Using `h1` as your selector, specify the following:

- Use a 16-point sized, sans serif font.
- Make the text bold.
- Change the color to a bright color (see the inside cover for a color chart).

3. Using `h2` as your selector, specify the following:

- Use a 14-point sized, sans serif font.
- Make the text bold.
- Change the color to a dark color (see the inside cover for a color chart).

4. Using `p` as your selector, specify the following:

- Use a 12-point sized font.
- Indent the first line of each paragraph by 25 pixels.

5. Create a universal class called "`seealso`", specify the following:

- Use a 12-point sized, sans serif font.
- Give it a yellow background color.

6. Save the file.

7. Open the `index.html` file.

8. Add the `link` tag to the header of the page to reference the external style sheet you just created (`styles.css`).

9. Save the file.

10. Open your Web browser and choose FILE | OPEN PAGE (or OPEN FILE or OPEN, depending on the browser you're using). Locate the file `index.html` you just saved. You should see changes in the page, according to the specifications in your style sheet.

11. If you need to make changes, return to your text editor. After making any changes, save the file and switch back to the browser. Choose REFRESH or RELOAD to preview the changes you just made.

12. If you are using the Woolwich Historical Society, you can compare your files to the following code and Figure 15-1.

index.html

```
<head>
     <title>Welcome to the Woolwich Historical Society,
located in Woolwich, Maine</title>
<link rel="stylesheet" type="text/css" href="styles.css">
</head>
```

. . . the rest of the code remains unchanged.

styles.css

```
h1 {font-family: sans-serif;
    font-size: 16pt;
    color: #ff0000;
    font-weight: bold}
h2 {font-family: sans-serif;
    font-size: 14pt;
    color: #660000;
    font-weight: bold}
p {font-size: 12pt;
    text-indent: 25px}
.seealso {font-family: sans-serif;
    font-size: 12pt;
    background-color: #ffff33}
```

Tip

If you run into problems, first ensure you're using at least a version 4 of Netscape or Internet Explorer. If you are using Netscape, you should also check that JavaScript is enabled in your Preferences. Finally, compare the code against the examples to make sure the syntax is correct.

Summary

Cascading style sheets hold significant promise in the future of Web design and development. This project gave you practice creating a basic external CSS style sheet, and referencing that style sheet from a Web page.

15

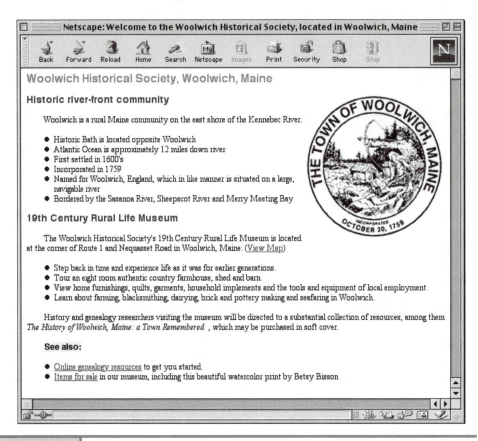

Figure 15-1 The result of this CSS style sheet can be seen when the HTML page that references it is viewed within a browser

Note

For extra practice, reference the external CSS style sheet from all the pages you created. In addition, try adding an internal and inline style sheet to one of the pages.

Mastery Check

1. What would you use as a selector if you wanted to add a style to all the Level 3 headlines on your page?

2. Name three ways you can reference a color in CSS.

3. What property can be used to add a colored background behind an element?

4. What is a universal class?

5. What tag is used to add an internal style sheet to a Web page?

Learning More

- *Cascading Style Sheets, Designing for the Web,* by Håkon Wium Lie and Bert Bos (published 1999 by Addison Wesley)

- *Cascading Style Sheets: The Definitive Guide,* by Eric Meyer (published 2000 by O'Reilly & Assoc.)

- *Cascading Style Sheets: Programmer's Reference,* by Eric Meyer (published 2001 by Osborne/McGraw-Hill)

- **style.webreview.com** is an amazing reference for cascading style sheets that lists all the specifications, as well as which ones are supported by which browsers and platforms.

- **www.w3.org/Style/CSS** is the W3C's CSS Web site, complete with testing tools and a validator (**jigsaw.w3.org/css-validator**).

15

- Newsgroup for authors of CSS: **news:comp.infosystems.www.authoring.stylesheets.**

- The House of Style (**www.westciv.com/style_master/house**) includes tutorials, books, links, a browser compatibility guide, help, and other resources to guide you in learning all about style sheets.

- HTML Writer's Guide CSS FAQ: **www.hwg.org/resources/faqs/cssFAQ.html.**

- Dave Raggett's Intro to CSS: **www.w3.org/MarkUp/Guide/Style.**

Module 16

Making Pages Available to Others

Goals

- Select possible domain names for your site

- Determine the most appropriate type of hosting for your site

- Recognize the differences between search engines and search directories

- Understand the basics of uploading your site to a host computer

- Understand the importance of testing your site

- Identify ways to publicize your Web site

Throughout the course of this book, you've created and viewed Web pages on your personal computer. At some point you'll, undoubtedly, want to show your Web pages to other people. To do that, your site must be transferred or *uploaded* to a host computer with 24-hour access to the Internet, where it has a suitable domain name or URL. Then, to drive traffic to that site, you need to consider submitting your site to search engines and other marketing techniques.

Domain Names

Before diving into the actual meat of this module, I want to mention domain names briefly. Many people underestimate the power of a guessable and memorable domain name. Consider a company called Acme Landscaping Incorporated. While it may seem logical to its business owners to purchase the domain name *alinc.com*, this is probably not the first thing a potential customer would guess.

Tip

Visit **www.networksolutions.com** to check for domain name availability.

acmelandscaping.com would be my first guess, but if that were already taken, I might try *acmelandscapers.com*, *acmelawns.com* or even something like *beautifullawns.com*. If more than one of those were available, you might even register both. Purchasing multiple domain names is an inexpensive way to bring in some additional customers and build your brand identity online. Whenever appropriate, you might also purchase the same domain name ending with different extensions, such as *beautifullawns.com* and *beautifullawns.net*.

?Ask the Expert

Question: What are the valid characters for a domain name, and how long can a domain name be?

Answer: According to Network Solutions (**www.networksolutions.com**), you can use letters and numbers. You can also use hyphens, although they may not be at the beginning or end of your Web address. Spaces or other characters like question marks and exclamation marks are never allowed.

Your complete domain name (including the four-character extension— .com, .edu, .net, or .org) can be up to 26 characters long. Remember, "www" isn't included in the domain name you register, so you needn't count those characters. For example, *acmelandscaping*.com (19 characters) is acceptable but *acmelandscapingincorporated*.com (31 characters) isn't.

Finding a Hosting Provider

Many different options are available for those who want to publish a site on the Internet. For the purposes of this module, I group these options into two categories: personal site hosting and business site hosting.

Personal Site Hosting

When you want to publish a personal Web site and you aren't concerned about having your own domain name (such as wendywillard.com), you have a wide range of free options available. For example, all the following sites offer free Web space for personal sites to anyone who asks for it. If you currently have an e-mail account with any of these, you're already halfway there.

- Yahoo! GeoCities (**www.geocities.com**)

- AOL Hometown (**hometown.aol.com**)

- Tripod (**www.tripod.com**)

- Angelfire (**www.angelfire.com**)

- MSN (**communities.msn.com**)

Because these sites are largely targeting toward beginners, they make uploading and maintaining your site a breeze. Most use Web-based tools to do so, meaning you don't even need any additional software.

While the sites listed above offer free hosting to anyone who requests it, remember to check first with your current *Internet service provider (ISP)*. ISPs frequently throw in some free Web space with dial-up Internet connections. If none of these free options suit your purposes or if you need to register your own domain, move on to the next section about business site hosting.

Note

Be sure to check the terms of service before you sign up with any ISP to verify your site fits within the confines of the ISP's requirements. For example, the majority of ISPs prohibit sites distributing pornography or illegal copies of computer software. In addition, free ISPs usually limit the amount of space and/or bandwidth you can use. I mention these only to point out that restrictions do exist and you'd be wise to review all terms and details carefully to avoid incurring unexpected fees.

Business Site Hosting

On the business side, your options vary from onsite to colocated to offsite. In the case of *onsite hosting*, your business purchases a server, its software, and a dedicated Internet connection capable of serving your site to Web users 24 hours a day, 365 days a year. For small businesses, this isn't a viable option because it requires expensive start-up costs and onstaff Information Technology (IT) talent.

For businesses that already own the appropriate equipment and have an experienced Webmaster, but don't want to spend the money for an expensive, dedicated Internet connection, *colocation* is an option. In this case, you use your own equipment and personnel, but rent space and a high-speed Internet connection from a host company. Your equipment is housed in that space and can be reached any time of day by your personnel, thereby enabling you to maintain a higher level of control over your site as desired.

For the majority of small to mid-size business, *offsite hosting* is the most cost-effective and popular solution. This can be on either a *shared* or a *dedicated* server. While a shared server can be significantly less expensive than one dedicated to your needs, it may not be possible in all situations. For example, if your site runs custom Web applications, requires a high level of security or needs a large amount of space, a dedicated server is preferred.

Many levels exist within shared offsite hosting, and therefore, many different costs. For this reason, be wary of comparing apples to oranges. When you are considering two or more hosting providers, look closely at the fine print to be sure they offer similar services before making a final decision solely on price.

Here are some questions to ask when you look for business hosting.

- How much space on the server will I receive? How much extra do I have to pay if I go over that space?

- How much traffic can my site generate over a month? What are some average traffic rates for some similar sites you host? How much extra will I pay if the site generates more traffic than allowed?

- How many e-mail accounts will I receive with this account?

- Can I use my own domain name(s) (as opposed to www.hostcompany.com/mybusiness)? Will you help me register my domain? (If you haven't already registered one.) Will you charge extra if I have multiple domain names for a Web site? If so, how much more?

- What kind of access will I have to my Web site? (for example, FTP access for uploading files).

- What kind of support do you offer? (for example, If I need help adding password protection to my site, will you help me?) What hours is your support staff available?

- Can I load my own applications (database tools, e-commerce tools, and so forth) onto the server? What requirements or restrictions do you have regarding those? Are additional costs involved?

- What additional services do you offer? (for example, Can you also host my online store and, if so, for how much additionally? Can I use the Microsoft Front Page extensions if I want to?)

- How many Internet connections do you have? (The more connections a host has, the better chance your site has of staying "live" if one connection goes down.)

- How often do you perform backups? How easy is it for me to gain access to a backup if I need one?

- What are the start-up costs? What are the monthly costs? Are there any guarantees?

- Do you offer a service to measure statistics for my site, such as how many people have visited? If so, can I see an example?

- Can you also provide Internet access if I need it?

- Can you provide references?

Many services online let you compare different Web site host companies. To get started, you might try:

- **www.hostinvestigator.com**

- **www.hostsearch.com**

- **webservices.cnet.com/html/aisles/Web_Hosting.asp**

Or, try searching in Yahoo! for *web site host* to see lists of hosting companies. In the end, you'll probably get the best ideas about which hosting provider to use by asking friends or business associates.

Ask the Expert

Question: Thanks for all the info, but can't you tell me how much I should pay for these services?

Answer: Because so many different types of hosting are out there, the prices do vary greatly. But, because you asked, I'll give you some ranges. For small businesses, you can find basic hosting (with few perks or options) for as low as about $10 a month, although I would put the average at about $20–$40. Obviously, the cost goes up from there, with mid-sized businesses paying an average of $40–$100 a month, depending on what services are needed. Large businesses may pay significantly more but, again, this depends greatly on what types of services are needed.

16

Search Engines & Search Directories

Many times in this book, I directed you to search for more information on the Internet. The majority of Web surfers use a search engine or search directory at some point to locate information. If the Web were a large book, you might think of these as different types of indexes—some listing alphabetically, others by topic.

Search directories like Yahoo! (**www.yahoo.com**) organize huge lists of Web sites by category and enable you to search these listings by keyword. Search directories usually include short descriptions next to each listing and sometimes even editorial comment. Other popular search directories are Open Directory (**www.dmoz.org**), LookSmart (**www.looksmart.com**) and Snap (**www.snap.com**).

In addition to these large search directories, thousands of smaller search directories exist for specific topics. So, if your site sells children's clothing, submitting the site to search directories of children's products or those specifically for parents might be wise. Search for these keywords to locate related search directories.

Tip

A great way to find out where you should list your site is to check your competition. If you enter `link:competitor.com` into AltaVista's search engine (where competitor.com is replaced with the URL of your competitor's Web site), you can see all the sites that link to your competitor. Chances are good that if you want to acquire some of those customers from the competition, you could benefit by having links from those same sites.

Search engines maintain a large database of the content on the Web. You can search that database according to keyword, to return pages of results. Some search engines are now adding directory features, trying to give users the best of both worlds. Popular engines are AltaVista (**www.altavista.com**), Excite (**www.excite.com**), Lycos (**www.lycos.com**), and Go (**www.go.com**). A few of these engines now allow users to ask questions in sentence format, such as "How can I advertise my Web site?" The most popular of these is Ask Jeeves (**www.ask.com**).

Search engines and search directories don't have to conform to any set of standards, so any details or special techniques you may read about them are subject to change. To help you keep current on these issues, visit **www.searchenginewatch.com.**

Preparing Your Site for Its Public Debut

Before you upload your site to a host computer and submit it to directories and engines, tidying it up a little is best. Consider the following dos and don'ts.

Do:

- Make sure all your images have alternative text. Directories and engines can't see the images—they only "look" at the alternative text for descriptions.

- Give your pages descriptive 5–13 word titles, using keywords from the page. Directories and engines look at the titles of your pages and often use them to list your site. So "Page 2" would definitely not entice as many visitors as "Lawn Care Products for Sale."

- Repeat keywords throughout the page. On a page entitled "Lawn Care Products for Sale," you should include those same words in the headlines, body text, and alternative text for images on the page. This increases the relevancy of the page when someone searches for those words.

Don't:

- Stray from the topic. If a page is about lawn care products, don't include information about your favorite links or television shows on that same page. Extraneous information only weakens the relevancy of your pages because search engines typically show pages with the most relevant information at the top of the results list.

- Repeat keywords too many times. Search engines are known for dropping sites from their listings because of suspected spamming—a word repeated too many times on a page is a big red flag for spamming. Be realistic and honest. Use the words whenever they seem appropriate and you'll be fine.

- Use irrelevant keywords just to draw in people. Don't include keywords that aren't appropriate for your site. Users will get annoyed and complain, causing your site to be dropped from the search engine altogether.

Meta Tags

Finally, use `meta` tags to aid those engines or directories supporting them in identifying your content. `meta` tags are hidden instructions about your page, such as a description and keywords.

Note

Be aware that some engines and directories ignore `meta` tags altogether. For this reason, they shouldn't be relied on as the "be all and end all" of preparing your site.

These tags should be added to each page on your site in between the opening and closing `head` tags. Here's an example of how `meta` tags might be used on a page selling handmade children's clothing.

```
<head>
    <title>Wendy's Handmade Children's Clothing For Sale</title>
    <meta name="description" content="We sell handmade children's
clothing for boys and girls, sizes 6-12. Our children's clothing --
pants, shirts, dresses, and more -- is made to last generations.">
    <meta name="keywords" content="kids children clothing clothes
handmade pant shirt suit dress skirt">
</head>
```

Customize the content of these tags to identify a description that properly explains the purpose of your site in a sentence or two (25 words is a good place to start) and keywords that parallel what users will probably search for. Because most users search for words in lowercase, you can avoid using capital letters in your keywords. The number of keywords you can use varies according to the search engine or directory, so make sure your most important keywords are listed first.

You can also use the robots version of the meta tag to restrict a page from being indexed at all. This might be useful for a private page or a work in progress.

```
<meta name="robots" content="none">
```

Possible values for this tag include

1. all—Index the page and follow its links (default).

2. none—Don't index to index the page and not to follow any of its links.

3. index—Index the page.

4. noindex—Don't index the page.

5. follow—Follow all the links on the page.

6. nofollow—Don't follow all the links on the page.

The last four values can be used together as needed, so content="index,nofollow" would tell the engine to index the page, but not to follow any of its links.

Tip

Visit Web Developer (**www.webdeveloper.com/html/ html_metatags.html**) for more tips on using the latest meta tags.

Project 16-1: Adding Meta Tags

As discussed, one way to help boost your rankings in some search engines is to add keywords and descriptions to all your Web pages using meta tags. This project asks you to add these tags to some of the pages in the Woolwich Historical Society's Web site. Goals for this project include using

● Research related sites to determine appropriate keywords

● meta tags to add descriptions and keywords to Web pages

16

Step-by-Step

1. Visit **www.altavista.com** with your Web browser.

2. In the search box, enter keywords that might be appropriate for your organization. If you are using the Woolwich Historical Society, these might be "maine history", "maine genealogy", "woolwich history", "history museum maine", and so on.

3. View the Web sites listed on the first page of results to determine what keywords are included on their pages to make them rise to the top of the search results. If necessary, view the HTML source of the pages to view any `meta` tags.

4. Repeat this process in **www.excite.com** to see how different the results are.

5. Open the `index.html` file in your text editor (SimpleText on the Mac or Notepad on the PC).

6. Add `meta` tags to this page to identify the page's description and appropriate keywords.

7. Save the file.

Summary

Advertising your site is a necessary, but time-consuming, aspect of Web development. This project gave you practice with two techniques used for improving search engine rankings. In the end, bringing your site to the top of the search listings (and keeping it there) involves dedication and patience—and a bit of luck.

Note

For extra practice, try adding `meta` tags to all the pages you created. In addition, try performing the same searches in directories such as **www.yahoo.com** and **www.dmoz.com** to see how the results vary.

Uploading Your Pages

After your site is finished and you're ready to make it "live" or accessible by visitors on the Web, it's time to transfer the pages to the host computer. You can use file transfer protocol (FTP) programs to do so.

The concept of using an FTP program is similar to moving things around on your own personal computer. The key difference is, instead of moving files from one folder to another on your computer, you're actually moving them from one folder on your computer to another folder on a different computer.

Just as you can change settings and information about who has access to view or edit a file on your own computer, you can also make these changes on a host computer. For information about how these settings might work, checking with your ISP or host company is best.

Depending on what type of computer you have and who's hosting your site, you may use one of many different types of FTP programs. Or, you might use an FTP tool that comes with your HTML editor, if you have one. The next sections outline a few popular options.

Windows FTP Programs

One of the most popular FTP programs for the PC is WS-FTP. It comes in a free LE (lite) version or an inexpensive professional version, and is available for download from **www.ipswitch.com.**

To begin, you must choose which computer you want to access. If you want to upload your files to your Web server, enter that computer's information in the Session Properties screen that comes up when you first start the program (Figure 16-1). (You may need to click the button labeled NEW first, if a different computer's information is already filled into the blanks when you launch the program.)

Note

You should receive all the necessary information when you sign up for hosting service. If you're unsure, check your host company's Web site or call its customer support line for assistance.

After entering all the appropriate information, click the button labeled OK to connect to that computer. If your connection is successful, WS-FTP displays the company you're accessing, referred to as the *remote*

16

Enter your username, as specified
by your hosting provider

Enter the domain name or IP address
of the computer you're trying to access

Unless your hosting provider specifies
otherwise, leave this as "Automatic detect"

Enter your password,
as specified by your
hosting provider

Give your settings a name

When finished,
click this button

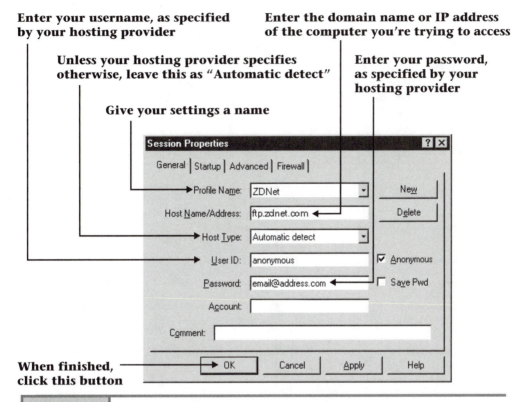

Figure 16-1 To begin, enter the information for the computer you want
to access

system, in the right window. Your local computer is visible in the left
window (Figure 16-2).

You can transfer files between these two computers by first clicking
the filename to highlight it, and then using one of the two arrows in the
center of the screen to move the file.

You can also navigate through the directory structure of either
computer by clicking the arrow at the top of the list of files to move back
to the previous directory. Double-click the name of a folder to view the
contents of that folder.

This is your computer

After highlighting a file on the remote system, click this arrow to download it to your personal system

This shows which directory you're currently in on the local system

This shows which directory you're currently viewing on the remote system

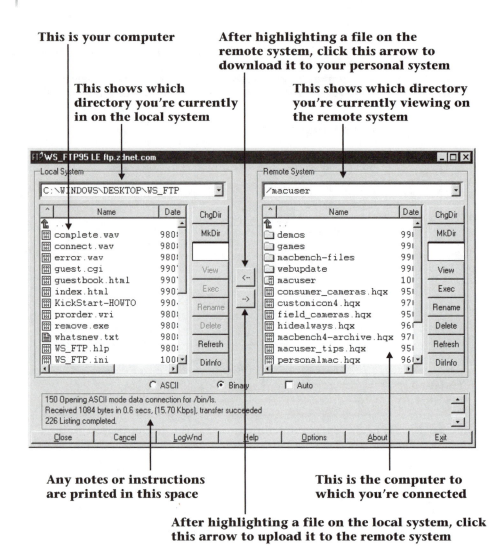

Any notes or instructions are printed in this space

This is the computer to which you're connected

After highlighting a file on the local system, click this arrow to upload it to the remote system

Figure 16-2   Once you're connected to another computer, it's displayed in WS-FTP's right menu and referred to as *remote system*

16

Tip

Notice near the bottom of the screen that you can transfer files in two different ways: *ASCII* or *binary* (the AUTO option attempts to help you choose between these two). HTML and text files should be transferred in ASCII mode, while graphic, multimedia, and most other file types should be transferred in binary mode. This is true regardless of what FTP program you are using.

For more information about using WS-FTP, visit **www.ispwitch.com.** Or, if you prefer, try one of these other great Windows FTP programs.

- CoffeeCup Free FTP (**www.coffeecup.com**)

- CuteFTP (**www.globalscape.com**)

- FTP Voyager (**www.rhinosoft.com**)

Macintosh FTP Programs

When working on my Mac, I use Vicomsoft FTP Client 3. This excellent FTP program is available in shareware and profession versions, which can be downloaded from Vicomsoft's Web site (**www.vicomsoft.com**).

To start the process, you have to enter all the information about the computer you intend to access. For example, you need the computer's name (domain name or IP address), your username and password. In Vicomsoft FTP Client, choose FILE | NEW SERVICE to set up a new connection (Figure 16-3).

Note

You should receive all the necessary information when you sign up for hosting service. If you're unsure, check your host company's Web site or call its customer support line for assistance.

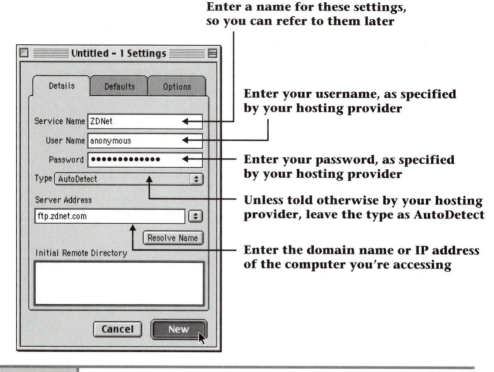

Enter a name for these settings, so you can refer to them later

Enter your username, as specified by your hosting provider

Enter your password, as specified by your hosting provider

Unless told otherwise by your hosting provider, leave the type as AutoDetect

Enter the domain name or IP address of the computer you're accessing

Figure 16-3 | After entering the necessary information, click the button labeled NEW to save your settings

After setting up the new profile, click the button labeled NEW to save the information. Then, select the name of the profile from the CONNECT menu at the top of the screen to access the other computer.

A window will display, showing your local hard drive on the left side and the computer you're accessing on the right side (Figure 16-4). You can drag-and-drop files from one side to the other, as you would in other folders on your Mac. Or, you can use the buttons next to each of the two windows to perform functions like renaming, moving, or deleting files.

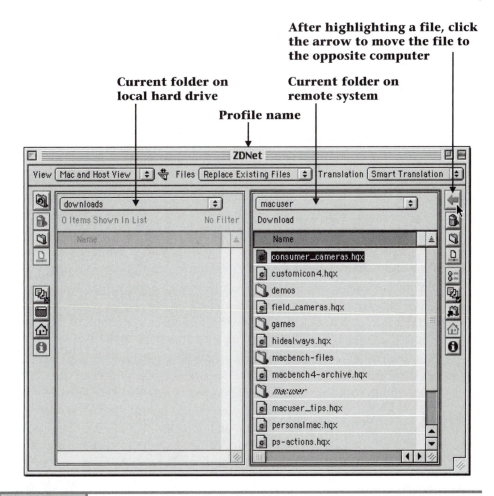

After highlighting a file, click the arrow to move the file to the opposite computer

Current folder on local hard drive

Current folder on remote system

Profile name

Figure 16-4   When you're connected to another computer, your local hard drive is shown on the left and the remote system is shown on the right

To upload or download a file, you must first highlight the file. Then, either drag it over to the other window or click the first button next to the current window. (When a file is highlighted, the button is labeled with an arrow. Otherwise, it's labeled with a folder and can be used to refresh the contents of the window.)

For more information about using Vicomsoft FTP Client, visit **www.vicomsoft.com.** Or, if you prefer, try one of these other great Macintosh FTP programs.

- Fetch (**www.dartmouth.edu/pages/softdev/fetch.html**)

- Interarchy (**www.stairways.com**)

- NetFinder (**www.ozemail.com.au/~pli/netfinder**)

- Transmit (**www.panic.com**)

Web-based FTP

If you are using a free service to host your Web page, you probably have FTP capabilities through that company's Web site. This is called *Web-based FTP* because you don't need any additional software to transmit the files—in fact, you transmit the files right from within your Web browser.

For example, Figure 16-5 shows the FTP capabilities for users of Yahoo! GeoCities. To use this Web-based FTP, click the first button labeled BROWSE and locate the file on your hard drive you'd like to upload. If you want to upload more than one file, use the additional Browse buttons to select multiple files. When you finish, click the button labeled Upload Files. Depending on the size of the files and the speed of your connection, you may experience a delay as the file is uploaded to Yahoo! GeoCities' servers.

> *Hint*
> Check with your hosting provider to see if it provides Web-based FTP service for your site.

Once your files are uploaded, you can use Yahoo! GeoCities' File Manager to move, rename, or delete files, as well as to create and edit folders. Notice on the right side of the screen in Figure 16-5, instructions are included for those who want to use separate FTP programs, like the ones discussed in previous sections.

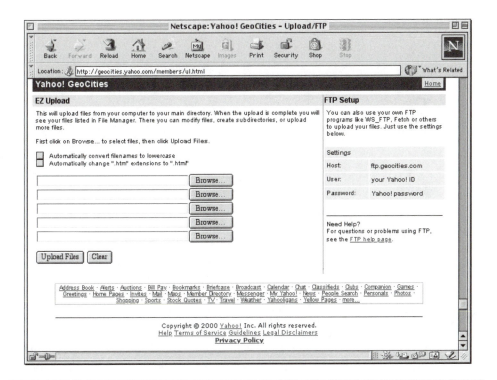

Figure 16-5 If available, Web-based FTP can be an easy way to upload your files to a Web server (Reproduced with permission of Yahoo! Inc. © 2000 by Yahoo! Inc. YAHOO! and the YAHOO! logo are trademarks of Yahoo! Inc.)

Testing Your Site

After your site is uploaded to the server, you want to run through each page once more, to verify everything transferred as expected. In addition, test to make sure all the links work and images appear.

Once you've made a cursory check, it's time to check for cross-browser and cross-platform consistency. Throughout the book, I have mentioned the importance of checking your pages in multiple browsers and on multiple computer systems to make sure they appear as you intended. However, if you weren't able to do so before because you didn't have another computer or browser handy, now's the time.

Tip

Finding errors? Remember to check out Resource C: Troubleshooting.

Even if you don't have more than one type of computer or browser, now that your pages are live, you can ask friends or family to test them for you. Have them record what type of browser they're using, what size monitor they have, what size screen resolution they're using and what computer operating system they're running. That way, when they report bugs or errors on your pages, you'll have help in determining the problem.

Submitting Your Site

After your site is live, you can begin submitting its URL to search engines and search directories. When you submit your site to a search directory, you typically have to fill out a form detailing information about the site and its purpose. To begin the process, visit a directory and look for links where you can "Suggest a Site" (Yahoo!) or "Add URL" (Open Directory) to get your site listed. Be aware, though, changing a listing in a directory is difficult, so be sure to enter the correct information the first time. It can take as long as eight to twelve weeks (Yahoo!) for your site to appear in a directory.

By contrast, submitting your site to an engine simply involves entering the URL of your Web site and, perhaps, a contact e-mail address. Just like with directories, you should look for a link labeled "Add URL" or "Add a Site". Your listing typically appears within a few days, but it may take as long as a week or so.

The different types of engines vary greatly according to how they index your site. Because most engines give results based on how relevant pages are to search terms, you might rank 10th on one day or $1,000^{th}$ on another. The only way to keep your site current in the engines is to resubmit it often.

There are two schools of thought regarding how to submit your site to search engines and search directories. First, you can do this manually, by visiting each of the top eight to ten search engines or search directories (as well as any other smaller directories you choose) and submitting your URL.

Tip

You can use a site like **submit-it.com** to help you organize the submission process when submitting your site to multiple search engines and search directories.

Second, you can pay someone else to do it for you. Unfortunately, finding a reputable service to do this is difficult and it can be costly. Be wary of companies willing to boost your site to the "top ten" for a fee. These companies may bring you to the top ten of a popular engine for a single day or, even worse, to the top ten of some unknown search engine. If you do hire a company to help you with this, look for one willing to submit and resubmit your site over a period of six to nine months. For a complete checklist of what to ask these services before signing up, visit Paul Bruemmer's article on the Clickz Network entitled "Getting Listed: Doing It Right" (**gt.clickz.com/cgi-bin/gt/cz/cz.html?article=1719**).

Either way, this is a time-intensive process for whoever does it and there's no magic solution. Some surveys (such as this one: **www.workz.com/Attract/se_survey1.asp**) show that unless you spend about 60 minutes a week resubmitting your site to a few engines, you are unlikely to see an increase in your ranking.

Note

Because many search engines and search directories have their own set of rules and guidelines, reading through any tips or help files they provide before submitting your site is important. For example, on some sites, if you submit your site too often, they actually remove it from their listings altogether.

Marketing Tips

In addition to submitting your site to search engines and search directories, you can do many other things to promote your Web site on- and offline.

- **Exchange links with related sites.** Consider asking sites with related content for links, in exchange for a link to their site from yours. Don't forget about organizations you belong to like your local Chamber of Commerce or an industry association. These are great places to exchange links. Another place you can exchange links is with a group of related sites, called a *Web ring*. Visit **www.webring.com** for some examples.

- **Create newsworthy content.** Everyone loves free publicity, and with the thousands of media outlets both on- and offline, you should be able to get a little publicity yourself. If you have an interesting product or a new twist on an old idea, tell someone! E-mail news agencies, send out a press release, write to your local paper, contribute to an association's newsletter . . . and don't forget to plug your Web site.

- **Use your customers and tell everyone you know.** Give out free pins, bumper stickers, pens, or anything with your Web site address to your existing customers. If your services and products are good, they'll have no problem telling others about them. In addition, spread the word through industry events where you can network and sell your business.

- **Don't forget traditional advertising!** If you have stationery, add your Web site address. If you already run radio or print ads, include your Web site address. Consider running a special ad promoting your new or revamped Web site.

- **If you have the budget, consider paid online advertising.** Banner ads and paid listings in directories can be beneficial if targeted toward the right audience. Sometimes a less-expensive alternative might be to sponsor a related nonprofit Web site. For example, if you sell school supplies, consider sponsoring a nonprofit homework help site. Another alternative is to sponsor free e-mail or Internet Service Providers. Juno (**www.juno.com**), whose Internet service is free, generates revenue entirely through advertisements shown to all its users.

● **Most important, create useful content.** If your site is boring, or otherwise useless, people won't come and they won't help you promote it. While the best marketer for *your* business is a satisfied customer, the best marketer for *your competition* is a dissatisfied one.

Making the Site Live!

As a final step in creating your Web site, research possible hosting solutions. Refer to the beginning of the module for links and tips on finding personal and business hosting.

Tip

If you simply want to test the site you created to learn HTML in this book, I suggest signing up for a free site with Yahoo! GeoCities (**geocities.yahoo.com**). You can then follow the onscreen instructions to use Yahoo!'s Web-based FTP or use any of the popular FTP programs.

After selecting a hosting provider, use an FTP program to transfer your Web site to the server. Test the pages in several browsers and on different computer systems to confirm you successfully created and uploaded your Web site. For practice, try making a change to one of the pages after viewing it live. Then, re-upload the page and choose REFRESH or RELOAD in your browser to review the change.

If appropriate, add your site to search engines and search directories, and continue with other marketing techniques. Remember, promoting your Web site is an ongoing task and requires frequent maintenance.

Summary

Congratulations! If you've successfully uploaded your pages to a server and made them live, you certainly should be proud. To compare your sites to others created by readers of this book, visit **www.willardesigns.com/ htmlbook**. If you need help, refer to Resource *C:* Troubleshooting or visit **www.willardesigns.com/htmlbook/bbs**.

Tip

Ready to learn about more Web technologies? Check out Obsorne's Web site (**www.osborne.com**) for information regarding additional books in the Beginner's Guide series.

☑ Mastery Check

1. How many characters are permitted in a domain name?

2. What does FTP stand for?

3. Why is it unrealistic for most small businesses to host their own Web sites?

4. In which format should HTML and text files be transferred?

5. Identify three ways you can get started marketing your new Web site.

Learning More

Many online tutorials can help you learn more about transferring files on the Internet. Check with your hosting provider because it probably will have additional help files on this subject. Here are some of the most popular:

- **Yahoo! GeoCities FTP Help** (**help.yahoo.com/help/us/geo/gftp**)

- **ZDNET: Help & How-To: File Transfer Protocol** (**www.zdnet.com/zdhelp/stories/main/0,5594,2302088,00.html**)

- **AOL's FTP Help** (**www.aol.com/nethelp/ftp/ftp.html**)

- **Web Know How** (**www.webknowhow.net**) contains online tutorials, as well as help with finding a Web host.

Search Engines & Search Directories

This module only scratched the surface of a complex issue for Web developers—marketing a site on the Internet. I recommend you check out some of the following sources of additional information to help improve your site's standing in the market.

1. Search Engine Watch (**www.searchenginewatch.com**) is considered one of the best places to look for information about improving your site's rankings online. It includes search engine tips and techniques, reviews, tests, resources, and the latest headlines.

2. The Search Engine Guide (**www.searchengineguide.com**) gives search engine and directory news, marketing information, and general tips.

3. keywordcount.com helps you analyze the most popular words on your Web site, as well as compare them to your competition.

4. Web Marketing Info Center (**www.wilsonweb.com/webmarket**) gives advice and links for articles about marketing on the Web.

5. The Clickz Network (**www.clickz.com**) is a large network of information about effective marketing of Web sites both on and offline.

6. Position Agent (**www.positionagent.com**) enables you to search by keyword for your site in ten of the top engines and directories at once.

In addition, the search engines and search directories themselves can be a great place to look for information about advertising your site. Most of them have sections of their site dedicated to answering users' questions about this very topic. Here's a list of the key engines and directories.

- Alta Vista (**www.altavista.com**)
- AOLNetfind (**search.aol.com**)
- AskJeeves (**www.ask.com**)
- Excite (**www.excite.com**)
- Go (**www.go.com**)
- Google (**www.google.com**)
- HotBot (**www.hotbot.com**)
- Infoseek (**infoseek.go.com**)
- LookSmart (**www.looksmart.com**)
- Lycos (**www.lycos.com**)
- NBC (**www.NBCi.com**)
- Netscape (**www.netscape.com**)
- Open Directory (**dmoz.org**)
- SearchMSN (**search.msn.com**)
- Snap (**www.snap.com**)
- Yahoo! (**www.yahoo.com**)

Part 3

Resources

Resource A

HTML 4
Reference Table

This resource should serve as a quick reference table for the tags learned in this book and is broken up into sections according to the different types of tags discussed throughout the modules. Because the scope of this book is at a beginner's level, I decided not to discuss a few HTML tags. If you come across a tag not listed here or in the index, try visiting an online tag library such as

● **www.zdnet.com/devhead/resources/tag_library**

● **www.webflex.nl/support/htmltag**

Note

The latest version of the HTML specifications can be found on the W3C's Web site: **www.w3c.org.**

Generic Attributes

The following groups of attributes can be used by a large number of tags in HTML. In the rest of the tables in this reference, a code is listed in the attribute column on a particular tag if it accepts any of the following groups of generic attributes.

● Core Attributes (*core) provide rendering and accessibility information to elements.

● Event Handlers (*events) provide a way of triggering an action when an event occurs on a page. Note: Not all event handlers are listed.

● International Attributes (*intl) provide a way of rendering documents using multiple language or character sets.

Group Type: Core

Attribute	Uses
accesskey	Assigns a keyboard shortcut to the element.
class	Assigns a category label to an element.
ID	Assigns a unique identifier to an element.
style	Gives instructions on how to render an element.
tabindex	Assigns the tab order of an element.
title	Gives a brief description of an element.

Group Type: Events

Attribute	Uses
onClick	Triggers an event when the element is clicked.
onDblClick	Triggers an event when the element is double-clicked.
onMouseDown	Triggers an event when the pointer is pressed down over an element.
onMouseUp	Triggers an event when the pointer is released over an element.
onMouseOver	Triggers an event when the pointer is passed over an element.
onMouseOut	Triggers an event when the pointer moves away from an element.
onKeyPress	Triggers an event when a key is pressed and released immediately.
onKeyDown	Triggers an event when a key is pressed and held down.
onKeyUp	Triggers an event when a key that was pressed is now released.

Group Type: Intl

Attribute	Uses
dir	Indicates the direction of the content flow
lang	Indicates the language of the content.

Basic Page Structure

Basic Element	Attributes	Uses	Opening/Closing	Notes
<!--...-->	n/a	Inserts comments into the page that aren't seen when the page is viewed in the browser.	required/required	n/a
!DOCTYPE	n/a	Indicates version of X/HTML used. Must be placed on first line of document.	optional/illegal	1
body	*core, *events, *intl	Encloses the content of the document.	optional/optional	1, 8
	alink	Specifies the default color of an active link on the page.	n/a	3
	background	Defines a background image for the page.	n/a	3
	bgcolor	Specifies the default background color of the page.	n/a	3
	link	Specifies the default color of the links on the page.	n/a	3

Basic Element	Attributes	Uses	Opening/Closing	Notes
body	text	Specifies the default color of the visited links on the page.	n/a	3
	vlink	Specifies the default color of the visited links on the page.	n/a	3
	topmargin, leftmargin	Specifies the size in pixels of the top and left margins.	n/a	4, 5
	marginheight, marginwidth	n/a	n/a	4, 6
div	*core, *events, *intl	Identifies a section (or division) of the page.	required/required	n/a
	align	Aligns the section to the page.	n/a	3
h1 … h6	*core, *events, *intl	Creates six levels of headline (h1 being the largest and most important.	required/required	n/a
	align	Aligns the headline on the page.	n/a	3
head	*intl	Contains the header information for the page (such as the title and information for search engines).	optional/optional	1, 8
hr	*core, *events	Separates sections with a horizontal rule.	required/illegal	2
	align	Aligns the rule on the page.	n/a	3
	noshade	Displays the rule with a solid color, without shading.	n/a	3
	size	Specifies the height of the rule.	n/a	3
	width	Specifies the width (or length) of the rule.	n/a	3
html	*intl	Contains and identifies the document.	optional/optional	1
meta	*intl	Gives information about the document.	required/illegal	2
	content	Contains specified information.	n/a	n/a

Basic Element	Attributes	Uses	Opening/Closing	Notes
meta	http-equiv	Assigns a header field, which then can be used to transfer the user to another page or otherwise process the document.	n/a	n/a
	name	Defines what type of information the content attribute specifies.	n/a	n/a
span	*core, *events, *intl	Defines a section of content.	required/required	n/a
title	*intl	Gives a name to your page that will be displayed in the title bar of the browser.	required/required	8

Working with Text

Basic Elements	Attributes	Uses	Opening/Closing	Notes
acronym	*core, *events, *intl	Specifies an acronym	required/required	7
address	*core, *events, *intl	Formats the contact information for a page.	required/required	n/a
b	*core, *events, *intl	Makes text bold	required/required	n/a
basefont	n/a	Defines the default font characteristics for a page.	required/illegal	2, 3
	color	Specifies the default font color.	n/a	3
	face	Specifies the default font face.	n/a	3
	size	Specifies the default font size.	n/a	3
big	*core, *events, *intl	Formats the text as one size larger than the default size.	required/required	n/a
blockquote	*core, *events, *intl	Sets off a block of text indenting it on both sides.	required/required	n/a

Basic Elements	Attributes	Uses	Opening/Closing	Notes
br	*core, *events, *intl	Causes a line break.	required/illegal	2
	clear	Causes text to stop wrapping around an image and start again on the next line.	n/a	3
cite	*core, *events, *intl	Formats a short quote or reference.	required/required	n/a
code	*core, *events, *intl	Formats text as code (usually in a monospaced font).	required/required	n/a
del	*core, *events, *intl	Formats text as deleted by marking a line through it.	required/required	7
	cite	References another document with a URL.	n/a	n/a
	datetime	Identifies the date and time of the deletion.	n/a	n/a
dfn	*core, *events, *intl	Specifies a definition.	required/required	7
em	*core, *events, *intl	Gives emphasis to text (usually by making it italic).	required/required	n/a
font	n/a	Formats text characteristics.	required/required	n/a
	color	Specifies the font color.	n/a	3
	face	Specifies the font face.	n/a	3
	size	Specifies the font size.	n/a	3
i	*core, *event, *intl	Formats text as italic.	required/required	n/a
ins	*core, *event, *intl	Formats text as inserted since the last change.	required/required	7
	cite	References another document with a URL.	n/a	n/a
	datetime	Identifies the date and time of the insertion.	n/a	n/a
kbd	*core, *events, *intl	Formats text as something the user should type on his or her keyboard.	required/required	7
p	*core, *events, *intl	Specifies a paragraph of text (inserts a blank line).	required/optional	2

A

Basic Elements	Attributes	Uses	Opening/Closing	Notes
pre	*core, *events, *intl	Identifies text as preformatted (usually displayed in a monospaced font).	required/required	n/a
q	*core, *events, *intl	Formats a short quotation.	required/required	7
s, strike	*core, *events, *intl	Formats the text as strikethrough.	required/required	3
samp	*core, *events, *intl	Formats text as a sample computer output, usually in a monospaced font.	required/required	n/a
small	*core, *events, *intl	Formats the text as on size smaller than the default size.	required/required	n/a
strong	*core, *events, *intl	Gives stronger emphasis to text, usually by making it bold.	required/required	n/a
sub	*core, *events, *intl	Formats the text as subscript.	required/required	n/a
sup	*core, *events, *intl	Formats the text as superscript.	required/required	n/a
tt	*core, *events, *intl	Formats the text as teletype or monospaced.	required/required	n/a
u	*core, *events, *intl	Underlines text.	required/required	3
var	*core, *events, *intl	Formats the text as variable.	required/required	n/a

Working with Links

Basic Element	Attributes	Uses	Opening/Closing	Notes
a	*core, *events, *intl	Creates links and anchors.	required/required	n/a
	coords	Defines the size of a hot spot in an image map.	n/a	n/a
	href	Specifies the location (URL) of the link.	n/a	n/a
	name	Identifies an anchor.	n/a	n/a

Basic Element	Attributes	Uses	Opening/Closing	Notes
a	shape	Defines the shape of a hot spot in an image map.	n/a	n/a
	target	Identifies the target window where the link will be displayed.	n/a	n/a
base	n/a	Identifies defaults for the document.	required/illegal	2
	href	Specifies the default location of the link.	n/a	n/a
	target	Specifies the default window in which the link should load.	n/a	n/a
link	*core, *events, *intl	Indicates a relationship between the current document and another resource (such as a style_sheet).	required/illegal	2
	href	Specifies the location of the resource.	n/a	n/a
	rel	Specifies the type of resource.	n/a	n/a
	type	Defines the MIME type.	n/a	n/a

Working with Images and Multimedia

Basic Element	Attributes	Uses	Opening/Closing	Notes
applet	n/a	Embeds a Java applet into a page.	required/required	3
	align	Aligns the applet on the page.	n/a	3
	alt	Defines text description.	n/a	3
	code, codebase	Defines the location (URL) of the applet's code.	n/a	3
	height	Defines the height, in pixels, of the applet.	n/a	3

A

Basic Element	Attributes	Uses	Opening/Closing	Notes
applet	hspace	Defines, in pixels, the amount of blank space to the right and to the left of the applet.	n/a	3
	name	Defines the name of the applet.	n/a	3
	vspace	Defines, in pixels, the amount of blank space above and below the applet.	n/a	3
	width	Defines the width, in pixels, of the applet.	n/a	3
area	n/a	Defines links and anchors within an image map.	required/illegal	2
	coords	Specifies the size of the hot spot.	n/a	n/a
	href	Specifies the location (URL) of the link.	n/a	n/a
	nohref	Specifies that a hot spot isn't linked.	n/a	n/a
	shape	Defines the shape of a hot spot in an image map.	n/a	n/a
	target	Identifies the target window where the link will be displayed.	n/a	n/a
embed	*core, *intl	Embeds an object in a page.	required/required	4, 7
	align	Aligns the object on the page.	n/a	n/a
	autostart	Defines whether the object begins playing as soon as it's loaded.	n/a	n/a
	controls	Defines how the controls for the object appear.	n/a	n/a
	height	Specifies the height, in pixels, of the object.	n/a	n/a
	loop	Specifies how many times an object plays.	n/a	n/a
	src	Identifies the source file of the object.	n/a	n/a

Basic Element	Attributes	Uses	Opening/Closing	Notes
embed	width	Specifies the width, in pixels, of the objects.	n/a	n/a
img	*core, *events, *intl	Embeds an image in a page.	required/illegal	2
	align	Aligns the image on the page.	n/a	3
	alt	Specifies a text description of the image.	n/a	3
	border	Defines the thickness of the border around the image.	n/a	3
	height	Defines the height of the image in pixels.	n/a	3
	hspace	Defines, in pixels, how much blank space is present to the right and left of an image.	n/a	3
	ismap	Identifies the image as a server-side image map.	n/a	3
	vspace	Defines, in pixels, how much blank space is present above and below an image.	n/a	3
	src	Defines the location of the image file.	n/a	3
	usemap	Identifies the image as a client-side image map and specifies the location (URL) of the map properties.	n/a	n/a
	width	Defines the width of the image in pixels.	n/a	n/a
map	*core	Defines the properties of a client-side image map.	required/required	n/a
	name	Names the map.	n/a	n/a
object	*core, *events, *intl	Embeds an object in a page.	required/required	7
	align	Aligns the object on the page.	n/a	3

Basic Element	Attributes	Uses	Opening/Closing	Notes
object	border	Defines the thickness of the border around the object.	n/a	3
	classid, codebase	Defines a URL indicating how the object should be implemented.	n/a	n/a
	codetype, type	Specifies the MIME type of the code referenced by the classid attribute.	n/a	n/a
	height	Defines the height, in pixels, of the object.	n/a	n/a
	hspace	Defines, in pixels, the amount of blank space to the left and right of the object.	n/a	3
	name	Defines the name of an object.	n/a	n/a
	standby	Defines the message to show while the object is loading.	n/a	n/a
	usemap	Identifies the object as a client-side image map and specifies the location (URL) of the map properties.	n/a	n/a
	width	Defines the width, in pixels, of the object.	n/a	n/a
	vspace	Defines, in pixels, the amount of blank space to appear above and below the object.	n/a	3
param	n/a	Contains parameters for an object.	required/illegal	2, 7
	name	Defines the parameter's name.	n/a	n/a
	type	Defines the parameter's MIME type.	n/a	n/a
	value	Defines the parameter's value.	n/a	n/a
	valuetype	Defines the value type.	n/a	n/a

A

Creating Lists

Basic Elements	Attributes	Uses	Opening/Closing	Notes
dd	*core, *events, *intl	Defines the description of a term in a definition list.	required/optional	2
dl	*core, *events, *intl	Creates a definition list.	required/required	n/a
	compact	Compacts the list.	n/a	3
dt	*core, *events, *intl	Defines a term in a definition list.	required/optional	2
li	*core, *events, *intl	Defines an item in an ordered or unorderd list.	required/optional	2
	type	Specifies the style of the list.	n/a	3
	value	Specifies the initial value of the first item.	n/a	3
ol	*core, *events, *intl	Created an ordered list.	required/required	n/a
	compact	Compacts the list.	n/a	3
	start	Specifies the starting number.	n/a	3
	type	Specifies the style of the list.	n/a	3
ul	*core, *events, *intl	Creates an unordered list.	required/required	n/a
	compact	Compacts the list.	n/a	3
	type	Specifies the style of the list.	n/a	3

Using Tables

Basic Element	Attributes	Uses	Opening/Closing	Notes
caption	*core, *events, *intl	Defines a table caption.	required/required	3
col	*core, *events, *intl	Specifies subgroups of colums within a column group, to allow them to share attributes.	required/illegal	2, 7
	align	Aligns the sub-column group horizontally.	n/a	n/a

A

Basic Element	Attributes	Uses	Opening/Closing	Notes
col	span	Specifies the number of columns the sub-column groups spans.	n/a	n/a
	width	Specifies the width of the columns, using percentages or pixels.	n/a	n/a
	valign	Aligns the sub-column group vertically.	n/a	n/a
colgroup	*core, *events, *intl	Defines a group of columns.	required/optional	2, 7
	align	Aligns the column group horizontally.	n/a	n/a
	span	Specifies the number of columns the group spans.	n/a	n/a
	width	Specifies the width of the columns, using percentages or pixels.	n/a	n/a
	valign	Aligns the column group vertically.	n/a	n/a
table	*core, *events, *intl	Creates a table.	required/required	n/a
	align	Aligns the table on the page.	n/a	3
	bgcolor	Specifies the background color of the table.	n/a	3
	border	Specifies the thickness, in pixels, on the border around the table.	n/a	n/a
	cellpadding	Specifies the amount of space around the content within the cells.	n/a	n/a
	cellspacing	Specifies the amount of space between cells.	n/a	n/a
	cols	Identifies the number of columns.	n/a	n/a
	frame	Defines which of the table's edges are visible.	n/a	7
	height	Specifies the height of the table, in pixels or percentages.	n/a	4
	rules	Defines which of the table's interior seams are visible.	n/a	7

Basic Element	Attributes	Uses	Opening/Closing	Notes
table	width	Specifies the width of the table, in pixels or percentages.	n/a	n/a
tbody	*core, *events, *intl	Defines the table's body.	optional/optional	1, 7
	align	Aligns the cell contents horizontally.	n/a	n/a
	valign	Aligns the cell contents vertically.	n/a	n/a
td, th	*core, *events, *intl	Defines an individual cell (td) or header cell (th).	required/optional	2
	align	Aligns the cell's contents horizontally.	n/a	n/a
	bgcolor	Defines the cell's background color.	n/a	3
	colspan	Defines how many columns the cell spans.	n/a	n/a
	height	Defines the height of the cell, in pixels or percentages.	n/a	3
	nowrap	Specifies the content of the cell should stay on a single line.	n/a	3
	rowspan	Defines how many rows the cell spans.	n/a	n/a
	valign	Aligns the cell's contents vertically.	n/a	n/a
	width	Defines the width of the cell, in pixels or percentages.	n/a	3
tfoot	*core, *events, *intl	Defines the table's footer.	required/optional	1, 7
	align	Aligns the cell contents horizontally.	n/a	n/a
	valign	Aligns the cell contents vertically.	n/a	n/a
thread	*core, *events, *intl	Defines a table's header.	required/optional	1, 7
	align	Aligns the cell contents horizontally.	n/a	n/a
	valign	Aligns the cell contents vertically.	n/a	n/a
tr	*core, *events, *intl	Defines a table row.	required/optional	1

Basic Element	Attributes	Uses	Opening/Closing	Notes
tr	aligns	Aligns the content of the row's cells horizontally.	n/a	n/a
	bgcolor	Specifies a background color for the row.	n/a	3
	valign	Aligns the content of the row's cells vertically.	n/a	3

A

Developing Frames

Basic Element	Attributes	Uses	Opening/Closing	Notes
frame	n/a	Creates frames.	required/illegal	2
	border	Defines the thickness of the border(s) between frames.	n/a	4
	border color	Defines the color of the border(s) between frames.	n/a	4
	frameborder	Specifies whether the border(s) between frames are visible.	n/a	n/a
	name	Defines a name for the frame, so it can be used as a target window.	n/a	n/a
	noresize	Specifies the user cannot alter the frame's size.	n/a	n/a
	margin height	Defines the size of the frame's top and bottom margins.	n/a	n/a
	marginwidth	Defines the size of the frame's right and left margins.	n/a	n/a
	scrolling	Defines when the scroll the scroll bars appear in the frame.	n/a	n/a
	src	Defines the initial document (URL) that should be loaded into the frame.	n/a	n/a
frameset	n/a	Creates a layout for a set of frames.	required/required	n/a

Basic Element	Attributes	Uses	Opening/Closing	Notes
frameset	border	Defines the thickness of the border(s) between frames.	n/a	4
	bordercolor	Defines the color of the border(s) between frames.	n/a	4
	cols	Defines the number and size of the columns.	n/a	n/a
	frameborder	Specifies whether the border(s) between frames are visible.	n/a	n/a
	rows	Defines the number and size of the rows.	n/a	n/a
iframe	n/a	Creates an inline, floating frame.	required/required	7
	align	Aligns the frame in the page.	n/a	3
	frameborder	Defines whether the frame's border is visible.	n/a	n/a
	height	Defines the height of the frame.	n/a	n/a
	name	Defines the name of the frame.	n/a	n/a
	scrolling	Defines when the scroll bar appears in the frame.	n/a	n/a
	src	Defines the initial source document (URL) to be loaded into the frame.	n/a	n/a
	width	Defines the width of the frame.	n/a	n/a
noframes	n/a	Provides alternative content for non-frames-capable browsers.	required/required	n/a

Employing Forms

Basic Element	Attributes	Uses	Opening/Closing	Notes
button	*core, *events, *intl	Creates a button	required/required	n/a
	name	Defines the name of the button.	n/a	n/a
	value	Specifies the value or type of button.	n/a	n/a
fieldset	*core, *events, *intl	Creates a group of controls.	required/required	7
form	*core, *events, *intl	Creates a form where users can enter information.	required/required	n/a
	action	Specifies the location (URL) of the script to process the form.	n/a	n/a
	enctype	Specifies the MIME type.	n/a	n/a
	method	Defines how the form will be processed.	n/a	n/a
input	*core, *events, *intl	Creates types of input controls for users.	required/illegal	2
	accept	Defines the file types allowed in a file upload control.	n/a	n/a
	alt	Defines an alternative text description.	n/a	n/a
	checked	Specifies the input control should be checked when the page is loaded.	n/a	n/a
	disabled	Specifies the input control cannot be used.	n/a	n/a
	maxlength	Defines the maximum number of characters a user can enter in a text field or password box.	n/a	n/a

Basic Element	Attributes	Uses	Opening/Closing	Notes
input	name	Defines the name of the input control, used when processing the form.	n/a	n/a
	size	Defines the size of a text filed or password box.	n/a	n/a
	src	Defines the location (URL) of an image used in an input control.	n/a	n/a
	readonly	Specifies a user can read, but cannot edit, a control.	n/a	7
	type	Identifies the type of input control (text, checkbox, and so forth).	n/a	n/a
	usemap	Identifies the control as a client-side image map and specifies the location (URL) of the map properties.	n/a	n/a
	value	Defines the initial value of an input control.	n/a	n/a
label	*core, *events, *intl	Specifies a label for an input control.	required/required.	7
	align	Aligns the label.	n/a	3
	for	Identifies to which input control the label belongs.	n/a	n/a
option	*core, *events, *intl	Creates choices in a select menu.	required/optional	1
	disabled	Specifies the specific option as viewable, but not selectable.	n/a	7
	selected	Defines the option as selected by default when the page is loaded.	n/a	n/a
	value	Defines the initial value of the option, used when processing the form.	n/a	n/a
select	*core, *events, *intl	Creates a menu with choices users can select.	required/required	n/a

Basic Element	Attributes	Uses	Opening/Closing	Notes
select	disabled	Specifies the menu as viewable, but not useable.	n/a	7
	name	Identifies the name of the menu, used when processing the form.	n/a	n/a
	multiple	Enables users to select multiple choices.	n/a	n/a
	size	Defines the number of choices visible in the menu when the page loads.	n/a	n/a
textarea	*core, *events, *intl	Creates an input control where users can enter multiple lines of text.	required/required	n/a
	cols	Defines the height of the text area, in the number of character columns visible.	n/a	n/a
	disabled	Prevents users from entering text in the area.	n/a	7
	name	Identifies the name of the text area, used when processing the form.	n/a	n/a
	readonly	Specifies the text area as viewable, but not editable.	n/a	7
	rows	Defines the width of the text area, in the number of character rows visible.	n/a	n/a

Using Style Sheets and Scripts

Basic Element	Attributes	Uses	Opening/Closing	Notes
noscript	n/a	Defines the content displayed in browsers that don't support forms.	required/required	n/a
script	n/a	Contains scripts, such as those written in JavaScript, executed in the page by the browser.	required/required	7

Basic Element	Attributes	Uses	Opening/Closing	Notes
script	language	Identifies the script language.	n/a	n/a
	src	References an external script, by giving its location (URL).	n/a	n/a
	type	Specifies the MIME type of the script.	n/a	n/a
style	*intl	Adds internal style sheet to a page.	required/required	7
	media	Specifies the media type in which the page will be displayed (such as screen, print, all, and so forth).	n/a	n/a
	title	Identifies the title of the style.	n/a	n/a
	type	Identifies the MIME type.	n/a	n/a

Notes:

1. Optional in HTML; Required in XHTML.

2. XHTML requires all tags be closed, even when the closing tag is listed as optional or illegal in HTML. Place a space and a slash before the final bracket to close these tags, as in the following example: `<img src="photo.jpg" />`.

3. These tags and/or attributes are deprecated in HTML 4. While the W3C favors other tags over the use of these, they still enjoy wide support among popular browsers.

4. Not part of the official HTML 4 specification.

5. Supported only by Internet Explorer.

6. Supported only by Netscape.

7. Browser support varies widely and, in some cases, is nonexistent.

8. Only one such tag is allowed per page.

Resource B

Special Characters

In HTML, characters that use the shift key should be rendered by entities instead of being typed out. Entities can be in the form of numbers or named, but all begin with an ampersand and end with a semicolon. Some entities aren't supported by all browsers, so be sure to test your pages in several browsers to ensure they appear as you intend. For more information, visit **www.htmlhelp.com/reference/charset**.

Note

This table lists the most popular entities. Most nonstandard or minimally supported entities aren't included here.

Standard HTML Entites

Character	Numbered Entity	Named Entity	Description
	&#32;	n/a	Space
!	&#33;	n/a	Exclamation point
"	&#34;	&quot;	Double quote
#	&#35;	n/a	Number symbol
$	&#36;	n/a	Dollar symbol
%	&#37;	n/a	Percent symbol
&	&#38;	&amp;	Ampersand
'	&#39;	n/a	Single quote
(	&#40;	n/a	Opening parenthesis
)	&#41;	n/a	Closing parenthesis
*	&#42;	n/a	Asterisk
+	&#43;	n/a	Plus sign
,	&#44;	n/a	Comma
-	&#45;	n/a	Minus sign
.	&#46;	n/a	Period
/	&#47;	n/a	Forward slash (virgule)
:	&#58;	n/a	Colon
;	&#59;	n/a	Semicolon
<	&#60;	&lt;	Left angle bracket (less than symbol)
=	&#61;	n/a	Equals sign

Character	Numbered Entity	Named Entity	Description
>	&#62;	&gt;	Right angle bracket (greater than symbol)
?	&#63;	n/a	Question mark
@	&#64;	n/a	"At" symbol
[	&#91;	n/a	Opening bracket
\	&#92;	n/a	Backslash
]	&#93;	n/a	Closing bracket
^	&#94;	n/a	Caret
_	&#95;	n/a	Underscore
`	&#96;	n/a	Grave accent, no letter
{	&#123;	n/a	Opening brace (opening curly bracket)
|	|	n/a	Vertical bar
}	&#125;	n/a	Closing brace (closing curly bracket)
~	&#126;	n/a	Tilde (equivalency symbol)
™	&#153;	™ (not widely supported)	Trademark symbol
			Nonbreaking space
¡	&#161;	&iexcl;	Inverted exclamation
¢	&#162;	&cent;	Cent sign
£	&#163;	&pound;	Pound sterling
¤	&#164;	&curren;	General currency sign
¥	&#165;	&yen;	Yen sign
¦	&#166;	&brvbar;	Broken vertical bar
§	&#167;	&sect;	Section sign
¨	&#168;	&uml;	Umlaut, no letter
©	&#169;	&copy;	Copyright symbol
ª	&#170;	&ordf;	Feminine ordinal
«	&#171;	&laquo;	Left double angle quote (guillemotleft)
¬	&#172;	&not;	"Not" symbol
?	&#173;	&shy;	Soft hyphen
®	&#174;	&reg;	Registration mark

Character	Numbered Entity	Named Entity	Description
¯	&#175;	&macr;	Macron accent
°	&#176;	&deg;	Degree symbol
±	&#177;	&plusmn;	Plus or minus symbol
²	&#178;	&sup2;	Superscript two
³	&#179;	&sup3;	Superscript three
´	&#180;	&acute;	Acute accent, no letter
µ	&#181;	&micro;	Micro symbol
¶	&#182;	&para;	Paragraph symbol
·	&#183;	&middot;	Middle dot
¸	&#184;	&cedil;	Cedilla
¹	&#185;	&sup1;	Superscript one
º	&#186;	&ordm;	Masculine ordinal
»	&#187;	&raquo;	Right double angle quote (guillemotright)
¼	&#188;	&frac14;	Fraction one-fourth
½	&frac12;	Fraction one-half	Fraction one-half
¾	&#190;	&frac34;	Fraction three-fourths
¿	&#191;	&iquest;	Inverted question mark
À	&#192;	&Agrave;	Capital A, grave accent
Á	&#193;	&Aacute;	Capital A, acute accent
Â	&#194;	&Acirc;	Capital A, circumflex accent
Ã	&#195;	&Atilde;	Capital A, tilde
Ä	&#196;	&Auml;	Capital A, dieresis, or umlaut mark
Å	&#197;	&Aring;	Capital A, ring
Æ	&#198;	&AElig;	Capital AE dipthong (ligature)
Ç	&#199;	&Ccedil;	Capital C, cedilla
È	&#200;	&Egrave;	Capital E, grave accent
É	&#201;	&Eacute;	Capital E, acute accent

Character	Numbered Entity	Named Entity	Description
Ê	`&#202;`	`&Ecirc;`	Capital *E*, circumflex accent
Ë	`&#203;`	`&Eulm;`	Capital *E*, dieresis, or umlaut mark
Ì	`&#204;`	`&Igrave;`	Capital *I*, grave accent
Í	`&#205;`	`&Iacute;`	Capital *I*, acute accent
Î	`&#206;`	`&Icirc;`	Capital *I*, circumflex accent
Ï	`&#207;`	`&Iuml;`	Capital *I*, dieresis, or umlaut mark
Ð	`&#208;`	`&ETH;`	Capital Eth, Icelandic
Ñ	`&#209;`	`&Ntilde;`	Capital *N*, tilde
Ò	`&#210;`	`&Ograve;`	Capital *O*, grave accent
Ó	`&#211;`	`&Oacute;`	Capital *O*, acute accent
Ô	`&#212;`	`&Ocirc;`	Capital *O*, circumflex accent
Õ	`&#213;`	`&Otilde;`	Capital *O*, tilde
Ö	`&#214;`	`&Ouml;`	Capital *O*, dieresis, or umlaut mark
×	`&#215;`	`&times;`	Multiply sign
Ø	`&#216;`	`&Oslash;`	Capital *O*, slash
Ù	`&#217;`	`&Ugrave;`	Capital *U*, grave accent
Ú	`&#218;`	`&Uacute;`	Capital *U*, acute accent
Û	`&#219;`	`&Ucirc;`	Capital *U*, circumflex accent
Ü	`&#220;`	`&Uuml;`	Capital *U*, dieresis, or umlaut mark
Ý	`&#221;`	`&Yacute;`	Capital *Y*, acute accent
Þ	`&#222;`	`&THORN;`	Capital THORN, Icelandic
ß	`&#223;`	`&szlig;`	Lowercase sharp *s*, German (sz ligature)
à	`&#224;`	`&agrave;`	Lowercase *a*, grave accent

Character	Numbered Entity	Named Entity	Description
á	&#225;	&aacute;	Lowercase *a*, acute accent
â	&#226;	&acirc;	Lowercase *a*, circumflex accent
ã	&#227;	&atilde;	Lowercase *a*, tilde
ä	&#228;	&auml;	Lowercase *a*, dieresis, or umlaut mark
å	&#229;	&aring;	Lowercase *a*, ring
æ	&#230;	&aelig;	Lowercase ae dipthong (ligature)
ç	&#231;	&ccedil;	Lowercase *c*, cedilla
è	&#232;	&egrave;	Lowercase *e*, grave accent
é	&#233;	&eacute;	Lowercase *e*, acute accent
ê	&#234;	&ecirc;	Lowercase *e*, circumflex accent
ë	&#235;	&euml;	Lowercase *e*, dieresis, or umlaut mark
ì	&#236;	&igrave;	Lowercase *i*, grave accent
í	&#237;	&iacute;	Lowercase *i*, acute accent
î	&#238;	&icirc;	Lowercase *i*, circumflex accent
ï	&#239;	&iuml;	Lowercase *i*, dieresis, or umlaut mark
ð	&#240;	&eth;	Lowercase eth, Icelandic
ñ	&#241;	&ntilde;	Lowercase *n*, tilde
ò	&#242;	&ograve;	Lowercase *o*, grave accent
ó	&#243;	&oacute;	Lowercase *o*, acute accent
ô	&#244;	&ocirc;	Lowercase *o*, circumflex accent
õ	&#245;	&otilde;	Lowercase *o*, tilde
ö	&#246;	&ouml;	Lowercase *o*, dieresis, or umlaut mark

Character	Numbered Entity	Named Entity	Description
÷	&#247;	&divide;	Division symbol
ø	&#248;	&oslash;	Lowercase *o*, slash
ù	&#249;	&ugrave;	Lowercase *u*, grave accent
ú	&#250;	&uacute;	Lowercase *u*, acute accent
û	&#251;	&ucirc;	Lowercase *u*, circumflex accent
ü	&#252;	&uuml;	Lowercase *u*, dieresis, or umlaut mark
ý	&#253;	&yacute;	Lowercase *y*, acute accent
þ	&#254;	&thorn;	Lowercase thorn, Icelandic
ÿ	&#255;	&yuml;	Lowercase *y*, dieresis, or umlaut mark

B

Resource C

Troubleshooting (FAQ)

This resource lists some of the most common problems encountered when writing HTML. If none of these answers solve your problem, try running your page through an online validator, such as the one offered by the W3C at **validator.w3c.org.** A service like this tests your page against the HTML specifications and prints a list of errors that makes it easy to locate problems.

Or, you could use Dave Raggett's HTML Tidy program (also available from the W3C at **www.w3.org/People/Raggett/tidy**). This handy program actually attempts to fix any problems on your page, if possible. It can also print a list of errors to alert you to things you can look for in the future.

My Page Is Blank in the Browser!

Yikes! You lost everything? No, don't worry—it's probably all there, but an unclosed tag or quote somewhere may be causing the browser to ignore everything else on the page. If you have Netscape, try viewing the HTML source of the page from within the browser. If an unclosed tag or quote is the problem, Netscape highlights the location of the error by changing its color or causing it to blink.

In my experience, the number one cause for a page displaying blank or empty in a browser is an unclosed `table` tag. So, if your page uses tables, go back through the code and identify each opening and closing `table` tag to make sure you didn't leave one off accidentally.

The number two cause for a missing section of a page is an unclosed quotation mark. For example, in the following code, the lack of closing quotes in the first `a` tag causes all the text after it to be considered part of the link URL. No text is displayed in the browser until another set of quotes is encountered that can be considered the closing quotes for the first link.

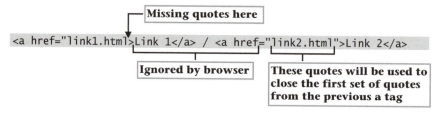

All I See Is Code in the Browser!

This occurs when the page doesn't have an HTML extension (such as `.htm` or `.html`) or when the page is saved in a format other than text-only. If you encounter this problem, return to your text editor and save the file again, making sure to choose "Text Only" or "ASCII Text" from any list of format types. When naming the file, be sure the text editor doesn't add a `.txt` extension because only `.htm` or `.html` extensions are recognized as HTML by a browser. Finally, make sure your page includes an opening and closing `html` tag.

My Images Don't Appear!

When images don't appear in a page, they are often replaced with a question mark graphic or a broken image symbol. Here's a quick checklist to run through if you encounter this problem.

1. **Check filenames.** Perhaps you named a file image.jpg but, in the HTML, you referenced it as IMAGE.JPG. Any difference at all causes the image to appear "broken" in the browser. In addition, be sure your filename doesn't include spaces because those also cause problems.

2. **Check file locations.** If you tell the browser your image is in the photos folder when you write your HTML, make sure to upload the image to that folder. If the image is in a different folder, the browser won't be able to find it.

3. **Check file types.** Remember, most graphical editors can view only GIF and JPEG files (although newer ones can also view PNG files). Other file types, such as BMP or TIFF, may be displayed as a broken image if the browser doesn't understand them.

4. **Check `img` tags.** It's common for beginners to write out *image* instead of `img` when referencing an image. The tag is `img`, however, not *image* and, therefore, you must write it as such.

I Tried to Change the Font, But Nothing Happened!

First, make sure the font name is spelled correctly. If it is spelled correctly, make sure you actually have that font running on your system. Try launching your word processor to see if the font is available in that program. If it isn't, chances are good that you don't have that font loaded on your system. You might try a different font or download the font in question. And, remember, your users may not have that font either.

When I Used a Special Character, It Doesn't Appear!

This happens for one of two reasons:

1. **Missing ampersand and/or semicolon.** Don't forget all entities—whether named or numbered—must begin with an ampersand and end with a semicolon.

2. **Lack of browser support.** Certain browsers don't support some entities. If you double-checked that you're typing the entity correctly and it still doesn't appear, it might not be supported by your browser.

In something like a trademark symbol, which is not supported by all the browsers, try using the superscript tag (`<sup>`) instead, as in the following example:

```
My Product<sup>TM</sup>
```

My Links Don't Work!

If your links don't work, check to make sure you typed them correctly. For example, a link to another Web site should look something like this:

```
<a href="http://www.willardesigns.com">WILLARDesigns</a>
```

While a link to another page in your site might look like this:

```
<a href="contactme.html">Contact Me</a>
```

Be sure to surround the link name with quotes and, if you are linking to another Web site, don't forget the `http://`.

Unfortunately, if you are linking to another person's Web site, it may be beyond your control to ensure the link works all the time. If a user clicks a link to another site from one of your pages and that site is unavailable, the link won't work. For this reason, it's important to check your links often, making sure they haven't become extinct. You might also contact the owner of the page you're linking to, as the owner might be able to provide a specific link address he or she can guarantee won't change.

Tip

You can use services to check for dead links on your site. One example is Web Site Garage's Tune Up (**www.websitegarage.com**).

My Page Looks Great in One Browser, But Terrible in Another!

Unfortunately, I must say this is a common problem. In most cases, though, the page's developer never takes the time to look at the site in another browser and, therefore, never knows how bad the page looks. Take heart—you're halfway to making your page look great in both browsers, just because you know there's a problem! Here are a few things to consider when you have this problem.

1. **Did you use Microsoft Word or Microsoft Front Page to create your page?** These programs sometimes create proprietary code that works great in Internet Explorer, but terrible in Netscape. You can use a validation service (such as **validator.w3c.org**) to identify any code that isn't HTML 4.0-compliant. In addition, some HTML editors, like Dreamweaver, have a function to delete all the

Microsoft HTML code from a Microsoft Word document. If that doesn't work, keep reading. . . .

2. **Did you use cascading style sheets or other features of Dynamic HTML (DHTML)?** These newer technologies are supported differently by Netscape and Internet Explorer. In fact, many versions of Netscape don't support these technologies at all, and those that do, support them with varying success. This means you may have to create two versions of your pages—one for Internet Explorer users and one for Netscape users—or just know your pages will look differently according to the browser used.

Finally, remember some HTML tags are rendered differently by some browsers. Even though you may have coded your page perfectly, there's a good chance it still might look different when viewed in certain browsers. The best advice I can offer you on this topic is to test, ask your friends to help you test, and test some more. Previewing your page in as many different browsers and computer systems as possible can help to ensure you know how it will look to the largest number of users.

When I Link My Images, They Have Little Colored Dashes Next to Them!

This happens when the browser finds a carriage return before it finds the closing a tag for a link, as in the following example:

```
<a href="home.html">
<img src="home.gif" alt="Return to the Home Page" width="25" height="25">
</a>
```

To eliminate those little dashes next to your images, run all the code on a single link, like this:

```
<a href="home.html"><img src="home.gif" alt="Return to the Home Page"
width="25" height="25"></a>
```

Strange Characters Are at the Top of My Page!

If you used a word processor to write your HTML, you may end up with some characters you didn't type up at the top of your page when you view it in a browser. This occurs when the page contains hidden formatting instructions. To avoid this, return to your file in the editor and save it in Text Only or ASCII Text format, with an `.html` or `.htm` extension.

I Updated My Web Page, But I Don't See the Changes in the Browser!

First, double-check that you saved the file. If you did, indeed, save your changes, and clicking the REFRESH or RELOAD button doesn't help, try forcing a reload by choosing FILE | OPEN PAGE or FILE | OPEN LOCATION, and then selecting the file in question. This ensures the browser is looking at the latest version of the file.

In some cases, you may also need to clear the browser's cache on disk. The *cache* is a place where browsers store temporary copies of Web page files, to avoid having to go back to the server to retrieve them multiple times. You can access your browser's cache by choosing EDIT | PREFERENCES | ADVANCED in Netscape and TOOLS | INTERNET OPTIONS in Internet Explorer.

My Whole Page Is _____ (Fill in the Blank)

For example, your whole page could be bold or linked or orange, and so forth. Even though this may look like a terrible error, it's relatively easy to

C

fix. Most likely you're just missing a closing tag somewhere. For example, if your whole page is a giant link, look in your code for the place you actually wanted to create a link to be sure you included the closing a tag. Or, if all the text on your page is bold, look to make sure you included a closing b tag. Typing something like this is actually quite common,

```
<b>Welcome to WILLARDesigns.<b>
```

where, at first glance it looks great, but a second look shows the closing tag is actually missing a slash. It should look like this:

```
<b>Welcome to WILLARDesigns.</b>
```

My Page Has a White Background in Internet Explorer, But Not in Netscape!

The latest versions of Internet Explorer set the default background color of Web pages to white, while Netscape's default is gray. If you only test your pages in Internet Explorer and forget to specify a background color in the body tag, Netscape users may complain that your pages look drastically different. To avoid this problem, always specify a background color in the body tag, even if you only want that color to be white.

```
<body bgcolor="#ffffff">
```

Tip

When you do specify a background color, be sure to set the text color to something readable. This is a common reason for "blank" pages: the text and background are the same color!

My Tables Look Fine in One Browser, But Terrible in Another!

First, make sure you have closed your `table` tags, and all `tr` and `td` tags have opening and closing versions. Consider the following example:

```
<tr>
  <td>Cell 1
  <td>Cell 2
<tr>
  <td>Cell 3
  <td>Cell 4
```

While some browsers can be forgiving when they encounter sloppy HTML that doesn't include closing tags, others refuse to display the content at all. The key to making tables that look good across multiple platforms is to use proper HTML and to test it in several browsers ahead of time.

```
<tr>
<td>Cell 1</td>
  <td>Cell 2</td>
</tr>
<tr>
  <td>Cell 3</td>
  <td>Cell 4</td>
</tr>
```

I Still Have Questions!

If the previous sections haven't answered your questions, here are a few more things to try:

1. **Take a break.** Looking at HTML code for hours on end can be quite straining, regardless of how experienced you are. If you're

having trouble, take a break and don't come back to the problem page until you feel rested enough to look at the issue with fresh eyes.

2. **Check for typos.** This may sound easy, but with HTML it's not. I can't tell you how many times I struggled with a certain page, only to find out three days later that it was all because I misspelled a tag or left out a quote. Printing the page and highlighting anything that seems like a potential problem area helps me. Also, reading the code on paper as opposed to on the screen can sometimes help you look at it differently. As much as 90 percent of HTML problems brought to my attention by students or co-workers involve typos!

3. **Start fresh.** Begin a new HTML page and add to it from the problem page, piece by piece. For example, first add the header and title tag. Then save the page and try it in the browser. If that works, add something else. While this may take a while, it certainly can help you identify exactly where the problem lies if you didn't already know.

4. **Reread the module.** If you're having trouble with tables, try returning to that module and, perhaps, even recreating some of the examples. After all, practice makes perfect, right? Well, at least it helps. . . .

5. **Ask someone else.** You could try posting your problem HTML on a troubleshooting bulletin board online to see if anyone else has had the same problem. I've set up a bulletin board on my Web site for this very subject. If all else fails, feel free to post your question at **www.willardesigns.com/htmlbook/bbs**. Be sure to check out the other questions first to see if a problem similar to yours has already been answered.

Resource D

Locating Images, Clip Art, Multimedia, Software, etc.

This resource gives a list of places to find images, clip art, multimedia, scripts, and code. Unfortunately, because this information changes so frequently, I cannot confirm all the following links will work when you try to access them. So, I keep an updated version of this list in the resources section of my Web site: **www.willardesigns.com/resources.**

Images, Clip Art, & Multimedia

- Corbis: Image Licensing for Creative Professionals (**www.corbis.com** and **www.corbisimages.com**)

- Comstock (**www.comstock.com**)

- Corel GraphicCorp (**www.graphiccorp.com**)

- Microsoft Clip Gallery Live (**cgl.microsoft.com/clipgallerylive**)

- Photodisc Digital Stock Photography and Animations (**www.photodisc.com**)

- The Publisher's Depot (**www.publishersdepot.com**)

In addition, try typing "clip art," "stock photography," or "royalty free" in Yahoo! (**www.yahoo.com**) or another search directory for countless links in this topic area.

Software

This section includes Web site links for the software mentioned in this book, as well as a few others in related categories.

HTML Editors

- Adobe GoLive★ (**www.adobe.com/products/golive**)

- Allaire HomeSite (**www.allaire.com/products/homesite/index.cfm**)

- Bare Bones BBEdit (**www.barebones.com**)
- Macromedia Dreamweaver★ (**www.macromedia.com/software/dreamweaver**)
- Microsoft FrontPage★ (**www.microsoft.com/frontpage**)
- Sausage Software's HotDog (**www.sausage.com/software/family.html**)

★WYSIWYG HTML Editors

Graphics Editors

- Adobe Photoshop (**www.adobe.com/products/photoshop**)
- Adobe Illustrator (**www.adobe.com/products/illustrator**)
- Corel Draw (**www.corel.com/draw9**)
- Corel Photo-Paint (**www.corel.com/paint9**)
- Jasc Paint Shop Pro (**www.jasc.com**)
- Macromedia Fireworks (**www.macromedia.com/software/fireworks**)
- Macromedia Freehand (**www.macromedia.com/software/freehand**)

Animation & Multimedia Editors

- Adobe LiveMotion (**www.adobe.com/products/livemotion**)
- Apple QuickTime (**www.apple.com/quicktime**)
- BoxTop Software's GIFmation (**www.boxtopsoft.com/gm.html**)
- Macromedia Director (**www.macromedia.com/software/director**)
- Macromedia Flash (**www.macromedia.com/software/flash**)

D

- Macromedia SoundEdit16
  (**www.macromedia.com/software/sound**)

- RealProducer Plus
  (**www.realnetworks.com/products/producerplus)**

Scripts and Code

- HTML Goodies (**www.htmlgoodies.com**)

- JavaScrip.com (**www.javascript.com**)

- JavaScript Source (**javascript.internet.com**)

- Matt's Script Archives (**www.worldwidemart.com/scripts**)

- Scripts.com (**www.scripts.com**)

- WebDeveloper (**www.webdeveloper.com**)

- WebReference (**www.webreference.com**)

- ZDNet Developer (**www.zdnet.com/developer**)

- Cnet's Builder.com (**www.builder.com**)

Resource **E**

File Types

This table includes some of the popular file types you might encounter when creating Web pages.

MIME Type	File Extension(s)	Name & Description
application/excel	.xl .xls	Microsoft Excel (spreadsheet)
application/futuresplash	.spl	Flash 1.0 file (animation)
application/mac-binhex40	.hqx	Macintosh Binhex format (file compression)
application/msword	.doc .word	Microsoft Word document (word processing)
application/octet-stream	.exe	Windows/DOS programs
application/pdf	.pdf	Adobe's Portable Document Format (postscript/printer-friendly files)
application/postscript	.ai .eps .ps	Postscript document
application/rtf	.rtf	Rich Text Format (word processing)
application/vnd.m-realmedia	.rm	RealMedia file (audio and video)
application/x-director	.dcr .dir .dxr	Macromedia Director file (presentation/animation/multimedia)
application/x-javascript	.js	JavaScript file
application/x-macbinary	.bin	Macintosh binary file (file compression)
application/x-shockwave-flash	.swf	Macromedia Flash 2.0+ file (presentation/animation/multimedia)
application/x-stuffit	.sit	Stuffit Archive (file compression)
application/zip	.zip	ZIP archive (file compression)
audio/basic	.au .snd	AU/μlaw (basic audio)
audio/vnd.m-realaudio	.ra .ram	RealAudio file

MIME Type	File Extension(s)	Name & Description
audio/x-aiff	.aif .aiff .aife	Audio Interchange File Format
audio/x-mpeg	.mp3	MP3 audio file
audio/x-mpegurl	.m3u .mp3url	MP3 text file (links to sound file)
audio/x-wav	.wav	Windows Waveform audio format
audio/x-midi	.mid	Musical Instruments Digital Interface (MIDI) sound files
audio/x-pn-realaudio	.ra .ram	RealAudio file
audio/x-pn-realaudio-plugin	.rpm	RealAudio plug-in page
image/gif	.gif	Graphic Interchange Format (GIF)
image/jpeg	.jpeg .jpg	Joint Photographer's Expert Group (JPEG)
image/pict	.pic .pict	Macintosh picture
image/tiff	.tif .tiff	TIFF image
image/x-bitmap	.xbm .bmp	Windows Bitmap Format (BMP)
text/html	.html .htm .shtm .shtml	Hypertext Markup Language document (HTML)
text/plain	.txt	Plain text document (no formatting)
text/xml	.xml	Extensible Markup Language document (XML)
video/vnd.m-realvideo	.rv	RealVideo file
video/quicktime	.qt .mov	*QuickTime* refers both to the file format and the helper application or plug-in used to play it

E

MIME Type	File Extension(s)	Name & Description
video/x-msvideo	.avi	Audio/Video Interleave Format is the standard non-streaming Microsoft Windows Video format
video/mpeg	.mpg .mpeg .mpe	MPEG Video file

Resource F

Mastery Checks Answers

Module 1: Getting Started

1. What does HTML stand for?

> HTML stands for Hypertext Markup Language.

2. What does the word "camp" in the following URL signify?
http://www.choppoint.org/camp/index.html

> **C.** folder name

3. Why is it important to know who your target audience is before developing your web site?

> Knowing your target audience can greatly affect how you design and develop your Web site, since this knowledge can drive decisions regarding such features as what screen size and browsers to develop for, the level of complexity offered by the site, the navigation style, the page structure, the content organization, and colors.

4. What does WYSIWYG mean?

> WYSIWYG stands for What-You-See-Is-What-You-Get, and means that theoretically your users will see the same thing you see when you are creating files.

5. What is the easiest way to learn HTML from your favorite web sites?

> The easiest way to learn HTML from the pros is to use the View | Source command within your Web browser to view the HTML source code from professional Web pages.

Module 2: Basic Page Structure

1. What file extension should HTML files have?

> `.html` or `.htm`

2. What is this tag missing?

> the final bracket >

3. At the very least, which tags should be included in a basic HTML page?

> `<html>`, `<head>`, `<title>`, `<body>` and the `!DOCTYPE` identifier

4. Which word in this tag is the attribute? What is the value of that attribute?

> `size` is the attribute. "+1" is the value of that attribute.

5. What might cause a random character such as ? or Ö to mistakenly appear in a web page?

> a curly quote or other character that should have been rendered using a character entity

6. How can you make line breaks appear within the content of a web page?

> use `<br>`

Module 3: Color

1. What is the difference between decimals and hexadecimals?

> Decimals are based on 10, whereas hexadecimals are based on 16.

2. Which color do the first two numbers in a six-digit hexadecimal code refer to?

> red

3. How many colors are there in the web-safe palette?

> 216

4. Which color is not web-safe?

> **C.** #FFCC44

5. How do you change the background color of a web page?

> Use the `bgcolor` attribute of the `body` tag.

Module 4: Working with Text

1. List 2 characteristics of the h tag.

> The h tag is available in varying levels of size and importance, from h1 to h6. It forces a line break before and after it is used in the page. The align attribute can be added to change the alignment of the heading.

2. What is the difference between physical and logical styles in HTML?

> Logical styles name how text is to be used in the page, but not how it will look. Physical styles tell exactly how the text should look when rendered in the browser.

3. How can you change the font that the text on a web page is rendered in?

> Use `<font face="name of font">`, where the value of the attribute includes the font name(s).

4. How do you close the br tag?

> The br tag is opened and closed in the same tag: `<br />`

5. List 2 characteristics of the `blockquote` tag.

> The `blockquote` tag indents text on both the left and right side. It forces a line break before and after it is used in the page.

6. List 2 ways to align text.

```
<p align="left, right, center or justify"> or
<div align="left, right, center or justify">
```

Module 5: Working with Links

1. Which tag and attribute are used to give a name to a section of text on a web page that you want to link to?

```
<a name="sectionname">
```

2. Which of the following would be classified as an absolute link?

```
<a href="http://www.choppoint.org/camp/store.html">
```

3. How do you link to a newsgroup?

```
<a href="news:alt.html">
```

4. Which attribute allows you to change the color of the links on your page after someone has clicked them?

```
vlink
```

5. How can you tell the browser to launch a link in a new window?

```
<a href="link" target="_blank"> or <a href="link"
target="NewWindowName">
```

Module 6: Working with Images

1. Why is it good to provide the height and width of an image in the HTML?

When you provide the height and width of an image in the HTML, the browser is able to leave the proper amount of space for the image and then display the rest of the page. If you do not provide these measurements in the HTML, many browsers will wait to display the page until all of the images on the page have downloaded.

2. What are the two types of image maps?

Client-side and server-side

3. How can you make the border invisible on a linked image?

Add the `border` attribute to your `img` tag and set the value to 0.

4. How can you add some buffer space around images?

Use the `hspace` and `vspace` attributes with the `img` tag.

F

5. How do you add an image to the background of a web page?

Add the `background` attribute to the `body` tag, specifying the name and location of the image file in the value.

Module 7: Working with Multimedia

1. What is the difference between a plug-in and a helper application?

A plug-in helps the browser display a file, whereas a helper application does it for the browser.

2. What is the simplest and most widely supported way of referencing multimedia in your web pages?

Link to them, using the `a` tag.

3. When you want to embed multimedia within a web page, which tag is recommended by the W3C for doing so?

`<object>`

4. What can you do for visitors whose browser does not support the object tag?

You can include the `embed` tag within the `object` tag. In addition, you can include other HTML within the `object` tag, in case the browser does not support either the `object` tag or the `embed` tag.

5. What is a Java applet?

A mini application, written in the Java programming language, that can be run within a web browser.

Module 8: Creating Lists

1. What are three types of lists in HTML?

Ordered, unordered, and definition lists.

2. What tag is used to denote list items in ordered and unordered lists?

`<li>`

3. What term is used to describe the process of including one type of list inside of another?

nesting

4. The definition description tag (`<dd>`) is used after which other tag in a definition list?

`<dt>`

5. How can you change an ordered list from using Arabic numbers to capital Roman numerals?

Add `type="I"` to the `ol` tag.

Module 9: Using Tables

1. Identify what is wrong with this table structure.

It is missing `tr` tags to define the table rows.

2. Which attribute is used to alter the amount of space between the content within a cell and the cell's edges?

`cellpadding`

3. What term is used to refer to a table completely contained within another table?

nested

4. What tags are used to group and align table rows?

`thead`, `tfoot`, and `tbody`

5. Since tables are often rendered differently by the various browsers, what is the best way to verify that your tables work properly?

View them in a variety of browsers on different computer systems.

F

Module 10: Developing Frames

1. What is wrong with the following HTML code?

The frame and frameset tags are switched. The correct code
should look like this:

```
<frameset rows="200,*">
 <frame src="links.html" />
    <frame src="intro.html" />
</frameset>
```

2. What could you add to `<frameset>` to create three columns of
equal width?

`cols="*,*,*"` or `cols="33%,33%,33%"`

3. Fix the mistakes in the following line of HTML code.

The `name` and `src` attributes should be switched. The correct
code should look like this:

```
<frame src="links.html" name="links" />
```

4. Fill in the blanks in the following XHTML-compliant HTML code.

The correct code should look like this:

```
<frameset rows="20%,80%">
 <frame src="links.html" noresize="noresize" />
    <frame src="intro.html" />
</frameset>
```

5. When nesting frames, which `frameset` tag should be closed first?

The most recently opened `frameset` tag should be closed first.

6. Which tag is used to include content for non-frames-capable browsers?

`<noframes>`

Module 11: Employing Forms

1. To process forms, what attribute is required in the `form` tag?

`action`

2. Name two optional attributes used in the `form` tag to customize how the form is processed.

`method` **and** `enctype`

3. What attribute is used to set the keyboard shortcut for a control?

`accesskey`

4. What two attributes allow you to restrict form elements from being altered by the user?

`disabled` **and** `readonly`

5. What tag is used to group form elements?

`<fieldset>`

Module 12: Creating Your Own Web Graphics

1. Fill in the blank: Colors usually appear _____ on a PC than on a Mac.

Colors usually appear <u>darker</u> on a PC than on a Mac.

2. When designing for 640 by 480 screen resolutions, what is the largest width the page's graphics should be?

600 pixels

3. How many colors can a GIF contain?

256 colors or less

F

4. What term is used to classify the type of compression JPEG uses?

lossy

5. Fill in the blank: Selecting the best file format for an image is a balance between aesthetics (how good the file looks) and

_____.

Selecting the best file format for an image is a balance between aesthetics (how good the file looks) and <u>file size (how quickly it will download)</u>.

Module 13: Web Content

1. How do most people "read" Web pages?

Most people scan Web pages for important information.

2. Where should the most important information on a Web page be?

Web pages should be written in the inverted pyramid format, where all of the most important information is at the top of the page.

3. Give two characteristics of effective and usable link labels.

Effective and usable link labels should be short, concise, descriptive and not buried in lengthy text segments.

4. Fill in the blank: A postscript file is one that contains instructions for _____ the file.

A postscript file is one that contains instructions for <u>printing</u> the file.

5. Name three things to consider when designing a printable version of a Web page.

When designing a printable version of a Web page, be sure to consider the page's size and layout, color and reference information.

Module 14: JavaScript

1. What are two ways that JavaScript differs from HTML?

JavaScript is case sensitive; HTML is not. In JavaScript quotes are required; in HTML quotes are optional. JavaScript has a distinct format that must be adhered to; HTML is very forgiving about spacing and formatting.

2. What can you type into Netscape's location bar to bring up the JavaScript troubleshooting console?

javascript:

3. What is one way that you can tell a JavaScript method apart from an object?

Methods are last in a chain of events, and are followed by a set of parenthesis, as in `document.write()`, where `document` is an object and `write()` is a method.

4. Fill in the blank: JavaScript is case-_____.

JavaScript is case-<u>sensitive</u>.

5. Give an example of a JavaScript event handler.

The following are all JavaScript event handlers: onAbort, onBlur, onChange, onClick, onFocus, onLoad, onMouseOver, onMouseOut, onSelect, onSubmit.

Module 15: Cascading Style Sheets

1. What would you use as a selector if you wanted to add a style to all the level 3 headlines on your page?

h3

2. Name three ways you can reference a color in CSS.

hexadecimal color, RGB color, predefined color name

F

3. What property can be used to add a colored background behind an element?

background-color

4. What is a universal class?

A universal class is one that can be added to several different tags.

5. What tag is used to add an internal style sheet to a Web page?

<style>

Module 16: Making Pages Available to Others

1. How many characters are permitted in a domain name?

26 characters are permitted in a domain name, including the four characters that make up the entension (for example, .com).

2. What does FTP stand for?

FTP stands for File Transfer Protocol.

3. Why is it unrealistic for most small businesses to host their own Web sites?

Hosting your own Web site requires the purchase and maintenance of hardware, software and dedicated high-speed Internet access, as well as on-site IT talent. The high costs of this make it unrealistic for most small businesses.

4. Which format should HTML and text files be transferred in?

HTML and text files should be transferred in the ASCII format.

5. Identify three ways you can get started marketing your new Web site.

There are many examples given throughout Module 16 of ways to market your Web site. Refer back to the material listed and pull out those options that will work the best for your business.

Index

Creating Internet Professional™

The need for high-quality Internet talent i
the professional service firms supporting t
experts within the next year. However, the
Internet-ready job candidates and the dem
Internet skills gap.

iGeneration is the Solution

One way to bridge the Internet skills gap i
new generation of Internet professionals. T
iGeneration offers the skills and job conne
career. The program is designed to create i
knowledge and tools you need to design ar

The program's three steps – assessment, tr
financial aid, career guidance and certificat
development. iGeneration differs from exis
iGeneration-certified professionals with en
database.

iGeneration Professional Certification prov
to become a practicing Internet Professiona
Creative Producer, Visual Designer), techni
Security Specialist) and business (e.g. Busi

Go to igeneration.com to take a s
your Internet career today. To spe
counselor please call (866) 263-85